ENGAGING THE EMOTIONS
IN SPANISH CULTURE AND HISTORY

Engaging the Emotions in Spanish Culture and History

EDITED BY
Luisa Elena Delgado,
Pura Fernández, and
Jo Labanyi

VANDERBILT UNIVERSITY PRESS
NASHVILLE

© 2016 by Vanderbilt University Press
Nashville, Tennessee 37235
All rights reserved
First printing 2016

This book is printed on acid-free paper.

Library of Congress Cataloging-in-Publication Data on file
LC control number 2015014683
LC classification number DP48 .E635 2015
Dewey class number DDC 946—dc23

ISBN 978-0-8265-2085-2 (hardcover)
ISBN 978-0-8265-2086-9 (paperback)
ISBN 978-0-8265-2087-6 (ebook)

Cover image: Julio Romero Torres, *Conciencia tranquila*
(Clear Conscience, 1897). Courtesy of Museo Nacional Centro de
Arte Reina Sofía, Madrid.

Contents

Illustrations   vii

Acknowledgments   ix

Introduction
Engaging the Emotions—Theoretical,
Historical, and Cultural Frameworks   1

1   **Reasonable Sentiments**
Sensibility and Balance in Eighteenth-Century Spain   21
Mónica Bolufer

2   **"How Do I Love Thee"**
The Rhetoric of Patriotic Love
in Early Puerto Rican Political Discourse   39
Wadda C. Ríos-Font

3   **Emotional Readings for New Interpretative
Communities in the Nineteenth Century**
Agustín Pérez Zaragoza's *Galería fúnebre* (1831)   56
Pura Fernández

4   **Emotional Contagion in a Time of Cholera**
Sympathy, Humanity, and
Hygiene in Mid-Nineteenth-Century Spain   77
Rebecca Haidt

5   **"Hatred alone warms the heart"**
Figures of Ill Repute in the Nineteenth-Century
Spanish Novel   95
Lou Charnon-Deutsch

6   **"You will have observed that I am not mad"**
Emotional Writings inside the Asylum   111
Rafael Huertas

7   **A Sentient Landscape**
    Cinematic Experience in 1920s Spain   120
    Juli Highfill

8   **The Battle for Emotional Hegemony
    in Republican Spain (1931–1936)**   141
    Javier Krauel

9   **Love in Times of War**
    Female Frigidity and Libertarian Revolution in the Work
    of Anarchist Doctor Félix Martí Ibáñez   159
    Maite Zubiaurre

10 **From the History of Emotions
    to the History of Experience**
    A Republican Sailor's Sketchbook in the Civil War   176
    Javier Moscoso

11 **Affective Variations**
    Queering Hispanidad in Luis Cernuda's Mexico   192
    Enrique Álvarez

12 **Sentimentality as Consensus**
    Imagining Galicia in the Democratic Period   210
    Helena Miguélez-Carballeira

13 **Emotional Competence and the Discourses of Suffering
    in the Television Series *Amar en tiempos revueltos***   225
    Jo Labanyi

14 **From Tear to Pixel**
    Political Correctness and Digital Emotions
    in the Exhumation of Mass Graves from the Civil War   242
    Francisco Ferrándiz

15 **Public Tears and Secrets of the Heart**
    Political Emotions in a State of Crisis   262
    Luisa Elena Delgado

    Afterword
    Shameless Emotions   283
    Antonio Muñoz Molina

    Contributors   287

    Index   291

Illustrations

1.1.	Goya, "Because She Was Sensitive"	22
1.2.	"The Three [Basque Provinces] Make One"	30
1.3.	"The Ill-Fated Margarita"	33
1.4.	Goya, "And They Are Like Wild Beasts"	34
3.1.	Illustration to *Milady Herwort y Miss Clarisa o Bristol, el carnicero asesino*	61
3.2.	Illustration to *Las catacumbas españolas*	69
3.3.	Illustration to *La princesa de Lipno o el retrete del placer criminal*	71
5.1.	Gavarni (Sulpice Guillaume Chevalier), in Eugène Sue, *El judío errante*	99
5.2.	Caricature of Jakob Rothschild	102
7.1.	Rotary printing press in *El misterio de la Puerta del Sol*	132
7.2.	Trolley advertisements in *El misterio de la Puerta del Sol*	133
7.3.	Aerial shots of the countryside and the Puerta del Sol in *El misterio de la Puerta del Sol*	136
10.1.	Luis Sarabia, *Apuntes*, "When I Arrived"	181
10.2.	Luis Sarabia, *Apuntes*, "Call to Arms"	181
10.3.	Luis Sarabia, *Apuntes*, "The 'Gato Negro'"	182
10.4.	Luis Sarabia, *Apuntes*, "My Daughter's Birthday"	185
10.5.	Luis Sarabia, *Apuntes*, "Victory"	186

13.1.	Andrea and Antonio with image of Franco in *Amar en tiempos revueltos*	235
13.2.	The roof terrace in *Amar en tiempos revueltos*	236
13.3.	Isidro, José, and Pura form an unorthodox "Holy Family" in *Amar en tiempos revueltos*	237
14.1.	Official commemoration and public mourning at Paracuellos del Jarama	245
14.2.	The relative of a victim of Francoism takes a picture with his smartphone, Calera y Chozas (Toledo)	253
14.3.	Reburial organized by the Foro por la Memoria at Menasalbas (Toledo)	256
14.4.	Pedro Cancho with a portrait of his murdered grandfather, Milagros (Burgos)	257
14.5	Forensic ritual of emotional identification with exhumed victims, Casavieja (Ávila)	258

Acknowledgments

This book forms part of the Spanish government–funded projects FFI2010-17273 (Ministry of Science and Innovation) and FEM2013-42699 (Ministry of Economy and Competitiveness), both directed by Pura Fernández. We thank those who participated in the two conferences organized by the editors of this book at the Center for the Humanities and Social Sciences (CCHS) of Spain's National Research Council (CSIC) in 2010, and at New York University's King Juan Carlos I of Spain Center in 2011, which helped to shape the conception of this volume. The conference in New York was made possible by grants from the Acción Complementaria de Investigación of the Spanish government (FFI2009-06748-E/FILO), the Program for Cultural Cooperation between Spain's Ministry of Culture and US Universities, and the Humanities Initiative of New York University, which also generously contributed to the publication costs of this book. Pura Fernández wishes to acknowledge her debt of gratitude to Eduardo Manzano, director of the CCHS, for his belief in and support of this interdisciplinary project, and to her colleagues in the Cultural History of Knowledge research group at the same institution. Luisa Elena Delgado wishes to thank Marta Segarra and Helena González (Centre Dona i Literatura, University of Barcelona) for their invitation to participate in the conference "Polítiques de les emocions: Diàlegs des del gènere i la sexualitat" (University of Barcelona/Barcelona Center for Contemporary Culture) in 2014. This participation, as well as the ongoing project on communities and emotions developed at the center, helped her to shape her contribution to this volume. Jo Labanyi would like to thank Rosa María Medina Domènech for many stimulating conversations on the role of the emotions in Spanish culture, and Luisa Passerini and the other members of the international research team Europe: Emotions, Identities, Politics (2002–2004), which introduced her to thinking about the emotions in the first place. We also wish to thank our contributors for accompanying us on this journey of several years, because their inspiring work made it so much more gratifying. Our special thanks are owed to Michael Ames of Vanderbilt University Press for his support of this project and his efficiency in bringing it to fruition.

INTRODUCTION

Engaging the Emotions
Theoretical, Historical, and Cultural Frameworks

This book aims to contribute to the history and critical interpretation of the emotions in relation to modern Spain, considering their evolution and their social and cultural significance from the second half of the eighteenth century to the present. It does not claim to offer a comprehensive historical account; rather, we have commissioned original essays by scholars whose work has been relevant to the history of the emotions, even though in some cases they may not have seen that as their primary object of study. In bringing them together in this volume, we want to constitute the history of the emotions as a consciously articulated field in the study of Spanish culture and history, and we hope that this first attempt to do so will generate further work that explores the many topics and issues not addressed here.

In this respect, we are building on developments in other parts of the world. The year 2008 saw the creation of Centers for the History of Emotions at Germany's national research agency, the Max Planck Institute in Berlin, and at Queen Mary University of London. Since 2011, the Australian Research Council has funded a Centre of Excellence for the History of Emotions at the Universities of Adelaide, Melbourne, Queensland, Sydney, and Western Australia. None of these centers includes Spain as an object of study. In the last few years, however, this corpus of international research has attracted increasing attention in Spain (Moscoso Sarabia and Zaragoza Bernal 76–79), and we are delighted that the collaborative Spanish-US research project directed by the editors of this book from 2009 to 2011 has been part of this process. Other emotion-related research groups currently producing interesting work in Spain are Emocríticas, led by Rosa María Medina Doménech at the University of Granada; and HIST-EX, led by Javier Moscoso, a contributor to this volume, at the Center for the Humanities and Social Sciences of Spain's National Research Council (CSIC). In November 2014, just before this book went to the publisher, the Spanish journal *Cuadernos de Historia Contemporánea* published a monographic issue devoted to the emotions as a category of historical analysis, recognizing that Spanish scholars could benefit from familiarity with this new strand of research. The issue focuses on the methodological and theoretical issues raised by international scholarship in the field, with just one article (tracing the emotional cartography of three Spanish Republican exiles in the United States) devoted to Spanish culture, from a transatlantic perspective (Rodríguez-López and Ventura Herranz). Its publication indicates a growing interest in Spain in the history of the emotions, and that much more work remains to be done.

We too have felt it important to consider interconnections between Spain and other parts of the world. Transnational relations between Spain and Latin America are explored by several contributors. Wadda Ríos-Font discusses the evolution of the concept of patriotic love elaborated by the Puerto Rican deputy to the Cortes de Cádiz, Ramón Power y Giralt; Enrique Álvarez explores the complexity of the Republican exile poet Luis Cernuda's expressions of love for Mexico and Mexican bodies; Francisco Ferrándiz considers how the transnational circulation of images of the disappeared in Latin America has affected the public display of emotions by relatives of the victims of the Francoist terror. The relation of Spanish culture to broader European trends is also explored in several essays, notably those by Mónica Bolufer on Enlightenment sensibility; by Pura Fernández on the early nineteenth-century transnational literature of horror; by Rebecca Haidt on the mid-nineteenth-century discourse of hygiene; and by Lou Charnon-Deutsch on the nineteenth-century pan-European construction of Jesuits, Jews, and Freemasons as objects of hate. It is interesting that there should be so many examples of Spain's insertion into European cultural circuits in the nineteenth century, whose categorization as the "age of nationalism" has led to a tendency to study it in national terms.

In addition to making connections across national boundaries, we have made a point of bringing together work by scholars in a range of disciplines: history, literary and cultural studies, anthropology, and the history and philosophy of science—and we are especially grateful to Antonio Muñoz Molina for providing the Afterword, from the perspective of a creative writer. In several cases, the contributors have chosen to write on material that does not fall squarely within their discipline. Thus we have a historian writing on literary texts; literary scholars writing on history, politics, cinema, television, or the history of medicine; historians of science writing on personal letters or graphic art; and an anthropologist writing on photography and the new media.

That the study of emotions should encourage work that crosses boundaries is not surprising, since the emotions refuse the organization of experience in tidy categories, undoing the binary oppositions inside/outside, individual/collective, mind/body, thought/feeling, and reason/emotion that have been erected to contain them. All the essays in this volume show the emotions to be a form of thought and knowledge, and a major component of social life—including in the nineteenth century, which attempted to relegate them to a feminine intimate sphere. Several of the essays refer to Raymond Williams's concept of "structure of feeling" (128–35) as the key to understanding a particular historical period because it runs deeper than the expression of ideas: "thought as felt and feeling as thought" (132). As Sara Ahmed insists, emotions are not "in" the subject or object but result from their contact (6). They emerge at the interface between the self and the outside world, and this is what makes them a kind of thought: "Emotions are intentional in the sense that they are 'about' something: they involve a direction or orientation towards an object. . . . The 'aboutness' of emotions means they involve a stance on the world" (Ahmed 7). Following Ahmed, this volume examines emotions "not as interior psychological states, but as social and cultural practices" (9). This means considering not so much what emotions are as what they do (Ahmed 4).

The essays collected here draw on a wide range of sources (literary, political, legal, journalistic, medical, activist, visual, and audiovisual). In some cases, the aim is to explore social, cultural, and political practices. When the aim is to analyze the workings of the textual sources themselves, the stress is on their social context and social effects. As Javier Moscoso notes in his essay, one cannot access the inner emotions of others; one can only examine the experiences that gave rise to them and the expressions that they generated. In any case, there is no such thing as purely inner or individual emotion, since all periods have a repertoire of emotional codes that shape not only the expression of emotions but the emotions themselves; indeed, it can be argued that the expression of the emotion (even if only to oneself) is what constitutes it at such. Emotions involve thought since they are reflexive: to feel fear means to be able to attach the word "fear" to what one is feeling—and here we need to remember that the vocabulary for the emotions in different languages packages them in different ways (as discussed below).

Furthermore, new forms of social relationship and shared leisure practices generate the need for the resulting new emotional experiences to be expressed in language, as, for example, in the case of the cinema theaters that became established entertainment venues in the 1920s—enclosed collective spaces that paradoxically fostered intimacy and self-absorption. In this volume, Juli Highfill analyzes how avant-garde writers explored the potential of such intensely physical experiences, showing how poetic language and the break with traditional artistic models were a necessary adaptation to the emotional codes of a world being transformed by technological modernity. The sensorial magnification created by the illusion of movement and the spatial effects created by the projection of light and shadow onto the screen, producing an intangible collective sensory invasion that activated spectators' emotions, shaped a new language and expressive modes. The fact that emotions cannot be separated from their expression means that they are performative: they fulfill a function, they communicate a message, they ask for a response. Rafael Huertas shows how this is true even in the case of the letters written by inmates of the mental asylum at Leganés, addressed to inaccessible interlocutors. How the communication is received by its interlocutors (when it is received), and who those interlocutors are, remain of course beyond its author's control—a problem intensified in the world of new digital media, which allow expressions of emotion to go viral, as Ferrándiz notes. But this issue is not entirely new: emotions have always depended on their circulation, as is graphically shown by Charnon-Deutsch's study of the circulation in nineteenth-century Spain, as in Europe generally, of hate discourse against Jesuits, Jews, and Freemasons through the vehicle of popular fiction. In this sense, the history of emotions is bound up with the history of the technologies that allow them to circulate, not least the technology of the printed book, which contributes to the emotional experience of reading through its physicality, as Fernández discusses in her essay.

A key issue in the volume is the way that emotions make it impossible to separate mind from body, given the importance of the senses in generating emotional responses. Highfill's discussion of the strong physical sensations afforded by the new technology of cinema examines how this made cinema viewing as much as a matter of tactility as of vision. As Highfill shows, the sensorial bombardment offered by cinema, which so fascinated writers limited to the printed page, was a product of modernity's celebration of speed. The thrills of cinema that writers sought to reproduce were often connected to travel, especially aerial travel; motion was the source of emotion; films were "moving pictures" in the double sense of the term (Bruno). Nonetheless, Fernández shows how, almost a century before, Agustín Pérez Zaragoza's *Galería fúnebre* (*Funereal Gallery*, 1831) used horror to produce similar intense physical effects in its "reader-spectators," thanks to the work's immersion in a popular culture of phantasmagoria and other optical effects that assaulted the senses. But the sensorial aspect of emotion is not just the product of technology; it is a key component of orality, where the quality of the voice is as important as what is said, and in fact gives meaning to what is said. Fernández and Ríos-Font remind us of the continuing importance in the nineteenth century of reading out loud and of political oratory, respectively. Indeed, the spoken word has a close affinity with music in its capacity to affect the nervous system, placing mind and body in communion, as eighteenth-century thinkers noted (Gouk and Hills 30–31). The performative capacity of voice, sound, and image in collective spectacles creates an atmosphere of shared emotions, stimulating sensorial experience through the fusion of the material and the immaterial, the real and the virtual, as Highfill discusses in her essay on twentieth-century modernism.

The fact that emotions are performative—addressed to an audience—allows them to construct "emotional communities" founded on common values and desires, a topic developed in Fernández's essay. In this sense, emotions have a social and socializing function. This is particularly true in the case of cultural offerings issued in installments, which create a set of intense expectations and passionate involvement over time, for example, the 1831 twelve-volume collection of horror stories analyzed by Fernández, the mid- and late nineteenth-century popular fiction discussed by Charnon-Deutsch, and the twenty-first-century television series examined by Jo Labanyi. The category of emotional communities, coined by Max Weber and explored by Rosenwein in relation to the Middle Ages, deserves more attention in the modern period—particularly since it enmeshes with Benedict Anderson's classic analysis of the importance of the press and the realist novel for nation formation, a role taken up in the twentieth and twenty-first centuries by radio and subsequently television, and now the Internet as discussed by Ferrándiz and Luisa Elena Delgado in their contributions. Ferrándiz highlights how the ritual posing before the camera of victims' relatives at the opening of Civil War mass graves constructs emotional communities that are no less emotionally and politically significant for being ephemeral.

Charnon-Deutsch's contribution reminds us that negative emotions such as hatred can also bind emotional communities together. Although the Jesuits were the object of hatred for left-wing writers of popular serialized fiction, and Jews and Freemasons for their conservative equivalents, Jesuits and Jews in particular were made virtually indistinguishable through their physical stereotyping. Alarmingly, as Charnon-Deutsch notes, this persistent hate mongering—more nuanced in late nineteenth-century realist fiction but nonetheless present—not only became normalized through endless repetition but was a marketable commodity. She follows Ahmed in insisting that hatred does not reside in the hating subject nor in the hated object but in "hate-producing contact zones." Her essay is an object lesson in how emotions expressed in fiction have real effects in the world, showing literature to be a form of emotional practice. This contrasts with the fact that, since the nineteenth century, literary criticism has fostered the idea of critical reading as a cognitive act whose goal is the production of meaning. The essays by both Fernández and Charnon-Deutsch illustrate the importance of popular and mass cultural products for an understanding of the "structure of feeling" of a given historical period. Products classified as "banal" in literary histories but consumed massively—like the nineteenth-century "penny dreadful" and the small-format romantic or erotic novellas that would reach mass audiences in the early twentieth century—were considered dangerous because of their capacity to move (to set in motion, to affect) their readers, especially when these included women and the lower classes. However, as Bolufer indicates, in the eighteenth century that same capacity to move readers had been considered positive by politicians and thinkers, who emphasized the superiority of works that could shape public opinion through the successful mobilization of emotions by comparison with those that admonished it with sermons.

Building on the insights of sociologist Pierre Bourdieu, Monique Scheer has elaborated the concept of emotional practice, stressing that practice is a bodily as well as a mental phenomenon (Plamper 25). In his introduction to Patricia Clough's edited volume *The Affective Turn*, Michael Hardt suggests that the reason affect has become a current object of study (since the mid-1990s) is that it demonstrates unequivocally the impossibility of thinking of body and mind as separate (Clough ix). Affect studies insist on the embodied nature of the emotions, seeing them as a form of embodied knowledge. However, the strand of affect studies originating in cognitive science, most notably represented by Massumi, risks setting up bounded categories of its own through its insistence on distinguishing between "affect" (the preconscious impact of the outside world on the body), "sensation" (awareness of this impact at a physical level), "feeling" (a still somewhat undefined awareness that is part physical, part mental), "emotion" (an interpretation that gives a name to the emotion concerned, and is thus an amalgam of feeling and thought), and finally "thought" (which analyzes the emotion and the situation that has given rise to it). Massumi arranges these responses in a temporal sequence according to the speed of the reaction, with affect kicking in first and thought last. This temporal grid risks giving the impression of a teleological linear process, in which the destiny of affect (body) is to end up producing an emotion (mind). Indeed, Ruth Leys has accused Massumi of reinforcing the body/mind split (456–58).

In practice, the neurological experiments discussed by Massumi suggest that affect is not the first stage of what will become emotion, but that the two follow different trajectories (23–27). His analysis also shows that the various stages of his temporal sequence cannot be separated out, since they are inextricably entangled with each other; indeed, the temporal lag between the various stages is so minimal that consciousness cannot perceive it. For this reason, Ahmed (6) and Teresa Brennan (4–6) choose not to make fine distinctions between "affects" and "emotions," while remembering that "affect" supposes a visceral energetic charge. Moscoso in this volume also concludes that the terminological distinctions are not helpful for his analysis, since the various levels of response are entangled in his object of study (a sailor's sketchbook made during the Spanish Civil War). Moscoso also notes that different terms are used in different academic communities, "affect" now being in vogue in North America, "sensibility" being preferred in France, and "emotions" used in the rest of the world. This raises the issue of translation, since Spanish "afecto" (affection, fondness) does not mean the same as English "affect," while English "emotion" is often best translated in Spanish as "sentimiento" (feeling), and Spanish "emoción" can be close to English "excitement." By contrast, the adjective "affective" does continue to be used in English as synonymous with the Spanish "afectivo" (pertaining to the emotions). In this volume, we have not wanted to get into this terminological minefield but have simply asked our contributors to clarify their terminology where there was a possibility of confusion. Leys has expressed worries about the fact that the present-day fascination with "affect," while important for showing the limits of intentionality, suggests an interest in presenting human behavior as driven by preconscious forces. This book's concern with the emotions as a major aspect of social and indeed political life—which we do not want to present as lacking in intentionality—also makes undue use of the term "affect" inappropriate. Like most critics (Ahmed; Brennan; Harding and Pribram), we have therefore opted for "emotion" as an umbrella term that has the merit of following everyday usage.

In a recent issue of *Cuadernos de Historia Contemporánea* on the history of emotions, Ute Frevert reminds us that, if the body is "the prime location of experiencing and expressing emotions" (39), bodies are "objects of historical reconfiguration" (43); Jan Plamper similarly notes that the body is a historical, plastic, and socially adapted surface (25–26). The embodied character of the emotions requires us to think about their historical specificity. We have arranged the essays in this volume in chronological order of the period treated, since we want to stress that emotions are historically conditioned. Additionally, we need to consider how the terminology used to describe the emotions has changed over time. The modern term "emotion" was not used in English before the sixteenth century (Trigg 7). The word "emoción" was first officially recognized by the dictionary of the Real Academia Española in 1843, as Bolufer notes in this volume, in the decade following abundant use of the term in the Romantic historical novels of the 1830s, with Mariano José de Larra leading the way. One of the research objectives of the Center for the History of Emotions at the Max Planck Institute is to clarify the terminology used to describe emotions, feelings, and affects, regarded as fundamental to an understanding of European intellectual history, although currently—as noted above—its projects do not include Spain.

Prior to the eighteenth century, the most frequent term was "passions," which were seen as external forces (often anthropomorphized as "demons") that invade and possess the self. This was a bodily possession—of which there are residues in the mid-nineteenth-century medical notion of "emotional contagion" discussed by Haidt. The historical evolution from the concept of the "passions" to that of "emotion," documented in a broad context by Thomas Dixon, is traced in Bolufer's essay with regard to Spain. In addition to charting the emergence in the eighteenth century of a new discourse of sensibility, seen—unlike the passions—as arising spontaneously from within the individual and as being a source of virtue, Bolufer shows how the semantic field of the term "sentimiento" (feeling) shifted as it increasingly came to denote pleasant feelings rather than sorrow. Toward the end of the eighteenth century, as she notes, a divergence started to appear between "sensibility"—the basis of sociality and expected of men and women—and "sentimentality," associated with women and the domestic sphere. This shift meant a decline in the value attributed in the eighteenth century to friendship (mostly but not necessarily between men) as a civic virtue; Bolufer notes that the notion of friendship as a social expression of emotion is enshrined in the term "Amigos del País" (Friends of the Country) used to designate eighteenth-century Spain's economic societies, conceived as emotional communities. In tracing such subtle semantic shifts, Bolufer draws heavily on literary texts, showing their value as a source for cultural history, as well as on political and legal documents, and on various kinds of self-writing. Her essay shows that Spanish writers who reflected on the emotions were conversant with European moral philosophy and sentimental novels, though the Spanish sentimental novel was more moralistic thanks to censorship.

Teresa Brennan has observed that today's interest in affect is, in a way, a return to the premodern understanding of the passions as something that enters the body from outside, refusing the inner/outer distinction created by the modern understanding of "emotion" as a property of the self, indeed as its innermost core (2, 16–19). Indeed, Bolufer notes that the term "afectos" was used in the premodern period. The modern term "emotion" parallels the rise of liberal political theory, in turn predicated on the capitalist definition of the autonomous individual as the owner of property, including property in one's person (Macpherson). Emotions consequently came to be seen as possessions, not in the sense of the self being possessed by outside forces, but in the sense of "things" that one "has." The eighteenth-century concept of sensibility, discussed by Bolufer, already supposed that sensibility was the innermost authentic self. But it differed from the concept of emotion that would develop in the Romantic period in that it was not seen as pitting the individual against society, but as binding him or her to it: sensibility supposed sympathy—the ability to "feel with" others. Sensibility was thus the basis of Enlightenment sociability, a civic virtue. As such, it worked in tandem with reason, as its complement. This made women, seen as naturally possessing sensibility unlike men who needed to learn it, the model of civic virtue—even as they were excluded from civic rights.

The gendering of this model had substantial consequences, explored by Bolufer, who notes that gender studies' stress on the self as a construction has been crucial to the development of emotion studies. Bolufer proposes that, if in the Western world generally what broke the Enlightenment belief in the complementarity of reason and sentiment was the French Revolution, in Spain the break was clinched by the War of Independence, with women's active participation in the struggle to expel Napoleon's occupying troops giving rise to a fear of women as emotionally violent and out of control. This, she suggests, encouraged the construction of reason and emotion as opposites, the former (seen as positive) associated with men, and the latter (seen as negative) associated with women, who from this point were increasingly confined to the domestic sphere. Fernández's essay, however, captures a moment, in the early 1830s, when women's susceptibility to extreme emotion was cultivated as a model for men to follow, on the supposition that exposure to horror through their reading practices—in a period of chronic instability, with memories of the War of Independence still strong and the Carlist Wars looming—would allow them to develop defenses against the horror that history seemed to promise in the future. This model of female emotional competence in moments of historical conflict is found again in the twenty-first-century television series *Amar en tiempos revueltos* (*Loving in Troubled Times*), whose first season (2005–2006) is analyzed by Labanyi; here too the suggestion is that men can learn emotional competence from women. If popular fiction and soap opera have traditionally been associated with women because of their extreme emotionality, it is perhaps not only so as to dismiss them as inferior cultural products but also in sneaking recognition of the assumption that women have an emotional competence that men have been socialized to lack. What is extraordinary in Pérez Zaragoza's *Galería fúnebre* is that, as Fernández shows, he acknowledges this openly and regards women's emotional competence as a necessary tool for historical survival.

Haidt suggests that the mid-nineteenth century did not entirely break with the Enlightenment concepts of sympathy and humanity, grounded in the civic virtue of sensibility, which remained central to the reformist discourse of hygiene. We should remember that the evolution of emotional codes is not a straightforward linear process, since different emotional regimes—residual, dominant, and emergent, to use Raymond Williams's terminology (121–27)—tend to coexist in any one period. Haidt's discussion of mid-nineteenth-century medical discourse shows that, at precisely the time when emotions were becoming psychologized, medical reformers—"hygienists"—regarded the relation between emotions and the body as so fundamental that they considered that extreme emotionality made one vulnerable to contagious disease (cholera) and, conversely, that emotional balance made one immune to contagion. It was precisely in the nineteenth century that the idea of contagion in relation to social phenomena was consolidated; it was not just that diseases could be propagated because of excessive emotionality, but also that affect, beliefs, and attitudes too could spread like viruses, in a process of social contagion. It is somewhat paradoxical that emotions started to be valued as markers of individual singularity at the same time that emotional temperance and the capacity for self-regulation became essential not just for good citizenship and social order, but also for healthy bodies and minds. Of particular concern was the management of what Adam Smith had already in 1759 classified as "unsocial passions" (hatred and resentment but also other emotions like envy and jealousy). These and other negative affects were pathologized as "static signs of deficiency" instead of motivated affective stances (Ngai 127). As the social dimension of emotions came to be minimized, so too were their political effects: emotions that could be understood as responses to social inequalities or antagonisms were invalidated as psychological flaws or "private dissatisfactions" (Jameson 202). Moreover, as Sianne Ngai reminds us, negative emotions "are more likely to be stripped of their critical implications when the impassioned subject is a female" (130)—or, we could add, a racial or class other. The danger, it seems, was the possibility of an individual demanding, or even fantasizing about, occupying a place that did not "properly" belong to her or him in the existing social order, thus stripping the demand or fantasy of emotional legitimacy. We should remember here Charnon-Deutsch's warning that certain negative emotions, far from resisting normalization, were its tool, as in the case of hate mongering against scapegoats.

Richard Sennett has stated that Victorian fiction is characterized by "the constant attempt to formulate what it is that one feels" (Sennett 152), an observation that can be extended to nineteenth-century European fiction in general. Personal feelings are understood as the manifestation of an irreducible singularity in relation, and often in opposition, to the world. The extent to which that tension can be nonnegotiable is present in the letters written by inmates of the Leganés mental asylum analyzed by Huertas, where the authors' self-interpretation contrasts with the interpretation of their symptoms by society. "You will have observed that I am not mad" is the observation made to her doctors by a patient studied in Huertas's chapter. Yet madness is precisely what society (family; medical and legal authorities) saw in her, as in her fellow patients: often their confinement was prompted by excessive or inappropriate feelings (hysteria, melancholia, monomania) that were considered incompatible with successful socialization. Huertas's analysis of the letters written by patients at Leganés, between 1860 and 1936, shows how these emotional writings allowed their authors to construct or reconstruct a sense of self—one that was not recognized by the emotional norms of the day. As Roxana Pagés-Rangel has observed, letters, like autobiographies and memoirs, are shaped by the "discursive geographies" of the processes that give meaning to the modern subject (6). The analysis of letters allows us to identify the representational mechanisms of a new social, ethical, or ideological order, through a model of personal experience based on reflexivity and the exploration of interiority. In particular, personal letters and writings provide evidence of the effort to make the self legible through writing on the part of those who, like the inmates of Leganés, see themselves as marginal or deviant subjects in relation to a normative sociocultural and emotional environment. The link between the "truths of sentiment" and public morality that Jovellanos acknowledged in the late eighteenth century, as analyzed by Bolufer in her contribution, was no longer acceptable in the nineteenth century. Indeed, what was engraved in the heart often clashed with what was socially appropriate and had to be successfully confined to the private sphere or discarded altogether. Self-perception, no matter how eloquent, had to be aligned with social perception. When it was not, the result was at best affective disorientation and at worst a sense of not belonging, as in the impossible space of paratopia that Huertas describes in his essay.

The manipulation and expression of fear of social contagion materialized in the nineteenth century in the prolific production of popular fiction and in the construction of the liberal state, as Charnon-Deutsch and Haidt show. While Charnon-Deutsch discusses the contagious propagation of hate speech against social groups themselves regarded as infecting the social body, Haidt analyzes disagreements over whether the state or the church should be responsible for care of the diseased and infirm. In both cases, emotions are inextricably entwined with bodies. The expression of anxieties relating to economic and social health through the physical stereotyping of Jews or Jesuits inscribed emotions on the body in a tangible way. As inscriptions on the body, emotions can be seen as actions—actions that are not purely individual since they drive historical change (Medina Doménech 166). The individual body projects itself onto the collective body of the nation but also onto the collective body of the religious community in the form of the mystical body of Christ—a double projection whose conflicting demands jostle with each other in the liberal nation-formation project of Catholic Spain. Haidt insists on the double (medical/moral) therapeutic regime proposed by the secular hygienists Pedro Felipe Monlau and Francisco Méndez Álvaro as well as by the Catholic social reformer Concepción Arenal to shore up this duality in the emotional and hygienic management of civil society.

Many of the essays in the collection go against the grain of the increasing psychologization of the emotions in the course of the nineteenth and early twentieth centuries, separating them off from the body. This separation was, of course, never fully achieved. The hyphenated title of the "Psycho-Sexual" advice column run by the anarchist doctor Félix Martí Ibáñez in the magazine *Estudios* in the mid-1930s, discussed by Maite Zubiaurre, supposes that the psychological and the sexual are mutually constitutive; hence sexuality is an emotional matter and emotions may have a sexual basis. Álvarez also tackles the double nature of emotions, which are embodied and ineffable at the same time, in the context of personal and national displacement. His analysis of queer desire in Luis Cernuda's exile poetry, anchored in Stanley Fish's concept of "textual emotionality," explores the consequences of the interaction with a racial alterity that subverts the poet's attachments to a Spanish cultural imaginary, thus questioning the hierarchical ordering of the relationship between Spain and Mexico, North and South, subject and object, self and other, reason and feeling. The dissolution of the self in the dark body of a postcolonial male other inflects the literary representation of *Hispanidad* (Hispanicity) and indigenism, disturbing the homophobic rhetoric of both Spanish and Mexican nationalisms. The emotional encounter with racial alterity analyzed by Álvarez can be seen as a counterpart to the reverse encounter with Spain, discussed by Ríos-Font, of the Puerto Rican deputy Ramón Power y Giralt during his participation in the Cortes de Cádiz from 1809 to 1813, in which he played a major role as its first vice-president. As Ríos-Font shows, his experience of political subalternity during the parliamentary debates produced a shift of loyalties, as his patriotic love transferred itself from Spain to the Puerto Rican soil, anticipating the telluric foundational fictions of Puerto Rican national identity. Álvarez observes that Cernuda's emotional attachments are to the Mexican landscape as well as to Mexican male bodies. The chapters on Cernuda and Power y Giralt show how love of one's country (whether native or adopted) needs material anchors, despite being regarded as a particularly elevated emotion.

Álvarez's essay is also usefully read together with that by Delgado, in that both touch on personal masculine shame as linked to national shame, albeit from different angles. Taken together, these two chapters provide a reflection on expressions of embarrassment and the fine line between shame and pride. Delgado's essay considers public acts of apology in relation to what saying or feeling sorry does and, more important, what it commits the nation to do (Ahmed 116). The issue of sexual shame is further raised by Zubiaurre's discussion of Martí Ibáñez's anarchist advice column, which stands out for its refusal to respond in terms of shame to those seeking help to resolve a sexual dilemma perceived as shameful.

If, as Peter Burke suggests, "Most ambitious of all is the attempt to study fluctuations in the intensity of emotions at different periods" (42), then extreme conditions such as war or epidemics are key objects of analysis. It is not just a matter of detecting "a change in the intensity of feelings, not just a change in vocabulary, awareness or code," but a matter of "measuring the intensity of emotion in the past" (42). Haidt's contribution shows how fears of emotional contagion were made acute by the cholera epidemics of the 1830s and 1850s. Civil war, in both the nineteenth and twentieth centuries, is a repeated motif in the volume. Power y Giralt's time in Spain, where he died without returning to Puerto Rico, coincided with the War of Independence against Napoleonic occupation, which was a civil war in that it pitted Spaniards against Spaniards. As noted above, the horror stories of Pérez Zaragoza are seen by Fernández as a response to the horrors of the War of Independence and to the threat of dynastic civil strife that would materialize with the Carlist Wars. The capacity of the extreme emotional intensity of civil war to upset the categorization and ordering of emotions is seen in Zubiaurre's study of the contradictions in the medical writings of the anarchist intellectual Martí Ibáñez, who, despite rejecting shame as a moral category, regarded militiawomen as shamefully sapping male revolutionary vigor and thus upsetting the emotional economy needed in combat, predicated on male emotional excess and curtailment of the female libido. By taking male revolutionary emotion as the yardstick against which all other forms of emotion should be measured, Martí Ibáñez classified female desire as inferior and threatening, despite his generally sympathetic attitude toward women's emotional and sexual emancipation—evidenced in his legalization of abortion as deputy secretary for health and social welfare in the Catalan government early in the Civil War. At the same time, Zubiaurre shows how, in his advice column, Martí Ibáñez took the side of a female schoolteacher who, having resisted her would-be fiancé's advances, gave herself to a stranger during an air raid—a case study in how the circumstances of civil war could produce an emotional cataclysm in those subjected to its unbearable emotional intensity. There is a striking parallel between Martí Ibáñez's alarm at women's presence in combat and the anxieties produced by women's role in the War of Independence discussed by Bolufer, despite the very different historical moments.

The Spanish Civil War is, beyond doubt, the event in Spanish history that has generated the most passionate responses—then and since. Indeed, almost all writings on the Civil War—regardless of their political stance and even when they stress their objectivity—are driven by a passion that fuses intellectual endeavor with emotional commitment and shows feelings to be a kind of thought. At the same time, the war produced a perception of the country—by foreigners and by Spaniards themselves—as ruled by passions easily inflamed and prone to violence, thus being inhospitable to democracy. Javier Krauel's essay demonstrates that the political debates of the Second Spanish Republic of 1931–1936 were also debates over the role of the emotions in public life, and that the inability of liberal Republicans to recognize the importance of the emotions was a contributing factor to the failure of their democratic project (though what triggered the Civil War was, of course, the right-wing military rebellion of 18 July 1936). The concern of liberal intellectuals with the emotional conduct of citizens and their calls for emotional restraint are hardly specific to Spain, however. Indeed, the idea that passions are incompatible with democracy is one that runs through the history of modern and contemporary political thought. The fear of citizens' grievances and emotional attachments being mobilized by extremist demagogues is one shared by many public figures. This is particularly the case with left-wing thinkers, given that it has traditionally been the right that has been able to appreciate and deploy for its own purposes the emotions generated by moments of crisis (two obvious examples would be the Weimar Republic and the years preceding the Civil War in Spain). It is therefore logical that liberal writers in the press who were committed to the reforms legislated in Spain between 1931 and 1933 should have been concerned with the emotional conduct of their readers, which they attempted to regulate by linking reasoned judgment to civic duty. Krauel shows how Republican intellectuals' emphasis on rationality as the vehicle through which to legislate a new regime into being was a struggle to assert "emotional hegemony" and democratic normalcy. In a similar manner, half a century later the Transition to democracy would also construct the normalcy of a new regime through the avoidance of excessive emotions, strict adherence to legal procedures, and the virtual erasure of noninstitutional forms of democratic participation.

Needless to say, the view of the public sphere and political processes as rational, uncontaminated by affective oscillations, and dependent on self-restraint has important gender and class implications given that, since the nineteenth century, unrestrained and destructive passion has been linked to women and the lower classes. The anxieties raised by women's involvement in the War of Independence and Martí Ibáñez's demonization of militiawomen are eloquent examples of the fear of women's emotionality, as is the gendered nature of the 1931 parliamentary debate on women's suffrage, analyzed by Krauel. Fear of a supposed working-class emotional excess is illustrated, as Krauel notes, by Republican intellectuals' failure to appreciate that the anger behind anarcho-syndicalist peasant revolt had its reasons. Moreover, since the nineteenth century crowds and protesters had been characterized as driven by unconscious motives that get channeled into uncontrollable and destructive emotions (Le Bon). Republican intellectuals were not impervious to this notion, which persists throughout the contemporary period. As Gould states: "The corporate media, politicians and others with a vested interest in maintaining the status quo frequently describe social justice activists as driven by emotion . . . and protest activities as irrational and childish, rather than a legitimate mode for expressing social grievances" (19).

Moscoso's analysis of the unpublished sketchbook of a Republican sailor in the Civil War takes another tack: rather than explore the explosive emotions that surface in moments of conflict, he focuses on how one particular combatant tried to make sense of a chaotic, violent reality by drawing pictures of it. As forms of sense making, these pictures do not so much reflect experience as construct it via narrative and rhetorical—that is, performative—conventions that make it communicable. For this reason, Moscoso argues, emotions are essentially theatrical. As Joan W. Scott indicates (86), individuals do not "have" experience, but it is through experience that subjects constitute themselves. The inseparability in these sketches of emotions, sensations, and prior knowledge binds the emotions to the body and to thought. Moscoso's essay offers a theoretical reflection on the question of how to study emotions in the past. He concludes that the cultural history of emotions cannot consist of the attempt (impossible even in the present) to access the inner world of others; rather, it is a matter of trying to understand the mechanisms through which an articulate experience could be constructed.

As is well known, since the late 1990s Spain has seen intensive attempts—through activism and cultural production—to come to terms retrospectively with the suffering caused by the Spanish Civil War and its repressive aftermath, studied here by Labanyi and Ferrándiz. Like Moscoso, Labanyi examines the use of narrative—literally theatrical in this case—to make sense of suffering, through analysis of the first season of the television series *Amar en tiempos revueltos* (*Loving in Troubled Times*, 2005–2006), which covers the period from the February 1936 Popular Front election victory to the end of the Second World War in 1945. One of the problems with much of the now massive literary and cinematographic production on the Francoist repression during and after the Civil War is its appeal to a facile sentimentality that encourages intense identification with the suffering of victims, to an extent that occludes critical analysis of the factors that caused that suffering. While recognizing the limitations of emotions as a tool of historical understanding, Labanyi's essay proposes that the series, although highly melodramatic, mobilizes its viewers' emotions as instruments of critical judgment, by training them to assess the relative strengths and weakness of different emotional regimes, each with its own political connotations.

To this end, Labanyi draws on the concept of emotional competence theorized by Eva Illouz, whose arguments are also picked up by Delgado. Illouz's proposition is that, if for Freud, writing in the early twentieth century, historical progress was based on the repression of emotion, late capitalist modernity has made emotion into a form of capital, whose management is the key to personal and public success. Delgado develops Illouz's stress on how late capitalist modernity has broken down the division between public and private by saturating both with the constant expression of emotion and, in particular, the performance of suffering. Labanyi focuses rather on emotional competence as a discourse of empowerment preferable to religious notions of redemption through suffering or the privileging of victimhood into which today's memory movement sometimes lapses. Although Ferrándiz does not mention Illouz, her arguments are not unrelated to his discussion of the expressions of emotion at the opening of mass graves from the Civil War that have taken place in Spain since 2000. Acutely aware of the possibility of misuse of digital images of exhumations—whether images of the corpses being unearthed or of the displays of grief of the relatives present—Ferrándiz stresses the value of the public display of emotion by victims' relatives as a form of dignification. At the same time he notes the disagreements between different historical memory associations over protocols for the expression of emotion. Ferrándiz's main stress is on the performative nature of emotions, analyzing the typology of different poses that have emerged as a result of the practice of photographing or video-recording relatives at the gravesite. His analysis of how the "emotive poses" adopted by victims' relatives at exhumations are affected by their digital reproduction and circulation in the global mediasphere illustrates graphically how intimate emotions are socially produced—in this case, through the intersection of the local and the global, and of past and present.

It can, of course, be argued that the recent emotional and affective turns in the academic world are another instance of Illouz's proposition that late capitalist modernity has made emotion into a form of capital. The counterargument, to which we subscribe, is that ignoring emotions and affects will not erase their role in today's "emotional capitalism" (Illouz 5). Consequently, the best course of action seems to be to engage critically with the ideological and political dimensions of dominant emotional scripts. The deconstruction of the reason/passion dichotomy undertaken by emotion and affect studies has resulted in an important critical reconsideration of the emotional dimensions of collective actions and of politics (Walzer; Cvetovich; Kingston and Ferry; Hall; Nussbaum). The attention to the role that emotions and affect play in politics (broadly understood) also allows for a reassessment of the way power and ideology operate: "Indeed, affect theory calls into question any notion of ideology which ignores that ideas take hold, or fail to, depending on the affective charge generated by coming into contact with them" (Gould 33). The political deployment and mobilization of emotions is explored in relation to key historical moments in several of the essays in this volume, in particular those by Ríos-Font, Krauel, Helena Miguélez-Carballeira, and Delgado. Ríos-Font and Delgado explore the concept of patriotic love and conflicting emotional allegiances at crucial transitional moments: the beginning of a new understanding of the nation (the political debates on the 1812 Constitution) and the end of what has been called the regime of 1978 (marked by calls to modify the 1978 Constitution and by the proindependence movement in Catalonia). Ríos-Font's analysis of the political positions developed over time by Ramón Power y Giralt as Puerto Rico's deputy to the Cortes de Cádiz serves as a powerful reminder of the complexities of national bonds and as a reflection on what permits or disallows self-identification with a given political community. If Spain merited being Power y Giralt's object of patriotic love, it was thanks to his expectation that the reformulation of the state would be based on the principles of equality and fraternity for all its territories—particularly for those who, because of their conditions of subalternity, could not self-identify fully as Spaniards. The change in Power y Giralt's rhetoric, as he came to realize that the Americas would always be perceived as occupying a hierarchically inferior position to the metropolis, underlines what happens when the nation fails to give back the love invested in it by a subject or groups of subjects. Power y Giralt's initial sense of indignation and final alienation is symbolic of the consequences of ignoring citizens' demands and replacing affective bonds with legal obligation.

Delgado explores the concept of patriotic love, conflicting emotional loyalties, and national allegiance as a legal requirement in the context of today's "España de la crisis" (Spain of crisis), considered by many as the end of the regime instituted by the 1978 Constitution. It is interesting to compare Power y Giralt's trajectory—from hopeful convergence with the new political principles discussed in the Cádiz Cortes to disillusionment with the treatment that the colonies, and in particular Puerto Rico, received from the metropolis—with similar trajectories experienced by many Catalan politicians who today support independence from Spain. The rhetoric of patriotic love has been mobilized (very successfully) by the Catalan proindependence movement as well as (rather unsuccessfully) by the conservative Spanish government. The latter's obdurate opposition to changes to the 1978 Constitution that would allow for a different relationship of Catalonia to the Spanish state, as well as its insistence on mandating emotional loyalty to the nation by legal means, has had the unintended consequence of fueling the fire of secession. Delgado's analysis of political dissent and current challenges to abstract demands for patriotic love extends to the new social movements that have emerged out of the 15 May 2011 occupations of public space. The fact that the successful deployment of so-called negative emotions (anger and indignation) by the up-and-coming party Podemos is perceived by established political forces as a threat to democratic coexistence should be considered in the context of the current critical reevaluation of the role of emotions in social movements and contentious politics, and in the light of the historical pathologization of protest movements.

Both Delgado and Miguélez-Carballeira explore the emotional habitus of the regime of 1978 (the Transition) and its present-day consequences in terms of what Berlant (*Cruel*; "Subject") calls the consolidation of a national sentimentality that displaces antagonistic class and ideological positions onto a utopian space of unconflicted identities. In the context of the emotional public sphere that characterizes contemporary Western societies—and Spain is no exception—the dominant cultural practices of the regime of 1978 have seemed to come from the place imagined by Dorothy in *The Wizard of Oz*: somewhere over the rainbow "where there is no trouble" (Berlant, "Subject" 60). The anxieties and suffering that undoubtedly have afflicted a country marked by internal conflicts and violence were made to seem to belong exclusively to the past or were displaced onto marginal elements of society. Miguélez-Carballeira's analysis demonstrates that the bland sentimentality that characterized the affective atmosphere of the official "CT" (Culture of the Transition) is particularly visible in relation to Galicia—as perceived from within Galicia and by the rest of Spain—whose image has rested since the nineteenth century, and still today, on the presumption of a sentimental, feminized, and politically docile cultural identity. Her essay examines how mainstream cultural practices and policy (in and outside Galicia) have perpetuated such perceptions of Galicia's feminized sentimentality, but are now being contested from the margins of institutionalized representations, specifically through the work of a popular music group that operates through parody. Her study points to the fine line between the repetition that constructs identity and the repetition that destabilizes it through parody. Her study also shows that we need to distinguish between emotions that disempower (sentimentality) and emotions that empower (indignation, as discussed by Delgado); it is not just a matter of being seen as emotional, but of the particular emotion that one is assigned. The adjudication to Galicia of sentimentality works both ways: when seen alongside more "belligerent" nonstate identities (Basque or Catalan), Galicia is much less criticized by supporters of a single Spanish national identity but also much less politically visible. Miguélez-Carballeira's analysis invites further reflection on the types of emotional scripts that sustain national narratives, including the specific emotions associated with strong national identities and their gender and class implications. Together with the essays by Álvarez, Ríos-Font, and Delgado, her chapter suggests the need for alternative conceptual frameworks to contemplate the existence within national identities of multifaceted, and often conflicting, affective components.

The current economic and political crisis in Spain has brought to the fore the crucial importance of emotions and affects in democratic politics, and their role in generating the energies needed for social and political change. Indignation (at untenable levels of unemployment, the proliferation of corruption cases, and government opacity) has been channeled from street demonstrations to the creation of new political and civic alternatives (Podemos, Ciudadanos, Guanyem, Ganemos, Plataforma de los Afectados por las Hipotecas). The voices that caution against the excesses of emotion in "populist" political alternatives and that align mainstream options with reason and normalcy could take note of theorists like Berlant who acknowledge that "non-rationality" has always been at the heart of the political (Berlant, "The Epistemology"); that is to say, intertwined with reason, within and beside cognitive sense making (Gould 24–25). In this context, it is understandable that there are those who do not regard the return of passionate politics as positive, given Spain's history of violent internal conflict. From the long history of military uprisings throughout the nineteenth and much of the twentieth century to the different proindependence movements, the rhetoric of insecurity and hatred has been entwined with the exaltation of patriotic love, with all-too-well-known results. Interestingly, the recognition by new social movements of the value of passions for democratic politics and social change comes with the return to key concepts that take us back to the Enlightenment: the notion of sensibility, for example, often invoked as a key ingredient of a new political culture in Spain (Monedero). In the same vein, suggestions have recently been made in Spain that citizens need to be educated in both reason and passion, as well as in empathy (Gomá Lanzón; "Nueva sensibilidad").

In her major 2013 study of political emotions, philosopher Martha Nussbaum has continued her previous exploration of emotions in relation to social justice within liberal democracies, emphasizing the importance of love in forging enduring communities. In 2012, at the worst moment of the economic crisis, the Spanish government had distinguished Nussbaum with the Príncipe de Asturias award in the Social Sciences. Many years before, in 1981, at the beginning of the democratic period, the Spanish philosopher María Zambrano had received the same award, created that year. It is very possible that Nussbaum did not know who Zambrano was, but she surely would have identified with her message, developed in 1930 as Krauel reminds us in this volume, that liberalism's morality fails to engage with essential human problems because it does not take into account feelings, emotions, and passions. Zambrano continued to articulate her philosophical reflections on love, freedom, visceral truths, and the reasons of the heart throughout her very long exile in several different countries. Strikingly in advance of her time, her proposition was that, if we listen to visceral truths and the rhythms marked by our hearts, we can through them listen to the social situation of a country, the flow of everyday life, the invisible movement of people. By contrast, she argued, the visceral truths and emotional reasons that are ignored will always come back, often violently and uncontrollably. By bringing the passions back into Spanish cultural history—to paraphrase the title of Kingston and Ferry's book on emotions in politics—we hope to reverse the dynamics so perceptively and poetically described by Zambrano. It is our goal, therefore, to contribute to an appreciation of the importance of the emotions not just as an object of academic study, and not just as a key component of subjectivity, but also as a tool to understand the identifications, misrecognitions, and antagonistic demands that are always operative within communities and civic life.

WORKS CITED

Ahmed, Sara. *The Cultural Politics of Emotion*. New York: Routledge, 2004.
Anderson, Benedict. *Imagined Communities: Reflections on the Origin and Spread of Nationalism*. 2nd rev. ed. London: Verso, 1983.
Berlant, Lauren. *Cruel Optimism*. Durham, NC: Duke UP, 2011.
———. "The Epistemology of State Emotion." *Dissent in Dangerous Times*. Ed. Austin Sarat. Ann Arbor: U of Michigan P, 2005. 46–78.
———. "The Subject of True Feeling." *Cultural Pluralism, Identity Politics and the Law*. Ed. Austin Sarat and Thomas Kearns. Ann Arbor: U of Michigan P, 1999. 49–84.
Brennan, Teresa. *The Transmission of Affect*. Ithaca, NY: Cornell UP, 2004.
Bruno, Giuliana. *Atlas of Emotion: Journeys in Art, Architecture, and Film*. New York: Verso, 2002.
Burke, Peter. "Is There a Cultural History of the Emotions?" *Representing Emotions: New Connections in the History of Art, Music and Medicine*. Ed. Penelope Gouk and Helen Hills. Aldershot, UK: Ashgate, 2005. 35–47.
Clough, Patricia T., ed. *The Affective Turn: Theorizing the Social*. Durham, NC: Duke UP, 2007.
Cvetkovich, Ann. "On Affect and Protest." *Political Emotions: New Agendas in Communication*. Ed. Janet Staiger, Ann Cvetkovich, and Ann Reynolds. New York: Routledge, 2010. 4–12.
Dixon, Thomas. *Passions to Emotions: The Creation of a Secular Psychological Category*. Cambridge: Cambridge UP, 2003.
Frevert, Ute. "The Modern History of Emotions: A Research Center in Berlin." *Cuadernos de Historia Contemporánea* 36 (2014): 31–55. *revistas.ucm.es/index.php/CHCO/article/view/46681/43817* (accessed 28 November 2014).
Gomá Lanzón, Javier. "Visión culta y corazón educado: Lecciones de la crisis." *Cultura/s* (supplement of *La Vanguardia*) 22 October 2014: 3–5.
Gouk, Penelope, and Helen Hills. "Towards Histories of Emotions." *Representing Emotions: New Connections in the History of Art, Music and Medicine*. Ed. Penelope Gouk and Helen Hills. Aldershot, UK: Ashgate, 2005: 15–34.
Gould, Deborah. "On Affect and Protest." *Political Emotions: New Agendas in Communication*. Ed. Janet Staiger, Ann Cvetkovich, and Ann Reynolds. New York: Routledge, 2010. 18–44.
Hall, Cheryl. *The Trouble with Passion: Political Theory beyond the Reign of Reason*. New York: Routledge, 2005.

Harding, Jennifer, and E. Deidre Pribram, eds. *Emotions: A Cultural Studies Reader.* New York: Routledge, 2009.

Illouz, Eva. *Cold Intimacies: The Making of Emotional Capitalism.* Cambridge: Polity, 2007.

Jameson, Fredric. *The Political Unconscious: Narrative as a Socially Symbolic Act.* Ithaca, NY: Cornell UP, 1981.

Kingston, Rebecca, and Leonard Ferry. *Bringing the Passions Back In: The Emotions in Political Philosophy.* Vancouver: U of British Columbia P, 2008.

Le Bon, Gustave. *The Crowd: A Study of the Popular Mind.* Trans. Robert Nye. New York: Dover, 2002. Trans. of *La Psychologie des foules,* 1895.

Leys, Ruth. "The Turn to Affect: A Critique." *Critical Inquiry* 37 (2011): 434–72.

Macpherson, C. B. *The Political Theory of Possessive Individualism.* Oxford: Clarendon Press, 1962.

Massumi, Brian. *Parables for the Virtual: Movement, Affect, Sensation.* Durham, NC: Duke UP, 2002.

Medina Doménech, Rosa María. "Sentir la historia: Propuestas para una agenda de investigación feminista en la historia de las emociones." *ARENAL: Revista de Historia de las Mujeres* 19.1 (2012): 161–99.

Monedero, Juan Carlos. *Dormíamos y despertamos: El 15 M, la reinvención de la democracia.* Madrid: Nueva Utopía, 2012.

Moscoso Sarabia, Javier, and Juan Manuel Zaragoza Bernal. "Historias del bienestar: Desde la historia de las emociones a las políticas de la experiencia." *Cuadernos de Historia Contemporánea* 36 (2014): 73–88. *revistas.ucm.es/index.php/CHCO/article/view/46722/43854* (accessed 28 November 2014).

Ngai, Sianne. *Ugly Feelings.* Cambridge, MA: Harvard UP, 2005.

"Nueva sensibilidad y nueva cultura política." Dossier in *El Estado Mental* 3: *Post-todo* (July–August 2014): 4–51, 132–44.

Nussbaum, Martha C. *Political Emotions: Why Love Matters for Justice.* Cambridge, MA: Harvard UP, 2013.

Pagés-Rangel, Roxana. *Del dominio público: Itinerarios de la carta privada.* Amsterdam: Rodopi, 1997.

Plamper, Jan. "Historia de las emociones." *Cuadernos de Historia Contemporánea* 36 (2014): 17–29. *revistas.ucm.es/index.php/CHCO/article/view/46680/43816* (accessed 28 November 2014).

Rodríguez-López, Carolina, and Daniel Ventura Herranz. "De exilios y emociones." *Cuadernos de Historia Contemporánea* 36 (2014): 133–38. *revistas.ucm.es/index.php/CHCO/article/view/46684/43820* (accessed 28 November 2014).

Rosenwein, Barbara H. *Emotional Communities in the Early Middle Ages.* Ithaca, NY: Cornell UP, 2006.

San Martín, Olga R. "Una asignatura llamada empatía." *El Mundo* 11 November 2014. *www.elmundo.es/espana/2014/11/03/5456aa0aca4741b5118b457e.html* (accessed 10 December 2014).

Scott, Joan W. "La experiencia como prueba." *Feminismos literarios.* Ed. Neus Carbonell and Meri Torras. Madrid: Arco Libros, 1999. 77–112.

Sennett, Richard. *The Fall of Public Man.* New York: Vintage, 1978.

Smith, Adam. *The Theory of Moral Sentiments*. 1759. Ed. Knud Hakoossen. Cambridge: Cambridge UP, 2002.

Trigg, Stephanie. "Introduction: Emotional Histories—Beyond the Personalization of the Past and the Abstraction of Affect Theory." *Exemplaria* 26.1 (2014): 3–15.

Walzer, Michael. *Politics and Passion: Toward a More Egalitarian Liberalism*. New Haven, CT: Yale UP, 2004.

Weber, Max. *Economía y sociedad: Esbozo de sociología comprensiva*. Vol. 1. Ed. Johannes Winckelmann. Intro. and trans. José Medina Echavarría. Mexico City: Fondo de Cultura Económica, 1993.

Williams, Raymond. *Marxism and Literature*. Oxford: Oxford UP, 1977.

Zambrano, María. *Persona y democracia: La historia sacrificial*. 1958. Barcelona: Anthropos, 1992.

CHAPTER ONE

Reasonable Sentiments
Sensibility and Balance in Eighteenth-Century Spain

MÓNICA BOLUFER

Etching number 32 in Goya's *Caprichos* series, published in 1799, is entitled "Porque fue sensible" ("Because She Was Sensitive"; see Fig. 1.1). It depicts a deeply sorrowful woman locked in a dark cell, barely illuminated by weak rays of light that filter in through a small window. A few years later, the accounts of the Spanish people's uprising against the Napoleonic invasion would reinforce two of the ideas suggested by the etching: the dangers inherent in sensibility and its particular association with women, both already characteristic of a Romantic vision of the emotions. In a fine study of Spanish sentimental fiction, Ana Rueda used this image to represent the growing distrust of sensibility and of its power to solve moral and social conflict that developed at the dawn of the nineteenth century ("'Virtue in Distress'" 201). However, in the previous century, there was a moment when the Enlightenment concept of "sensibility" was conceived as being able to reconcile reason and sentiment, although this ideal was wrought with tensions that Goya's etching—and, as we shall see later, the episode that inspired it—embody.

In effect, the eighteenth century constitutes, in Spain as in the rest of Europe, a key period in the formation of new emotional codes, which in certain respects anticipate those of the nineteenth century and in others clearly differ from them. It was in the eighteenth century that the earlier discourse on the passions as domineering impulses was toned down in favor of a more pleasant image of feelings as spontaneous affective manifestations, signs of an innate natural morality not at odds with Providence. When Gaspar Melchor de Jovellanos (1744–1811)—man of letters, politician, and friend of Goya—declared in his "Memoria sobre educación pública" ("Report on Public Education"), written in 1802 during his exile in Majorca, that moral truths are "verdades de sentimiento" (truths of sentiment; 455) engraved in human hearts as the true expression of God's will, he was echoing ideas widespread among enlightened Spaniards, supported by readings of key texts in European moral philosophy like those of Shaftesbury, Hutcheson, David Hume, Adam Smith, and Condillac (Gies 216–19; Polt). According to Jovellanos, although reason helps us to "discernir y conocer la ley

Figure 1.1. Goya, "Because She Was Sensitive." *Los caprichos.* Courtesy of the Trustees of the British Museum.

moral" (assess and know moral law), behavior must be guided above all by such "verdades de sentimiento": "El hombre, por decirlo así, las halla antes en su espíritu, las siente más bien que las conoce, o las conoce y ve de una ojeada y sin necesidad de profundas reflexiones. Una luz clara que el Criador infundió en su corazón, se las descubre, y una voz secreta que excitó en su interior, se le anuncia y recuerda poderosamente aun en medio del tumulto de las pasiones" (Man, we might say, encounters them sooner in his spirit, feels them rather than knows them, or knows and sees them at first glance with no need for deep reflection. A clear light infused in his heart by the Supreme Creator reveals them to him, and a secret inner voice aroused by Him announces and evokes them even amid the passions' turmoil; Jovellanos, "Memoria" 455).

In this period, such feelings were not referred to as "emotions," a term that, as historians know well, was not used to refer to feelings before the nineteenth century (*emoción* makes its first appearance in a Spanish dictionary in 1843 (*Nuevo diccionario* 413). In the early modern period, the words used most often to speak about states of the heart or mind were "afectos" (affects), "afecciones" (affections), or "pasiones" (passions), understood as passing—and often undesirable—commotions or disturbances (Dixon 1–6, 62–68; Tausiet and Amelang 8–9). The new idea of an inner impulse that inspires moral judgment emerged with the change of meaning undergone by the concept "sentimiento" (sentiment), previously defined as "opinion" or "sorrow," which increasingly came to be used to mean both the act of perceiving objects through the senses (as theorized by sensist epistemology) and a feeling of the heart, as defined in the 1791, third edition of the Real Academia Española's *Diccionario de la lengua castellana:* "La percepción del alma en las cosas espirituales con gusto, complacencia o movimiento interior" (Perceptions of the soul in spiritual matters with pleasure, complaisance, or inner movement; 759). Since this was a relatively new usage, in a 1792 preface to her Spanish translation of a French philosophical novel, María Rosario Romero felt the need to clarify her language to her readers: "por la palabra sentimiento no se ha de entender solamente el que se recibe de alguna pesadumbre, sino también por el gusto y complacencia que recibe el alma, según las diferentes impresiones" (by the word "sentiment" we must understand not only that provoked by sorrow, but also the pleasure and complaisance received by the soul, according to different impressions; 18). But above all, these new meanings were evidenced, in Spain as in other countries, by growing use of the term "sensibility" to designate not only the capacity to react to stimuli—the "involuntaria y como maquinal" (involuntary and almost machinelike) sensibility of which the poet and jurist Meléndez Valdés speaks in 1798 (1084)—but also the capacity to experience emotions through sympathy or affinity with the feelings of another, which awakens compassion that in turn incites action: a "sensibilidad oficiosa" (officious sensibility) that "inspira dulcemente virtudes sociales y domésticas" (sweetly inspires social and domestic virtues; 1099).

In this chapter, I hope to underscore the differences between this eighteenth-century emotional style of sensibility and that of Romanticism, two markedly different cultures, although the former contains within it the paradoxes and tensions that will end up exploding in the form of open contradictions in the latter.[1] At the same time, I will attempt to point out some specificities of the Spanish case within the context of eighteenth-century European sentimental culture. My approach will be based on a history of the emotions that has a longer and more complex trajectory than the current "affective turn" in the English-language humanities and social sciences tends to acknowledge (Burke 36–38; Tausiet and Amelang 19–24). Specifically, I will draw on several historiographical traditions—some of them too abruptly dismissed and others not mentioned in a fine and now classic essay by Barbara Rosenwein (821–23, 831–32)—including the legacy of the French Annales school (from Lucien Febvre to Roger Chartier) and of British and French scholarship on the history of the family (Lawrence Stone, Philippe Ariès, Jean-Louis Flandrin). But, above all, I am indebted to the insights of cultural history and gender history, which have been crucial in dismantling a residual notion of the emotions as basic natural facts, universal in time and space and immune to change, whose history would simply be that of the "repression" or "tolerance" of preexisting spontaneous impulses. By contrast, the works of Knott, Carter, Barker-Benfield, Rosenwein, Reddy, Morant, and de la Pascua Sánchez, among others, have explored the ways in which the emotions mediate between the individual and the social (Bourke 124) by analyzing the cultural construction of emotional codes, and the shaping and expression of personal and social experience through the use and manipulation of the languages and resources made available by them. The material discussed in this chapter will include eighteenth-century Spanish sentimental literature, plus other documents ranging from political reports and legal papers to personal writings (memoirs, autobiographies, and letters). Taken together, these sources can help us understand, at least partially, not only how sentiments were expressed in writing, but also how a specific language (that of sensibility) was used in ways that, in keeping with William Reddy's notion of "emotives," were neither completely constative nor totally performative, but "at once managerial and exploratory" (Plamper 240). In other words, this is a language likely to have produced particular ways of feeling and of relating to others, while being flexible enough to accommodate individual and collective appropriations and reworkings (Bolufer, "La realidad y el deseo").

Although the contrary has sometimes been argued, sentimental literature was not unknown in Spanish society in the eighteenth century; rather, there was an active process of reception, consumption, appropriation, and production of sentimental genres. New forms of drama and comedy—including the comédie larmoyante (lachrymose comedy)—were introduced in select aristocratic and literary circles such as the Madrid *tertulia* (salon) of the Marquesa de Sarria, Josefa de Zúñiga, in the 1750s and that of Pablo de Olavide in Seville in the 1770s (Fuentes 104–9). Promoted by the state in its efforts at aesthetic and moral reform of the theater, these new theatrical forms would reach a broader public in the century's last two decades, through original works but especially through versions of French and German plays (García Garrosa, *La retórica*; "Unión de voluntades"). In the 1790s, the sentimental novel began to develop, also through adaptations of English works such as those of Samuel Richardson (*Pamela*, 1794–1795; *Clara Harlowe*, 1794; *Carlos Grandison*, 1798), and Henry Fielding (*Amelia*, 1796; *Tom Jones*, 1796), and of French works such as Stéphanie de Genlis's *Adela y Teodoro* (1782), Jeanne-Marie Leprince de Beaumont's *La nueva Clarisa* (1797), and Gatrey's *La filósofa por amor* (1799). These adaptations were later supplemented by the belated production of original novels in Spanish, including very successful works such as Pedro de Montengón's *Eusebio* (1786–1788), Antonio Valladares de Sotomayor's *La Leandra* (1797–1807), and Gaspar Zavala y Zamora's *Oderay* (1804) and *La Eumenia* (1805), continuing throughout the nineteenth century and outliving the birth of realism (Rueda, *Cartas*). Such novels, usually marketed via subscription, were extremely successful with a broad and varied public, including a high percentage of women readers (ranging between 14 percent and 28 percent, remarkable in a country with low literacy rates).[2]

State and inquisitorial censorship kept a close watch on the novel, refusing printing licenses and controlling access to works in foreign languages. Finally, a formal ban on the genre (only partially effective) was decreed in May 1799. As a result, Spanish authors, translators, and publishers of sentimental fiction tended to defend the genre even more emphatically than their European counterparts. To counter those who distrusted the novel for its power to stimulate the imagination, they presented it as an excellent instrument of moral education, precisely because of its power to touch and move its readers, helping them to identify and educate their feelings—as Alfonso, the protagonist of José Mor de Fuentes's *La Serafina* (1798), claims of "Clarisa y sus semejantes, que están brotando por todos sus renglones la moral más acendrada" (Clarissa and its likes, whose every line exudes the most distilled morality; Mor de Fuentes, *La Serafina* 1: 100). At the same time, translators went to great lengths to adapt their versions to "las costumbres nacionales" (national customs) and to stress (crucial in a Catholic country) the basic equivalence between natural morality and divine Providence. For example, the translator of *Pamela*, Ignacio García Malo, not only bowdlerized the text (more radically than the French version from which he worked) of any allusion to sensuality but also Christianized its heroine in his prologue, coming close to martyrological hagiography in his praise of her chastity (García Malo, *Pamela* 5: vi).

Sentimental rhetoric was not, of course, limited to explicitly "sentimental" genres. It also pervaded other types of texts, from moral and didactic literature to political speeches and medical treatises. And the public that enthusiastically received sentimental ethics and aesthetics was broad and diverse: male and female, more or less educated, ranging from aristocrats, politicians, intellectuals, and artists like Jovellanos (who owned all of Richardson's major works) or Goya (who subscribed to the Spanish version of *Clarissa*), to broad sectors of the middle and even popular classes—in the latter case, in a society with low literacy rates, largely through the theater rather than the novel. These heterogeneous reading publics may have appreciated different aspects of the code of sensibility: its claim to universality as a virtue allegedly transcending class, and its implicit ability to convey distinction as the alleged attribute of educated and refined people.

How did the affective models proposed by sentimental literature influence the ways in which people assigned meaning to their feelings and relations? Unsurprisingly, this is more difficult to evaluate, since private writings, even if we assume that shifts in the way people narrate their emotions alter their subjective experience (Bourke 120), are often opaque or ambiguous in this respect. On the one hand, at the end of the century letters exchanged by married couples or lovers timidly incorporated inflections of the new sentimental language into the amorous formulas inherited from earlier moral and religious literature or from the baroque novel (de la Pascua Sánchez, *Mujeres solas* 124–25, 291–92). At the same time, private correspondence between intimate male friends displayed a language of even higher affective intensity clearly influenced by the sentimental style—as seen, for example, in the letters of Jovellanos and Meléndez Valdés, who address each other as "muy amado" (beloved) and "mi dulcísimo amigo" (my sweetest friend), and revel in their mutual "sentimiento" (sentiment), "íntimo amor" (intimate love), and tenderness (Meléndez Valdés 1175–82,

1207–8), or in those sent by Goya to Martín Zapater where he addresses him as "amigo y amigo y más amigo" (friend and friend and closest friend), and "querido de mi alma" (dear to my soul; Goya 65, 68, 121). On the other hand, different types of ego documents—autobiographies, diaries, moral advice—were shaped by the model not so much of sentimental confession (as in Rousseau's *Confessions*, dismissed by Jovellanos in 1794 as "impertinencias bien escritas, muchas contradicciones y mucho orgullo" (well written impertinences, many contradictions, and much pride; *Diario* 632) as of other kinds of writing (the testimonial of professional or learned merits, the aristocratic genre of advice to one's children) in which there is scant room for affective experiences. Decades later, a tone of containment and reserve dominates in the style of José Blanco-White (1775–1841), who, although describing himself as a deeply sensitive individual, in 1821 declared his wish to avoid sentimental exhibition: "No poseo el cinismo intelectual que me permitiría, como a Rousseau, exponer mi corazón desnudo a la mirada de los demás" (I lack the intellectual cynicism that would allow me, like Rousseau, to expose my naked heart to the gaze of others; *Cartas* 79–80). Much rarer is the explicit treatment of subjectivity found in Antonio Alcalá Galiano (1789–1865) who, in his memoirs, written past the midcentury, boasted of a "sensibilidad extremada" (extreme sensibility) and constructed a life narrative deeply influenced by sentimental fiction (367–68).

With some peculiarities and a degree of time lag, then, the Spanish culture of sensibility shares with its European counterparts some fundamental features that differentiate it from the regime of Romantic sensibility. Although sentiments are naturalized as impulses that need to be given an outlet, it is understood and often explicitly declared that they should be educated and channeled. On the other hand, sentiments are not yet seen as closely linked to personal identity in the sense of an autonomous self, conscious of its own individuality and singularity, and confronting an exterior world of social conventions and obligations. On the contrary, sentiments are interpreted as the bonding agent that creates society, binding the individual to others through empathy and benevolence, that is, constructing a "socially tuned self," in Sarah Knott's felicitous phrase (5). While private life is seen as the most suitable (but not the only) sphere for the expression of the emotions, this private dimension where feelings can blossom is still not exclusively identified with domestic and family space. Rather, it is connected with a broader notion of sociability (a crucial concept in Enlightenment thought and culture) that includes and particularly favors elective relationships: salons (tertulias), academies, and other voluntary or informal circles, friendship bonds, and small networks.

Correspondingly sensibility in the eighteenth century is not yet seen as a specifically feminine inclination, but rather as a positive yet ambivalent gift (partly natural, partly the result of education) that, when properly balanced with reason, defines the respectable moral subject and citizen—male (the *hombre de bien* or "true gentleman") as well as female (Haidt; Carter; Bolufer, "'Hombres de bien'"). This does not mean that sensibility was ungendered: women were credited with being more spontaneously sensitive, while men had to educate themselves in order to become so. However, only with time would sensibility become more clearly feminized and associated with domesticity, being presented as a weakness that the male should repress in public while cultivating it in the "emotional refuges" provided by homosocial circles (Gómez Castellano; Vincent-Buffault; Sierra 24).

The collection of stories *Voz de la naturaleza* (*Voice of Nature*), by Richardson's translator Ignacio García Malo (1760–1812), published with great and lasting success in six volumes between 1787 and 1792 (a seventh volume appeared in 1803), offers an excellent example of this new eighteenth-century sentimental culture. Its author was a state functionary, known in literary circles for his translations, in particular that of Richardson's *Pamela* (1794–1795, reprinted in 1799). His *Voz de la naturaleza*—though loosely inspired by Richardson's novels and French collections of moral and sentimental stories (Marmontel, Arnaud), as he admits (*Voz* 136)—is nonetheless an original work, characterized by an intense moral purpose and strong concern with stylistic renovation. Its title makes use of a personification frequently found in Enlightenment literature, fictional as well as moral, pedagogical, and medical. The "voice of nature" (like the "secret voice" Jovellanos speaks of) is that of the natural morality inscribed in the hearts of all human beings, which makes itself heard through the sentiments. It is not seen as an imperious call that must be followed whatever the cost, but rather as mediated by education, whose role is stressed in shaping a more refined "second nature." To this end, García Malo enthusiastically defends the superior moral value of sentimental fiction over treatises and sermons—too verbose, solemn, and explicitly didactic—on account of its power to move the public: "Para instruirlo [al hombre] se requiere no solamente darle ideas puras que lo iluminen, sino imágenes sensibles que le hagan descubrir la verdad" (In order to instruct [Man], not only are pure ideas required to illuminate him, but also sensible images that enable him to discover truth; 135); this phrase, quoted from Fénelon's *Télémaque*, opens García Malo's "Advertencia al lector" ("Address to Readers"). Thus, the power of sentimentality as a moral and aesthetic code lies in the fact that it conceals its own cultural rhetoric by appearing as an immediate, transparent embodiment of feeling: "No se hallarán en esta obra rasgos de elocuencia y erudición, sino sentimientos exprimidos [expresados] naturalmente y sin artificio. La voz de la razón es la que únicamente persuade, y ésta es la que habla en toda mi obra" (No traits of eloquence and erudition will be found in this work, but sentiments expressed naturally and without artifice. The voice of reason is the only one that can persuade, and it is the voice that speaks throughout my work; 136).

The twelve stories that make up García Malo's volume transmit the Enlightenment ideal of sensibility as a complex balancing act. Those who allow themselves to be carried along by the blind force of passion are severely punished and compared to irrational beasts. Thus, in "Flora y Teodoro" ("Flora and Teodoro") the protagonist's protector, an exemplary religious man, on his deathbed counsels his protégé to distrust the sentiments of others and "vencerse a sí mismo" (conquer himself). Although throughout the text the author uses a language full of military metaphors exhorting combat against the passions, suggesting that ecclesiastical discourse weighed more heavily on the sentimental imaginary than Enlightenment thinkers themselves liked to admit, the work's prevailing moral vision is more optimistic and confident, affirming the possibility of reconciling reason and sentiment.

This delicate balance is expressed above all through the contrast between two different feelings. On the one hand, amorous "passion" is understood as an alienating impulse: "este tirano de los corazones" (this tyrant of the heart; 2) that "perturba los sentidos y la razón, quitando al hombre la facultad de dominarse a sí mismo" (disturbs the senses and reason, depriving man of self-control; 34). On the other hand, sentiment founded on virtue is represented through the recurring metaphor of the harmonious concord of musical instruments, as, for instance, in the description of the love between Estanislao and Leonor, the protagonists of the ninth story: "Parecía que la naturaleza había formado dos corazones tan conformes que se movían a un mismo impulso, así como dos instrumentos templados unísonamente" (Nature seemed to have formed two hearts so in accord that they moved in unison, like two instruments tuned to the same pitch; 107–8).

Failure to understand that this "natural affection" refers to the docile affinity of souls, the sentiment proclaimed as the basis of conjugal union, has led to distorted interpretations of the Enlightenment concept of "marriage of inclination," which has often been understood too literally as emblematic of a new society that extols virtue over birthright, and spontaneous emotion over social convention (Reddy 153; Morant and Bolufer, *Amor, matrimonio* 106–41, "Hombres y mujeres" 147–50). However, in literature as well as in life and memory practices, the sentiments are not drastically opposed to, but rather mixed with, aspirations for material well-being and social propriety. For instance, in his memoirs, written in 1790–1810, Jovellanos grounds his discussion of his parents' union (carefully planned so as to resolve a long-standing dispute between families) on the assumption that marriage should not be guided by purely economic reasons, nor by unreflective passion, but rather should reconcile personal virtues with familial convenience and social order, as the bases of a profitable, happy life together, which in the case of his parents had retrospectively given rise to a solid conjugal affection ("Memorias familiares" 206, 208, 213–14).

Marriage is thus represented as the most useful civil status and at the same time the happiest one for the man and woman adequately formed in the values of sensibility, as happens with Alfonso and Serafina and countless other literary characters. And the plots of Spanish literary texts, whether original or translated, show even more agreement on this matter than their French or British counterparts: most novels and comedies finish when their virtuous protagonists, having overcome the obstacles that separated them, can at last fulfill their love, that is, when they marry or are about to do so (very few works explore their conjugal relations). Contrary to the nineteenth century, it is extremely hard to find tragic or transgressive endings that do not resolve the conflict between individual choice and social coercion. This does happen, however, in the case of García Malo's stories "La desventurada Margarita" ("The Ill-Fated Margarita") and "El brigadier y Carlota" ("The Brigadier and Carlota"), whose heroines are punished for their sins against virtue and honor by starving to death or being locked up for life in a convent, respectively, as it does also in "Anselmo y Elisia" ("Anselmo and Elisia"), the love of whose title characters, impossible because of social convention, ends up consuming them. Generally, though, it is assumed that love, if based on virtue and merit, cannot but have a happy end. Marriage is thus represented, in sentimental literature and also in political and juridical texts, as the state that is both the most beneficial for society and the most suited to human nature, the bond that harnesses reason to sentiment and individual happiness to social order, as Meléndez Valdés would explain at length in his *Discursos forenses* (*Prosecutor's Addresses*; 1047).

In effect, in eighteenth-century discourse on sensibility, the emotions (including love), even when they are seen as an intense, intimate experience, are not presented as the essential core of an identity conceived as a radical, irreducible singularity—a notion that is central to the concept of the modern subject. Rather, sentiments are described in literature and theorized philosophically as the basis of sociability, understood in a double sense: as an innate human tendency and as a relational practice between people who share similar tastes and values (Bolufer, "Lo íntimo"). In this sense, sensibility would play a key role in generating alternative bonds and senses of belonging (though sometimes reinforcing and justifying traditional ones) between "emotional communities" (often additionally connected by social and political commitments), in a period of gradual erosion of longstanding filiations of social estate or lineage. This is evidenced in the importance attached to marriage of inclination as the foundation of society, but also in the related role of another sentiment that was central to moral reflection, literary fiction, and life practices: friendship, presented as a source of sentimental pleasure—the pleasure of elective affinities. In her *Cartas selectas* (*Selected Letters*, 1800), a moral and pedagogical essay allegedly translated from the English, Rita Caveda y Solares (1760–?), a member of the cultivated Asturian nobility and a friend of Jovellanos, included friendship among the "disposiciones del corazón" (heart's dispositions), presenting it as a demanding relationship that combines sentimental expansion and utility, emotion and reflection: a sentiment that does not exclude but on the contrary *demands* the rational consideration of the object of esteem (36–41). That is, emotions (those of close friendship, in this case) were often theorized as having cognitive potential, not opposing but complementing reason. In a more lyrical vein, sentimental fiction, although it focused preferentially on the power of love, also evoked friendship as a "delicioso comercio entre dos almas que se explayan y comunican mutuamente sus penas y sus gustos" (delightful commerce between two souls that speak at length and mutually communicate their sorrows and their pleasures), as Gaspar Zavala y Zamora wrote in *La Eumenia* (*Obras* 101)—note the use of the term "commerce," applied in the eighteenth century to both mercantile and social exchange, in this case referring to sentimental bonds. In select Enlightenment circles, amicable sentiments also took on the broader sense of "friend of the nation," as exemplified by the Sociedad Bascongada de Amigos del País (Basque Society of Friends of the Nation; see Fig. 1.2), a key center of Enlightenment ideas in Spain, originating around 1760 in a small circle of Basque nobles linked by existing bonds of kinship, friendship,

Figure 1.2. "The Three [Basque Provinces] Make One." Emblem of the Basque Society of Friends of the Country.

and ideological affinity, which made the concept of friendship the raison d'être of their reformist projects and activities (Trojani xiii–xvii, 178–91). Thus, sensibility was seen and constructed as the keystone of sociability, which should radiate out in concentric circles from intimate relations to broader forms of association, blurring the limits between the private and the public, the social and the political.

If the naturalization of sentiment (conjugal and amicable) did not entail its unequivocal assignment to the private realm (and privacy itself was symbolically identified with friendship as much as with domesticity), neither did it attach it to an exclusively feminine sphere. However, the new emotional style discriminated between the sentimental inclinations of men and women and the uses they should make of their emotions. Although sensibility was considered intrinsic to the human condition and desirable in all moral and refined individuals, it was taken for granted that in women it came more naturally—"esta amable virtud que vosotras recibísteis de la naturaleza y que el hombre alcanza apenas a fuerza de reflexión y studio" (that pleasant virtue that you [women] received from nature and that man barely attains by force of reflection and study), Jovellanos declared in his 1788 "Elogio de Carlos III" ("Praise of Carlos III"; 684) at a solemn session of the Madrid Sociedad de Amigos del País at which both its male members and those of its Ladies' Committee were exhorted to exercise their respective patriotic duties in complementary ways. While in women conjugal and maternal feelings were depicted as innate vocations, for men, although the measured display of familial sentiment was valued and encouraged, it was admitted that their nature steered them more toward passionate or inconstant love. Therefore, women were charged with educating male sentiments in order to mould a civilized society, while, paradoxically, they were intensively trained in this allegedly spontaneous inclination.

This idea that women—"naturally" chaste, self-contained, and sensitive—should curb men's passional excesses, making men responsible subjects in their public and private duties, is also a leitmotif in novels and comedies, among them, Zavala y Zamora's *La Eumenia* (1787) and Cándido María Trigueros's *El precipitado* (*The Hasty Man*; written 1773, printed 1785, first staged 1803). It emerges in a particularly rich way in a hugely successful novel published in 1798 on the cusp of the nineteenth century, *La Serafina* by José Mor de Fuentes, who would later translate two classics of European sentimental literature, Goethe's *Werther* and Rousseau's *Nouvelle Héloïse*. Comprising letters that the male protagonist Alfonso sends to a friend narrating the stages of his falling in love with and courting of Serafina, the novel is articulated as a psychological self-examination by a male subject who analyzes what he terms his "most extraordinary" passions (García Garrosa, "Una lectura," "De *El cariño perfecto*"). Alfonso, who has a taste for European theater, poetry, and fiction and a propensity for writing verse, considers himself a sensitive soul who is repelled by crude carnal pleasure—"vivo casi únicamente para el espíritu" (I live almost solely for the spirit; Mor de Fuentes, *La Serafina* 1: 28)—and manages to conquer his sensuality with an intense effort of self-control. This is inspired by his love for Serafina, which is different from the fleeting infatuations, from those "encendimientos de sangre y acaloradas de imaginación" (burnings of the blood and fires of the imagination; 1: 139) that he had previously experienced. In contrast to Alfonso, who appears strongly individualized in his awareness of acute singularity and moral superiority over the "vulgo" (common people; 1: 18), the heroine offers a more diffuse profile—a peculiarity of Spanish sentimental fiction. She is always seen through the eyes of her beloved, as an angel, goddess, or Dulcinea, a prototypical incarnation of the virtues attributed to her sex. Her own personal feelings are barely mentioned, although Alfonso praises her generically for her "inestimable sensibilidad y espíritu sobrehumano" (inestimable sensibility and superhuman spirit; 1: 15), and her "natural propensión al amor" (natural inclination for love; 1: 21).

In strong contrast to Rousseau's concepts of the "natural man" or "noble savage," Alfonso maintains that civilization and education must subdue and polish man's rough nature for the better of society: "Digan los amantes de la tosquedad lo que quieran, el espíritu del hombre necesita labrarse para adquirir las prendas que le distinguen esencialmente de los irracionales" (No matter what lovers of roughness say, man's spirit needs to be sculpted for him to acquire the qualities that set him apart from irrational beasts; 2: 51). In this crucial process of producing civilized man through hard discipline, woman (particularly as beloved and wife) is charged with a vital role, graphically conveyed in the following passage:

> El hombre es de suyo desmandado y montaraz, y no mediando siquiera aquel grado ínfimo de cultura que vulgarmente se llama crianza, para enfrenar sus arrebatos, amansar su fiereza y suavizar su natural y desabrida selvatiquez, viene a ser más feroz e insociable que los mismos irracionales. La mujer se aparece, desde luego, más bien librada en esa parte, pues por lo común predominan en su espíritu los impulsos compasivos y decorosos, que son el cimiento de la sociedad, y suplen, hasta cierto punto, los medios artificiales de la educación. (2: 51)

(Man is inherently unruly and uncouth, and without a minimal degree of culture commonly called *breeding* to restrain his outbursts and temper his natural, ill-conditioned brutishness, he ends up being wilder and more unsociable even than irrational beasts. Woman is certainly better equipped in this respect, because in her spirit compassionate and decorous impulses, which are the foundation of society, generally prevail, partly making up for the artificiality of the education process.)

Marriage and conjugal love thus provide a metaphor for the state of society, seen as the fulfillment of a necessarily sociable and sentimental human condition, attained largely thanks to woman's role as mediator. However, if men are alerted against letting their feelings overrule their reason, thus becoming effeminate—"El hombre puede ser sensible, pero con mesura, sin traicionar nunca la fortaleza viril que constituye su verdadera naturaleza" (Man can be sensitive, but with measure, without ever betraying that manly fortitude which is his true nature; Mor de Fuentes, La Serafina 1: 124)—the same innate sensibility that bestows on women a certain moral superiority also exposes them to the dangers of an excessive sentimentality: "la mujer, en mi opinión, es el mejor y el peor de los vivientes . . . por los dones inestimables o las frenéticas extravagancias de su espíritu" (woman, in my opinion, is the best and worst of beings . . . on account of the inestimable gifts or frenzied extravagances of her spirit; 1: 19).

The paradox formulated so clearly by Mor de Fuentes's male protagonist expresses the moral ambiguity that sensibility, and its gendering, already held on the brink of the new century's start, which takes us back to the image with which we began. The inspiration for Goya's *Capricho* 32 has been attributed to the impact on the painter and his contemporaries in 1798 (the year of *La Serafina*'s publication) of the murder of a respectable merchant, Santiago Castillo—a friend of Goya and of the case's public prosecutor, the poet Juan Meléndez Valdés—at the hands of his wife's lover, with her acting as accomplice. Public opinion passionately followed the suspects' arrest, trial, and execution, which was witnessed by Leandro Fernández de Moratín, author of the well-known sentimental comedy on marriage *El sí de las niñas* (*The Maidens' Consent*, 1806) (Bolufer and Gomis). In many ways, the case reveals both the Enlightenment's eagerness to make sensibility the basis of moral judgment and social relationships, and the worries that by that time were starting to be expressed at its possible excesses. In his charges, the prosecutor appealed to the concept of marriage not only as the foundation of society, but as "una perspectiva de bien y de purísimas delicias" (a prospect of well-being and purest joys; Meléndez Valdés 1028). The legal process also expressed the idea that the emotional response—individual and collective—provoked by the crime, while being a sign both of the magistrate's own sensibility and of social consensus regarding marriage as an affective and social bond, need not cloud reason. If the prosecutor admitted to being moved by his affective proximity to the victim and by his communion with a unanimously horrified society, this, he maintained, did not impede him from assessing the facts, nor should the judge himself, in this or any other case, let his compassion for the criminals prevent him from making the law prevail when severe punishment was needed (Meléndez Valdés 1051, 1067–68, 1081–84).

Figure 1.3. "The Ill-Fated Margarita." Illustration to García Malo, *Voz de la naturaleza*, 1831.

The defense lawyer, while rejecting the "vulgar" reaction that passionately called for the death penalty, declared that he trusted the judge, despite his sensibility for the victim, to weigh the extenuating circumstances. The prosecution and defense both debated the appropriate terms to describe the wife's sentiments. While Meléndez Valdés reproached her for inhuman coldness, lacking pity or remorse and contrasting with the victim's "noble corazón, nacido para la amistad y las más honestas afecciones" (noble heart, born for friendship and the most honest affections; 1028), the defense minimized her guilt, attributing it to the madness of an impassioned love. Goya appears to adhere to this benevolent interpretation; his etching "Porque fue sensible" seeks the spectator's commiseration: a saddened, solitary woman whose unnamed crime is linked to an excess of sensibility. The image is reminiscent of the illustrations to sentimental novels, for example, that reproduced here as Figure 1.3, which depicts "la desventurada Margarita" in an 1831 edition of García Malo's *Voz de la naturaleza*.

This rupture in the precarious balancing of reason and passion that typified the eighteenth-century ideal of sensibility, together with the progressive assignment of the "sentimental" to the female domestic sphere and its resulting devaluation, are, as is well known, part of a wider European and American phenomenon strongly influenced by the

Figure 1.4. Goya, "And They Are Like Wild Beasts." *Los desastres de la guerra.* Courtesy of the Trustees of the British Museum.

French Revolution (Reddy 142, 173–210). In Spain, the preventive measures of border closing and intensification of ideological vigilance to avoid revolutionary contagion projected a growing suspicion onto foreign and sentimental literature, which brought about, as we have seen, the ban on novels in 1799 for fear of their potential moral and political disruptive effects. However, it was the Peninsular War (known in Spanish as the War of Independence) that definitively called into question the code of sensibility (Rueda, "'Virtue in Distress'" 201), in a complex process that entailed the redefinition of national, political, class, and gender identities (Castells, Espigado, and Romeo 40–52). From 1808 to 1814, the exceptional circumstances of war allowed the irruption of women of different social conditions into the public arena of politics and even military combat, as well as the appearance of "the people" as a political subject. Both women and "the people" were charged with representing the nation symbolically, and images of the former in particular were displayed as instruments to legitimate rebellion against French rule and to generate a mass war effort by appealing to men's virility and patriotism, while at the same time they were regarded with a certain distrust.

For the supporters of Napoleonic government in Spain (*afrancesados*), the resistance of part of Spanish society would be the product of an irrational attachment to the church and monarchy or of an impassioned reaction to unfounded rumors, which would allow the simultaneous discrediting and excusing of women involved in the popular insurrection. Thus, José Marchena, writing in the *Gaceta de Madrid* on 21 February 1810, dismissed popular women's participation in the uprising of 2 May 1808, on account of their excessive sensibility: "en el transtorno de una revolución, que equivale a decir en un incendio general, el fuego [hace] mayores estragos en sus cerebros, más preparados que los nuestros para este género de combustión" (in the turmoil of revolution, that is, in a general conflagration, fire causes more havoc in their brains, more prepared than ours for this kind of combustion; 213). On the other hand, the patriotic rhetoric of those opposing the Napoleonic occupation would present women's participation in the war as a product of their natural passion, saluting such involvement on account of its capacity to galvanize national resistance against the invader, but at the same time fearing both its female and plebeian components (Molina and Vega 135; see Fig. 1.4) Finally, for foreign observers, this undesirable double presence in the public arena of politics and war would contribute to the construction of a stereotype of Spaniards as excessive in their passions and lacking in the sort of rational control required of civilized nations, opening the door, from the 1820s, to Orientalist constructions of Spain that had been absent from earlier accounts (Andreu).

When, in the 1830s, a now aged Mor de Fuentes recalled in his autobiography the events of 1808, he evoked the women who participated in the fighting not as delicate Serafinas but as "furias infernales" (infernal furies; "Bosquejillo" 389), given over to the "frenzied extravagances" that, in his novel of four decades earlier, he had already to some degree presented as the dark side of the sentimental ideal. The precarious and contradictory balance of eighteenth-century culture, in which sensibility had been viewed, despite many ambiguities and tensions, as a necessary complement of reason, a moral foundation, and social bonding agent, thus gave way to a more problematic dichotomous vision, in which reason and sentiment figured, to a greater extent, as a clear-cut binary opposition that mapped onto other binary oppositions—male/female, culture/nature, public/private—laying the ground for the culture of Romanticism.

NOTES

Research for this chapter has been undertaken in the framework of the research project HAR2014-53802-P, funded by the Spanish MINECO. I wish to thank Jo Labanyi, Luisa Elena Delgado, Pura Fernández, Gloria Espigado, and María Sierra for their suggestions and comments on earlier versions.

1. I deliberately avoid the category "emotional regime" developed by William Reddy (129), which implies a degree of dominance and political enforcement absent, in my view, from late eighteenth-century sentimentalism, which was rather an emerging code coexisting with other competing cultures or "emotional communities" (courtly restraint and dissimulation, Christian notions of the passions, among others). See de la Pascua Sánchez, "Tradición y cambio"; Bolufer, "De la cortesía a la civilidad."
2. Fourteen percent of subscribers to *Clara Harlow* were women, the figures being 16.6 percent for *Adela y Teodoro*, 18 percent for *Amelia Booth*, and 27.8 percent for *La nueva*

Clarisa. Figures for female illiteracy in Spain during the second half of the end of the eighteenth century oscillate between 30 percent and 90 percent, with sharp differences according to class and between rural and urban environments.

WORKS CITED

Alcalá Galiano, Antonio. *Obras escogidas*. Ed. Jorge Campos. Biblioteca de Autores Españoles 83–84. Madrid: Atlas, 1955.

Andreu, Xavier. "La mirada de Carmen: El mite oriental d'Espanya i la identitat nacional." *Afers* 48 (2004): 347–67.

Barker-Benfield, George. *The Culture of Sensibility: Sex and Society in Eighteenth-Century Britain*. Chicago: U of Chicago P, 1992.

Blanco-White, José. *Autobiografía*. Ed. Antonio Garnica. Seville: U de Sevilla, 1975.

———. *Cartas de España*. Ed. Antonio Garnica. Seville: Fundación José Manuel Lara, 2004.

Bolufer, Mónica. "De la cortesía a la civilidad. Modelos en tensión." *La Corte de los Borbones: Crisis del modelo cortesano*. Ed. José Martínez Millán, Concepción Camarero Bullón, and Marcelo Luzzi. Vol. 3. Madrid: Polifemo, 2013. 1439–64.

———. "'Hombres de bien': Modelos de masculinidad y expectativas femeninas, entre la ficción y la realidad." *Cuadernos de Ilustración y Romanticismo* 15 (2007): 7–31.

———. "Lo íntimo, lo doméstico y lo público: Representaciones sociales y estilos de vida en la España ilustrada." *Studia Historica: Historia Moderna* 19 (1998): 85–116.

———. "La realidad y el deseo: Formas de subjetividad femenina en la época moderna." *Mujer y deseo: Representaciones y prácticas de vida*. Ed. María José de la Pascua, María Rosario García-Doncel, and Gloria Espigado. Cádiz: U de Cádiz, 2004. 357–82.

Bolufer, Mónica, and Juan Gomis. "Literatura popular y delitos 'privados' en los orígenes de la opinión pública: A propósito del caso Castillo." *Estudis: Revista de Historia Moderna* 37 (2011): 217–33.

Bourke, Joanna. "Fear and Anxiety: Writing about Emotion in Modern History." *History Workshop Journal* 55 (2003): 111–33.

Burke, Peter. "Is There a Cultural History of the Emotions?" *Representing Emotions: New Connections in the Histories of Art, Music and Medicine*. Ed. Penelope Gouk and Helen Hills. Aldershot: Ashgate, 2005. 35–47.

Carter, Philip. "Tears and the Man." *Women, Gender and Enlightenment*. Ed. Sarah Knott and Barbara Taylor. London: Palgrave, 2005. 156–73.

Castells, Irene, Gloria Espigado, and M. Cruz Romeo, eds. *Heroínas y patriotas: Mujeres de 1808*. Madrid: Cátedra, 2009.

Caveda y Solares, Rita. *Cartas selectas de una Señora a una sobrina suya, entresacadas de una obra inglesa impresa en Filadelfia*. Madrid: García, 1800.

Deacon, Philip. "La historia de la traducción española de *Amelia* de Henry Fielding." *La traducción en España (1750–1830): Lengua, literatura, cultura*. Ed. Francisco Lafarga. Lleida: U de Lleida, 1999. 335–44.

de la Pascua Sánchez, María José. *Mujeres solas: Historias de amor y de abandono en el mundo hispánico*. Cádiz: Diputación de Cádiz, 1998.

———. "Tradición y cambio en el lenguaje de los afectos: El discurso literario." *Ayer* 78 (2010): 47–68.

Dixon, Thomas. *From Passions to Emotions: The Creation of a Secular Psychological Category*. Cambridge: Cambridge UP, 2003.
Fuentes, Yvonne. *El triángulo sentimental en el drama del Dieciocho (Inglaterra, Francia, España)*. Kassel: Reichenberger, 1999.
García Garrosa, María. "De *El cariño perfecto* (1798) a *La Serafina* (1802 y 1807): Las tres versiones de una novela de José Mor de Fuentes." *Revista de Literatura* 71 (2009): 461–96.
———. "Una lectura 'sentimental' de *La Serafina* de José Mor de Fuentes." *Revista de Literatura* 67 (2005): 349–71.
———. *La retórica de las lágrimas: La comedia sentimental española (1751–1802)*. Valladolid: U de Valladolid, 1990.
———. "'Unión de voluntades' y 'Ajuste de intereses': El matrimonio en el teatro sentimental del siglo XVIII." *Boletín de la Biblioteca Meléndez Pelayo* 78 (2007): 129–51.
García Malo, Ignacio, trans. *Pamela Andrews o la virtud premiada: Escrita en inglés por Tomas [sic] Richardson, traducida al castellano, corregida y acomodada a nuestras costumbres por el traductor*. 2nd ed. Madrid: Pedro Pereyra, 1799.
———. *Voz de la naturaleza*. Ed. Guillermo Carnero. London: Tamesis, 1995.
Gies, David T. "Sensibilidad y sensualismo en la poesía dieciochesca." *Ideas en sus paisajes: Homenaje al profesor Russell P. Sebold*. Ed. Guillermo Carnero, Enrique Rubio, and Ignacio Javier López. Alicante: U de Alicante, 1999. 215–24.
Gómez Castellano, Irene. *La cultura de las máscaras: Disfraces y escapismo en la poesía española de la Ilustración*. Madrid: Iberoamericana; Frankfurt: Vervuert, 2012.
Goya, Francisco de. *Cartas a Martín Zapater*. Ed. Mercedes Águeda and Xavier de Salas. Madrid: Istmo, 2003.
Haidt, Rebecca. *Embodying Enlightenment: Knowing the Body in Eighteenth-Century Spanish Literature and Culture*. New York: St. Martin's, 1998.
Jovellanos, Melchor Gaspar de. *Diario 1º*. Vol. 6 of *Obras completas*. Ed. José Miguel Caso. Oviedo: Instituto Feijoo de Estudios del Siglo XVIII; Ayuntamiento de Gijón, 1994.
———. "Elogio de Carlos III." *Obras completas*. Vol. 10. *Escritos económicos*. Ed. Vicent Llombart and Joaquín Ocampo Suárez-Valdés. Oviedo: Instituto Feijoo de Estudios del Siglo XVIII; Ayuntamiento de Gijón; KRK Editores, 2008. 669–85.
———. "Memorias familiares (1790–1810)." *Obras*. Ed. Miguel Artola. Biblioteca de Autores Españoles 87. Madrid: Atlas, 1956. 206–20.
———. "Memoria sobre educación pública." *Obras completas*. Vol. 13. *Escritos pedagógicos (1º)*. Ed. Olegario Negrín Fajardo. Oviedo: Instituto Feijoo de Estudios del Siglo XVIII; Ayuntamiento de Gijón; KRK Editores, 2010. 435–532.
Knott, Sarah. *Sensibility and the American Revolution*. Williamsburg: Omohundro Institute of Early Modern American History and Culture; U of North Carolina P, 2009.
Marchena, José. *Obra española en prosa (historia, política, literatura)*. Ed. Juan Francisco Fuentes. Madrid: Centro de Estudios Constitucionales, 1990.
Meléndez Valdés, Juan. *Obras completas*. Ed. Antonio Astorgano. Madrid: Cátedra, 2004.
Molina, Álvaro, and Jesusa Vega. "Imágenes de la alteridad. El "pueblo" de Goya y su construcción histórica." *La guerra de la Independencia en la cultura española*. Ed. Joaquín Álvarez Barrientos. Madrid: Siglo XXI, 2008. 131–58.
Montengón, Pedro de. *Eusebio*. Ed. Fernando García Lara. Madrid: Editora Nacional, 1984.

Morant, Isabel. "Las costumbres del amor y la diferencia de sexos en la novela de la modernidad." *Las huellas de Foucault en la historiografía: Poderes, cuerpos y deseos*. Ed. Henar Gallego Franco and María Isabel del Val Valdivieso. Barcelona: Icaria, 2013. 135–62.

Morant, Isabel, and Mónica Bolufer. *Amor, matrimonio y familia: La construcción histórica de la familia moderna*. Madrid: Síntesis, 1998.

———. "Hombres y mujeres en el matrimonio: Deseos, sentimientos y conflictos." *La historia de las mujeres: Perspectivas actuales*. Ed. Cristina Borderías. Barcelona: Icaria, 2009. 133–62.

Mor de Fuentes, José. "Bosquejillo de la vida y escritos de D. José Mor de Fuentes." *Memorias de tiempos de Fernando VII*. Ed. Miguel Artola. Madrid: Atlas, 1957. 375–428. Biblioteca de Autores Españoles 97–98.

———. *La Serafina*. Madrid: Repullés, 1807. Rpt. of *El cariño perfecto, o Alfonso y Serafina*. Madrid: Cano, 1798.

Nuevo diccionario de la lengua castellana. Paris: Vicente Salvá, 1846.

Plamper, Jan. "The History of Emotions: An Interview with William Reddy, Barbara Rosenwein, and Peter Stearns." *History and Theory* 49 (2010): 237–65.

Polt, John H. R. "Jovellanos and His English Sources: Economic, Philosophical and Political Writings." *Transactions of the American Philosophical Society* ns 54.7 (1964): 1–74.

Real Academia Española. *Diccionario de la lengua castellana*. 3rd ed. Madrid: Viuda de Joaquín Ibarra, 1791.

Reddy, William. *The Navigation of Feeling: A Framework for the History of the Emotions*. Cambridge: Cambridge UP, 2001.

Romero, María Rosario, trans. *Cartas de una peruana: Escritas en francés por Madame de Graffigny y traducidas al castellano con algunas correcciones, y aumentada con notas, y una carta para su mayor complemento por* . . . Valladolid: Viuda de Santander e hijos, 1792.

Rosenwein, Barbara H. "Worrying about Emotions in History." *American Historical Review* 107.3 (2002): 821–45.

Rueda, Ana. *Cartas sin lacrar: La novela epistolar y la España Ilustrada, 1789–1840*. Madrid: Iberoamericana; Frankfurt: Vervuert, 2001.

———. "'Virtue in Distress' in the Spanish Sentimental Novel: An Unsustainable Model of Rational Sensibility." *Eve's Enlightenment: Women's Experience in Spain and Spanish America, 1726–1839*. Ed. Catherine M. Jaffe and Elizabeth F. Lewis. Baton Rouge: Louisiana UP, 2009. 197–217.

Sierra, María. *Género y emociones en el Romanticismo: El teatro de Bretón de los Herreros*. Zaragoza: Institución Fernando el Católico, 2013.

Tausiet, María, and James S. Amelang. *Accidentes del alma: Las emociones en la Edad Moderna*. Madrid: Abada, 2009.

Trojani, Cécile M. *L'Écriture de l'amitié dans l'Espagne des Lumières: La Real Sociedad Bascongada de Amigos del País, d'après la source épistolaire*. Toulouse: Presses Universitaires du Mirail, 2001.

Vincent-Buffault, Anne. *Histoire des larmes (XVIIIe-XIXe siècles)*. Marseille: Rivages, 1985.

Zavala y Zamora, Gaspar. *Obras narrativas*. Ed. Guillermo Carnero. Alicante: U de Alicante; Barcelona: Sirmio, 1992.

CHAPTER TWO

"How Do I Love Thee"
The Rhetoric of Patriotic Love in Early Puerto Rican Political Discourse

WADDA C. RÍOS-FONT

The Cortes de Cádiz (1809–1814) can be considered the birthplace of the modern Spanish state, and the Constitution of 1812 its foundational code. In its very first lines, the document bluntly declares that Spain is not, and cannot be, the patrimony of any person or family. With this bold stroke, its authors transfer sovereignty from the king to the nation, understood as an abstract and composite entity made up of the voluntary "reunion" of all Spaniards (Articles 1 and 2, *Constitución* 4). Having thus created the nation-state, in the following articles the Cádiz deputies laid down its fundamental laws. One of the cornerstones of the new regime is the invention, indeed the *proclamation*, of a new affective relationship between citizen and state. The first article of the Constitution's second chapter (Article 5) describes *los españoles* as all free individuals born and domiciled in Spanish domains, naturalized foreigners, and freed slaves. In other words, while the Constitutional Commission linked Spanish nationality to specific territories (explicitly in the plural, *las Españas*), it chose not to define this identity in terms of ethnicity.[1] Instead, it conceived the nation as a community of associates consenting to be bound by common law. Article 6, significantly the first clause that touches on Spaniards' responsibilities, immediately specifies the relationship that must bind them all: "el amor de la patria es una de las principales obligaciones de todos los españoles, y asimismo el ser justos y benéficos" (love of the fatherland is one of the principal duties of all Spaniards, as is being just and charitable; 5). This obligation is listed *before* those of being faithful to the Constitution, obeying laws, respecting established authorities, paying taxes, and taking up arms to defend the nation (Articles 7, 8, and 9).

The Spanish nation-state was not, therefore, imagined as ethno-national, but rather as a collective civic arrangement ensuing from the (at least theoretical) decision of its heterogeneous members to belong, manifested through behaviors intended to express a grounding emotion: patriotic love. Although the terms *patriotism* and *nationalism* are commonly conflated, it is useful to remember that they have divergent histories that begin to converge only at the dawn of the so-called Age of Nations. Like patriotic civic states, nationalist states will command their citizens' love; but this love will be different, both in object and in nature, from the sentiment to which the Cádiz deputies refer. As Maurizio Viroli explains, "Patriots and nationalists have not only recommended different ideals as objects of our love: the republic, in the case of the patriots, the nation as a cultural and spiritual unity in the case of the nationalists; they have also endeavored to instill or strengthen in us different types of love: a charitable and generous love in the case of patriotism, an unconditional loyalty or an exclusive attachment in the case of the nationalists" (2). In the sense in which Cádiz delegates could understand it, patriotism was not love of kindred, but love of *political* brotherhood.

The representatives immediately struggled with the question of how to legislate an emotion. In the brief discussion of Article 6 held on 21 September 1811, when it was brought to the floor, Representative Vicente Terrero Monesterio, from the province of Cádiz, asked for the whole item to be deleted, since love of country was instinctively arrived at through *sinderesis*, a moral faculty that presumably drove individuals to do good and abhor evil. Valencian representative Joaquín Villanueva y Astengo thought that, being an interior virtue, patriotic love could not be regulated, since only *actions* stemming from the sentiment (or lack thereof) could be subject to the law. Representative Pedro Inguanzo y Rivero, from Asturias, similarly observed that Article 6 would be appropriate if the congress were drafting a "catecismo político" (political catechism) (*Diario* 3: 1741), but not in a collection of "leyes fundamentales" (foundational laws). As an "acto interno" (internal act), patriotic love related to religion and natural law rather than civil legislation. Catalan representative Antonio Capmany y Montpalau added that the article could not function as a precept, but only as advice; furthermore, the Nation had already proved, through its heroism in the War of Independence, that it did not need such entreaties. Without considering patriotic love innate, these deputies balked at the attempt to rule over that which could only be interpretively ascertained from outer expressions or behaviors. All of the article's critics regarded patriotism as a strong emotion crucial in eliciting the substantial sacrifices dictated to Spaniards in subsequent articles, but none of them could see a clear way to bring it out of the intangible web of representation and into the concrete sphere of the juridical. Deputies who spoke in favor of the article found ways to step around this conundrum. Representative Felip Aner d'Esteve, also from Catalonia, alluded to the distinction between the undoubtedly patriotic "Nacion" (Nation; 1740)—a general entity—and "los españoles" (Spaniards)—particular individuals among whom some "se han olvidado de este amor á la Pátria" (have forgotten this love of Fatherland).[2] From this perspective, the feeling was fully realized in its expression by actual persons and could thus be monitored and regulated. Representative Domingo Dueñas y Castro, from Granada, noted that love of country was no more innate than love of God, and the latter was nevertheless mandated in the first commandment. These interventions seemingly resolved the challenge of how to legislate over affect, and Asturian Agustín Argüelles y Álvarez, who was presiding, asked for an immediate vote. Article 6 was swiftly approved.

None of the participants in the discussion defined too precisely the exact nature of *amor a la patria*. The session's transcript nonetheless reveals the discursive field in which it was inscribed. Terrero referred to it as a quality of *rationality*; Villanueva brought up the domain of *virtues*. Aner added that "este amor á la Pátria es la obligacion que puede hacer felices é independientes á los Estados" (this love of the Fatherland is the *duty* that can make States *happy* and *independent*; 1740, my emphases). Representative Antonio Alcaina Guirao of Granada invoked parallels between *religion* and *fatherland*: "teniendo el hombre relacion con Dios, de quien recibe el ser; á la religion, que le hace feliz; á la Pátria, al Rey, de quien es súbdito" (as Man is in relationship to God, from Whom he receives being; to religion, which makes him happy; to Fatherland [and] King, of which he is a subject; 1741). Most important, the language of the article itself metonymically associates love of country with *justice* and *charity* toward others, thereby projecting the abstract *patria* back on its people. As Viroli points out, "classical antiquity transmitted to modernity a political patriotism based on the identification of *patria* with *respublica*, common liberty, common good. . . . [It] must commend a particular type of love, that is, *pietas* or *caritas*" (19). Peter R. Campbell, in his analysis of the cult of patriotism in eighteenth-century France, relates it to the discourse of sensibility, a sentimental disposition of the soul to be touched or moved toward the common good: "the language of sensibility made it possible for people to articulate their feelings for the community of their fellows—for the *patrie*" (25). Certain political values were projected onto the linguistic domain of patriotic love: "*Patrie* [Fatherland] is associated with *bien public* [public good], *république* [republic], *nation* [nation], *société* [society], *communauté* [community], *citoyen* [citizen], *liberté* [liberty], *égalité* [equality], *lois* [laws], *roi* [king], *vertu* [virtue], and *bienfaisance* [charity]" (26). But two are especially important: "The concepts of *equality* and *fraternity* are inherent in the concept of patriotism, this powerful sentiment that springs from love of humanity" (15, my emphases). As well as devotion to the state, patriotism entails a love of one's compatriots that creates, rather than emanates from, ethno-cultural kinship. In spelling out causal relationships between emotion and specific behaviors (like submission to law, taxes, and armed service), the Spanish Constitution construed patriotic love as a type of public investment. In linking these behaviors to a shared emotion, it aimed to create a community based on empathy.

As much as defining a new sentiment, however, the Constitution demarcated its appropriate object in a manner consistent with the tradition of Spanish Enlightened Despotism. Bourbon reforms attempted to modernize Spain by weakening regional and foral diversity through territorial reorganizations that emphasized the (sometimes newly created) province as administrative unit within an increased centralization of the state. The underlying tension between the ethnic and the civic was already apparent in the writings of Fray Benito Feijóo y Montenegro, who in his 1729 essay "Amor de la patria y pasión nacional" ("Love of the Fatherland and National Passion") advocated for the identification of *patria* with a contractual state: "la Patria á quien sacrifican su aliento las almas heroycas, á quien debemos estimar sobre nuestros particulares intereses, . . . es aquel cuerpo de Estado donde, debaxo de un gobierno civil, estamos unidos con la coyunda de unas mismas leyes. Así, España es el objeto propio del amor del Español" (the Fatherland to which heroic souls sacrifice their breath, which we must revere above our particular interests, . . . is that body of State where, under a civil government, we are joined by the yoke of a single set of laws; 237). The generous affection it required was the polar opposite of the "desordenado afecto que no es relativo al todo de la República, sino al proprio, y particular territorio" (*disorderly affection* not related to the whole of the Republic, but to our own and particular territory; my emphasis).

Generically, patriotism found a perfect channel in oratory, described by nineteenth-century Spanish literary historians as a form of the "bello-útil, el discurso oratorio, que á la vez que conmueve con los arrebatos del sentimiento convence con los argumentos de la razón" (beautiful [and] utilitarian, oratorical discourse, which at once *moves* with the raptures of feeling and *convinces* with the arguments of reason; Vidart 283, my emphases). Perhaps no text better embodies the importance of patriotic discourse to nation building than the preliminary speech to the Constitution delivered by Argüelles the Divine—so called because of his famed grandiloquence—symbolically offering the document to the (absent) king on 24 December 1811, the day of its approval. In his powerful words, the Constitution contains

> verdades tan santas, tan sencillas y tan necesarias a la gloria y felicidad de la nación y del Rey, cuyos derechos nadie compromete más que los que aparentan sostenerlos, oponiéndose a las saludables limitaciones que le harán siempre padre de sus pueblos y objeto de las bendiciones de sus súbditos. . . . Preséntele a la nación, que impaciente y ansiosa por saber su suerte futura, reclama del Congreso el premio de sus heroicos sacrificios. Dígale V. M. que en esta ley se contienen todos los elementos de su grandeza y prosperidad, y que si los generosos sentimientos de amor y lealtad a su inocente y adorado rey la obligaron a alzarse para vengar el ultraje cometido contra su sagrada persona, hoy más que nunca debe redoblar sus esfuerzos para acelerar el suspirado momento de restituirle al trono de sus mayores, que reposa majestuosamente sobre las sólidas bases de una Constitución liberal. (128)

(truths so holy, so simple, and so necessary to the glory and happiness of the nation and the King, whose rights no one jeopardizes more than those who pretend to support them, opposing the healthy limitations that will forever make him father of his peoples and target of his subjects' blessings. . . . Present it to the nation which, impatient and anxious to know its future fate, demands from Congress the reward for its heroic sacrifices. Your Majesty must tell it that this law contains all the [requisite] elements for its greatness and prosperity, and that if generous feelings of love and loyalty for its innocent and adored king compelled it to rise and avenge the outrage committed against his sacred person, now more than ever it must redouble its efforts to hasten the longed-for moment of restoring him to the throne of his elders, which rests majestically on the solid foundations of a liberal Constitution.)

Disguised as gifting to Fernando VII the very law that dispossessed him of absolute sovereignty, the speech's emotional rhetoric redefines the underpinnings of the nation.

In this paragraph, the climax of a lengthy textual crescendo, Argüelles stresses the paternal relationship between the king and his subjects, a family tie that *naturally* inspires love, loyalty, *adoration*, and sacrifice as a means to shared glory. Through this common paternity, the monarchy's subjects undergo a smooth textual transition from the plural *peoples* (*pueblos*) to the singular *nation*: they become, in effect, a national fraternity. If *selfless love* is the emotive origin of the new state, it is as much required of the nation as implicitly demanded of the father-king, the addressee of all the imperative verbs (*preséntele, dígale*). The metaphor of the nation as family not only grounds the new model of shared sovereignty but also provides an existing ideal of mutuality as the model of patriotic love.

Against this background, the question emerges of how this patriotic love story unfolds in the furthest reaches of the Spanish empire. If the new Spanish fatherland beckons its citizens to abandon their passions for the *país* and surrender themselves to the love of *patria*, what happens to the feeling and discourse of patriotism when the país needs to be built as much as the nation? This question is particularly relevant in the case of Puerto Rico, which at the dawn of the nineteenth century still had to *begin* imagining itself as a community. Like other American territories, the island welcomed the 1808 call from Spain to send a representative to the Junta Suprema Central Gubernativa del Reino (Supreme Governing Central Junta of the Kingdom)—to which it was the first Spanish possession to swear allegiance—and subsequently in 1810 to the Cortes. The reason for this enthusiasm can be found in the 1808 summons itself:

> Considerando el rey, nuestro señor, don Fernando Séptimo, y en su real nombre la Junta Suprema Central Gubernativa del Reino que esta isla no es propiamente una colonia o factoría, como las de otras naciones, sino una parte esencial integrante de la monarquía española y deseando estrechar de un modo indisoluble los sagrados vínculos que unen esta isla y demás dominios de América con los de España y corresponder al mismo tiempo a la heroica lealtad y patriotismo de que acaba de dar tan decidida prueba a la Madre Patria . . . , se ha servido su majestad declarar . . . que los reinos, provincias e islas que forman estos dominios deben tener representación nacional inmediata a su real persona y constituir parte de la Junta Central Gubernativa del Reino por medio de sus correspondientes diputados, y que para que tenga efecto esta soberana resolución ha de nombrar esta isla un individuo que la represente. (Caro de Delgado 23–24)

(Considering the king, our lord Fernando VII, and in his royal name the Kingdom's Supreme Governing Central Junta that this island is not properly a colony or factory, as those of other nations, but an essential constitutive part of the Spanish monarchy, and desiring to tighten indissolubly the sacred bonds that tie this island and the rest of the American domains with those of Spain, and to reward at the same time the heroic loyalty and patriotism of which it has just given the Motherland clear proof . . . , his majesty has seen fit to declare . . . that the kingdoms, provinces, and islands composing these domains shall have national representation immediate to his royal person, and constitute part of the Kingdom's Governing Central Junta through their corresponding deputies, and that in order for this sovereign resolution to take effect, this island shall name an individual to represent it.)

The proclamation once again appeals to *heroic loyalty*, *patriotism*, and the *sacred ties* between the *mother* country and its possession. To Puerto Ricans, however, most attractive was the prospect of leaving behind the status of *colony or trading post* to become an *essential, constitutive part of the Spanish monarchy*, a reward long sought through visible acts of loyalty.[3] At the time, Puerto Rico in fact hardly qualified for the name of *colonia*, if by that one means a civil settlement with established agriculture and trade.

The island's particularity at the start of the nineteenth century cannot be overemphasized, as it predetermined the ways in which it embraced constitutional nation building in Spain. Since the Spanish "discovery," it had gone through many cycles of population and depopulation, and its main importance was still the geographical location that made it a naval way station and key military post. In 1811, it still had only 183,000 inhabitants. Unlike other Spanish American territories, it was not home to a sufficiently established creole class, the "pioneers" that Benedict Anderson (47) has identified behind separatist impulses. Its inhabitants were isolated from each other—as late as the 1830s, the trip from the city of Ponce on the south coast to San Juan on the north coast was usually made by sea. The printing press had arrived in 1806, but overregulation and censorship meant that for prolonged periods the government's *Gazeta Oficial* was the only allowed periodical; thus written forums for native islanders, always moderated by metropolitan officials, could not function to create the "deep, horizontal comradeship" Anderson attributes to protonational groups. Far from the *imagined community* he posits, the island remained closer to Mary Louise Pratt's *contact zone*: "the space of colonial encounters . . . in which peoples geographically and historically separated come into contact with each other and establish ongoing relations, usually involving conditions of coercion, radical inequality, and intractable conflict" (6). In the opinion of Ramón Power y Giralt, the island's first representative in the Cortes de Cádiz, Puerto Rico's circumstances made it, among American colonies, "una excepción . . . un caso singularísimo" (an exception . . . a most singular case; Caro de Delgado 167) requiring development stimulus rather than independence.[4] This determined his decision to invest fully in the project of Spanish patriotism, despite supporting secession for other territories. For him, the matter at hand was not to dissolve the relationship with the metropolis, but to achieve equality and fraternity within it.

Two beliefs underlay his choice. First, the notion that it was not the nation itself that was to blame for present conditions, but rather colonial governor-generals who used authoritarian rule for personal gain. In Puerto Rico, the posts of civil governor, captain general, and treasury intendant (*intendente*) were concentrated in the same person, who therefore held military, executive, legislative, juridical, and economic power, oftentimes brutally. The invitation to *immediate* or *unmediated* national representation offered a way not just to negotiate directly with the peninsula, but to participate in the very reformulation of the metropolitan state. The second belief underlying Power y Giralt's choice was that natural resources were too scarce for Puerto Rico to thrive on its own. To foster growth, he placed his hopes on exploiting the island's position as the northeasternmost Spanish territory, at the epicenter of a nautical zone bordered by Europe and North, Central, and South America—a purpose for which Spanish merchant marine structures and markets were indispensable. Accordingly, upon his arrival in Cádiz in 1809, Power y Giralt immediately sought to accomplish three objectives: first, the establishment of a democratic civic state with equal peninsular and overseas representation; second, the limitation of the governor-general's powers; and third, the approval of economic concessions encouraging skilled white immigration from various nations and establishing the island as a virtual free port.

Owing to all the above, as a matter of political strategy Spain was deemed the appropriate object of Puerto Ricans' love. Nonetheless, it did not escape Power y Giralt and his electors that material progress depended on the solidification of a local bourgeoisie with genuine ties to the island. Furthermore, although Puerto Ricans did not have a historical sense of identity equivalent to that of Catalans, Basques, or Galicians, or to the collective self-awareness of an already significantly developed Cuba (and thus there was little preexisting regionalism to be weakened in the name of the nation), the centuries of despotism endured did generate a communal sense of subalternity that undermined their resolute self-identification as Spaniards. These contradictions foreshadowed an uneven political evolution whose accidents can be traced through the tortured appropriation of the language of patriotism that begins with the island's first politician. With the país as embryonic as the patria, the narrative of Hispanic brotherhood adopted in the service of the latter eventually yielded to a tale of tormented, uncertain, and ultimately unrequited love.

From his arrival in Cádiz, Power y Giralt followed the patriotic script. His letter of September 1810 to the San Juan City Council, informing of the parliament's imminent inauguration and his own election as its first vice president, is coded in a celebratory grandiloquence in clear connection to that of Agustín Argüelles's 1812 speech:

> Llegó por fin el momento deseado por la Nación y aquel día feliz memorable en que el Pueblo Español se ve en posesión de todos sus derechos. La mañana del 24 del corriente día prefijado para la apertura del augusto congreso que va á pronunciar los Decretos para la salvación de la Patria y su futura felicidad, ha sido la de mayor júbilo, y entusiasmo patriótico que haya podido enagenar los corazones de todos los Españoles de ambos mundos. . . . He merecido [d]el augusto Congreso que por una mayoría considerable de votos se me haya elegido para vice-Presidente de él, y esta particular distinguida demostración que ha señalado al representante de Puerto Rico, llena mi corazón de reconocimiento y estrecha cada vez más los vínculos que han unido siempre á mis amados compatriotas con sus generosos y nobles hermanos de la Metrópoli. (131–32)

(Here at last is that moment the Nation desired, that joyous memorable day when the Spanish People finds itself in possession of all its rights. The morning of the 24th of this month, designated for the opening of the august congress that will deliver the Decrees that will save the Fatherland and ensure its future happiness, has been full of the greatest jubilation and patriotic enthusiasm that can enrapture the hearts of all Spaniards from both worlds. . . . I have been deemed by the august Congress worthy of being elected its vice President by a considerable majority of votes, and this special recognition that has singled out the representative from Puerto Rico fills my heart with appreciation and increasingly strengthens the ties that have always united my beloved compatriots with their generous and noble brothers from the Metropolis.)

Like Argüelles, Power y Giralt composes a highly personal climactic text that associates love of the *res publica* and familial love. But where Argüelles still underlines the vertical filiation between king and subjects, Power y Giralt emphasizes horizontal brotherly ties—here referring to *our metropolitan brothers* just as he will elsewhere to "nuestros hermanos de América" (our American brothers; 144). This coming together of brethren is the basis of a new nation, with capital letters and in the singular (*la Nación, el Pueblo Español*), that will guarantee equality to all. Curiously, his emotional metaphor is as loaded as that of the Spaniard. According to the *Diccionario de Autoridades*, already in the eighteenth century the term *vincular* (to bind) designated the legal incorporation of previously separate goods into a single estate: "sujetar, ù gravar los bienes a vìnculo, para perpetuarlos en alguna familia" (to hold or commit goods to a bundle, so as to keep them within a family in perpetuity). If brotherly love was the model of patriotic love, neither Argüelles nor Power y Giralt would have it forgotten that family entailed a contract to provide for next of kin. In a related vein, by using the verb *enajenar* (to alienate)—"dar a otro alguna cosa, transfiriendo en él el señorío o domínio" (give something to someone else, transferring possession or dominion to this person)—to describe how the constitutional parliament's ceremonial opening enraptures the hearts of *all* Spaniards, Power y Giralt suggests, even in advance of debates about sovereignty and representation, the necessary renunciation of local identities that the Cádiz majority considered necessary for the success of a single political apparatus.

There is, of course, another sense of the word *enajenar*—"sacar a alguien fuera de sí," literally to *alienate* in the psychological sense, to *estrange* someone from his or her self (*Diccionario de la lengua española* [*DRAE*])—that denotes self-division and intimates the future evolution of the tropes of patriotism in Power y Giralt's works. Very soon, the deputy has to face the fact that the transatlantic fraternity he envisioned was illusory; as this happens, the affective metaphor shifts meanings. In early 1811, with revolution sprouting in Gran Colombia, to which Power y Giralt had strong personal ties,[5] parliamentary debates focused on representative apportionment. The point of discord was a royal decree of February 1810 calling for one deputy for each fifty thousand inhabitants of the peninsula versus one for each American district capital, thereby guaranteeing peninsular Spaniards a permanent majority. To add insult to injury, the former were to be popularly elected, and the latter chosen by city councils. Affronted American delegates contested Spain's pretense that overseas territories were *essential* and *integral*. Their protest in Cádiz accompanied emergent insurrection across the Atlantic.

In his "Reflecciones . . . acerca del estado presente de la América" ("Reflections . . . on the Present State of America") and "Voto sobre la igualdad de representación" ("Vote on Equal [Congressional] Representation"), written in January, Power y Giralt backed the Americans, deploying in their support the old familial image, now with far-from-celebratory connotations. He portrays a "Madre Patria devorada por la guerra más sangrienta" (Motherland devoured by the bloodiest war; 144) who nevertheless prepares to ravage rather than nurture her justly insubordinate children: "¿Pues que la sangre de nuestros hermanos habrá de derramarse habiendo medios de reconciliarnos con ellos?" (Well, shall our brothers' blood be spilt while there are still means of reconciliation?). The subject positions he assigns and assumes in these pieces reveal a change in his relationship to the great Spanish lineage. While on the one hand the metropolis has resumed the hierarchical parental role, on the other all references to the American brotherhood are made strictly in the third person: "la América . . . no ha mejorado su suerte" (America . . . has not improved its lot); "luego que los naturales de aquellos países tengan una seguridad de que ya no serán vejados" (as soon as the natives of *those* countries are assured that *they* will no longer be humiliated; my emphases). Occupying an in-between position, Power y Giralt is a nautical *flaneur*: "El servicio de mi profesión [naval officer] me ha conducido alternativamente a muchos de los principales puntos de ambas Américas, y esta concurrencia accidental unida a otras varias, me han hecho conocer el corazón y opiniones de sus naturales" (The exercise of my profession has every so often taken me to many of the capital locations of both Americas, and this chance occurrence, added to some others, has allowed me knowledge of the heart and opinions of their inhabitants; 152). He presents himself as mediator, and phrases his advice to the metropolis in terms reminiscent of another archetypal family drama, that of the prodigal son:

> Me abstendré de mirar como una rebelión las ocurrencias de Caracas, puesto que yo he visto aquella ilustre Ciudad y a todas sus Provincias dar las más señaladas pruebas de su acendrado patriotismo y lealtad. . . . Pero si por desgracia no se hallase exenta de toda objeción la conducta de Venezuela, siempre dicta la política que V. M. con mano indulgente corra un denso velo. . . . El representante del fidelísimo, del guerrero Puerto Rico, ruega a V. M. que . . . se sirva publicar una amnistía general . . . [y] espera igualmente que todos sus apreciables compañeros de España y América, unirán sus ruegos para que se adopte esta medida . . . que a su parecer es la única capaz de restablecer la unión con una Provincia hermana nuestra. (145)

> (I will not look on the events of Caracas as a rebellion since I have seen that illustrious City and all its Provinces give the most notable proof of their pure patriotism and

loyalty.... But if Venezuela's conduct were unfortunately not exempt from any and all objection, politics still dictates that Your Majesty draw a thick veil over that with forgiving hand.... The representative of the most faithful, valiant Puerto Rico begs Y.M. to... publish a general amnesty... and similarly hopes that all his esteemed peers from Spain and America will join him in the plea for adoption of this measure... which is, in his view, the only one that can reestablish unity with a sister Province.

He sums up his appeal in highly expressive terms stated, as in Argüelles's discourse, in a pleading imperative: "dígase a Venezuela que la Patria llora su separación y no enjugará sus lágrimas hasta verla estrecha y más tierna e indisolublemente unida con sus hermanos que lo ha estado jamás" (pray tell Venezuela that the Fatherland laments its separation and will only wipe dry its tears after seeing it more tightly, tenderly, and indissolubly connected to its brothers than ever before; 146, my emphasis). As if conscious of the sudden inadequateness of the repertoire of patriotism to this circumstance, Power y Giralt also becomes insistently apologetic; after specifying that "faltaría a mi deber si... tratase de expresar otros sentimientos que los que me animan" (I would fail in my duty if... I tried to express other feelings than those inspiring me; 143), he concludes by imploring of His Majesty "[que] se haga por lo menos la justicia de creer que sólo el amor de la Patria y el deseo de estrechar más y más indisolublemente los lazos fraternales de la unión entre todas las partes de esta inmensa Monarquía, es quien ha movido mi corazón hacia los principios expresados" (to at least do me the justice of believing that only love of Fatherland and a desire to tighten ever more indissolubly the fraternal bonds of union among all parts of this immense Monarchy have moved my heart toward the principles expressed; 146–47).

The Cortes did issue a compromise decree on representation that they (vainly) hoped would assuage unrest in the continent. Predictably drafted by Power y Giralt himself, the text returned once more to the topos of fraternity:

> Las Cortes generales y extraordinarias confirman y sancionan el inconcuso concepto de que los dominios españoles de ambos hemisferios forman *una sola y misma monarquía, una misma y sola nación, y una sola familia*, y que por lo mismo los naturales *que sean* originarios de dichos dominios europeos ó ultramarinos son iguales en derechos a los de esta Península, quedando a cargo de las Cortes tratar con oportunidad y con un particular interés de todo cuanto pueda contribuir a la felicidad de los de Ultramar, como también sobre el número y forma que deba tener para lo sucesivo la representación nacional en ambos hemisferios. (133, my emphases)

(The general and extraordinary Courts confirm and sanction the indisputable concept that Spanish dominions of both hemispheres constitute *one and the same monarchy, one and the same nation, and a single family*, and that for this reason those natives *who may be* originary from said European or overseas dominions are equal in rights to those from this Peninsula, and it falls to the Courts to negotiate opportunely and with particular interest everything that *might contribute* to the happiness of those from Overseas, as well as the number and form that national representation *may* henceforth take in both hemispheres.)

The irony is, of course, that a presumably uncontested concept needs to be confirmed and sanctioned, and that while the principle of fraternity is declared in the indicative, the principle of equality is immediately qualified by a number of subjunctives. Despite Power y Giralt's recurrent evocation of national commonality, the distance between the sense of fulfillment of his 1810 letter and the indefinite postponement of his 1811 utterances is abysmal. If, as he first espoused it, patriotism's emotional register was that of sensibility, here it is infused with a sense of hopeless urgency that brings it closer to the passions of Romanticism.

I alluded earlier to the budding self-alienation underlying Power y Giralt's discourse, and this is finally most evident when he writes distinctly in the name of Puerto Rico. The euphoria of the 1810 letter was also largely absent in February 1811, when Power y Giralt appealed to the Cortes to overturn a decree granting the island's governor-general Salvador Meléndez Bruna full power against suspected secessionist conspirators to "proceder a la detención de toda clase de personas . . . confinarlas y trasladarlas a donde más bien le parezca" (proceed to the arrest of any type of person . . . lock them up and transfer them where [you] may see fit; 158). Protesting the incontrovertible "lealtad heroica de aquel pueblo que hace trescientos años acredita su patriotismo" (heroic loyalty of that people, who have been proving their patriotism for three hundred years; 160), the delegate denounces the fact that there are still "provincias en que el ciudadano español no es verdaderamente libre" (provinces where the Spanish citizen is not truly free) at a time when "debía esperarse que no hubiese un solo español entregado al capricho arbitrario de la tiranía" (it would be expected that there not be a single Spaniard at the mercy of the capricious whim of tyranny; 157). It is notable that where he had referred in 1810 to "el Pueblo Español" (the Spanish People), here the noun "pueblo" squarely designates Puerto Rico (although he will again, on selected occasions, apply it to the nation). Power y Giralt returns to the family image but it now symbolizes the islanders' marginalization from the benefits of citizenship: "Cada ciudadano trémulo y consternado espera en todos los momentos ver asaltado el sagrado asilo de su domicilio: cada uno teme verse arrancado del seno de su patria, de los brazos de una tierna esposa, o de una amante familia, para ser confinado a una región de horror" (Each trembling and dismayed citizen expects at any moment to see the sacred shelter of his home raided: each one fears to see himself torn from his land's bosom, from the arms of a tender wife, or a loving family, to be banished to a realm of horror; 158–59). Being torn from home and its relationships is akin to being expelled from the nation, banished from the reign of justice promised by the constitution then being drafted. Although the order is repealed immediately, the incident triggers a vicious rivalry between Power y Giralt and Meléndez Bruna, who will from this point on never cease plotting against the deputy.

In April 1811, Power y Giralt presented to the Cortes a document entitled "Exposición y peticiones" ("Exposition and Petitions") outlining a series of proposals to improve living conditions in Puerto Rico. Quite interestingly the very first paragraph, describing the island's current backwardness, stages the breakdown of the ideals of enlightened sensibility as the former *júbilo* gives way to affliction: "Al considerarse el mérito distinguido de tantas virtudes cívicas y las pocas ventajas de que hoy gozan los habitantes de la Isla, . . . el hombre ilustrado y sensible se aflige sobremanera" (Considering the distinguished merit of so many civic virtues and the scarce advantages presently enjoyed by the Island's inhabitants, . . . an enlightened and sensitive man is exceedingly distressed; 165). One might anticipate new invocations of the language of fraternity and kinship in an attempt to *convince* the parliament by *moving* them to empathy with their island fellows. Convince he did, as most of the petitions were indeed approved; however, Power y Giralt never again portrayed European and American Spaniards as bound by brotherly love. The "Exposición y peticiones" feature a new protagonist, the peasant or *labrador* clearly related to the *jíbaro* that the privileged Puerto Rican classes fashioned as an archetypal ethnic figure precisely in the 1810–1820 period.[6] And this figure comes with its own emotional repertoire.

Power y Giralt tells the story of the "lastimosa miseria en los Labradores . . . un Pueblo fiel y generoso, que acostumbra siempre sacrificarlo todo a su obediencia sin límites, pero que al mismo tiempo espera obtener del Gobierno supremo el remedio universal de sus enfermedades políticas" (pathetic misery of the Laborers . . . a faithful and generous People who customarily sacrifice everything to boundless obedience, but at the same time expect to obtain from the supreme Government the universal remedy for their political maladies; 166–67). The collective image soon turns into an embodied singular: "el Labrador permaneció siempre miserable" (the Laborer remained forever wretched; 167). The island needs a provident administration "que aplique a su fomento muchos desvelos, protección y auxilios" (to apply much effort, protection, and assistance to its development; 171), but its absence "reduce al Labrador más honrado al triste y amargo extremo de violar la ley . . . para poder darle salida a las producciones de una tierra, cuya fertilidad había aumentado el infeliz, a expensas de mil afanes y sudores" (reduces the most honest Laborer to the sad and bitter need to break the law . . . so as to be able to export the products of a land whose fertility the poor soul has increased at the expense of a thousand worries and toils; 169). In other words, the Puerto Rican peasant is forcibly and *bitterly* excluded from the regime of justice, transformed almost by default into an outlaw. Turned away from a motherland he *obeyed*, he now loves the land he will arduously *fecundate*. As in the February appeal, the only family invoked is the peasant household endangered by colonial greed and tyranny: "El Labrador que sólo posea una vaca para el alimento de sus tiernos hijos, el que tenía sólo una yunta de bueyes con que cultivar la pequeña propiedad que le hacía existir; éstos infelices que parece debieran haberse substraído a la tiranía de tan riguroso tributo . . . tampoco pudieron eludirlo porque el interés ahogaba todos los clamores de la indigencia desvalida" (the Farmer who may own only one cow for his tender offspring's sustenance, and who had but a single yoke of oxen with which to plow the small property that kept him alive; these wretches who should have avoided the tyranny of such a rigorous tax . . . could not evade it because special interests drowned every clamor of helpless indigence; 173–74). This is still an affective semantic field, but the language of sensibility is diluted among notions of illness, destitution, and suffering: "vejado atrozmente el Labrador" (the Laborer atrociously humiliated; 174), the island remains in "el mayor quebranto" (the worst affliction; 171). In his conclusion, Power y Giralt vainly struggles to return to the linguistic domain of patriotism: "Desde este momento pongo en manos de V. S. la suerte futura del Pueblo a quien represento, y la felicidad de doscientos mil habitantes que por la bondad de carácter y por su acendrado amor a la causa de la Patria, deben merecerla su particular protección" (As of this moment I leave in Your Lordship's hands the future fate of the People I represent, and the happiness of two hundred thousand inhabitants whose benevolent disposition and pure love of the Fatherland should earn them its special protection; 179). However, this happiness is no longer envisioned as a transatlantic fraternity, but simply as "hacer florecer aquella hermosa posesión reducida hasta ahora a la nulidad más deplorable" (making flourish that beautiful possession, hereto reduced to the most deplorable nullity).

The evolution just outlined shows that, by the time Argüelles made his abovementioned speech in December 1811, Power y Giralt had all but abandoned the discourse of exalted patriotism. Only once more does he approximate his 1810 elation: in a new letter dated 9 March 1812 announcing to the San Juan Council the Constitution's proclamation. He communicates this news with "mi corazón inundado del más puro placer y mi alma fuertemente conmovida" (my heart flooded with the purest pleasure and my soul profoundly moved; 215). His words on this occasion are nevertheless much more cautious and tentative than when he first disembarked in Cádiz. While he rejoices at the promulgation of the "suspirado Código que dichosamente ha fijado sobre bases indestructibles la forma política de la Monarquía y los derechos sagrados del pueblo" (longed-for Code that has felicitously secured on indestructible foundations the political form of the Monarchy and the sacred rights of the people), the concrete consequences he forecasts have more to do with the end of the rule of terror than with the achievement of *égalité* and *fraternité*. He welcomes the security newly afforded to "la vida, el honor, la libertad, la propiedad de todos y cada uno de los individuos que componen el dilatado Imperio Español" (the life, honor, freedom, and property of each and every individual composing the vast Spanish Empire), and these references to *individuals* and the *distances* between them replace talk of national brothers and the ties that bind them. The greatest advantage of the new code—at least the one described in most detail—seems to be placing citizens "al abrigo de toda tiranía. Con ella se ha derrocado el abominable Coloso del despotismo . . . ominoso que nos condujo hasta el mismo borde del más hondo precipicio . . . con ella queda para siempre aprisionado el horrendo monstruo de la arbitrariedad. . . . Defendida cual merece la inocencia, jamás podrá en lo adelante verse confundida bajo las apariencias del crimen" (under protection from all tyranny. With it the abominable Colossus of the ominous . . . despotism that brought us to the very edge of the deepest abyss has been overthrown . . . with it the horrid monster of arbitrariness is forever incarcerated. . . . Innocence safeguarded as it deserves to be shall never again be tarred with the appearance of crime; 215–16). Here too a text whose starting point was patriotic sensibility morphs into a grotesque evocation of strife and fear. Only timidly at the end, and once again in a vague future tense, does the hope of some sort of national communion reappear, curiously phrased in the words of another islander: "las palabras del ilustre obispo de Mallorca, que yo me complazco en repetir. . . . Ya somos libres y ahora indudablemente seremos españoles" (the words of the Illustrious Bishop of Majorca, which I take pleasure in repeating. . . . *We are free at last, and now we will undoubtedly be Spanish*; 216).

In his last known letter (1813) Power y Giralt, already sick with yellow fever and needing his expense allowance (unpaid because of the governor's interference), describes himself as "enfermo y sin recursos en un pays extraño" (ill and penniless in a strange country; cited in Álvarez Curbelo). Remarkably, this phrase conveys not only homesickness but a feeling of foreignness in the peninsula. The word *país* here is quite telling, for although Power y Giralt consistently used it with the meaning of region or territory, it remains the opposite of the Nación and Patria to which he devoted his life. País is what remains divisive within the nation, yet ironically it is what Power y Giralt most succeeds in constructing—far from the surrender of local identity suggested in his 1810 letter. Out of the collapse of his patriotic discourse in the face of the fatherland's repudiation there emerges a new object for a love that is neither patriotic (inspired by the republic) nor exactly nationalist (inspired by "cultural and spiritual unity"), but aroused by the land itself. Much has been made of "tellurism" as a historically dominant current in Puerto Rican letters: a nostalgic attachment to the tropical landscape and its hero, the *jíbaro*, as myths of origin, a paradise lost to disenfranchisement.[7] As a foundational fiction, it was already present in Power y Giralt's words. From his performative efforts to become *Spanish* once and for all, the rhetoric that ultimately survived refers to the Puerto Rican país for which he spoke: "entre todas las Antillas . . . la más feraz y salubre" (among all the Antilles, the most fertile and nourishing; 165). The ways in which the deputy constructed—and unwittingly *deconstructed*—the concepts of país and patria articulate Puerto Rican identity discourse through the present.

NOTES

1. The acknowledgment of diversity in constructing nationality was a concession to American deputies at a time of incipient unrest, when many saw the new constitution as the only hope for the empire's survival. Accordingly, it should be noted that nationality was not identical to *citizenship*, a special status that conferred, among other privileges, the rights to vote and to run for office and that excluded, except in extraordinary circumstances, those of African descent (although not indigenous Americans, already recognized by the *Leyes de Indias*). Nevertheless, although there was a racial component to this distinction,

as King explains, its main purpose was political and economic: to ensure the numerical superiority of peninsulars over Americans in government. Although perhaps making a virtue out of necessity, the 1812 Constitution's authors minimized the ethnic component of nationality.

2. Here and throughout the text, all quotations from primary sources maintain the spelling and accentuation of the original.
3. Most notable among these is Puerto Rico's resistance to the attempted British invasion of 1797, specifically mentioned in the Junta summons. The islanders' victory over the attackers, involving both regular armies and popular militias, marks an important milestone in Puerto Rican history, since in reward for this show of fidelity Carlos IV bestowed on the city of San Juan the epithet of *Muy Noble y Muy Leal* (Most Noble and Loyal), along with several economic privileges.
4. Except where otherwise noted, all quotations from Power y Giralt are from Caro de Delgado's compilation of his work.
5. A lifelong naval officer, between 1801 and 1809 Power y Giralt was a captain in the Costa Firme mail corps, sailing between San Juan, Puerto Cabello, and La Guayra. Dávila has speculated that he had friends and connections in Venezuela's revolutionary circles.
6. Scarano compellingly analyzes the archaeology of the jíbaro as a strategy on the part of elite Puerto Rican creoles—who were landowners rather than peasants—to develop a local identity "mask" behind which to exercise oppositional politics:

    The Puerto Rican–as–*jíbaro* trope was initially tied to the politics of a historically young, ascendant elite; as such, it formed part of the arsenal that this group used to advance a particular socioeconomic and political—that is, class—project. . . . In the 1810s and 1820s . . . its meanings proved a bit opaque and difficult to decipher by those whom the masqueraders assumed to be the 'natural' audience, that is, other constitution enthusiasts, among whom liberal creoles predominated, and their absolutist rivals, a group dominated by conservative Spaniards. But, in time, the masquerade's intent became more widely understood, and the Puerto Rican–as–*jíbaro* trope assumed a key role in the liberals' protracted struggle to fashion and solidify a Puerto Rican ethnicity, a proto-nation. By the middle of the nineteenth century, the trope had acquired the transparency and clarity necessary for its symbolic anchoring of the nation. (1403–4)

7. In her comprehensive history of Puerto Rican literature, Rivera de Álvarez traces the history of these motifs beginning in the 1820s with the satirical depiction of local customs in the Puerto Rican countryside in Miguel Cabrera's *Coplas* (*Peasant Songs*) and continuing uninterrupted through the twentieth century (104). González, perhaps the critic who has most emphasized the pervasiveness of tellurism, criticizes it, like Scarano, as the (false) construction of a national image on the part of the elites. For González, tellurism does not represent a disinterested lyrical sensibility toward the Puerto Rican tropical landscape, but a very concrete historical yearning for the land lost under US rule; that is, a means of material production whose ownership passed into foreign hands (33). Power y Giralt, whose family owned one of the most important sugar mills on the island, was himself, of course, a member of the dominant class. Nevertheless, his nostalgia for the land can be understood not so much as a denial of the least privileged classes (he was one of the

earliest champions of abolitionism), but rather as a turn to an element available for identity construction that could not be associated with Spanish nationality or the Spanish state.

WORKS CITED

Álvarez Curbelo, Sylvia. "El Reino en orfandad: Las instrucciones de los cabildos a Ramón Power y Giralt (1809–1813)." Academia Puertorriqueña de Jurisprudencia y Legislación, Proyecto Cádiz. *academiajurisprudenciapr.org/cadiz/coleccion-documental/ponencias/el-reino-en-orfandad-las-instrucciones-de-los-cabildos-a-ramon-power-y-giralt-1809-1813/* (accessed 30 June 1914).

Anderson, Benedict. *Imagined Communities: Reflections on the Origins and Spread of Nationalism*. 2nd ed. New York: Verso, 2006.

Argüelles, Agustín de. *Discurso preliminar a la Constitución de la Monarquía Española*. Gerona: Oliva, 1820.

Campbell, Peter R. "The Language of Patriotism in France, 1750–1770." *Journal of French Studies, e-France* 1.1 (2007): 1–43.

Caro de Delgado, Aida. *Ramón Power y Giralt: Diputado puertorriqueño a las Cortes Generales y Extraordinarias de España, 1810–1812; Compilación de documentos*. San Juan: Printed by the author, 1969.

Constitución política de la Monarquía Española. Madrid: Imprenta Nacional, 1820.

Dávila, Arturo V. "Ramón Power: Apuntes biográficos." *Revista del Instituto de Cultura Puertorriqueña* 17 (1962): 30–36.

Diario de sesiones de las Cortes Generales y Extraordinarias: Dieron principio el 24 de setiembre de 1810 y terminaron el 20 de setiembre de 1813. 9 vols. Madrid: Imprenta de J. A. Garcia, 1870–1874. Digital facsimile. *www.constitucion1812.0rg/ficha.asp?id=27&tipo_libro=3* (accessed 30 June 2014).

Diccionario de Autoridades. 1726–1739. Madrid: Instituto de Investigación Rafael Lapesa; Real Academia Española. *web.frl.es/DA.html* (accessed 30 June 2014).

Diccionario de la lengua española (DRAE). 22nd ed. Madrid: Real Academia Española, 2001. *www.rae.es/recursos/diccionarios/drae* (accessed 30 June 2014).

Feyjóo y Montenegro, Fray Benito Gerónimo. *Teatro crítico universal*. Vol. 3. Madrid: Real Compañía de Impresores y Libreros, 1773.

González, José Luis. *El país de cuatro pisos y otros ensayos*. Río Piedras: Ediciones Huracán, 1989.

Información sobre reformas en Cuba y Puerto Rico celebrada en Madrid en 1866 y 67, por los representantes de ambas islas. 2nd ed. 2 vols. New York: Imprenta de Hallet y Breen, 1877.

Iriarte, Tomás de. *Guzmán el Bueno: Colección de obras en verso y prosa*. Vol. 7. Madrid: Imprenta Real, 1805.

King, James L. "The Colored Castes and American Representation in the Cortes de Cádiz." *Hispanic American Historical Review* 33.1 (1953): 33–64.

Pratt, Mary Louise. *Imperial Eyes: Travel Writing and Transculturation*. New York: Routledge, 1992.

Rivera de Álvarez, Josefina. *Literatura puertorriqueña: Su proceso en el tiempo*. Madrid: Ediciones Partenón, 1983.

Scarano, Francisco A. "The *Jíbaro* Masquerade and the Subaltern Politics of Creole Identity Formation in Puerto Rico, 1745–1823." *American Historical Review* 101.5 (1996): 1398–431.

Sommer, Doris. *Foundational Fictions: The National Romances of Latin America*. Berkeley: U of California P, 1991.

Varela Suanzes, Joaquín. *Las Cortes de Cádiz: Representación nacional y centralismo*. Alicante: Biblioteca Virtual Miguel de Cervantes, 2005. *www.cervantesvirtual.com/FichaObra.html?portal=0&Ref=15810* (accessed 30 June 2014).

Vidart, Luis. *La historia literaria de España*. Madrid: Tipografía de la Revista Contemporánea, 1877.

Viroli, Maurizio. *For Love of Country: An Essay on Patriotism and Nationalism*. New York: Oxford UP, 1997.

CHAPTER THREE

Emotional Readings for New Interpretative Communities in the Nineteenth Century
Agustín Pérez Zaragoza's Galería fúnebre *(1831)*

PURA FERNÁNDEZ

> Sólo recuerdo la emoción de las cosas,
> y se me olvida todo lo demás
> (I only remember the emotion of things,
> and I forget everything else)
>
> —ANTONIO MACHADO, *PROSAS COMPLETAS* (1188)

On 6 November 2003, the Spanish media announced the official engagement of the heir to the throne, now King Felipe VI, to the journalist Letizia Ortiz.[1] The news caused a sensation, thanks to the secrecy surrounding the relationship and the future queen's divorced status and profession as the face of Spanish state television's main news program. Media reports highlighted the traditional exchange of gifts between the engaged couple, revealing that, when the crown prince announced that his gift to Letizia would be "a family jewel," she replied, "And mine . . . a literary jewel." As she declared, "It's a beautiful book I've been trying to find for some time, by Mariano José de Larra, a gorgeous 1850 edition of a chivalric tale set in the fifteenth century. A book I wanted him to have" since, as next day's report in *El País* stated, "their common 'passion' for literature has been one of the things that has most brought them together" (Galaz). The same article explained that it was an old edition of the journalist Larra's romance *El doncel de Don Enrique el Doliente* (*The Page of King Henry the Infirm*, 1834). The obstacles to the love relationship in the plot, the supposition that the protagonist is an alter ego of the author, and Larra's profession as journalist gave the gift additional symbolic capital, providing a tacit emotional code that allowed the new couple to connect with the Spanish public. Indeed, ISBN records show that at least thirteen of the eighteen editions of Larra's novel published in Spain since the 1970s have appeared since 2003, in which year it was reprinted at least four times.

The royal couple's union through literature parallels the passion belatedly discovered by Britain's Queen Elizabeth II in Alan Bennett's novel *The Uncommon Reader* (2007), whose title refers to Virginia Woolf's 1925 essay collection *Uncommon Reader*. Through her voracious thirst for novels, the British monarch is progressively humanized as she enters a vital, unruly, open emotional community—the Republic of Letters—in which she learns to feel and, thus, to *really* live, succumbing to the female passion most treated in nineteenth-century literature: that of Bovarism, defined by Daniel Pennac as a textually transmitted disease.

These two royal examples, one real and one fictional, exemplify a concept of reading as a means to knowledge through sensate and emotional experience. Yet, as Karin Littau notes, the emotions as an aesthetic and cultural category remain absent from theories of reading. From the eighteenth century, underpinned by Kantian aesthetics, a critical discourse emerged that exalted reading as a purely cognitive experience, distanced from pathos and everything associated with the bodily and sensorial (24). This binary thinking—generating the dichotomies high/popular, reflexive/entertaining, cognitive/affective, active/passive, resisting/facile, rational/emotional, select/mass—has made literature and its effects a matter of hermeneutics. The category "reader" is thereby reduced to that of an active (critical and objective) producer of meaning, distanced from the vital experience that Ramón Gómez de la Serna defined in 1909 as an "estado de cuerpo" (state of body).

Emotional Communities

In 1832, still under Fernando VII's absolutist rule, Larra reflected on the nature of the reading public: a cultural, social, and publishing category of increasing size and power thanks to the growth of the press and the still modest Spanish literary field. In his article "¿Quién es el público y dónde se le encuentra?" ("Who and Where Is the Public?"), he offered an acute analysis of the power of a capricious, unpredictable, sovereign readership, asking: "¿Será el público el que compra la *Galería fúnebre de espectros y sombras ensangrentadas* . . . o el que deja en la librería las *Vidas de los españoles célebres* y la traducción de la *Ilíada*?" (Is the public the reader who buys the *Funereal Gallery of Specters and Bloody Shadows* . . . or leaves on the bookstore shelves the *Lives of Famous Spaniards* and translations of the *Iliad*?; 21). Here Larra was picking up on a major social phenomenon that had taken the literary scene by storm the previous year: the twelve volumes published by Agustín Pérez Zaragoza y Godínez, a former civil servant under Carlos IV who supported French Enlightenment ideas and opposed absolutism and theocracy, going into exile in France after the defeat of the Napoleonic troops that had occupied the peninsula in 1808, and returning to Spain under the brief

1820–1823 period of constitutional rule. Pérez Zaragoza survived the repressive 1823–1833 "Ominous Decade" thanks to a chameleonic talent for writing, translating, and adapting educational, moral, and recreational works that helped eclipse his heterodox past (Cuenca; Pura Fernández).

Fernando VII's remarriage to the young María Cristina in December 1829 was followed by the March 1830 promulgation of the Pragmatic Sanction, abolishing the Salic Law that prevented a woman from inheriting the Spanish throne. This unleashed a struggle for the succession that would, between 1833 and 1876, give rise to three civil wars, pitting the newborn liberal state against the Catholic absolutist supporters of Fernando's brother Don Carlos. October 1830 saw the birth of Fernando's firstborn child, the future Isabel II (1844–1868), followed from March to November 1831 by publication of the twelve volumes of Pérez Zaragoza's *Galería fúnebre de historias trágicas, espectros y sombras ensangrentadas: Obra nueva de prodigios, acontecimientos maravillosos, apariciones nocturnas, sueños espantosos, delitos misteriosos, fenómenos terribles, crímenes históricos y fabulosos, cadáveres ambulantes, cabezas ensangrentadas, venganzas atroces y casos sorprendentes* (*Funereal Gallery of Tragic Stories, Specters, and Bloody Shadows: A New Work of Wonders, Marvelous Occurrences, Nocturnal Apparitions, Terrifying Dreams, Mysterious Ill-Doings, Dreadful Phenomena, Historical and Fabulous Crimes, Walking Corpses, Bloody Heads, Terrible Vengeances, and Extraordinary Episodes*). This suggestive work was advertised as a "Colección curiosa e instructiva de sucesos trágicos para producir las fuertes emociones del terror, inspirando horror al crimen que es el freno poderoso de las pasiones" ("Curious and Instructive Collection of Tragic Happenings Aimed at Producing Strong Emotions of Terror, Inspiring a Horror of Crime as a Powerful Brake on the Passions"; 1: 5). Its success coincided with news of the king's declining health and his female heir's first few months of life.

Against the backcloth of serious political tensions between the supporters of Don Carlos and those of the queen who sought out the more liberal sectors, each volume of the *Galería fúnebre* has a front cover proclaiming that its author dedicates it "a la augusta Real persona de S.M. Dª María Cristina de Borbón, Reina de las Españas, bajo la real protección del Rey" (to the august royal person of Her Majesty Doña María Cristina of the House of Bourbon, Queen of the Spains, under the royal protection of the King). To have secured this double distinction is surprising, given the author's past and the title and contents of a work that, the previous year, had been denied a printing license and that includes numerous explicit scenes of indecent assault, rape, necrophilia, sacrilege, incest, and a horrendous range of murders and acts offending social, moral, and religious principles. Even more surprising is the letter published on 8 July 1831 in *El Correo Literario y Mercantil* by Basilio Sebastián Castellanos and Julián Anento, accusing Pérez Zaragoza of unfair competition and usurpation of authorship by publishing a work most of which they were publishing as an "expanded translation" of an unknown Monsieur David's *La poderosa Themis o Los remordimientos de los malvados* (*The Powerful Themis; or, The Remorse of the Wicked*, 1830–1831) (Alonso Seoane 10–12).

Pérez Zaragoza's forceful reply ended the polemic by appealing to the queen's protection and to his peculiar status as original author, translator, and adaptor of certain stories by the French writer Cuisin (whose name was not mentioned during the hostile exchange). J. R. P. Cuisin, a military officer and polygraph, had in 1820 published in Paris two volumes entitled *Les ombres sanglantes: Galerie funèbre de prodiges, evénements merveilleux, apparitions nocturnes, songes épouvantables, délits mystérieux, phénomènes terribles, forfaits historiques, cadavres mobiles, têtes ensanglantées et animées, vengeances atroces et combinaisons du crime, puisés dans des sources réelles; Recueil propre à causer les fortes émotions de la terreur* (*Bloody Shadows: Funereal Gallery of Wonders, Marvelous Occurrences, Nocturnal Apparitions, Terrifying Dreams, Mysterious Wrongdoings, Dreadful Phenomena, Historical Misdeeds, Walking Corpses, Bloody Animated Heads, Terrible Revenge, and Motley Crimes, Taken from Real Sources; A Collection Intended to Produce Strong Emotions of Horror*), and *Les Fantômes nocturnes, ou les Terreurs des coupables; Théâtre de forfaits, offrant, par nouvelles historiques, des visions infernales de monstres fantastiques, d'images funestes, de lutins homicides, de spectres et d'échafauds sanglants, supplices précurseurs des scélérats* (*Nocturnal Phantoms; or, the Terror of the Guilty: Theater of Wrongdoing Based on Historical Events and Offering Infernal Visions of Fantastic Monsters, Dreadful Images, Murderous Ghouls, Specters and Bloody Gallows, Cautionary Torments of Villains*)—a compilation of novellas mostly reworked from other sources, aimed at an essentially female public.

This dispute over authorship points to the flooding of the Spanish literary market in the first third of the nineteenth century with translations and adaptations from French or English, presented as original creations that reflected the national character (López Santos 145–49). This practice often betrays a complex process of moral, cultural, and emotional mediation, as in the *Galería fúnebre*'s case. Cuisin's parody of Gothic tales, with a high degree of sexual titillation (López Santos 186–95), is given a historical and moral spin by Pérez Zaragoza, as indicated in the collection's subtitle "El historiador trágico de las catástrofes del linaje humano" ("Tragic Chronicles of Catastrophes of the Human Lineage").

The press of the time reveals the rush of subscribers attracted by a collection that advertised itself as offering extreme plots and emotions (Cuenca 16–23; Roas 89–90; López Santos 85–86). The (incomplete) list of subscribers published at the end of the twelfth volume (249–82) includes aristocrats and high palace dignitaries, civil servants, and members of the military, the liberal professions, and even the religious, by contrast with the modest list of bourgeois subscribers published in the series edited by Castellanos and Anento, whose request for royal approval of its dedication was rejected (Alonso Seoane 8). Most of the listed subscribers to the *Galería fúnebre* were men, as was normal, even with subscriptions to women's magazines, since those who subscribed were those able to enter into a contractual agreement. What interests me in this chapter is that Pérez Zaragoza's readers were habitually referred to at the time—by himself and others—as female.

Fernando VII's repressive regime (save for the brief 1820–1823 Trienio Liberal) imposed strict controls on the publication of literary works, and especially on translations of the so-called Female Gothic (Davison; Smith and Wallace); only four English "Female Gothic" authors secured translation, including Ann Radcliffe between 1819 and 1832 (Establier Pérez). Thus the *Galería fúnebre*'s suggestive title, its dedication to the queen, and its explicit appeal to a female readership in its publicity and prologue provoked a cultural commotion.

As Labanyi has noted ("Liberal Individualism" 8–9), literary production of the 1830s pays considerable attention to family relationships, with the textual unconscious projecting social, political, moral, and economic issues onto the family. But what happens when the most visible family unit, the royal couple, triggers a potential conflict of succession linked to the female condition of the heir to the throne—a conflict threatening to lead to yet another war in a country that, in less than three decades, had endured the Napoleonic invasion and ensuing fratricidal struggle, the end of the dream of freedom and progress signaled by the Constitution of Cádiz (1812), Fernando VII's restoration of absolutism (1814), successive waves of exiles (1814 and 1823), and loss of its major overseas colonies (1824)?

In the *Galería fúnebre*, as in the royal family, parental and fraternal relationships are the source of claustrophobic nightmares threatening the heroines, sometimes to the point of paroxysm as in the case of the novella *Leonisa, víctima de amor y de la hermosura o El desenfreno de las pasiones* (*Leonisa, Victim of Love and Beauty; or, Passion Unleashed*), written by Pérez Zaragoza for the *Galería fúnebre* but finally excluded, possibly because of the extremity of the plot in which the young female protagonist suffers the lecherous predations of her two brothers, who through deceit and incarceration trap her in a *ménage à trois*, provoking in her a brutal crisis of identity. Gothic sentimental novels could be read as parables of family relationships in which women have to be alert and develop passive-aggressive or even masochistic strategies in order to adapt and survive (Smith and Wallace 3), as, for example, in *Milady Herwort y Miss Clarisa o Bristol, el carnicero asesino* (*Milady Herwort and Miss Clarissa; or, Bristol, the Murderous Butcher*) (Fig. 3.1). This is a model of suffering close to the female education whose codes of pain and sacrifice inflect the sentimental novel of the Isabeline period, which, thanks to a generation of women writers, notably Pilar Sinués, created the paradigm of the *ángel del hogar* (angel of the hearth) as an adaptive resource within the bourgeois sphere (Charnon-Deutsch; Blanco). Macías-Fernández sets the *Galería fúnebre* in the context of the discourses of power relations and sexual politics of 1830s Spain, which resorted to Gothic-style political allegory—with helpless young women victimized by villains and virtuous men corrupted by ambitious, lascivious women—as a strategy for legitimizing bourgeois sexual morality (267). In contrast to the collection's plotlines, which systematically subject female virtue to male assault, the figure of Queen María Cristina appears in the dedication as the "madre tierna de tantos vasallos" (tender mother of her many vassals) who protects the throne's legitimacy as a symbolic incarnation of moral virtue.

Evolutionist explanations suggest that fear, anguish, and insecurity are effective weapons of survival, reminding us of danger and anticipating a threatening future

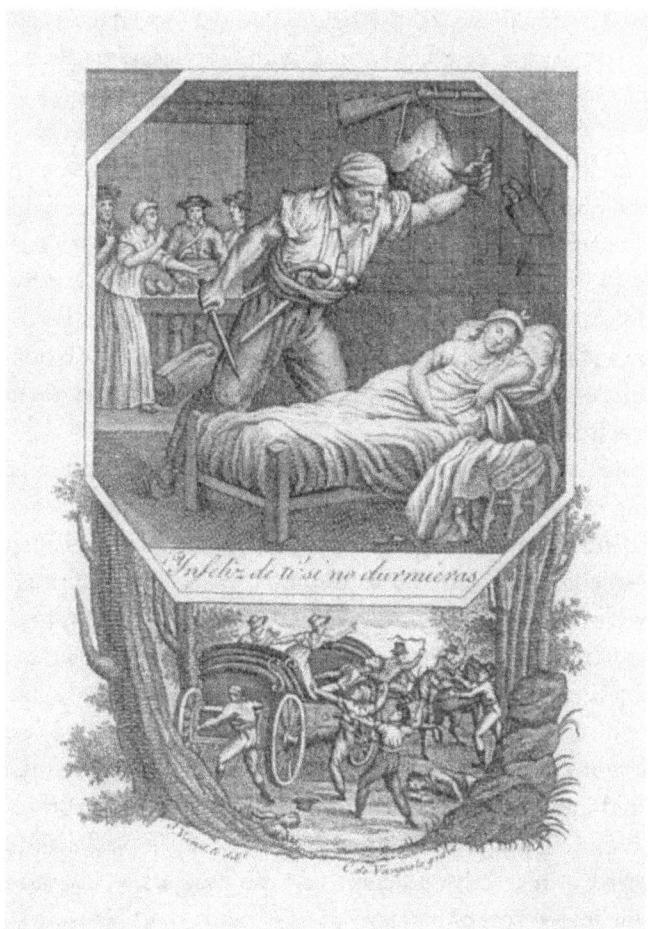

Figure 3.1. Illustration to *Milady Herwort y Miss Clarisa o Bristol, el carnicero asesino*, in Agustín Pérez Zaragoza's *Galería fúnebre*: "Woe on You Had You Not Been Asleep!" Courtesy of Biblioteca Nacional de España.

(Gubern 14–15). Additionally, the neurological experiments mentioned by Massumi show that the most frightening film scenes produced the greatest pleasure and emotional intensity (Labanyi, "Doing Things" 225). As Pérez Zaragoza declares in *Varinka, o efectos de una mala educación* (*Varinka; or, Effects of a Bad Education*), having to face her lover's terrible death snaps the female protagonist out of her haughtiness since "el dolor la ha hecho una mujer sensible" (grief has made her a sensitive woman; 9: 31). Historically, the fact that it is socially acceptable for women to express fear has freed them from rigid masculine emotional codes, allowing them to develop competence in what psychologists today call resilience in the face of trauma (Bourke). The history of civilization is built on fear, pain, and suffering, as Javier Moscoso notes (121). And these same emotions are the principal narrative agents of the novellas in the *Galería fúnebre*, in which, despite the remote settings, the most likely source of terror lies close at hand, ready to assault the female body, its sovereignty, and its agency. If Cuisin aimed to produce a "delightful terror" with his phantasmagorias, Pérez Zaragoza seeks to induce a "terror saludable" (salutary terror; 1: 17), resulting in "dulces efectos" (agreeable effects; 1: 54), because horror and danger can be pleasurable, as Amedeo discovers in the novella *La morada de un parricida* (*A Parricide's Abode*): "parecía gozar en su interior cierto encanto: el dolor gusta algunas veces de asociarse a unos espectáculos tan terribles" (he seemed to enjoy an inner delight; pain sometimes takes pleasure in associating itself with such terrible spectacles; 1: 99–100). Unlike the castrating silence imposed on individuals in the sociopolitical and intimate spheres, Pérez Zaragoza offers passional excess and delirium through cathartic representations. It is not just a matter of deciphering signs or assimilating ideas, but of experiencing bodily responses facilitated by sensorial hyperstimulation (1: 6).

The metaphor of the passionate female reader made women the protagonists of a debate spanning the whole century about the pernicious effects of fiction on women who equate art and life by reading literally—like Galdós's Isidora Rufete in *La desheredada* (1881)—thereby denying the autonomy of the subject (Catelli). But there is nothing passive about the paradigm of reading advocated by the *Galería fúnebre*; there is no forgetting of the self in the immersion in the word of the other, but an overexcitation of individual experience as a form of knowledge and agency. Romanticism dramatized the contradictions inherent in the development of individual consciousness and the construction of modern subjectivity based on models of reflexivity, the cultivation of interiority, and ideals of emancipation (Novella 20–21). In the new bourgeois order, the centrality of the subject resulted from the split between public and private spheres, which encouraged introspective practices and the progressive insertion of family and interpersonal life into spaces of privacy.

The visual and literary representation of the woman reader is a constant in the nineteenth century, as are the discourses on women's reading that effectively propose a *dispositio*: the confirmation of a new *modus legendi* which, as Petrucci observes (545), entails a new bodily freedom of movement, quite unlike the forced postures required by collective spaces such as the library or classroom, and characterized by an intense, intimate contact with the book, unhampered by any normalizing regulation. As shown by historical studies of the teaching and practice of reading, the latter was generally seen as a social art to be *performed* in collective spaces containing bodies in action (Botrel); an art to be shared, in which intonation, inflection of the voice, and gesture or bodily attitude complement a form of reading that is expressive, synaesthetic, modulated, and interpretative. It should be remembered that, in the nineteenth century, reading aloud—whether individual or collective—was still the norm for a public used to *hearing reading* (Botrel 588). The phrase "expressive reading" sums up the nineteenth-century art of reading, as exemplified in the widely circulated manuals of Ernest Legouvé, which insist that "[l]a lectura en voz alta exige tal perfección en los órganos, tanto tacto, gusto y sentimiento que es muy raro el saber leer bien" (reading aloud requires such perfection of the organs, whether touch, taste, or feeling, that the ability to read well is extremely rare), since readers have to pay attention to emphasis and intonation, abandoning themselves to every level of passion and achieving the particular tone required by feelings and emotions, so as to *affect* the text by imbuing it with their personality (Botrel 580). Legouvé's manual suggests that feeling is a bodily organ that exists alongside the other senses and, like them, is an instrument of knowledge.

As Rancière recalls when talking of the "paradox of the spectator," the role of the reader of literature has traditionally been seen as passive, since the word is seen as the opposite of action; appearance as the opposite of reality; activity as the opposite of passivity; the gaze as the opposite of knowledge. But, regardless of this binary vision, spectators are able to emancipate themselves, transforming the gaze into action, and interpreting the spectacle by forming an image of it or associating it with a lived experience. The capacity to be *affected* is cumulative. Thus the character Elvira in Pérez Zaragoza's novella *La princesa de Lipno o el retrete del placer criminal* (*The Princess of Lipno; or, the Retreat of Criminal Pleasure*; 2: 34) responds so strongly to the sounds and colors of the scene of horror in which she finds herself because she has been sensitized by the atrocities she has witnessed previously. In the same way, the further readers progress through Pérez Zaragoza's twelve volumes, the more keenly their senses are tuned. Readers become involved spectators who even appear in the narrative, as in *Milady Herwort y Miss Clarissa o Bristol, el carnicero asesino*: "El espectador se estremece, su corazón palpita, se oprime, suspéndese su respiración, teme interiormente aquel espectáculo, no se atreve a mirar" (The spectator shudders, his heart beats faster and contracts, he holds his breath, deep down fearing the spectacle, he dare not look; 1: 72).

Even though, in this quote, Pérez Zaragoza uses the masculine form to refer to the reader, his model of the ideal reader is explicitly female. His description of the female reader suggests an intimate act experienced unaccompanied in the privacy of the bedroom, in close material communion with the text's material manifestation: a small, easy-to-handle volume with high-quality illustrations promising an inexhaustible supply of emotional reactions—a boudoir format appropriate to the "economy of desire" that fetishizes the object, giving the product value not because of its practical function or materiality, but because of its social status and provision of emotional gratification (Haidt, "The Wife" 116). The book, as a commodity, takes on the provisional, subjective value conferred by its social life (Appadurai).

The *Galería fúnebre*'s success is explained by its belief in the ability of reading to contribute to interpersonal cohesion, in the intersubjective communication of a society of over five hundred sensitive readers equipped with an external organ that permits their emotional self-stimulation, that is, Pérez Zaragoza's Sociedad de Amigos (Society of Friends), which published its twelve volumes. Significantly, over a third of the first volume, designed to capture subscribers' interest, is taken up with Pérez Zaragoza's preliminary address to his readers—the mark of a great literary publicist.

The Weberian category "emotional community"—referring to ephemeral, shifting groupings, local and unorganized, with similar, shared forms of emotional expression—can be a useful tool for analyzing these small circles that practice empathic socialization through collective reading. Such circles, which for Maffesoli (57) constitute a kind of neotribalism, can create strong social bonds, especially in adverse circumstances, functioning as a virtual projection of the literary *tertulias* (gatherings), characteristic of the period, whose facilitation of the sharing and exchange of reading experiences made them "emotional refuges" (Reddy 24, 14–19). Decades later, the most popular Spanish writers of serialized fiction would foster such forms of cultural tribalism via group practices of sociability involving a commitment to read, buy, or subscribe to works that were often read aloud by a community sharing similar tastes, interests, and interpretative strategies—practices of sociability based on a common imagined library that stretched the emotions beyond their normal capacity. We are, in other words, dealing with an "interpretative community" as defined by Stanley Fish.

The stories told by Pérez Zaragoza show signs of orality, of expressive devices and functions designed for collective reading. In his "Introducción analítica" ("Analytical Introduction"), he refers to those practices of reading aloud at literary tertulias that lead to a sharing of emotions through the empathic capacity of the voice: "las caras macilentas, desencajadas y pintados en ellas el asombro y el espanto" (amazement and terror painted on their haggard, contorted faces; 1: 45). The traces of oral prosody in the novellas suggests that their value lay not so much in the story's novelty or originality as in its intercommunicative performative capacity; in the holistic power of the sounds and voices; in the "technologies of the word" that delegate to the voice the ability to produce the emotional transference that gives life to a text (Ong 47–48). This helps explain the length and success of the interminable serialized novels that flooded Spain from the 1840s, such as those of the successful social writer Wenceslao Ayguals de Izco or, from 1860, Enrique Pérez Escrich. Their dialogue format and expansive style, whose studied punctuation gives it great expressive force, make these texts "emotional scores" (Sánchez García), implying oral reading as a kind of collective spectacle in keeping with the tastes of an age marked by theatrical and musical culture, often linked to mystical sensory experiences like those that inflame and offset the life of Ana Ozores in Leopoldo Alas's *La Regenta* (1884–1885). These popular works condense with extraordinary intensity the "structure of feeling" that, as Raymond Williams has shown, defines particular historical moments, shaping cultural production and testifying to the historical variability of emotion. The very emotional density and inflation of the *Galería fúnebre*, grounded in specific historical and cultural circumstances, are the key to its instant success in its time, since it accorded with the emotional standards of an epoch, but also explain why its appeal was short-lived.

The model of reader-listener addressed by Pérez Zaragoza can be defined as a cultural subject who is the actor-spectator of a narrative exercise that seeks to stretch his—or rather her—sensory experience to the maximum. His text demands a performative, empathic, synaesthetic, corporeal reading, closely linked to the formulas of dramatic representation and collective spectacle. In some striking passages of his introduction, he evokes, with a startling visual rhetoric, how a young woman starts to feel impelled by her agitated reading of the *Galería fúnebre*—"obra nueva en su clase" (a new work in its class; 1: 52)—to act out a scene of panic whose protagonist is her body in action, like an automaton driven by the effects of an overstimulation that will have lasting effects: "Resonará continuamente a sus oídos el ruido espantoso de metales y cadenas; se paseará su imaginación por largos pasadizos . . . divisarán un cadáver amoratado, etc." (The terrifying clanking of metal and chains will keep ringing in her ears; her imagination will travel down long corridors . . . her eyes will make out a badly bruised corpse, etc.; 1: 28–29). Pérez Zaragoza, as the spectator of his own narrative spectacle's effects, describes how "ya veo erizados sus cabellos y palpitar agitadamente su corazón de una fuerte opresión; sus ojos, imagen del terror" (I can see her hair stand on end and her heart, strangled with emotion, throb wildly; her eyes, a picture of terror; 1: 42). His female reader "quédase inmóvil, tiembla, agítase más y más la palpitación de su corazón, y cae por último desmayada . . ." (halts, trembles, her heart pounding more and more, and finally falls in a faint . . . ; 1: 48). In short, in a perfect illustration of J. L. Austin's famous *How to Do Things with Words* (1962), Pérez Zaragoza insists on the performative nature of words, which produce effects. That is the *Galería fúnebre*'s chief promise to its readers: "verán en acción su sensibilidad" (they will see their sensibility in action; 1: 53). Indeed, an 1831 press article "Lectura aterradora" ("Terrifying Reading") testified to the collection's impact on female readers.

Beyond the parodic nature of these scenes of panic, Pérez Zaragoza insists that it is not enough to read: one has to *know how* to read (1: 6). And reading must mobilize all the senses to reach the emotional extremes that lead to true knowledge, which women and the young are best equipped to attain given their sensibility and impressionability, even though those same qualities can make them easy prey for the passions. According to Haidt, citing George Haggerty, the "primary formal aim of Gothic fiction is the emotional and psychological involvement of the reader [to] maximize affective potential by means of techniques we can call 'sublime'" ("Gothic Larra" 53), with the aim of producing "sympathetic feelings" ("How Gothic" 123). In all his writings, from those of a dissident nature to his encyclopedic educational manuals, Pérez Zaragoza proclaims his patriotic aim of forming the new generations without doing violence to their natural dispositions, through dissection of the human heart, reinforcing virtue by mixing instruction with pleasure.

Reading with the Body

In regarding women as his ideal readers, Pérez Zaragoza has in mind the modern reader resulting from the reading revolution produced in Europe by sentimental fiction, thanks in particular to Richardson, Rousseau, and Goethe, whose work shaped new forms of relationship to books and new ways of reading based on empathy, privacy, and at the same time the socialization of emotions through their sharing with like-minded readers (Whittmann 452–56). Reading as a perceptual activity involves the interaction between a mind and a body in space (Cavallo and Chartier 15). It is this body in a space of privacy that is addressed by Pérez Zaragoza's paratexts, but not in the sense of a passive surrender to the book, as the female reading experience has traditionally been seen, reproducing the androcentric cosmovision that has so angered feminist critics (Littau 219). When Hélène Cixous talks of the female reader, she has in mind the subject who, unlike the Cartesian model, writes and thinks with the body as a source of knowledge and creativity. This branch of feminist reception theory, represented also by Luce Irigaray, appeals to biology to exalt female hypersensibility and multierogeneity, resemanticizing what has been stigmatized by a medical and psychiatric tradition stretching from Havelock Ellis to Freud (Littau 223–32).

For Pérez Zaragoza, however, "reading with the body" has a social, indeed national dimension. He seeks to move and even maltreat the imagination of a public used to spectacles based on optical illusion and physical experiments, so as to destroy phantasmatic chimeras that have no basis in nature (1: 11), with the aim of providing a defense against possible adversity and combating superstition (1: 11–12). But above all he constructs a reflexive, emotionally *affected* model of the reader-spectator, to counter those ladies and young people whose self-absorbed detachment goes against the vigorous national spirit (1: 35–37). This negative prototype—an "ente sin alma" (soul-less being; 1: 31) whose "torpes órganos" (sluggish organs) cannot "soportar las fuertes emociones de un alma sensible" (bear the strong emotions of a sensitive soul; 1: 56)—is marked by indifference and coldness (1: 57); affectation, effeminacy, and elegance have caused the national character to degenerate (1: 37)—an additional contributing factor being inconsequential literary compositions that do not produce an emotional response (1: 34). Here Pérez Zaragoza is distinguishing between an effeminacy that weakens citizens' capacity to respond to threats, and the active female response to horror that he encourages in his readers, which trains them in resistance to danger. His model of the active female reader thus paradoxically offers a feminization of the reader (presumably including male readers too) that will save them—and the nation—from effeminacy.

In keeping with this aim, the atmosphere created in the *Galería fúnebre*'s stories provides a psychological frame for the evocation in the reader of the ever-present threat of horror: whether that of the carnage and destruction caused by wars, that of excessive violence, or that of the daily experience of absolutist power and control over citizens, who suffer a "terror pánico" (panic-stricken terror) as Pérez Zaragoza had declared in 1820, during the brief period of constitutional rule (Macías-Fernández 266). The insinuating threat of danger lodged in the memory of recent horrors motivates the writer's wish to create a "salutary terror"; as he comments, "todos los medios son buenos cuando se encaminan a purificar las costumbres" (all means are good when they seek to purify customs; 1: 18). The activation of sensibility "moves" the mind and leads to action, Pérez Zaragoza claims in his prefatory pages; for that reason he rejects the escapist fantastic stories—"sueños sepulcrales" (sepulchral dreams)—of Radcliffe (1: 27): "Lejos de faltarnos materia, ¿no tenemos bastante recorriendo las atrocidades que han cometido los puñales de otras épocas más modernas? . . . Las muchas y largas guerras de veinte y cinco años a esta parte, ¿no pueden darnos infinitos sucesos y desgracias para formar nuestra *Galería fúnebre*?" (Far from lacking material, don't we have enough simply by considering the atrocities committed in more recent times? . . . Don't the many long wars of the last twenty-five years offer an infinite supply of events and misfortunes for our *Galería fúnebre*?; 1: 39).

Reading becomes an act of emotional mediation that allows the stories told in the *Galería fúnebre* to be inflected by the reader's personal experience. In this intercultural exchange, what appears as cruelty and sadism when seen from one side of the battlefront becomes heroism or patriotic valor when seen from the other. The chronicle narrated in *Las catacumbas españolas* (*The Spanish Catacombs*) is a good example, as seen in the accompanying illustration included by Pérez Zaragoza (Fig. 3.2). Indeed, the previously mentioned Castellanos and Anento denounced the inclusion of this story in the *Galería* precisely because they found problematic a story that demonstrated the instability of a "historical truth" that swings between heroism/patriotic love and treason/felony, depending not only on which side is narrating the events, but also on the reassignation of patriotic values in the convulsive course of political events, eliminating stable emotional referents: "por ser un cuadro ridículo de horrorosos excesos supuestos en la gloriosa Guerra de la Independencia contra los franceses, cometidos por los partidarios que en aquella época fueron héroes defensores de la península y de nuestro amado Soberano, pues aunque algunos de ellos hayan posteriormente desmentido de sus intentos, en aquellos tiempos no por eso los deja de citar la historia como beneméritos en el año de 1808" (on account of its ridiculous depiction of supposed horrific excesses in the glorious War of Independence against the French, committed by those who at that time were heroes defending the peninsula and our beloved Monarch, since, although some of them later changed their position, that is no reason for history not to depict them as heroes in 1808; Castellanos and Anento cited in Alonso Seoane 11). Literary creation modifies one's relationship to one's situation in the world and generates a new imaginary that permeates one's perception of everyday experience and even one's view of lived historical experience; as Max Milner puts it, it is a machine for creating ways of seeing (13). This is what Pérez Zaragoza does in his *Galería fúnebre*. The fantastic offers the illusory artifice of a new space in which the relationship between the subject's desire and its object configures a new optics, which confuses the senses. The camera obscura, optical box, stereoscope, magic lantern, diorama, or exhibition of galvanism plays on spectators' bewilderment, offering a spectacle whose workings they cannot fathom and that presents reality as an unsolvable enigma (Milner 263). The success of these magic-technological spectacles created a "visual esperanto" or "common market of images" that contributed to interest in the use of certain literary discourses in the *Galería fúnebre* (Gian Piero Brunetta cited in Luis Miguel Fernández 16).

An example is the following passage of the previously mentioned novella *Milady Herwort y Miss Clarissa o Bristol, el carnicero asesino*: "Había cesado de nevar, pero unas nubes enormes arrojadas con violencia del norte al oeste cambiaban la luz a los objetos de un modo extraordinario y terrible, de manera que una oscuridad total hubiera causado menos pavor que estas mudanzas en la luz triste y opaca de una noche nevada, pues producían sobre el prisma de la imaginación una especie de fantasmagoría espantosa" (It had stopped snowing, but some huge clouds violently thrust from north to west altered the light cast on objects in an extraordinary, terrible fashion, so that total darkness would have caused less terror than these modulations to the gloomy, pearly light of a snowy night, which projected on the prism of the imagination a kind of frightful phantasmagoria; 1: 88–89). Pérez Zaragoza's prologue, like several of his novellas, is shot through with allusions to optical effects, magic spectacles, the visual illusions of cosmoramas, dioramas, and phantasmagorias, adding to the narrative and stylistic techniques that seek to physically *move* the female reader imagined by him.

Contrary to the paradigm of emotional moderation and tranquil sentiment that formed the basis of the Enlightenment ideal of sociability and affective relations, the *Galería fúnebre* offers the excess of a galvanic, hypnotic, haptic literature that seeks to "poner a prueba el valor y la sensibilidad de sus lectores" (put readers' stamina and sensibility to the test; 1: 61). It is a narrative that avoids "ejemplos fríos, a veces inverosímiles" (cold, sometimes implausible examples) that fail to impress those who are to be saved from unbridled passion (1: 11). Coldness is seen by the author as an extreme state of mind to be rejected as an initial disposition on the readers' part (1: 23, 30). On the contrary, readers are invited to cooperate by mobilizing their passions to "producir las fuertes emociones del terror" (produce the strong emotions of terror; 1: 23), as the author declares in his dedication to the queen. Pérez Zaragoza could not be further from the psychological culture identified with the Spanish Baroque, whose cold passions (secretiveness, deceit, dissimulation) are designed to ensure civil prudence in an unstable, deceptive world (Flor 15); or from the balanced "reasonable sentiments" of the Enlightenment (see Bolufer in this volume). The preliminary pages of the *Galería fúnebre* reject all inhibition, any desire for concealment or moderation during the cathartic reading experience.

As if in a cosmorama, the author-guide takes the reader-spectator on a tour of the catacombs of passion, displaying with an unsparing light the otherness that inhabits the subject beneath the veneer of civilization: "El lector que fuese codicioso de sensaciones fuertes, que nos siga a la luz opaca de nuestras lámparas lúgubres, hasta aquellas sinuosidades pérfidas y catacumbas infernales" (Let the reader eager for strong sensations follow the clouded light of our gloomy lamps, to those perfidious sinuosities and infernal catacumbs; 1: 39–40). Appealing to the life context of readers who need more intense stimulation thanks to the specific historical circumstances they have lived through in a convulsive Spain, Pérez Zaragoza evokes the discourse of a terror familiar to the social imaginary. The dark scenes he projects onto zones of personal safety are reminiscent of Goya's prints *Los desastres de la guerra* (*The Disasters of War*) or the sensationalist, violent engravings illustrating mass-produced popular broadsides, as, for example, in the illustration to *La princesa de Lipno o el retrete del placer criminal* (Fig. 3.3) or the stories narrated in *Las catacumbas españolas*, which make up a blood-curdling diorama designed to produce intense emotions.

Figure 3.2. Illustration to *Las catacumbas españolas*, in Agustín Pérez Zaragoza's *Galería fúnebre*: "Eternal God, Spare Your Virgins So Much Suffering." Courtesy of Biblioteca Nacional de España.

In his "Introducción analítica," Pérez Zaragoza asserts that "escribiré solo para las personas de una imaginación viva y exaltada por las impresiones fuertes, y de un alma sensible, que buscan con anhelo las emociones interesantes y aquellos golpes vigorosos que, dirigiéndose al momento a los resortes del corazón, le causan aquellos estremecimientos repentinos" (I will write only for those with a lively imagination inflamed by strong impressions and with a sensitive soul, who avidly seek out interesting emotions and strong surprise effects that set the heart racing; 1: 22–23). The reader becomes the agent of creative mediation par excellence, to rework the expression of Philippe Hamon

(30), who stresses the subjective component of the process of visual perception and mental elaboration by which a spectator makes an image exist, thus situating the gaze within specific sociocultural coordinates. It is to this kind of reader that Pérez Zaragoza dedicates "estas escenas trágicas tan sensibles, [que] estremecerán [a] mis lectores, [quienes] perderán sus facultades intelectuales, se inflamará su corazón, su espíritu sufrirá una saludable inquietud, y sea que las emociones que experimenten provengan de un gran terror, sea que resulten solamente de una viva sensibilidad, se recogerá siempre el fruto de una preciosa meditación" (these moving, tragic scenes [that] will startle my readers [who] will lose their intellectual faculties, their heart will pound, their spirit will be seized by a salutary anxiety and, regardless of whether their emotions are inspired by a great terror or simply by a keen sensibility, the outcome will always be a fruitful meditation; 1: 25).

Pérez Zaragoza appeals to the heightened sensorial stimulus that activates the sixth sense emphasized by the medical doctor Fabra Soldevila in his *Filosofía de la Legislación Natural fundada en la Antropología* (*Philosophy of Natural Legislation based on Anthropology*, 1838): the great sympathetic nerve that triggers action and is activated in situations of danger and stress. Thus, "las sensaciones de este sexto modo admirable de la facultad de sentir se han designado con un nombre especial y se llaman emociones" (the sensations of this admirable sixth mode of the faculty of feeling have been given a special name and are called *emotions*; Fabra Soldevila 54). Fabra Soldevila explains that dependent on the emotions are the natural instincts, moral affects (defined as simple, mild, and passive [69]), and passions, which are instinctive feelings that can produce strong, violent disturbances but are necessary to life because they are the origin of all human motivation (54, 69). He insists that the emotions (such as the imagination) are more extreme in women and children since their sensitive faculties are less offset by reason (62, 132–34). Women, he concludes are "más sensibles en lo exterior que los hombres" (more outwardly sensitive than men) and "acosadas de sensaciones más locales, y más efímeras" (assaulted by more local and more transient sensations; 133).

For Pérez Zaragoza, reading is "the school of the world" whose pedagogical formula is to mix instruction with pleasure in such a vivid way that the reader is moved (1: 13, 18). William Reddy has analyzed the biological-cognitive and cultural factors that link certain emotions with certain colors (for example, blood red or sinister black), thanks to their strong subjective or experiential character (5–12). Thus, as Pérez Zaragoza indicates in *Las catacumbas españolas*: "Si la Europa, ensangrentada por tantas guerras, estuviese dividida en tantos colores alegóricos que indicasen el grado de las calamidades que más pesaron sobre cada una de sus naciones, ¿no sería indudablemente el color de púrpura, el color de fuego el que designase a la España, habiendo sido el teatro donde más sangre ha corrido y el más frecuentemente abrasado por los fuegos de la guerra?" (If Europe, bleeding from so many wars, were divided into different allegorical colors to indicate the level of calamities that has befallen each of its nations, would not the color crimson, the color of fire, surely be the color assigned to Spain, having been the

Figure 3.3. Illustration to *La princesa de Lipno o el retrete del placer criminal*, in Agustín Pérez Zaragoza's *Galería fúnebre*: "Heaven Above, What Do I See!!! This Is No Illusion; My Death Is Certain." Courtesy of Biblioteca Nacional de España.

theater where the most blood has been spilled and the one most often razed by the fires of war?; 3: 133).

On the literary map of modernity traced by European Romanticism and its fascination for the Gothic, Pérez Zaragoza's collection appears to fit the image that northern Europe imposed on "romantic" Spain (Iarocci 204). The War of Independence made Spain the inspiration for the cultural discourse of modernity elaborated by Romanticism: as Iarocci notes (xii), "for the north, Spain did not *produce* romanticism; it simply *was* romantic." The novella *Las catacumbas españolas* projects this image of a Spain of dazzling light and passion, found in the novellas of Cuisin, who makes it a setting for the carnality, bravado, and vigor of a people threatened by an invasion that "acabó de inflamar los resentimientos de un pueblo de un carácter demasiado dispuesto a irritarse" (inflamed the resentments of a people overdisposed by nature to violent arousal; 3: 141–42). The funereal specters and bloody shadows of Pérez Zaragoza's tale represent the disasters of a war that led to civil conflict and brutal repression after victory over the invader.

Pérez Zaragoza transcribes Cuisin's vision of Spain as "el país de la mortandad" (the land of carnage; 3: 143): "Al ardor del clima se unía el ardor inquieto y sediento de la venganza: una desunión sorda ha sucedido al principio a la llegada de los franceses: la discordia agita los ánimos" (The heat of the climate was matched by a restless, ardent thirst for revenge: a muffled disunity initially followed the arrival of the French: discord sowed anxiety; 3: 141). The Spanish adaptor of Cuisin's story revels in the landscape inundated with mutilated bodies and rivers of blood—the consequence of "un proceder sanguinario" (brutal tactics; 3: 141) that stains the pages of history with "sombras ensangrentadas" (bloody shadows: 3: 174), peopling its fields with corpses frozen in postures that made them look like "los más espantosos autómatas del genio de la muerte" (the most horrendous automata of the genius of death; 3: 189). This paroxysm of violence, mediated by an expatriate who, on his return, courted the entourage of the new queen, reveals the true theater in which the terror advertised in the *Galería fúnebre* plays itself out. The dead bodies on the battlefield represent the human passions in a country strewn with blood and bones (3: 180); a nationwide cemetery where "los músculos [de los cadáveres] expresan allí aun por sus contorsiones terribles el sentimiento de la rabia o desesperación con que el paciente ha exhalado el último suspiro" (the horribly contorted muscles [of the corpses] still express the rage or despair felt by the victims as they breathed their last; 3: 188). The *Galería*'s emotional mode of representation opts for the blackest tone (1: 13), the most graphic depiction (1: 28), focusing obsessively on the memory of a war in which Spanish women showed "todo el furor devorador de las africanas" (the devouring fury of African females; 3: 147) but also experienced the galvanic force of the unleashing of emotions that allowed those who had lived in the shadows to become agents of history.

In 1838, the Leonese newspaper *Frai Gerundio*, during the first Carlist War of 1833–1839, recalled the *Galería fúnebre*, seeing a convulsed Spain as the ideal setting for horror, without need for recourse to literary substitutes, since one had only to consider the real-life scenes of cannibalism related by the "martyrs of Beceite" who had survived the Carlist terror and whose story was enough to overwhelm the sensibility of any spectator: "Si [Pérez Zaragoza] quería estremecer las almas sensibles con un espectáculo de horror, . . . si se proponía . . . apurar el órgano del sentimiento, no tenía más que coger el pincel de la muerte, y sombrearnos el cuadro de nuestros prisioneros en poder de la facción [carlista] royendo con el diente de la desesperación los huesos de sus finados compañeros, y desgarrando sus flacas carnes para vivir un día más: unos cadáveres vivos comiendo otros cadáveres muertos" (If [Pérez Zaragoza] wanted to make sensitive souls shudder with a spectacle of horror, . . . if his aim was . . . to exhaust the organ of sentiment, he had only to pick up the brush of death and paint the dark contours of our men taken prisoner by the Carlists, gnawing with the tooth of desperation the bones of their dead comrades and mutilating their emaciated flesh so as to live one day more: living corpses eating dead corpses; "Galería fúnebre" 191).

As a self-styled "tragic chronicler of the catastrophes of the human lineage," Pérez Zaragoza addresses real readers, especially female readers, promising them new sensorial experiences. In granting the female reader license to feel, he allows her to become the spectator of her own haptic responses to the text, starting with those produced by the tactility of the beautifully produced volume, and reinforced by the privacy of a space that, like a camera obscura, allows her to test the limits of her sensate experience. The emotional risks are offset by the comfortable sensation of forming part of a community of similar readers with whom to share furtive emotions, elective affinities that construct new forms of relationship and expression that in turn construct new forms of sociability—forms of relationship and expression that are also vehicles of resistance, not necessarily restrained by decorum, civilization, and reason, which, in the wake of war, terror, exile, and the loss of empire, appeared fragile and vulnerable. The intense emotions naturalized by the excesses of war gave visibility to women as new historical agents, including the soon-to-be-widowed Queen María Cristina, who would restore Pérez Zaragoza to administrative positions under her regency. The same naturalization of intense emotions also made affective responses paradoxically necessary to the hygiene of the passions, via the cathartic empathy permitted by reading practices that heighten sensorial experience and thereby provide a training for life, in an era when recent history had made horror a familiar experience for many.

NOTE

1. I would like to thank Jo Labanyi for her careful translation of my Spanish original.

WORKS CITED

Alonso Seoane, María José. "*La Poderosa Themis* y la *Galería fúnebre*: Una polémica en prensa en el contexto de la traducción de colecciones de relatos en España (1830–1831)." *Anales de Filología Francesa* 15 (2007): 5–16.

Appadurai, Arjun. "Introduction: Commodities and the Politics of Value." *The Social Life of Things: Commodities in Cultural Perspective*. Cambridge: Cambridge UP, 1986. 3–63.

"Base de datos de libros editados en España." Ministerio de Educación, Cultura y Deporte. *www.mecd.gob.es/cultura-mecd/areas-cultura/libro/bases-de-datos-del-isbn/base-de-datos-de-libros.html* (accessed 4 September 2014).

Bennett, Alan. *The Uncommon Reader*. London: Faber and Faber, 2007.

Blanco, Alda. *Escritoras virtuosas, narradoras de la domesticidad*. Granada: U de Granada, 2001.

Botrel, Jean-François. "Teoría y práctica de la lectura en el siglo XIX: El arte de leer." *Bulletin Hispanique* 100.2 (1998): 577–90.

Bourke, Joanna. *Fear: A Cultural History.* Emeryville, CA: Shoemaker and Hoard, 2006.

Catelli, Nora. *Testimonios tangibles: Pasión y extinción de la lectura en la narrativa moderna*. Barcelona: Anagrama, 2001.

Cavallo, Guglielmo, and Roger Chartier. "Introducción." *Historia de la lectura en el mundo occidental.* Trans. María Barberán et al. Madrid: Taurus, 1998. 11–53.

Charnon-Deutsch, Lou. *Narratives of Desire: Nineteenth-Century Spanish Fiction by Women.* University Park: Pennsylvania State UP, 1994.

Cuenca, Luis Alberto de. "Prólogo." In *Galería fúnebre de espectros y sombras ensangrentadas, o sea el historiador trágico de las catástrofes del linaje humano.* By Augustín Pérez Zaragoza. Madrid: Editora Nacional, 1977. 13–41.

Davison, Carol Margaret. "Haunted House/Haunted Heroine: Female Gothic Closets in 'The Yellow Wallpaper.'" *Women's Studies* 33 (2004): 47–75.

Establier Pérez, Helena. "La traducción de las escritoras inglesas y la novela española del primer tercio del siglo XIX: Lo histórico, lo sentimental y lo gótico." *Revista de Literatura* 143 (2010): 95–118.

Fabra Soldevila, Francisco. *Filosofía de la Legislación Natural fundada en la Antropología o en el conocimiento de la naturaleza del hombre y de sus relaciones con los demás seres.* Madrid: Imprenta del Colegio de Sordo-Mudos, 1838.

Fernández, Luis Miguel. *Tecnología, espectáculo, literatura: Dispositivos ópticos en las letras españolas de los siglos XVIII–XIX.* Santiado de Compostela: U de Santiago de Compostela, 2006.

Fernández, Pura. "Terror saludable para la higiene de las pasiones: Criminalidad femenina en la *Galería fúnebre* (1831) de A. Pérez Zaragoza." *Femme(s) et crime en Espagne (XIXe et XXe siècles).* Ed. Solange Hibbs-Lissorgues. Manage, Belgium: Lansman Éditeur, 2010. 85–103.

Fish, Stanley. *The Authority of Interpretative Communities.* Cambridge, MA: Harvard UP, 1980.

Flor, Fernando R. de la. *Secretos y disimulación en el Barroco hispano.* Madrid: Marcial Pons, 2005.

Galaz, Mábel. "Un anillo de brillantes y unos gemelos." *El País* 7 November 2003. elpais.com/diario/2003/11/07/espana/1068159605_850215.html (accessed 4 September 2014).

"Galería fúnebre de espectros y sombras ensangrentadas." *Frai Gerundio* 8 March 1838. 190–92.

Gómez de la Serna, Ramón. "El concepto de la nueva literatura." *Obras Completas.* Vol. 1. *"Prometeo" I. Escritos de juventud (1905–1913).* Ed. Ioana Zlotescu. Barcelona: Galaxia Gutenberg; Círculo de Lectores, 1996. 149–76.

Gubern, Román. *Metamorfosis de la lectura.* Barcelona: Editorial Anagrama, 2010.

Haidt, Rebecca. "Gothic Larra." *Decimonónica* 1.1 (Fall 2004): 52–66.

———. "'How Gothic Is It?': The *Galería fúnebre*, Panoramic Seeing, and Enlightenment Visuality." *Dieciocho* 26.1 (Spring 2003): 115–29.

———. "The Wife, the Maid, and the Woman in the Street." *Eve's Enlightenment: Women's Experience in Spain and Spanish America, 1726–1839.* Ed. Catherine M. Jaffe and Elizabeth Franklin Lewis. Baton Rouge: Louisiana State UP, 2009. 115–27.

Hamon, Philippe. *Imageries: Littérature et images au XIXé siècle.* Paris: José Corti, 2007.

Iarocci, Michael P. *Properties of Modernity: Romantic Spain, Modern Europe, and the Legacies of Empire.* Nashville: Vanderbilt UP, 2006.

Labanyi, Jo. "Doing Things: Emotion, Affect, and Materiality." *Journal of Spanish Cultural Studies* 3.11 (2010): 223–33.

———. "Liberal Individualism and the Fear of the Feminine in Spanish Romantic Drama." *Culture and Gender in Nineteenth-Century Spain*. Ed. Lou Charnon Deutsch and Jo Labanyi. Oxford: Clarendon Press, 1995. 9–26.

Larra, Mariano José de. "¿Quién es el público y dónde se le encuentra?" *El Pobrecito Hablador: Revista Satírica de Costumbres* 1 (18 August 1832): 8–23.

"Lectura aterradora." *Cartas Españolas o sea Revista Histórica, Científica, Teatral, Artística, Crítica y Literaria* 2 (September 1831): 71–72.

Littau, Karin. *Teorías de la lectura: Libros, cuerpos y bibliomanía*. Trans. Elena Marengo. Buenos Aires: Manantial, 2008.

López Santos, Míriam. *La novela gótica en España (1788–1833)*. Vigo: Academia del Hispanismo, 2010.

Machado, Antonio. *Prosas completas*. Ed. Oreste Macrí. Madrid: Espasa-Calpe, 1989.

Macías-Fernández, Paz. "Horror at Home: The Transgressions of the Body Politic in Agustín Pérez Zaragoza's *Galería fúnebre*." *La Chispa '97 Selected Proceedings: Eighteenth Louisiana Conference on Hispanic Languages and Literature*. New Orleans: Tulane UP, 1997. 265–77.

Maffesoli, Michel. *El tiempo de las tribus: El ocaso del individualismo en las sociedades posmodernas*. Trans. Daniel Gutiérrez. Mexico City: Siglo XXI, 2004.

Milner, Max. *La fantasmagoria: Saggio sull'ottica fantástica*. Trans. G. Guglielmi. Bologna: Il Mulino, 1982.

Moscoso, Javier. *Historia cultural del dolor*. Madrid: Taurus, 2011.

Novella, Enric. *La ciencia del alma: Locura y modernidad en la cultura española del siglo XIX*. Madrid: Iberoamericana; Frankfurt: Vervuert, 2013.

Ong, Walter J. *Oralidad y escritura: Tecnologías de la palabra*. Trans. Angélica Scherp. Mexico City: Fondo de Cultura Económica, 1987.

Pennac, Daniel. *Comme un roman*. Paris: Gallimard, 1992.

Pérez Zaragoza y Godínez, Agustín. *Galería fúnebre de historias trágicas, espectros y sombras ensangrentadas: Obra nueva de prodigios, acontecimientos maravillosos, apariciones nocturnas, sueños espantosos, delitos misteriosos, fenómenos terribles, crímenes históricos y fabulosos, cadáveres ambulantes, cabezas ensangrentadas, venganzas atroces y casos sorprendentes*. 12 vols. Madrid: Imprenta de D. J. Palacios, 1831.

———. *Leonisa, víctima de amor y de la hermosura o sea El desenfreno de las pasiones. Historia trágica. Versión libre del francés al castellano*. Manuscript 4438, Biblioteca Nacional de España. May 1831. 67 pp.

Petrucci, Armando. "Leer por leer: Un porvenir para la lectura." *Historia de la lectura en el mundo occidental*. Ed. Guglielmo Cavallo and Roger Chartier. Madrid: Taurus, 1998. 522–49.

Rancière, Jacques. *El espectador emancipado*. Trans. Ariel Dilon. Castellón: Ellago Ediciones, 2010.

Reddy, William M. *The Navigation of Feeling: A Framework for the History of Emotions*. Cambridge: Cambridge UP, 2001.

Roas, David. *De la maravilla al horror: Los inicios de lo fantástico en la cultura española (1750–1860)*. Pontevedra: Mirabel Editorial, 2006.

Sánchez García, Raquel. "La lectura como espacio de comunicación: Materialidad del texto y lectura en las publicaciones españolas del siglo XIX." *Senderos de ilusión: Lecturas populares* en *Europa y América Latina (del siglo XVI a nuestros días)*. Ed. Antonio Castillo and Verónica Sierra. Gijón: Trea, 2007. 303–22.

Smith, Andrew, and Diana Wallace. "The Female Gothic Then and Now." *Gothic Studies* 6.1 (May 2004): 1–7.

Weber, Max. *Economía y sociedad: Esbozo de sociología comprensiva*. 3rd ed. Vol. 1. Ed. Johannes Winckelmann. Intro. and trans. José Medina Echavarría. Mexico City: Fondo de Cultura Económica, 2014.

Whittmann, Reinhard. "¿Hubo una revolución en la lectura a finales del siglo XVIII?" *Historia de la lectura en el mundo occidental*. Ed. Guglielmo Cavallo and Roger Chartier. Trans. María Barberán et al. Madrid: Taurus, 1998. 435–72.

Williams, Raymond. "On Structure of Feeling." *Emotions: A Cultural Studies Reader*. Ed. Jennifer Harding and E. Deidre Pribram. New York: Routledge, 2009. 35–49.

CHAPTER 4

Emotional Contagion in a Time of Cholera
Sympathy, Humanity, and Hygiene in Mid-Nineteenth-Century Spain

REBECCA HAIDT

In the tumultuous first half of the nineteenth century, the drawing of sharp polarizations provided secure rhetorical structure in political discourses and literary conventions: the image of the "tyrant" opposed that of the "oppressed proletariat" (Zavala); "freedom" opposed "altar and throne" (Aymes 75). The conditions for such Manicheistic discursivity were set by a post-1789 hermeneutics of sublimation, leading generations of speakers and writers across the shifting political spectrum to advocate the avoidance of passional extremes; in other words, a hygienicist program. In the decades following the French Revolution, a group of doctors, philosophers, and writers known collectively as the Ideologues promoted the preservation of society by means of education and self-control. Ideologues such as Pierre Cabanis and Antoine Destutt de Tracy theorized hygiene as a "bio-medical programme . . . [to] heal civil society and encourage social improvement" through popularization (Quinlan 140–41). From its inception, hygiene was an educational, philosophical, and medical instrumentality for the training of citizens during unstable times. By the first years of the nineteenth century, it became foundational to a wide range of disciplines, including government administration (González de Pablo 281). Combining the physical and the moral in the governance and regulation of mind, will, and body, hygiene—as Cabanis argued in his 1802 *Rapports du physique et du moral de l'homme* (*On the Relations between the Physical and Moral Aspects of Man*)—proposed directing "habits of the mind and the will by the habits of the physical organs and the temperament" toward the regeneration of human nature (cited in Martin 159–60). A central contributory concept to postrevolutionary hygienicist thought was "sensibility," which joined study of the natural (animal and human) capacity to react physically to stimuli, with its role in "bridging . . . individual feeling and sociability, assuring sympathy and sentiment in the human community" (Quinlan 147). Cabanis conceptualized a sensibility that—beyond muscular irritability and physiological reactions to stimuli—would underlay superior forms of consciousness achieved through citizens' improved use of their faculties (Sánchez-Blanco 194). Sensibility, entwined with sympathy on a continuum along which "the same physiological communication that was imagined to account for somatic sympathy was used to explain the effects of the 'passions of the mind' on the sensations and impressions of the body" (Forget 283), underlaid early nineteenth-century liberal and republican reformist thinking about civil society, economics, and property.

Hygiene's wellspring of power was an Enlightenment conviction in the power of passions and feelings, and it formulated techniques and conventions for stimulating and equilibrating emotions within a larger program of avoiding social, moral, and political extremes. Yet insufficiently appreciated are the ways in which nineteenth-century frameworks of emotion intersected with scientific and administrative constructs (such as hygiene), and thus were shaped by eighteenth-century concepts such as sensibility and sympathy. In fact, hygiene was a comprehensive, multidisciplinary field transcending borders between centuries, languages, and fields. It grew from a spectrum of approaches developed by Enlightenment materialist and sensist philosophers and proved itself adaptable to programs in science, medicine, education, administration, economics, and engineering. Hygiene exemplified the permeability of Enlightenment ideas across the eighteenth and nineteenth centuries, entering the Spanish cultural sphere through the doctors, philosophers, and educators who taught modern disciplines in academies and institutes, redacted manuals in their areas of specialization, and translated foreign works of science and medicine (Sánchez-Blanco 151–52). These agents of transfer linked late eighteenth-century scientific and reformist thought, and post-1789 liberal praxes of philanthropy, education, and administration (Burguera 56). Although as early as 1784 Lorenzo Normante y Carcavilla's *Discurso sobre la utilidad de los conocimientos económico-políticos* (*Discourse on the Utility of the Study of Political Economy*) had promoted hygiene as an essential component within a larger "science of man" that might create public prosperity (Bolufer Peruga 39), by the 1830s and 1840s the ideas of the French Ideologues had wide-ranging impact in Spain through translations, editions, publications, and academic curricula (Volck-Duffy 241). For example, between 1816 and 1832 there were at least seven Spanish translations of works by Cabanis, published in Madrid, Barcelona, and Paris (López Piñero et al.); in 1820, Toribio Núñez's *Sistema de la ciencia social* (*System of Social Science*) acknowledged the usefulness of the Ideologues' "science of man" to Spanish reform efforts (Cepedello Boiso 149).

The Enlightenment did not disappear with Fernando VII's absolutism: liberal exiles, including the hygienists Mateo Seoane and Pedro Felipe Monlau, in London and Paris—Europe's major hubs of intellectual circulation—played a crucial role in the cross century cultural transfer of ideas about sensibility, sympathy, and medicine (Palacios Fernández and González Troyano 293–310; Valera Candel; Muñoz Sempere and Alonso García). After Fernando VII's death in 1833, these returnees ensured the integration of wider Enlightenment matrices of sensibility and hygiene into their initiatives, from the reorganization of university study to the projection of disentailments and constitutional government (Sánchez-Blanco 143). An earlier postrevolutionary hygienicist push toward the perfection of moral, physiological, and political systems thus inflects the Manicheanism of the mid-nineteenth-century social imaginary (González, "Los Tribunos" 168): nineteenth-century struggles around the constitution, judicial reform, freedom of the press, and economic liberalization reflect an eighteenth-century legacy of belief in the power of a sensing, feeling individual's role in the preservation and moral regeneration of society and nation. In this chapter, I will focus on the interweaving of an Enlightenment preoccupation with emotion (as crucial to the formation of moral and political judgment) into a specific instance of conflictivity in mid-nineteenth-century hygienicist discourse, within the context of the cholera epidemics of 1833–1835 and 1854–1856.[1] In particular, I will explore how two concepts bound into Enlightenment ideas about sensibility—sympathy and humanity—inform hygienicist thinking in texts by Pedro Felipe Monlau (1808–1871) and Francisco Méndez Álvaro (1806–1883), and intersect with the Christian conception of caregiving outlined in writings by Concepción Arenal (1820–1893).

Monlau and Méndez Álvaro, the most important midcentury Spanish hygienists, were protégés of the great early hygienist Mateo Seoane (1791–1870). Exiled in England after being condemned to death by the Fernandine regime (for his political and sanitarian activities during the Trienio Liberal of 1820–1823), Seoane entered the international intellectual and publishing community cultivated by Rudolph Ackermann. In Ackermann's circle, Seoane became an agent of European and transatlantic cultural transfers, translating and adapting a range of works and ideas for the Spanish-language market. As Tully notes, the Spanish émigrés in London shaped themselves as intellectuals and writers during a period in which literary culture "still follow[ed] key Enlightenment ideals whilst broadening the canon, both geographically and diachronically" (157). The Enlightenment ideal of hygiene as a key tool for the improvement of humanity spread widely during the decades following the French Revolution, as political turmoil combined with epidemics (yellow fever, cholera) to create a rapidly growing demand for programmatic means of preserving citizens. Doctors became crucial European intermediaries in the spread of hygienicist ideas, and in England Seoane was a tireless worker in the transfer of European paradigms into Spanish. Thus when the first cholera pandemic began to sweep toward Europe, the Fernandine regime realized that its aggressive purging of liberals from medical faculties had left Spain unprepared to face potential outbreaks, and the government approached Seoane—in exile in London—to translate and report on the British Board of Health's documents on cholera. Seoane agreed; the translation was published in Madrid in 1831 (López Piñero, "Las ciencias médicas" 216).

Monlau, a Catalan doctor and surgeon, was politically active as a Saint-Simonian liberal, editing periodicals such as *El Vapor* (1833–1836) and *El Propagador de la*

Libertad (1835–1838) before going into exile in France from 1837 to 1839. After his return to Spain, Monlau became a tireless popularizer of hygienicism and eventually obtained government posts from which to further his goals for public education. Méndez Álvaro edited and contributed to some of the most important medical periodicals (including *El Siglo Médico*), held government posts in sanitation and health bureaucracy, and promoted vitalist medical ideas associated with the Ideologue tradition (López Piñero, "Las ciencias médicas" 218). Arenal was an early defender of women's rights and the first woman to attend a Spanish university. A crusader for improved living conditions for women, laborers, and other marginalized populations (in 1863 she would become the first woman to hold the position of inspector of women's prisons), Arenal's reformist activities and publications were rooted in Christian doctrine and motivated by liberal philosophy.[2]

All three—Monlau, Méndez Álvaro, and Arenal—developed careers shaped by political upheaval and disease. If Arenal conceptualized caregiving within a framework of Christian charity, Monlau and Méndez Álvaro were linked by an inheritance of Enlightenment ideology and a professionalized approach to the preservation of humanity. The period's unsettlement and what Gilbert terms "cholera panic" (5) brought antagonisms into sharp relief: between contagionists and anticontagionists; and between those (such as Monlau and Méndez Álvaro) envisioning hospitalization and public beneficence as vehicles for scientific advances and medical professionalization, and those (such as Arenal) insisting on the centrality of religious faith to healing (Valenzuela Candelario and Rodríguez Ocaña 110–11). These oppositions reflect the breach between two contradictory logics of state action at midcentury: the one, demanding a strong secular apparatus that might address injustice and improve the lot of populations; the other, demanding minimal state interference in traditional religious spheres of action and private and commercial interests (López Castellano 4–5). However, as I will argue, these opposing discourses converge in a shared concern about emotion, thanks to the cross century continuity of an Enlightenment conviction in the moral necessity of affect and fellowship to any bridging of divisiveness. In the following pages, I will pay particular attention to the resonance of eighteenth-century preoccupations with emotional connectedness—"sympathy"—and fellow feeling—"humanity"—across Monlau's, Mendez Álvaro's, and Arenal's differing conceptualizations of caregiving during turbulent times.

Hygiene, Sympathy, and the Problem of "Emotional Contagion"

Now that "una enfermedad verdaderamente pestilencial" (a veritable plague) had made its way across the globe from remote India and Asia—stated the 1831 edition of Robert's *Carta histórico-médica sobre el cólera-morbo de la India importado a Moscú* (*Historical-Medical Letter on the Indian Cholera Imported to Moscow*)—it was the duty of "un médico amigo de la humanidad" (a doctor and friend to humanity) to give some account of cholera's causes, indicate hygienic measures against its ravages, and suggest potential remedies in case it should strike (Robert 1). By early summer of 1834 the epidemic approached Madrid, even as the liberal government was embroiled in the first Carlist rebellion. On 28 June 1834 the front page of *El Eco del Comercio*, acknowledging residents' anxiety, had accused anyone raising a public alarm of aiding the "enemies of the fatherland." Nonetheless, when on 29 June the press announced the decree of a *cordon sanitaire* between Toledo and Aranjuez, many in Madrid were disposed to panic. In mid-July there were bloody attacks on friars by fearful crowds led to believe that the religious had poisoned water supplies. At the end of July the government insisted on opening a new session of the Cortes to formalize Isabel II's succession, so as to claim some sort of stability in the midst of the epidemic and civil war.

Recalling those July days, the writer Ramón Mesonero Romanos commented that he and his friends discounted the rumors of cholera's impending arrival, trusting in Madrid's "notoriously healthy climate" (*Memorias* 124). An educated person, Mesonero understood the Hippocratic environmental paradigm underlying the modern etiology of disease. Yet Mesonero's calmness would stem further from his embrace of hygiene, which theorized control of the passions as one essential prophylactic against illness. "Uno de los principales medios para preservarse del Cólera es conservar el ánimo tranquilo y no tener aprensión de contraer esta enfermedad" (One of the principal ways of protecting oneself from cholera is to maintain equanimity and not fear contracting this disease), the Real Academia de Medicina y Cirugía of Cádiz had counseled in 1832 in its widely disseminated *Instrucciones relativas al cólera-morbo* (*Instructions on Cholera*; 8). The *Instrucciones* incorporate hygiene's totalizing vision for moral, psychic, and physiological health in directing individuals to seek out distractions conducive to a serene, happy disposition, such as walking, agreeable conversation, gatherings of friends in well-aired rooms, and so on (9).

Nonetheless, it was difficult *not* to feel intensely affected by others' suffering during the epidemic. In Paris in 1832, Heinrich Heine described his horror at the sick lying in the streets and the dead stacked like wood in marketplaces and squares, waiting for hauling to the public graves (Athanassoglou-Kallmyer 686). In Madrid, the *Boletín de Medicina, Cirugía y Farmacia* of 31 July 1834 called for a different system of hauling cholera dead to the cemeteries, alleging that several women, their emotions inflamed by the sight of carts stacked with victims' cadavers, had become infected from distress itself (72). A letter writer from Cádiz claimed in the 24 June 1834 issue of *El Eco del Comercio* that apprehension was the true cause of cholera contagion. One newspaper encouraged *madrileños* in early summer of 1854 to go on vacation without worrying about an outbreak, as cholera "sólo acomete a los que le temen" (only attacks those who fear it; Urquijo y Goitia, *La Revolución* 418).

Intense emotion had been considered a "mal" (sickness) for centuries, with origins in the Hippocratic theory of humoral balance and Galenic inclusion of the passions among the "nonnatural" causes of disease. Retaining the ancient conceptualization of passional equilibrium as necessary to health, Enlightenment philosophers integrated new evidence from anatomy and physiology to formulate *sensibilidad* (sensibility) as the natural emotional responsiveness of sensing beings within society and community, and theorized control over passionality as "a basis for the decent ethical life" (Griswold 14).[3] In his 1759 *Theory of Moral Sentiments*, Adam Smith posited that the capacity to imagine others' feelings—that is, sympathy—was at the root of moral judgment, for "it is by the imagination only that we can form any conception of [others'] sensations . . . and become in some measure the same person with" a fellow human being (47).[4] A medico-moral framework tying passions to sympathy was systematized in works such as Tissot's 1798 *De l'influence des passions de l'âme dans les maladies* (*On the Influence of the Passions of the Soul on Sickness*), translated into Spanish the same year (Novella, "Medicina" 712). Tissot stipulated that only proper direction of passionality could "harness the emotions for the social good" (Pinch 19) and preserve one from a "término fatal que una cuidadosa atención sobre sí mismo hubiera podido retardar" (fatal outcome that could have been prevented by careful attention to one's own state; Tissot, "Introducción" n.p.).

After 1789, the linking of imagination and emotion seemed particularly dangerous, in part because emotions long had been understood to spread from body to body by uncontrollable means. Smith had commented on the "transfusion" of emotions "from one man to another, instantaneously, and antecedent to any knowledge" of the transmission itself (50). Emotions are "contagious" in the sense that people have little ability to limit the natural human tendency to mimic ("transfuse") others' emotional experiences (Hatfield et al. 10). From the eighteenth century onward, medical writers had observed the involuntary nature of sympathetic imitation and warned of the potentially pathological spread of a consequent "moral contagion" (Mitchell 73). The transfusion of affective extremes among mobs, or among audiences roused by forceful speakers, were powerful reminders of the easy mechanism of multiple contagions (Forget 292). Thus a new framework for the control of the passions, one invested in the stability of political bodies through the minimization of emotional and moral contagions, informed postrevolutionary hygiene and centrally inflected hygienicist programs through most of the nineteenth century (Novella, "La higiene" 62).

Enlightenment preoccupations with sympathetic contagion informed disputes between contagionists and anticontagionists around the prevention of cholera. Through the epidemics of the 1830s and 1850s, medical professionals and government officials sharply debated the utility of isolationist measures in limiting cholera's spread. Anticontagionists argued for the suppression of information and the removal of interior cordons sanitaires. Their assertions relied, in part, on the supposed threat of emotional contagion: panic aroused by the mere mention of the term "cholera," they claimed, would suffice to bring on economic devastation and create conditions for infection (Rodríguez Ocaña, "La dependencia" 119). The government, municipal councils, and the political press generally wanted the terms "contagion" and "cholera" avoided in all public discussions, alleging that the emotional transfusion had caused more damage than cholera itself (Urquijo y Goitia, "Madrid" 42, citing 1854 documentation). Contagionists generally favored the liberalization of information, advocating a multi-pronged approach (publication of statistics on infection and mortality, cordons sanitaires, and hygienicist measures) against a disease whose transmission remained unclear and cure uncertain. Seoane, Monlau, and Méndez Álvaro were among the medical professionals signing a mid-1850s report criticizing commercial interests' lobbying against cordons sanitaires, and lamenting the predominance of private over the common interest (Urquijo y Goitia, "Madrid" 34). Indeed, even anticontagionists acknowledged that keeping citizens uninformed was to "faltar a uno de los deberes más sagrados del hombre . . . por sostener algún tiempo más el giro de los intereses" (neglect one of man's most sacred duties . . . so as to protect private interests in the short term; Rodríguez Ocaña, "La primera" 2433, citing an 1830s report on cholera in Jerez).

Nineteenth-century hygienists such as Monlau wrestled with the contagionist implications of Enlightenment sympathy. It is worth noting that Smithian sentimental theory opens the possibility of exclusion from fellow feeling: after all, one may be disinclined to imagine others' experiences (Hurtado 47–48). Smith had commented that those who feel "horror" at the sight of "beggars" and "wretches" with open sores are liable themselves to physical affect brought on by "the very force of this conception" (48–49). Therefore, a hygienicist program has the potential to work *against* the moral potential of sympathy in a society, if it emphasizes emotional transfusion's potential for contagion. Ramos Gorostiza suggests that hygienists and sanitary reformers were unwilling to imagine themselves in the place of the poor and marginalized, viewing them as morally contagious, alien creatures (28): Monlau, after all, advised readers to throw themselves into a pile of filth rather than walk near a prostitute and risk contamination by her "vices" (López Piñero, "El testimonio" 135). Nonetheless, Monlau's rhetorical framework reveals the persistence of an Enlightenment emotional register of sympathy. Though he excoriated prostitutes, Monlau, at the outset of his 1856 essay "Higiene industrial" ("Industrial Hygiene"), posited the fundamental dignity of impoverished workers, calling them "estas clases desheredadas" and "desgraciadas" (these disinherited, unfortunate classes; 64). He initiates his argument with an act of Smithian sympathetic suffering, affirming that "las condiciones físicas y morales en que por lo general viven las clases obreras son lastimosas" (the physical and moral conditions in which the working classes generally live are pitiful; 65). ("Lástima," of course, denotes commiseration, sympathy.) He reiterates moral sense philosophy in averring that one's physiological state is the basis of one's ability to feel "sentimientos de bienquerencia" (sentiments of kindness or benevolence) and to function for the good of society (105). Monlau's drive to study the social context of human suffering drew on the physiology and medical anthropology developed by Ideologues such as Cabanis (Calero Vaquera 126) and the utilitarianism of reformers such as Bentham and Chadwick (Ramos

Gorostiza 24–31), while his sympathetic approach to the miseries of industrial workers incorporated knowledge—widespread among Spanish medical professionals of the 1820s, 1830s, and 1840s—of Enlightenment philosophies treating questions of sensation, sentiment, and sympathy.

Beneficence, Charity, and the Question of "Humanity"

Hygiene was at the forefront of a wider nineteenth-century public health movement positing that the expertise of scientists, joined with a public emotional investment in "humanity," would generate concerted attacks on a range of common diseases (Melosi). In conceptualizing its project as consisting not just in control of the passions but in the regeneration of humanity, the discourse of hygiene lent itself to a spillage of images across discursive boundaries. What was referred to as "la cuestión social" (the social question) generated a new literature addressing pauperism by linking science and medicine to social and political advocacy through hygiene (González, *La pasión* 141). Hygienists demanded that society "responda a la miseria de las clases obreras" (respond to the misery of the working classes; Seoane cited in González, *La pasión* 137) and remedy "la insuficiencia con que generalmente retribuye la industria a los que, no teniendo renta ni capital, viven del trabajo de sus manos" (the insufficient remuneration generally given by industry to those who, without income or capital, support themselves through manual labor; Monlau, *Remedios* 56). They passionately invoked *humanidad* (humanity) in responses to the social question: Monlau (for example) through numerous essays and pamphlets, such as his 1841 *Memoria* recommending demolition of Barcelona's city walls and his 1845 *Remedios del pauperismo* (*Remedies to Pauperism*), Méndez Álvaro through his many articles on public beneficence and public hygiene published in medical journals through the 1840s and 1850s.

Monlau and Méndez Álvaro draw on an Enlightenment conceptual reserve in promoting public hygiene as a remedy to the social question. For example, in his *Memoria*, Monlau argued that, since only war—the "scourge of humanity"—led men to erect high walls, the confinement of populations in unsanitary conditions was produced by an inhumanity born of egoism and antithetical to the sympathy essential to human nature (4). Monlau supported his argument through recourse to notions with an eighteenth-century genealogy, such as happiness and liberty (5, 13), or tolerance and brotherhood: the influx of travelers and investors to an opened city would result in a "fraternal" mingling of habits, manners, and languages, creating "familiarity among men" (16).[5] In this text, Monlau insisted that common should outweigh private interest, particularly when resulting in an increase in salubrity and well-being (19). Thus the "well-being" of the *Pueblo* (People)—a synecdoche of humanity (19)—trumps the interests of property holders, who must resign themselves to the consequences of an urban expansion desired by the People and demanded by sanitary legislation (19). In his 1853 treatise "Consideraciones sobre la higiene pública" ("Considerations on Public

Hygiene"), Méndez Álvaro argued that humanity, in league with science, should regard urban sanitation as a sacred duty, especially in the present century, which recognized the rights of man (82).

Valis observes that the role of religion in relieving pauperism was inseparable from "the larger predicament of modernity" in Spain (93) and argues for the importance of Christian *communitas* and spirituality in nineteenth-century literary interventions into the social question. For example, she identifies a "harken[ing] back to the *caritas* of early Christianity, tempered by Enlightenment tolerance" (111) in Monlau's lament that in the nineteenth century, in the age of philanthropy and enlightenment, individuals were still dying of poverty in Europe (*Remedios* 57). Valis rightly captures a midcentury yearning to "put back the social in social body . . . to re-establish some sense of *communitas* among all classes and in particular a sense of responsibility among the better off" (113). Yet Monlau's emotional register stretches further than this midcentury yearning for communitas: his vision of the social is rooted in an enlightened medico-anthropological-moral understanding of the human. For example, when discussing the elevated mortality and sickness rates among workers in industrial cities such as Manchester and Birmingham, Monlau employs a hygienicist framework, attributing them to improvidence, poverty, and abjection (*Higiene industrial* 66–67). When Monlau prefers to call impoverished workers "las clases desgraciadas" (the unfortunate classes) rather than "las clases peligrosas" (the dangerous classes; *Remedios* 60), he is speaking as a professional who built a career on approaching the illness wracking the social body with not just spiritual concern, but social-scientific and progressive humanitarianism claimed since the Enlightenment as the province of hygiene.[6] Even as he defines Christianity as "hygiene canonized by God," Monlau equates hygiene with civilization, enlightenment, and the forward march of Humanity (*Elementos* 2: 704, 766). In arguing that Christian charity—that is, philanthropy (*Higiene industrial* 112)—is fundamental to the emotional health of humanity (*Elementos* 2: 724), Monlau blends a framework of communitas with an Enlightenment philosophical register entwining affect, science, and progress.

Likewise, Méndez Álvaro injected enlightened humanitarianism into his argument in favor of administrative control over beneficence in an 1849 series of articles published in the *Boletín de Medicina, Cirugía y Farmacia*. In the first installment, he pointed out that asylums are a strongly Christian tradition but public beneficence is human, found across all cultures as a necessary condition for social order ("Beneficencia pública I" 98). In the second article, he clarified that beneficence was made an essential part of man by the Creator, with charity placed in man's heart as a necessary condition of society ("Beneficencia pública II" 105). By grounding charity as a social impulse inherent in human nature, he frames the question of beneficence as one of (Enlightenment) sympathy—the natural inclination by which humans are drawn to each other through fellow feeling. Méndez Álvaro advocates the absorption of beneficence by government-sponsored hygiene—thereby becoming *public* beneficence—as one of the chief branches of state administration ("Beneficencia pública II" 106).

In part, Méndez Álvaro reiterates a position taken by Enlightenment doctors such as Cabanis, who had theorized a role within hygiene for the attack on an inadequate clerically distributed charity and the promotion of secular public responsibility for beneficence (Staum 116). Throughout the nineteenth century, government and religious stances on charity reform would clash over the presence—or lack—of spiritual and emotional support in secular institutions administering beneficence. Reformers such as Arenal campaigned against the expansion of state-controlled care, asserting that Christian home relief and religious control of asylums provided the poor with dignity in illness and death, and that it was a public responsibility to minister to patients' physical *and* spiritual needs (Shubert 44). As Antonio Balbín de Unquera asserted in an 1862 essay on beneficence (cited in Shubert 47), state-administered charity is bureaucratic, governed by regulations, inflexible; it lacks the benevolence and affection associated with home care; and the hierarchy set up to administer it "merely carries out its duty without sympathizing with the unfortunate."

Méndez Álvaro, however, countered such assertions by arguing that the secularized centralization of caregiving rises from a *naturally responsive mechanism* of human society and thus, when administered within a hygienicist program, improves on the Christian charitable tradition by being rooted in *sympathy*. He proposed that clergy and those lacking scientific knowledge should not be selected by the government to direct hospitals and asylums ("Beneficencia pública III [Continuación]"139) not only because they were not trained to reform institutions of beneficence but, fundamentally, because the clergy had *no social response* to the misfortunes of the poor and only attended to the needy when they were about to die ("Beneficencia pública III [Conclusión]" 202). In his view, the removal of clergy from control over institutions of beneficence served the interests of humanity doubly: trained professionals could use their work with the sick to gain experimental and statistical knowledge that might advance the progress of medicine; and sufferers would be tended within a (secular) program of care intent on preservation and improvement of the citizenry. Religious philanthropy—care ultimately responsive to the soul rather than the sensing body—thus should be removed as an official framework for care. Méndez Álvaro proposed that the "religious element" was best employed in home care, where its philanthropic sentiments were valuable ("Beneficencia pública II" 106). In their homes, surrounded by family and supported by clergy, the sick, as "human beings," would benefit from religious ministrations ("Beneficencia pública III [Conclusión]" 202); in hospitals, on the other hand, the sick were best treated by secular professionals whose goal was the improvement of humanity's lot.

Writing three years after Monlau's *Higiene industrial*, Concepción Arenal, in *La beneficencia, la filantropía, y la caridad* (*Beneficence, Philanthropy, and Charity*), countered Méndez Álvaro's claim, calling beneficence "la compasión oficial que ampara al desvalido por un sentimiento de orden y justicia" (official compassion that protects the needy out of a sentiment of order and justice; 43) and defining philanthropy as "la compasión, filosófica, que auxilia al desdichado por amor a la humanidad, y la conciencia de su dignidad y de su derecho" (philosophical compassion that aids the unfortunate through love of humanity and a sense of their dignity and rights; 43). Wishing to ground philanthropy in an affective field of operations, Arenal lent force to her contention by dichotomizing the official nature of (state-administered) beneficence and the spirituality inherent in (Christian) philanthropic *caridad* (charity). Her association of humanidad with philanthropic compassion might seem to suggest an underlying Enlightenment emotional register of sympathy; as might her insistence, in her 1863 *Manual del visitador del pobre* (*Manual for Ministrations to the Poor*), on the "enlace tan íntimo entre nuestras ideas, nuestros sentimientos y nuestras acciones" (intimate relationship among our ideas, sentiments, and actions; 7). However, Arenal quickly makes clear that philanthropic compassion for the suffering of the poor requires, not a (Smithian) emotional "transfusion" born of sensibility, but rather a rational distinction: "una idea exacta de nuestra posición respectiva" (an exact idea of our respective position; *Manual* 8). In a chapter titled "¿Qué es el dolor?" ("What Is Suffering?"), Arenal elaborates that the practitioner of *filantropía* should not imagine herself sympathizing with another's pain, but rather understand her own limitations and preparedness to face others' suffering. Arenal likens suffering to an "amigo triste, que ha de acompañarnos en el camino de la vida" (a sorrowful friend, who must accompany us on life's path; 9)—quite a different sort of "fellow feeling" from that provided by Enlightenment sensibility. Arenal sought to remedy "a broken world" dissolved into chaos through "social disharmony and economic distress" (Valis 136). Yet the emotional register of Christian spirituality was not diametrically opposed to the (secular) humanitarian feeling traceable in "official" responses to pauperism. Hygienicist discourse, such as that framing Méndez Álvaro's *Beneficencia pública* series, also channels emotional markers of "philosophical compassion" through the humanitarian nexus of medicine and sympathy inherited from the Enlightenment.

Infrastructure: Sympathy and Humanity across Boundaries

Bray comments that cholera, wherever it appeared, "tested municipal structures and their efficiency, and threw into cruel relief the shortcomings of administrative structures, political platforms and social mores" (176–77). A story appearing in a 17 August 1855 article in the *Gaceta de Madrid*, reporting from Cáceres during the second cholera outbreak, serves as illustration: the provincial governor, who had left on 8 August to visit a nearby city, returned five days later to discover that three hundred families had abandoned the town; the doctor, pharmacist, and most sanitary authorities had fled; and "no se oía más ruido que el producido por los sollozos y los ayes desgarradores de los parientes de las víctimas" (one heard nothing but the sobs and heartrending laments of the victims' relatives). Mesonero Romanos became ill during the epidemic of 1834; as he lay delirious, his mother and half his neighbors died. Throughout 1835, Mesonero published articles in the *Diario de Avisos* with proposals for sanitation and public hygiene (*Trabajos*). He wrote of Madrid's need to improve management of human and animal waste, prodding authorities to find a way to control the accumulation of refuse that brought stinking night soil carts and daytime obstructions ("Policía urbana" 17). In the wake of the first cholera epidemic, Mesonero wrote as an urban reformer; but his appeals tapped a long-established affective modality around regenerative humanitarianism within hygiene. After all, editorialized the *Boletín de Medicina, Cirugía y Farmacia* in its inaugural issue of 5 June 1834, the conservation of public health is one of the most necessary contributors to national prosperity.

From 1834 onward, agents of "science" mobilized public opinion around hygiene, sanitation, and urban administration in the name of "humanity" and the "nation." Professionals (doctors, engineers) and entities (local sanitation boards, newspapers, charitable institutions) worked as a controlling, authoritative collective to shape reaction to the crisis, providing the public with information about prevention, treatment, and infrastructure in reports and notices whose purpose was the patriotic preservation of order and health. As an article in the *Boletín Oficial de la Provincia de Badajoz* proclaimed grandly to members of the medical and scientific communities during the first months of the 1834 pandemic, to fight cholera was to safeguard the national destiny: "llegado es el tiempo . . . de prepararle al público para que sepa repelar la enfermedad que ha llenado de espanto a Europa . . . la humanidad, la religión y nuestro destino nos lo manda" (the time has come . . . to prepare the public to repel the disease that has filled Europe with terror . . . humanity, religion, and our destiny demand it; cited in Peral Pacheco and Pérez Torralba 147). Initially, such collective action fell under the heading of "policía urbana" (urban policy), a category that since the eighteenth century had framed discourses on issues such as public behavior and street lighting (Peral Pacheco and Pérez Torralba 147). However, returning émigrés brought with them years of experience in foreign public health movements and a commitment to developing infrastructures based on French and British models of hygiene and sanitation. For example, during his exile in London, Seoane had studied Benthamist doctrines, published articles in British medical journals, collaborated with the British Board of Health, and served as a physician at St. George's Hospital (Ramos Gorostiza 24–25). From the mid-1830s, doctors, engineers, pharmacists, and scientific authors intervened increasingly in public discourse promulgated through regional administrative bulletins, local newspapers, and translations of foreign works on hygiene. Between 1841 and 1860, over a thousand legal provisions seeking the regulation of hygiene were published and popularized through pamphlets and a growing number of professional journals (Lafuente and Saraiva 534). It should not surprise, then, that by 1853, one emotional marker of the province of hygiene—that of *humanity*—had entered the rhetorical framing of even steam-powered public works projects, according to Ángel Retortillo Imbrechs, who in one of the first issues of the *Revista de Obras Públicas* claimed that the application of steam to locomotion had extended the life of man and that railway engineering had improved the human condition morally and physically (25).

Monlau observed that the same modern civilization responsible for industrial progress also put humanity at risk through inequities and chaos (*Remedios* 60). In the face of modern unsettlement and dividedness, Monlau retained hygiene's earlier commitment to developing a national therapeutics of subdued extremes. There is no easy separation between eighteenth and nineteenth centuries, French or Spanish, in hygienicist invocations of humanity. Cabanis's postrevolutionary conviction that doctors might perfect society by seizing "all these invisible reins of human nature" (cited in Staum 162) slips across decades and translations into Méndez Álvaro's claim that hygiene is "la ciencia que considera todas las cosas humanas, todos los actos de la misma humanidad" (the science that considers all human things, all acts of humanity itself; "Higiene pública" 258). Even Arenal's alignment of compassion with Christian charity rather than state-sponsored beneficence indicates the slippage of a long-operative vocabulary of emotions across competing discourses on pauperism, patient care, and cholera, manifesting the continuing reconciliation of Enlightenment sensibility with antimaterialist thought during the first half of the nineteenth century and beyond (Calero Vaquera 126). Nineteenth-century anxieties around emotional and moral contagion reveal an extended time span for Smithian sympathy and emotional transfusion. By the time Monlau, Méndez Álvaro, and Arenal make their claims for distressed humanity, their shared hermeneutical framework is nearly a century old.

NOTES

1. On the cholera epidemic of 1833–1835, see Puerto and San Juan; Rodríguez Ocaña, "La primera"; Vidal Galache. On the epidemic of 1854–1856, see Urquijo y Goitia, "Madrid" and *La Revolución*.
2. For background on Monlau, see Granjel; Cuñat Romero. For Méndez Álvaro, see Fresquet Febrer; Moro Aguado. On Arenal, see Martín; Franklin Lewis; Lacalzada de Mateo.
3. On sensibility, see Vila, "Beyond" and *Enlightenment*.
4. On Smith and sympathy, see Frazer. Polt details how Smith was read in eighteenth-century Spain by Jovellanos and others.
5. For the semantic framework for terms such as "liberty" and "fraternity" during the mid-nineteenth century, see Aymes; Lapesa.
6. My interpretation here differs from scholarship emphasizing hygiene's repressive apparatus. See, for example, Rodríguez Ocaña, *Por la salud* 26; Campos Marín.

WORKS CITED

Arenal, Concepción. *La beneficencia, la filantropía y la caridad*. Madrid: Colegio de Sordo-Mudos y de Ciegos, 1861.

———. *Manual del visitador del pobre*. Madrid: Imp. de Tejado, a cargo de R. Ludeña, 1863.

Athanassoglou-Kallmyer, Nina. "Blemished Physiologies: Delacroix, Paganini, and the Cholera Epidemic of 1832." *Art Bulletin* 83.4 (2001): 686–710.

Aymes, Jean-René. "L'Écho en Espagne de la triade 'Liberté, Egalité, Fraternité' (1793–1848)." *Le Métissage culturel en Espagne*. Ed. Jean-René Aymes and Serge Salaün. Paris: Presses de la Sorbonne Nouvelle, 2003. 67–91.

Boletín de Medicina, Cirugía y Farmacia 5 June 1834.

Boletín de Medicina, Cirugía y Farmacia 3 July 1834.

Boletín de Medicina, Cirugía y Farmacia 31 July 1834.

Bolufer Peruga, Mónica. "'Ciencia de la salud' y 'Ciencia de las costumbres': Higienismo y Educación en el siglo XVIII." *Áreas: Revista Internacional de Ciencias Sociales* 20 (2000): 25–50.

Bray, R. S. *Armies of Pestilence: The Impact of Disease on History*. Cambridge: James Clarke, 2004.

Burguera, Mónica. "Liberalism and the Origins of the Social: Women, Poverty, and the Political Meanings of Philanthropy in Nineteenth-Century Spain (Madrid 1834–1843)." Diss. U of Michigan, 2008.

Calero Vaquera, María Luisa. "En los orígenes del concepto ideología: De la filosofía a la lingüística, del individuo a la sociedad." *Boletín Hispánico Helvético* 23 (Spring 2014): 109–40.

Campos Marín, Ricardo. "La sociedad enferma: Higiene y moral en España en la segunda mitad del Siglo XIX y principios del XX." *Hispania* 55.191 (1995): 1093–112.

Cepedello Boiso, José. "La influencia de Condillac y los ideólogos en la teoría del derecho española decimonónica." *La cultura del otro: Español en Francia, francés en España*. Ed. Manuel Bruña Cuevas et al. Seville: U de Sevilla, 2006. 148–56.

Cuñat Romero, Marta. "El higienista Monlau: Apuntes para una biografía contextual." Third Congress of the European Network on Theory and Practice of Biography. Florence, Italy. February 2011. Conference presentation. *www.uv.es/retpb/docs/Florencia/Marta%20Cunyat.pdf* (accessed 13 October 14).

El Eco del Comercio 49 (24 June 1834).

El Eco del Comercio 49 55 (28 June 1834).

El Eco del Comercio 49 60 (30 June 1834).

Forget, Evelyn L. "Evocations of Sympathy: Sympathetic Imagery in Eighteenth-Century Social Theory and Physiology." *History of Political Economy* 35 (2003): 282–308.

Franklin Lewis, Elizabeth. "La caridad de una mujer: Modernización y ambivalencia sentimental en la escritura femenina decimonónica." *Anales de Literatura Española* 23 (2011): 185–204.

Frazer, Michael. *The Enlightenment of Sympathy: Justice and the Moral Sentiments in the Eighteenth Century and Today*. Oxford: Oxford UP, 2010.

Fresquet Febrer, José Luis. *Francisco Méndez Álvaro (1806–1883) y las ideas sanitarias del liberalismo moderado*. Madrid: Ministerio de Sanidad y Consumo, 1990.

Gaceta de Madrid 958 (17 August 1855).

Gilbert, Pamela K. "On Cholera in Nineteenth-Century England." *BRANCH: Britain, Representation and Nineteenth-Century History*. Ed. Dino Franco Felluga. Extension of *Romanticism and Victorianism on the Net*. n.d. *www.branchcollective.org/?ps_articles=pamela-k-gilbert-on-cholera-in-nineteenth-century-england* (accessed 17 July 2014).

González, Román Miguel. *La pasión revolucionaria: Culturas políticas republicanas y movilización popular en la España del siglo XIX*. Madrid: Centro de Estudios Políticos y Sociales, 2007.

———. "Los Tribunos del Pueblo: La tradición jacobina del republicanismo histórico español." *Utopías, quimeras y desencantos: El universo utópico en la Espana liberal.* Ed. Manuel Suárez Cortina. Santander: U de Cantabria, 2008. 159–90.

González de Pablo, Ángel. "Sobre la configuración del modelo de pensamiento de la higiene actual: El caso español." *Dynamis* 15 (1995): 267–99.

Granjel, Mercedes. *Pedro Felipe Monlau y la higiene española del Siglo XIX.* Salamanca: U de Salamanca, 1983.

Griswold, Charles. *Adam Smith and the Virtues of Enlightenment.* Cambridge: Cambridge UP, 1999.

Hatfield, Elaine, et al. *Emotional Contagion.* Cambridge: Cambridge UP, 1994.

Hurtado, Jimena. "Adam Smith y la escuela del sentido moral: Continuidad y ruptura en la comunidad moral y política." *Ideas y Valores* 62.153 (December 2013): 45–72.

Instrucciones relativas al cólera-morbo, dirigidas por la Real Academia de Medicina y Cirujía de Cádiz y su Provincia. Cádiz: Imprenta de la Viuda e Hijo de Bosch, 1833.

Lacalzada de Mateo, María José. *Concepción Arenal: Mentalidad y proyección social.* Zaragoza: U de Zaragoza, 2012.

Lafuente, Antonio, and Tiago Saraiva. "The Urban Scale of Science and the Enlargement of Madrid (1851–1936)." *Social Studies of Science* 34.4 (August 2004): 531–69.

Lapesa, Rafael. "Algunas consideraciones sobre el léxico político en los años de Larra y Espronceda." *Homenaje a José Antonio Maravall.* Vol. 2. Madrid: CSIC, 1985. 393–414.

López Castellano, Fernando. "El buen samaritano no sabía economía política: De la primera ley de beneficencia al intervencionismo científico (1822–1920)." IX Congreso Internacional de la Asociación Española de Historia Económica. Murcia, 2008. Conference presentation. *www.um.es/ixcongresoaehe/pdfB3/El%20buen%20samaritano.pdf* (accessed 16 July 2014).

López Piñero, José María. "Las ciencias médicas en la España del siglo XIX." *Ayer* 7 (1992): 193–240.

———. *Mateo Seoane y la introducción en España del sistema sanitario liberal.* Madrid: Ministerio de Sanidad y Consumo, 1984.

———. "El testimonio de los médicos españoles del siglo XIX acerca de la sociedad de su tiempo: El proletariado industrial." *Medicina y sociedad en la España del siglo XIX.* Ed. Pedro Laín Entralgo. Madrid: Sociedad de Estudios y Publicaciones, 1964. 109–208.

López Piñero, José María, et al., eds. *Bibliographia medica hispánica IV (Libros y folletos, 1801–1850).* Valencia: U de Valencia, 1991.

Martín, Elvira. *Concepción Arenal.* Madrid: CEGAL, 1994.

Martin, Xavier. *Human Nature and the French Revolution: From the Enlightenment to the Napoleonic Code.* New York: Berghahn, 2001.

Melosi, Martin. "'Out of Sight, Out of Mind': The Environment and the Disposal of Municipal Refuse, 1860–1920." *Historian* 35 (August 1973): 621–40.

Méndez Álvaro, Francisco. "Beneficencia pública I: La Beneficencia como institución social." *Boletín de Medicina, Cirugía y Farmacia* 2nd ser. 170 (1 April 1849): 97–98.

———. "Beneficencia pública II: La Beneficencia como ramo de la administración." *Boletín de Medicina, Cirugía y Farmacia* 3rd ser. 171 (8 April 1849): 105–6.

———. "Beneficencia pública III: Estado actual de la Beneficencia en España (Continuación)." *Boletín de Medicina, Cirugía y Farmacia* 3rd ser. 175 (6 May 1849): 137–39.

———. "Beneficencia pública III: Estado actual de la Beneficencia en España (Conclusión)." *Boletín de Medicina, Cirugía y Farmacia* 3rd ser. 182 (24 June 1849): 201–2.

———. "Consideraciones sobre la Higiene Pública y mejoras que reclama en España la Higiene Municipal." 1853. *Francisco Méndez Álvaro (1806–1883) y las ideas sanitarias del liberalismo moderado*. Ed. José Luis Fresquet Febrer. Madrid: Ministerio de Sanidad y Consumo, 1990. 75–89.

———. "Higiene pública: Importancia de su Estudio." *Boletín de Medicina, Cirugía y Farmacia* 2nd ser. 85 (15 August 1852): 257–59.

Mesonero Romanos, Ramón. *Memorias de un setentón: Natural y vecino de Madrid*. Vol. 2. Madrid: Oficinas de la Ilustración Española y Americana, 1881.

———. "Policía urbana." *Trabajos no coleccionados*. Vol. 1. Madrid: Imprenta de los Hijos de M. G. Hernández, 1903. 15–19.

———. *Trabajos no coleccionados*. Vol. 1. Madrid: Imprenta de los Hijos de M. G. Hernández, 1903.

Mitchell, Peta. *Contagious Metaphor*. London: Bloomsbury, 2012.

Monlau, Pedro Felipe. *Elementos de Higiene Pública*. 2 vols. Barcelona: Pablo Riera, 1847.

———. "Higiene industrial: ¿Qué medidas higiénicas puede dictar el gobierno a favor de las clases obreras? Memoria." 1856. *Condiciones de vida y trabajo obrero en España a mediados del siglo XIX*. Ed. Antoni Jutglar. Barcelona: Anthropos, 1984. 57–143.

———. *Memoria sobre las ventajas que reportaría Barcelona, y especialmente su industria, de la demolición de las murallas que circuyen la ciudad*. Barcelona: Imprenta del Constitucional, 1841.

———. *Remedios del pauperismo*. 1845. Reprinted in *Enciclopedia del pauperismo*. Ed. Gonzalo Capellán de Miguel. Vol. 2. Cuenca: U de Castilla La Mancha, 2007. 47–62.

Moro Aguado, Jesús. *Francisco Méndez Álvaro: La higiene española en el siglo XIX*. Madrid: Consultores Editoriales, 1986.

Muñoz Sempere, Daniel, and Gregorio Alonso García, eds. *Londres y el liberalismo hispánico*. Madrid: Iberoamericana; Frankfurt: Vervuert, 2011.

Normante y Carcavilla, Lorenzo. *Discurso sobre la utilidad de los conocimientos económico-políticos, y la necesidad de su estudio metódico*. Zaragoza: Blas Miedes, 1784.

Novella, Enric J. "La higiene del yo: Ciencia médica y subjetividad burguesa en la España del siglo XIX." *Frenia* 10 (2010): 49–74.

———. "Medicina, antropología y orden moral en la España del siglo XIX." *Hispania* 70.236 (September–December 2010): 709–36.

Palacios Fernández, Emilio, and Alberto González Troyano. "La pluralidad y la polémica: Ensayistas y políticos de 1789 a 1833." *Se hicieron literatos para ser políticos: Cultura y política en la España de Carlos IV y Fernando VII*. Ed. Joaquín Álvarez Barrientos. Cádiz: U de Cádiz, 2004. 271–329.

Peral Pacheco, D., and T. Pérez Torralba. "Las enfermedades epidémicas en el *Boletín Oficial de la Provincia de Badajoz* en el siglo XIX (1833–1873)." *Norba: Revista de Historia* 20 (2007): 143–60.

Pinch, Adela. *Strange Fits of Passion: Epistemologies of Emotion, Hume to Austen.* Stanford, CA: Stanford UP, 1996.
Polt, John H. R. "Jovellanos and His English Sources: Economic, Philosophical and Political Writings." *Transactions of the American Philosophical Society* ns 54.7 (1964): 1–74.
Puerto, F. Javier, and Carlos San Juan. "La epidemia de cólera de 1834 en Madrid." *Estudios de Historia* 15 (1980): 9–61.
Quinlan, Sean. "Physical and Moral Regeneration after the Terror: Medical Culture, Sensibility and Family Politics in France, 1794–1804." *Social History* 29.2 (May 2004): 139–64.
Ramos Gorostiza, José Luis. "Edwin Chadwick, el movimiento británico de salud pública y el higienismo español." *Revista de Historia Industrial* 55.2 (2014): 11–38.
Retortillo Imbrechs, Ángel. "Caminos de hierro." *Revista de Obras Públicas* 1.3 (1853): 25–29.
Robert, L. J. M. *Carta histórico-médica sobre el cólera-morbo de la India importado a Moscú.* Trans. Juan Francisco de Bahí. 2nd ed. Barcelona: Antonio Brusi, 1831.
Rodríguez Ocaña, Esteban. "La dependencia social de un comportamiento científico: Los médicos españoles y el cólera de 1833–35." *Dynamis* 1 (1981): 101–30.
———. "La primera pandemia de cólera en España, 1833–35." *Jano* 30.728 (1986): 2421–34.
———. *Por la salud de las naciones: Higiene, microbiología y medicina social.* Madrid: Akal, 1993.
Sánchez-Blanco, Francisco. *La Ilustración goyesca: La cultura en España durante el reinado de Carlos IV (1788–1808).* Madrid: CSIC, 2007.
Shubert, Adrian. "'Charity Properly Understood': Changing Ideas about Poor Relief in Liberal Spain." *Comparative Studies in Society and History* 33.1 (January 1991): 36–55.
Smith, Adam. *The Theory of Moral Sentiments.* Indianapolis: Liberty Classics, 1976.
Staum, Martin S. *Cabanis, Enlightenment and Medical Philosophy in the French Revolution.* Princeton, NJ: Princeton UP, 2014.
Tissot, Claude-Joseph. *Del influxo de las pasiones del alma en las enfermedades, y de los medios propios para corregir sus malos efectos.* Trans. Francisco Bonafon. Madrid: Cano, 1798.
Tully, Carol. "Ackermann, Mora and the Transnational Context: Cultural Transfer in the Old World and the New." *Londres y el liberalismo hispánico.* Ed. Daniel Muñoz Sempere and Gregorio Alonso García. Madrid: Iberoamericana; Frankfurt: Vervuert, 2011. 153–64.
Urquijo y Goitia, José Ramón. "Madrid ante la epidemia de cólera de 1854–56." *Asclepio* 35 (1983): 27–52.
———. *La Revolución de 1854 en Madrid.* Madrid: CSIC, 1984.
Valenzuela Candelario, José, and Esteban Rodríguez Ocaña. "Lugar de enfermos, lugar de médicos: La consideración del hospital en la medicina española, siglos XVIII a XX." *Cuadernos Complutenses de Historia de la Medicina y de la Ciencia* 2 (1993): 107–31.
Valera Candel, Manuel. "Actividad científica realizada por los liberales españoles exiliados en el Reino Unido, 1823–1833." *Asclepio* 69.1 (January–June 2007): 131–66.
Valis, Noël. *Sacred Realism: Religion and the Imagination in Modern Spanish Narrative.* New Haven, CT: Yale UP, 2010.
Vidal Galache, Florentina. "La epidemia de cólera de 1834 en Madrid: Asistencia y represión a las clases populares." *Espacio, Tiempo y Forma* 5th ser. 2 (1989): 271–79.
Vila, Anne C. "Beyond Sympathy: Vapors, Melancholia, and the Pathologies of Sensibility in Tissot and Rousseau." *Yale French Studies* 92 (1997): 88–101.

———. *Enlightenment and Pathology: Sensibility in the Literature and Medicine of Eighteenth-Century France.* Baltimore: Johns Hopkins UP, 1998.

Volck-Duffy, Elisabeth. "Die Rezeption der Ideologues: Spanien zwischen 1800 und 1830; Bedeutende Vorläufer der zentralen Rezeption der vierziger und fünfziger Jahre." *Europäische Sprachwissenschaft um 1800: Methodologische und historiographische Beiträge zum Umkreis der "Ideologie."* Ed. Brigitte Schlieben-Lange. Vol. 2. Münster: Nodus, 1991. 241–56.

Zavala, Iris. "El discurso socialista romántico." *Romanticismo 2: Atti del III Congresso sul Romanticismo spagnolo e ispanoamericano (12–14 aprile 1984).* Genoa: Biblioteca di Lettere, 1984. 29–37.

CHAPTER 5

"Hatred alone warms the heart"
Figures of Ill Repute in the Nineteenth-Century Spanish Novel

LOU CHARNON-DEUTSCH

> When fictional characters begin migrating from text to text,
> they have acquired citizenship in the real world and have
> freed themselves from the story that created them.
> —UMBERTO ECO, *SIX WALKS IN THE FICTIONAL WOODS*

The events of 9/11 in the United States stimulated not only a heightened sense of nationalism but also a spate of conspiracy theories that fed off the anxieties of a politically underinformed and malleable segment of the American public. What is evident following incidents such as this is that conspiricism ignites opportunistically during moments of political upheaval, fueled by fears that the world is inflicted with evil forces that require the marshaling of great financial and military resources to extinguish. In the wake of the French Revolution of 1789, and continuing to the end of the nineteenth century, Spanish novelists enthusiastically exploited this fear in their conspiracy novels, assembling all imaginable evils into an overarching plot, a "comfortingly totalizing allegory that leaves nothing to chance" (Boym 97), whose villains were often Jesuits, Freemasons, and Jews. The climate of hatred that prevailed in their novels both reflected and inflamed animosity to these groups as debates about the economic and spiritual health of a politically unstable nation proliferated.

In studying together these conspiracy novels I have been guided by Sara Ahmed's thesis in *The Cultural Politics of Emotions* that hate resides neither in a subject who hates, nor in the object or person perceived as hateful. What is often repressed or erased in discussions of hatred is the history of its production and circulation that Ahmed locates in the contact between bodies rather than in bodies and psyches themselves, and these hate-producing contact zones are what interest me here. To arrive at this notion Ahmed uses an economic model derived from Marx's theory of the fetish. As the value of hate gets assigned to people or things through repeated signs and metaphors it becomes fetishized, which disguises the history of its production: stereotypes become "sticky" to use Ahmed's expression, and this leads to a misrecognition of hate's production and location in the political landscape. Useful in gauging the effects of these novels is also Ahmed's point that love is an attribute of hate. Hatred not only drives bodies apart; it attracts them toward something that comes to be regarded as the ultimate good: for example, a collective identity like the nation or another group to which people infected with hatred become attached as a reaction. Freemasons, Jews, and priests were the bogeymen of choice involved in the affective economy informing nineteenth-century popular fiction. As these groups come to be assigned the category of evil through the rhetoric that clung to them, the resulting hatred anchored group identities in a harmful, polarizing way, engendering subjects who grouped defensively to combat other groups imagined as threatening to the greater good of the nation. The more these signs circulated among an ever more literate and secular audience, the more affective they became, and, as this occurred, nations and other collectivities emerged in fiction as if they were subjects in need of nurturing and protection from the harm that other groups, notably Jews, Freemasons, and Jesuits, conspired to cause. The instability of the rhetoric of hate, its proclivity to elide with other signs and become attached to other subjects, only increased anxiety since the drive to differentiate between harmful and good bodies and concepts is never able to be conclusive, that is, to 'stick' permanently. When the characteristics associated with one group get displaced on another, new associations emerge and new claims, for "it is the failure of hate to be located in a given object or figure, which allows it to generate the effects that it does" (Ahmed 49).

For these reasons it is useful to study the representations of despised groups collectively. As Maurice Olender has suggested in reference to Jews and Jesuits, they are "allied in a specular relationship, understandable only from the standpoint of the Other, the always excluded third party" (22). This Other is the phantasm of a group imagined as a coherent identity, a "pure fiction" as Olender describes it, that in the nineteenth century plumbed the depths of Jewish, Freemason, and Jesuit perfidy; a phantasm that gained believers exposed to certain signs and metaphors endlessly repeated and refined thanks to the fiction of popular writers such as the ones cited here. Taken together, the dozens of anti-Jesuit, anti-Semitic, and anti-Freemason texts published in the nineteenth century demonstrate that hate mongering was a fashionable but also pernicious literary convention, a marketable commodity as the authority of the monarchy diminished and signs increased in their affective value, becoming commodified as an effect of the movement between them and their repetition in a greatly expanded press.

The most fascinating but poorly understood aspect of nineteenth-century stereotypes is the way they fed from and into the great conspiracy hoaxes of the modern era in Europe. The serial novel was the fertile ground where a number of these invented conspiracies intersected and fed off each other, and the Spanish tradition was not immune to this insidious trend. Any account of the transmission of hate in European literature invariably leads back to the anti-Jesuit *Monita secreta* (1613) and forward to the anti-Semitic *Protocols of the Elders of Zion* (1903). Both documents purport to be based on real events and include a list of protocols for acquiring world power, but both are forgeries, and their claims are false. Both the *Monita secreta* and the *Protocols* existed as conspiracy theories in some form prior and subsequent to their date of publication under their respective titles. Their titles, "monita" (Latin for advice) and "protocols," promise to reveal the secret strategies of despised groups, and of course the revelation of secret plots is a favorite device of fiction writers. But the main reason for their enduring appeal was their spurious justification for the fear and loathing that were the preconditions of hate circulating before and after the documents were published. Had there been no suspicions that Jesuits circulated secret protocols to further their ambition for world domination, and no fears that Jews harbored a secret plot to use their vast wealth to reestablish the kingdom of Zion on a world scale, these two documents would have languished as quaint fictions suitable only for a collection of occult writings. Such is sadly not the case: today new media have allowed hatred to circulate even more widely. Anti-Semitic blogs still cite the *Protocols* as evidence of Jewish world ambition, radical born-again Christians urge the faithful to read the *Monita* document as a warning against Jesuit world ambition, and daily debates still describe Freemasons as worshipers of Lucifer.

In the 1840s, when anticlerical literature was especially "virulento" (virulent; Caro Baroja 74), versions of the *Monita* were circulating widely in the Iberian Peninsula, some in essays, others incorporated into novels. In 1845 ex-Dominican Joaquín Rodríguez included portions of it in *Misterios de los jesuitas* (*Mysteries of the Jesuits*), part novel, part treatise that denounced the Jesuits' "proyectos de dominación" (projects of domination; 43). That same year saw the distribution of the pamphlet *Monita secreta de los jesuitas o instrucciones reservadas de los padres de la Compañía de Jesús* (*Secret Advice of the Jesuits or Reserved Instructions of the Fathers of the Company of Jesus*), falsely attributed to Claudio Acquaviva, and an anonymous Spanish writer summarized the *Monita*'s instructions in *El jesuita sagaz o consejos secretos que da un jesuita a los hermanos de la companyía a fin de que esta llegue a dominar al orbe entero* (*The Crafty Jesuit or Secret Advice Given by a Jesuit to the Company's Brothers So It May Achieve World Dominion*). The trend continued in the following decades with the Portuguese A. de Oliveira Pires's *Os jesuitas* (*The Jesuits*) (1873) and Fernando Garrido's ¡*Pobres jesuitas!* (*Poor Jesuits!*) (1881), which included a version of the *Monita* prefaced with a lengthy and damning exposé of Jesuit perfidy. It is tempting to categorize this craze to disseminate the *Monita* hoax as a French import and therefore to describe its anticlericalism as superficial, but to do so is to overlook explanations for its enduring popularity that had deep roots in Spanish liberal ideology. A comparative study of these texts reveals a deep-seated anxiety about the role of the church in civil society, the fear of ex–cloistered priests exerting influence during the Isabeline period, anger at the role of the church in the Carlist Wars,[1] distrust of the intrusion of confessional politics in family dynamics, and antagonism to papal interference in Spanish affairs. To resist the clergy and everything that it symbolized in Romantic literature (casuistry, hypocrisy, greed, subversive acts) was to champion progress, freedom, and individual rights. The Jesuits were an especially easy target because of their global ambitions. After Prime Minister Count of Toreno ordered the disbanding of the Jesuit Company on 4 July 1837, followed by the general suppression of religious orders in the 29 July 1837 *Ley de Exclaustración*, few Jesuits remained openly in Spain.[2] Anti-Jesuit animosity continued unabated in the 1840s, however, since many Spanish clerics had become ideologically linked with the insurgent Carlists whose values were overwhelmingly absolutist. The 1851 Civil Code that reauthorized religious orders on a limited scale kept the issue of ecclesiastical malfeasance alive, and anticlericalism drifted easily into realist fiction in the following decades.

Many anticlerical novels of the midcentury bore traces of the *Monita* conspiracy in their dark vision of clerical greed, hypocrisy, and political subterfuge, and their villains were explicitly modeled after Eugène Sue's infamous Jesuit villains Rodin and d'Agrigny, often depicted graphically with a globe symbolizing the reach of Jesuit power as in Pedro Martínez López's 1845 translation of Sue's novel (Fig. 5.1). Less frequent but just as incendiary, a number of ultraconservative writers contributed to the growing bank of conspiracy texts that by the end of the century coalesced into the anti-Semitic document *The Protocols of the Elders of Zion*. A radicalized vision of good and evil characterizes most conspiracy plots, but because good and evil are in a relationship of interdependence, as Slavoj Žižek points out (156), the signifiers of good and evil are prone to inversion. This is in fact what happened to the tales of perfidy that proliferated beginning in the 1840s, in which Jew, priest, and Freemason alternate as Machiavellian evildoers and pious heroes or victims. It was at this time that a new breed of writers clung fiercely to extremist political positions dogmatically preaching a gospel of good and evil infused with a kind of perverse idealism, inflammatory discourse, and a festering atmosphere of shared hatred. If the assumption is valid that hatred signifies the triumph of imagination over reality (Donskis 4), then it follows that Romantic prose fiction, that theme park of imaginary forces and factions, should have generated fantastical plots that pit evil against good in epic confrontations. The stereotyping of these groups was more than a narrative device emulating popular French culture. What is disturbing about Spanish conspiracy plots is their assignation of evil to entire groups that were the focus of intense political debate. The villain is not a rare instance of a man straying from the principles upheld by the group to which he belongs, but a personification of the group as a whole for which he acts as an extreme representative. It not only takes a wellspring of imagination to assign entire groups the category of radical evil; it implies a moral abrogation of the vision of others as humans, a failure of the ability to see the other in oneself, in addition to a slavish adherence to literary convention that was circulating even before these authors latched on to the serial craze imported from France.

Liberal novelists Estanislao de Cosca Vayo and Ceferino Tresserra exploited the same utopian socialist themes as their French models Eugène Sue and Alexandre Dumas, stocking their fictions with stereotypical images of clerical villainy resembling

Figure 5.1. Gavarni (Sulpice Guillaume Chevalier). In Eugène Sue, *El judío errante*. Trans. P. Martínez López. Paris: Admininstración de *El Correo de Ultramar*, 1845. 1: 132. Courtesy of John Hay Library, Brown University Library.

those Sue concocted to defame Jesuits in *Le Juif errant* (*The Wandering Jew*, 1844–1845). At the opposite end of the political spectrum, Antonio Navarro Villoslada's *El Ante-Cristo* (*The Antichrist*, 1845) and José Mariano Riera y Comas's *Los misterios de las sectas secretas* (*The Mysteries of the Secret Sects*, 1864–1865) bucked the liberal trend with their equally damning stereotypes of Jews and Freemasons. Taken together these typical midcentury conspiracy novels demonstrate how, for the serial writer, Jew, Jesuit, and Freemason were interchangeable figures of perfidy. The stereotyping that these novels swapped and shared corroborates Umberto Eco's claim that in nineteenth-century conspiracy fiction "hatred alone warms the heart" (436).

De Cosca Vayo's *El judío errante en España* (*The Wandering Jew in Spain*, 1844–1845), set during the first Carlist War (1833–1839), reads like a defense of the exclaustration of religious orders that occurred a few years earlier. Written from the perspective of a Jew seeking to avenge the horrors of the Inquisition, the condemnation of the Catholic clergy here is one of the fiercest to be found in European literature of the time. Hovering around the court with fawning pretense, hooded friars and their Jesuit cohorts await the opportunity to seduce the queen, like a vampire "que cuando chupa la sangre abanica con sus alas a la víctima dormida para hacer con el fresco más dulce y agradable el sueño" (that when it sucks blood fans the sleeping victim with its wings to cool the air so as to make her sleep more sweet and pleasant; 4: xiii). In the dark and dingy rooms of a convent situated on the Manzanares River, a group called the

Ángel Exterminador (Exterminating Angel) plots their insurrections. United in their ignorance, greed, and ambition, they are consumed by "ideas teocráticas y sangrientas" (bloody theocratic ideas; 4: 35). Evidence exists that the Ángel Exterminador Society, one of several comprising radical royalists associated with the Carlist movement, did in fact exist beginning around 1827 (Zavala 127). For example, Fernando VII rewarded its support of the crown, along with other royalist groups like the Bandas de la Fe, after the failed liberal coup of 1823. However, the group's activities were so shrouded in secrecy that very little reliable evidence documents the extent of its ultraconservative activities.

With their shifty, sinister looks, de Cosca Vayo's Angels display their perfidy on the surface of their bodies, taking on a racial profile similar to what Steven Gilman has outlined as the Jewish stereotype. The hypocritical "angel" giving the orders is Bishop Julián, who, with his small head, beady eyes, flat nose, and thick eyelids and lips, is at once sinister and frightening, reminiscent of a "tipo del sangriento Torquemada" (type of bloodthirsty Torquemada; 3: 222). Following him in rank is Fray Bruno, with his immense stomach, black teeth, filthy tunic stained with snuff, and lasciviousness painted on his face. The group's invocation of religious purity, regeneration, and adherence to Catholic doctrine is little more than a front to mask a lust for power. If they have taken up the banner of pretender to the throne Carlos de Borbón, it is not to strengthen the monarchy but to rule Spain by controlling the throne. To that end they devise tricks to instigate unrest, paying assassins to eliminate enemies and using the church's vast influences and financial resources to incite the credulous masses to blindly support them. If historical evidence of the involvement of this group is flimsy, what is known is that on 15 July 1834, large demonstrations took place in the streets of Madrid, flamed by unidentified political agitators. Over the next few days, demonstrations raged on, and on 17 July a mob attacked and killed fifteen Jesuits in the Colegio Imperial and assassinated dozens of Franciscans, Dominicans, and Mercedarians in other convents because of fears that they had brought on the cholera epidemic by poisoning the city wells. The following year convents were razed in Zaragoza, Reus, Murcia, and Barcelona as well, and sixty-seven priests and monks were killed (Moliner Prado 92). De Cosca Vayo has made the Exterminating Angels the source of the anticlerical violence of 1834–1835 to suit his didactic purposes. If only they had been educated in Enlightenment ideals, the violence of the 1830s could have been averted, according to de Cosca Vayo's reasoning. Instead they employ the revolutionary tactics of Marat and Robespierre to "regenerate" Europe with their retrograde religious intolerance.

Several years later (1862), Tresserra capitalized in on the popularity of Sue's Wandering Jew saga and blistering anticlericalism with the rambling serial *La judía errante* (*The Wandering Jewess*). Tresserra's novel purports to be a sequel to Sue's *Le Juif errant*, following the Jesuits, now disguised, to Spain, where in 1860 they plot to influence events both in Spain and abroad. Tresserra's version of Sue's Jesuit archvillain D'Agrigny is Brother Damian, the brains behind the plot, while his henchman is Negrín, a crypto-Jesuit described as a reptile in keeping with anticlerical descriptive convention. Negrín's portrait is worth quoting in full for its striking physiognomic detail that again evokes the stereotypical Jew:

> su frente era ancha, pero lisa é inclinada hacia atrás; sus parietales abultados, formando entre ellos y los pómulos salientes un hoyo desmesurado, y desde la parte superior central de las parietales hasta el occipúceo se presentaba su cabeza pelada como el cráneo de una calavera. Su boca era grande, y sus labios cerraban como una caja; es decir, el inferior oculto casi siempre debajo del superior, grueso y caído como la membrana de un reptil. Tenía los ojos grandes y salientes, saltones y movibles debajo unos párpados que se contraían con dificultad, permanecían constantemente arrugados debajo del arco sejijal. El color de sus pupilas era verde y circundaba el blanco del iris una estensa red de sangre. (Tresserra 183)

> (his brow was broad, but smooth and sloping backward; his parietal bones were protuberant, with an abnormally big crevice between them and his protruding cheek bones, and from the central upper part of his parietals to his occiput his head was bald like the cranium of a skull. His mouth was big, with his lips clamped shut like a chest, the lower lip almost always hidden by the upper one, fleshy and flabby like the membrane of a reptile. His eyes were large and bulging, dancing and mobile beneath eyelids that contracted with difficulty, permanently wrinkled under the frontal bone. His pupils were green, and the white of the iris was circled by an extensive web of blood vessels.)

Serial novelists exploiting quite opposite anxieties adopted the descriptive and plotting conventions of anticlerical novels to fashion the villains of their anti-Freemason and anti-Semitic conspiracy novels. For archconservative Navarro Villoslada, the Jew provided a handier scapegoat than the cleric to harness the fearsome specters of insurrection and economic instability of the midcentury. His "Ante-Cristo" Ezequiel Widergott (Widergott being German for "against God") is a greedy and enigmatic Jewish banker, a rejoinder to the benevolent Jews of Sue's *Le Juif errant* that made its debut in Spain the same year as Navarro Villoslada's *El Ante-Cristo*. Widergott's nefarious plan is to employ his vast fortune to bribe the College of Cardinals into selecting a renegade priest as pope and gain control of the Spanish crown by coercing the government into accepting a German prince financially indebted to him as Queen Isabel's consort. Once all the European monarchies line up under his control, he will be able to direct the course of history on a global scale. In this portrait of the squalid, money-lending Jew, Navarro Villoslada echoed the fears of French critics of Jewish banking like Alphonse Toussenel, who that same year complained in his alarmist treatise *Les Juifs, rois de l'epoque: Histoire de la féodalité financière* (*The Jews, Kings of the Era: A History of Financial Feudalism*, 1845) that the "Israelites" were conquering the

Figure 5.2. Caricature of Jakob Rothschild. *Le Rire* 4.180 (16 April 1898). Cover. Courtesy of Schmulowitz Collection of Wit and Humor, Book Arts and Special Collection, San Francisco Public Library.

world. With his vast web of international loans and mortgages, Widergott is the perfect example of Toussenel's Jewish financier, proof that Europe was "mortgaged to the domination of Israel" as Navarro Villoslada put it (73).

Plotters not just of European revolutions, Jews in some conservative circles had the entire globe in their sights, a concept that came to be known as the "Jewish peril," often depicted graphically as a giant octopus, spider, or serpent or with long boney fingers clasping a globe as he is in a caricature of Jakob Rothschild on the cover of *Le Rire* in 1898 (Fig. 5.2). As a commodity, the "Jewish peril" was regarded as having intrinsic truth value, and the means of its production were already blurred by the time the *Protocols* document as we know it today was published in 1903. However, long before that, already by the mid-nineteenth century, the Jew was regarded by some as a world menace in several ways: spreading the cholera plague as in the many versions of the Wandering Jew saga, inciting revolution in emerging European nation-states as depicted in Father Antonio Bresciani's *L'ebreo di Verona* (*The Jew of Verona*, 1850), or intervening in international affairs to gain control of the monarchy and the Vatican as in Navarro Villoslada's *El Ante-Cristo*.

Navarro Villoslada used a tried and true "sticky sign" familiar to readers of nineteenth-century fiction to signify Jewishness: by midcentury the Jew's character traits were "glued" onto his body. Widergott's face bears not just the sign of his pathognomonic racial difference, but of boundless greed and aspirations. His wide, wrinkled forehead "expresaba una ambición sin límites" (expressed a limitless ambition; 91); his face and hair "tan ensortijado y tan bermejo, como dicen que lo tuvo Judas Izcariot" (as curly and red as is said of Judas Iscariot; 22). Armed with "una mirada mágica, fascinadora, irresistible" (a magical, fascinating, irresistible gaze; 53), he is "un conjunto extraño de ambición, de maldad, de sarcasmo y de infortunio" (a strange combination of ambition, evil, sarcasm, and misfortune; 91). The banker's eagle-like countenance is so repulsive that the novel's heroine falls in a dead faint, followed by months of fever, after seeing it just once. Together with the anti-Semitic novels of the following decades, most notably Vicente de la Cruz's *Más pequeñeces . . . el cuarto estado* (*More Trivia . . . The Fourth Estate*, 1890) and Ubaldo Romero Quiñones's *Lobumano* (1894), one can see how it was but a short step to that "vademécum del antisemitismo europeo" (handbook of European anti-Semitism; Fernández 347), the defamatory document known throughout the world as *The Protocols of the Elders of Zion*.

Between 1797 and 1798, Augustin Barruel, a French ex-Jesuit who fled to England after the French Revolution, published his influential *Mémoires pour servir à l'histoire du jacobinisme* (*Memoirs Illustrating the History of Jacobinism*) in which he interrelated the triple conspiracy of the *philosophes*, the Freemasons, and the Bavarian *illuminati* to produce a masterpiece of conspiricism that became the "indispensable foundation of future anti-masonic writing" (Partner quoted in Pipes 71). Luis Fris Ducos, a fellow expatriate and Jesuit residing in Spain, borrowed Barruel's conspiracies in *Historia cierta de la secta de los Francmasones* (*True History of the Sect of Freemasons*), and so began the lengthy trajectory of anti-Freemason texts that informed novels like Riera y Comas's *Los misterios de las sectas secretas*. In his introduction to his *Misterios*, Riera y Comas claimed that Freemasons were destroying the Spanish nation despite the efforts of the Jesuits to save it. Its besieged Jesuit hero Father Vincencio battles the plotting Freemasons till the last but remains powerless to prevent the violent events of 1834–1835 that are the novel's historical referent. Riera y Comas's ire is directed not only at *comuneros*, *carboneros*, and Freemasons, the novel's principal conspirators, but other groups aligned with radical Catholics and proroyalist associations including Anilleros, Defensora de la Fe, and El Angel Esterminador (*sic*) whose history and motives Vincencio divulges to his pupil Aurelio in chapter-length phillipics. In an indirect rebuke to anti-Jesuit polemicists, however, Vincencio assures his young pupil that "en los designios y complots de las sociedades monárquicas no tuvieron participación alguna los Jesuitas" (the Jesuits played no part in the plans and plots of the monarchist societies; 506). Secret societies such as the Ángel Exterminador weaken the throne and result in a deep-seated hatred for ecclesiastics that, he asserts, was responsible for the burning of convents in 1820.[3] *Los misterios* imputes the responsibility for all the tragic events and conspiracies of the novel, including the burning of convents of July 1835, squarely to the Freemasons, while the secret society of Jesuits and their allies of which he is president, called the Sociedad de la Contramina (Countermine Society), is helpless to prevent the bloodshed. In other words, contrary to his opening pronouncement, Riera y Comas did not condemn *all* secret societies, only those to which he did not belong and that were dangerous to what Jesuits perceived as the common good.

Conspiracy novels did not die out in the second half of the century, but, with the techniques increasingly favored by a new generation of novelists such as indirect discourse and the psychological exploration of emotional states, a more complex portrait of Jew and Jesuit emerged after 1868. As Ignacio Javier López explains in his introduction to the edition of Pedro de Alarcón's *El escándalo* (*The Scandal*, 1875), philosophical debates about the role of religion in a secular society that were percolating after the 1868 revolution inspired a more probing examination of the "religious question" including the equally fraught "Jewish question" that Pura Fernández examines in "La literatura del siglo XIX y los orígenes del contubernio judeo-masónico-comunista" ("Nineteenth-Century Literature and the Origins of the Judeo-Masonic-Communist Conspiracy"). Debates in the Parliament about religious freedom and the role of the Catholic Church as the state religion tempted a new generation of fiction writers to wade into the question. Religion, for example, became the focus of writers like Alarcón who straddled Romanticism and realism (Alarcón 20), as well as novelists like Benito Pérez Galdós whose engagement with realist techniques as well as liberalism was more sustained. Alarcón's confessional novel explores atheism, spirituality, morality, justice, and scandal against the backdrop of twelve hours in the life of a playboy confessing to a Jesuit priest. Eager to put behind him his more radical past, it was around this time that Alarcón cast his political lot with the *moderados* (the more conservative wing of Spanish liberalism), and became a staunch defender of what came to be known as the "novela de tesis" (thesis novel). His 1877 speech on his acceptance into the Royal Academy, "Discurso sobre la moral en el arte" ("Discourse on Morality in Art"), sealed his fate among generations that followed who found his moral positions distasteful. An immense success during the first few years after it was first published in 1875, *El escándalo*, like most "arte al servicio de la moral" (art in the service of morality; Alarcón 55), fell into oblivion during the Restoration and after.

While Alarcón's Jesuit Father Manrique has a starring role with his lengthy interrogations and comments on the protagonist's moral vagaries, resulting in a spectacular conversion, *El escándalo* does not explore the priest's own subjectivity and so does not venture much beyond the clichéd portraits that populate the novels of Jesuit apologists like Riera y Comas or Father Luis Coloma. As wise fonts who dispense knowledge, their Jesuits deal with the souls of the troubled, never experiencing themselves the spiritual crises of the souls they cure. At the other extreme, in contrast, is the greatest novel of priestly crisis written in nineteenth-century Spain, Leopoldo Alas's *La Regenta* (*The Judge's Wife*, 1884–1885). Alas's pseudo-Jesuit Fermín succumbs to human frailty from which so many fictional Jesuits before and after are blissfully immune. Fermín has never taken the investiture as a Jesuit because his mother has other ambitions for him, pulling him out of his Jesuit training and eradicating his fantasy of becoming a missionary. Nevertheless, the novel casts him as a would-be Jesuit who reads Jesuit literature in preparation for his sermons and is regarded with suspicion by the men of Vetusta. The town's playboy Mesía warns anyone who will listen about the "absorbente" (all-absorbing) Jesuitism of the famed Magistral: "Sobre todo don Fermín había sido un poco jesuita. '¡Jesuita! ¡El casuismo! . . . ¡El Paraguay! . . . ¡Caveant consules!'" (Above all don Fermin had been something of a Jesuit. "Jesuit! Casuitry! . . . Paraguay! . . . Caveant consules!"; 205). Here and elsewhere *La Regenta* recycles the loathing nourished by a generation of Romantic serial writers, even while it also digs deeper into a priest's psyche than any other writer had previously ventured to give readers a portrait of an emotional trajectory that, as Timothy Mitchell asserts, concords with current psychotherapeutic practice (52).

Readers of *La Regenta* found cause to sympathize with a priest pushed into a vocation-less role, but any sympathy for Fermín's psychological dilemma is colored by his misdeeds as church procurer, attempted seduction of a married woman, and manipulator of his Catholic flock. And other writers more biased and in some cases less talented than Alas fell into the same anti-Jesuit mold of Tresserra and de Cosca Vayo far into the late decades of the century that saw the waning of the feuilleton. Writing nearly a half century after Sue's Jesuitphobic *Le Juif errant*, Jacinto Octavio Picón in *El enemigo* (*The Enemy*, 1887) took up the crusade in a novel that reads like a rebuttal of Alarcón's *El escándalo* (1875), and Vicente de la Cruz in *Más pequeñeces . . . El jesuita* (*More Trivia . . . The Jesuit*, 1890) explicitly did battle with Father Coloma's *Pequeñeces* (*Trivia*, 1890–1891) by tracing the consequences of Jesuit meddling in private family life. Equally destructive is the meddling of Vicente Blasco Ibáñez's Father Pauli, who insinuates himself into the lives and loves of the characters in his novel *El intruso* (*The Intruder*, 1904). But the longest, and by far most acrimonious, of all anti-Jesuit screeds is found in Blasco Ibáñez's two-volume *La araña negra* (*The Black Spider*, 1897), a late *novela por entregas* (serialized novel) that delves deeper into Sue's grab bag of Jesuit tricks than any other work to fashion a world of unbridled Jesuit power and ambition.

In *La araña* the Jesuits' "sublimidad para el mal" (sublime talent for evil; 969) extends from the 1820 uprisings through the 1868 revolution and into the early years of the Restoration. A map stretching from the north of Spain to the Canary Islands and the Antilles, studded with crosses spreading like a "red que envolvía el territorio español, dándole el aspecto de un insecto enredado en fúnebre telaraña" (net enveloping the national territory, giving it the appearance of an insect trapped in a deadly spider's web; 106), pinpoints the cities, towns, and centers of high Jesuit influence and interest during these periods. Besides extracting a vast fortune from Madrid's wealthy families, its villain Father

Claudio sets his sight on the highest post of the Society of Jesus, plotting to poison the current superior general. When his plot fails, the superior general sends a Jesuit assassin from Rome to poison and replace him as vicar general of the order in Spain, the implication being that when one powerful Jesuit is taken down, another will always replace him. In the never-ending cycle of Jesuit malfeasance, the "ejército invencible" (invincible army) of Jesuits will forever be victorious over the "escandalosa doctrina que se llama democrática" (scandalous doctrine called democracy; 21). Blasco Ibáñez meticulously records dates, political events, and historical names to ensure readers grasp the political gravity and reality of Jesuit influence in the Spanish public as well as private sphere, and the longevity of their unrestrained meddling that includes theft, assassination, imprisonments, seductions, sedition, and every imaginable Machiavellian trickery. Like Sue, Blasco Ibáñez was working from a set of assumptions about Jesuitism that interpreted the 1614 *Monita secreta* as a Jesuitic blueprint for world domination. Inclusion of the *Monita secreta* libel as an appendix to the novel, even though it was by then widely known to be a forgery, ensured that the legacy of 1840s anti-Jesuitism remained alive to stoke the hatred that raged on into the twentieth century.

Biographer Ramiro Reig dubbed *La araña negra* a joke and a failed novel, "algo así como el que se mete en esas montañas del miedo que suele haber en los parques de atracciones" (something like a ride on one of those scary helter-skelters found at fairgrounds; 39). Yet the hatred spewing from every chapter of *La araña negra* is truly breathtaking, an insidious projection of the anticlerical sentiment of the pro-Republican sector of Valencia for whom republic and progress were synonymous with anticlericalism (Alós Ferrando 46). This tour de force of Jesuitphobia was fortunately unmatched in virulence by anti-Semitic works by most of Blasco Ibáñez's contemporaries. As Spain limped toward reassessing its past relations with Jews, writers of fiction disseminated biblical and historical representations of Jews, and, in the wake of the Spanish Moroccan war (1859–1860), when the Spanish military and journalists came into contact with Sephardic communities, contemporary Jewish characters also began to appear in fiction with greater frequency, some in positive roles. Still the "Jewish question" found detractors bent on staunching the spreading tolerance toward Jews after 1868. Vicente de la Cruz's two anticlerical but equally anti-Semitic novels *Más pequeñeces . . . El jesuita* (*More Trivia . . . The Jesuit*, 1890) and its sequel, *Más pequeñeces . . . El cuarto estado* (1890), and Ubaldo Romero Quiñones's *Lobumano* (1894) followed in the footsteps of the anti-Semitic Navarro Villoslada. Sunk deep into the Spanish psyche, anti-Semitism found its way even into the fiction of some of the most gifted and admired realist novelists in the 1890s. Emilia Pardo Bazán's abject leper Felipe in *Una cristiana* (*A Christian Woman*, 1890) presents the same "atávico antisemitismo" (atavistic anti-Semitism) that Pura Fernández has shown is "revestido de los mismos atributos de un siglo a otro" ("clad in the same attributes from one century to another"; 312), and Galdós's Francisco of the *Torquemada* series (1889–1895) is "a burlesque farce of the projections of Spain upon the Jew" (Schyfter 56).

The one exception repeatedly cited that delved deeply and sympathetically into a Jewish character is Galdós's early novel *Gloria* (1876). Its very uniqueness has made it a standout classic among the hundreds of novels that broach the topic of religion in nineteenth-century fiction. Undoubtedly its serious exploration of Daniel Morton's identity crisis as a Jew forced to choose between his religion and the woman he loves deserves its accolade as an avatar of religious tolerance. A close reading of *Gloria*, nevertheless, reveals that the religious question was not as much a revolutionary exploration of Jewish identity as Galdós's cognitive tool for gauging the divisive political situation of contemporary Spain (Lewis 268). Tom Lewis has argued that the fact that Daniel's religious idealism is unviable given Spanish social reality forces readers to infer a mediating ideological matrix. By framing the novel around an irresolvable conflict, Galdós maneuvers the reader into inferring a pragmatic solution for the political conflicts of his times: "we may consider the textual organization of *Gloria* as an ideological dispositio, for it compares and contrasts contradictory ideological positions from the vantage point of an unspoken ideology whose vitality and validity we are meant inferentially to discover" (Lewis 277). In short, Daniel is the accusing finger, Spain the patient in need of a cure.

While many in Galdós's generation suppressed the most acrimonious anticlerical and anti-Semitic rhetoric that had infected the Spanish novel during the Romantic period, as is evident in *La araña negra* the conspiratorial imagination continued during the years when classical realism dominated Spanish fiction. The reasons for its survival bring us back to the issue of hate and fear and their connection to a new world order. Throughout the century Spaniards were becoming more aware of the precariousness of the monarchy, the international rhetoric of freedom, and especially the power of wealth to, as one of Tresserra's characters puts it, "buy a European crown." Controlling the globe, many believed, could now be done by those whose legitimacy stemmed from wealth rather than birthright, and groups could unite across political and geographic borders to spearhead vast conspiracies. Jesuits, Freemasons, and Jews remained handy scapegoats, alternating as the sign of the possibility of the end or at least the control of the monarchy. The emerging mass media of the nineteenth century, with its unprecedented capacity to spread ideas internationally, fed off these figures at a time when markets were in fact becoming globalized, which is why the plots of all the conspiracy novels including those mentioned here revolved around the issue of securing vast wealth and power. Fredric Jameson, speaking about stereotypes, has argued that envy and loathing are the two fundamental forms of group relationship. Group loathing, he writes, "mobilizes the classic syndromes of purity and danger, and acts out a kind of defense of the boundaries of the primary group against this threat perceived to be inherent in the Other's very existence" (quoted in Chow 56). Rather than arguing that deploying stereotypes is some cognitively predictable psychological defense, as Jameson seems to suggest, I would agree with Rey Chow that the loathsome images deployed in these books are evidence of a "normative practice that is regularly adopted for collective purposes of control and management" (54), in other words, a deliberate duplication of images that can have real material effects. Seeing the interchangeability of Jew, Freemason, and Jesuit in these texts, and their similar preoccupation with money and power, prompts me to argue not just that the stereotypes are false, but that they cannot be divorced from discussion of the changing economic landscape of nineteenth-century Europe written on the bodies of the imaginary abject sinners who dominated the popular fiction of the nineteenth century.

NOTES

1. After Fernando VII died without leaving a male heir, a series of civil wars (1833–1839, 1846–1849, and 1872–1876) erupted that were spearheaded by those who supported Fernando's brother Carlos's claim to the throne over those of Fernando's daughter Isabel II. Estanislao de Cosca Vayo in his novel *El judío errante en España* (*The Wandering Jew in Spain*, 1845–1846) was one of several novelists who interpreted the conflicts of 1833–1839 as the overarching result of greedy and violent Jesuit conspirators.
2. According to Revuelta González, only three hundred Jesuits remained in Spain after the closing of the last convents in 1839 ("La Compañía" 303).
3. 1820–1823, known as the Trienio Liberal, was a time of considerable anticlerical violence. This included the assassination of the bishop of Vich, Ramón Estrauch, and several dozen priests in Catalonia and Valencia (Revuelta González, "El anticlericalismo" 164).

WORKS CITED

Ahmed, Sara. *The Cultural Politics of Emotion*. New York: Routledge, 2004.
Alarcón, Pedro Antonio de. *El escándalo*. Ed. and intro. Ignacio Javier López. Madrid: Cátedra, 2013.
Alas, Leopoldo. *La Regenta*. 2 vols. Ed. Gonzalo Sobejano. Madrid: Castalia, 1981.
Alós Ferrando, Vicente R. *Vicente Blasco Ibáñez, biografía política*. Valencia: Diputació de València; Institució Alfons el Magnànim, 1999.
Barruel, Agustin. *Mémoires pour servir à l'histoire du jacobinisme*. Hamburg: Fauche, 1797–1799.
Blasco Ibáñez, Vicente. *La araña negra: Obras completas*. Vol. 5. Ed. Arturo del Hoyo. Madrid: Aguilar, 1977.
Boym Svetlana. "Conspiracy Theories and Literary Ethics: Umberto Eco, Danilo Kiš and the Protocols of Zion." *Comparative Literature* 51.2 (1999): 97–122.
Bresciani, Antonio. *L'ebreo di Verona*. Milan: Serafino Muggiani, 1872.
Caro Baroja, Julio. *Historia del anticlericalismo español*. Intro. Jon Juaristi. Madrid: Caro Raggio, 2008.
Chow, Rey. *The Protestant Ethnic and the Spirit of Capitalism*. New York: Columbia UP, 2002.
Coloma, Luis. *Pequeñeces*. 1890–1891. Madrid: Catedra, 1975.
Cubbit, Geoffrey. *The Jesuit Myth: Conspiracy Theory and Politics in Nineteenth-Century France*. Oxford: Clarendon Press, 1993.

de Cosca Vayo, Estanislao. *El judío errante en España: Novela original española*. Madrid: Madoz y Sagasti, 1845–1846.
de la Cruz, Vicente. *Más pequeñeces . . . El cuarto estado*. Madrid: Juan Muñoz Sánchez, 1890.
———. *Más pequeñeces . . . El jesuíta*. Madrid: Juan Muñoz Sánchez, 1891.
de Oliveira Pires, A. *Os jesuitas: Romance historico do seculo XVIII*. Lisbon: Editora de Romances Instructivos, 1873.
Donskis, Leonidas. *Forms of Hatred: The Troubled Imagination in Modern Philosophy and Literature*. Amsterdam: Rodopi, 1993.
Eco, Umberto. *The Prague Cemetery*. Trans. Richard Dixon. Boston: Houghton Mifflin Harcourt, 2011.
———. *Six Walks in the Fictional Woods*. Cambridge, MA: Harvard UP, 1994.
Fernández, Pura. "La literatura del siglo XIX y los orígenes del contubernio judeo-masónico-comunista." *Judíos en la literatura española*. Ed. Iacob M. Hassán and Ricardo Izquierdo Benito. Cuenca: U de Castilla–La Mancha, 2001. 301–51.
Fris Ducos, Luis. *Historia cierta de la secta de los Francmasones*. Madrid: Francisco Martínez Dávila, 1815.
Garrido, Fernando. *¡Pobres jesuitas! Orígen, doctrinas, máximas, privilegios y vicisitudes de la Compañía de Jesús desde su fundación hasta nuestros días. Seguido de la Monita secreta o instrucciones ocultas de los jesuitas*. 2nd ed. Madrid: Mendizábal, 1881.
El jesuita sagaz o consejos que da un jesuita a los hermanos de la Compañía a fin de que ésta llegue a dominar el orbe entero. Vitoria: Imprenta de Engaña y Compañía, 1845.
Lewis, Tom. "Galdós's *Gloria* as Ideological Dispositio." *Modern Language Notes* 94.2 (1979): 258–82.
Mitchell, Timothy. *Betrayal of the Innocents: Desire, Power, and the Catholic Church in Spain*. Philadelphia: U of Pennsylvania P, 1998.
Moliner Prada, Antonio. "Anticlericalismo y revolución liberal (1833–1874)." *El anticlericalismo español contemporáneo*. Ed. Emilio La Parra López and Manuel Suárez Cortina. Madrid: Biblioteca Nueva, 1998. 69–125.
Monita secreta de los jesuitas o instrucciones reservadas de los padres de la Compañía de Jesús. Madrid: Miguel de Burgos, 1845.
Navarro Villoslada, Francisco. *El Ante-Cristo: Obras completas*. Vol. 5. Iruña: Mintzoa, 1992.
Olender, Maurice. *Race and Erudition*. Trans. Jane Marie Todd. Cambridge, MA: Harvard UP, 2009.
Pardo Bazán, Emilia. *Una cristiana*. Madrid: España Editorial, 1890.
Pérez Galdós, Benito. *Gloria*. Madrid: Pérez, 1877.
———. *Las novelas de Torquemada: Torquemada en la hoguera; Torquemada en la cruz; Torquemada en el purgatorio; Torquemada y San Pedro*. 1889–1895. Madrid: Alianza Editorial, 1970.
Picón, Jacinto Octavio. *El enemigo*. Madrid: F. Fernández, 1887.
Pipes, Daniel. *Conspiracy: How the Paranoid Style Flourishes and Where It Comes From*. New York: Free Press, 1997.
Reig, Ramiro. *Vicente Blasco Ibáñez*. Madrid: Espasa Calpe, 2002.
Revuelta González, Manuel. "El anticlericalismo español en el siglo XIX." *Religión y sociedad en España (siglos XIX y XX)*. Madrid: Casa de Velázquez: 2002. 155–78.

———. "La Compañía de Jesús restaurada (1815–1965)." Part 2 of *Los jesuitas en España y en el mundo hispánico*. Ed. Teófanes Egido. Madrid: Marcial Pons, 2004. 279–460.

Riera y Comas, José Mariano. *Misterios de las sectas secretas: Novela histórica interesante por su plan y su objeto, adecuada a los sucesos políticos de estos tiempos en España*. Barcelona: Imprenta Hispana de Vicente Castaños, 1866.

Rodríguez, Joaquín. *Misterios de los jesuitas*. 4 vols. Madrid: Sociedad Tipográfica de don Benito Hortelano, 1845.

Romero Quiñones, Ubaldo. *Lobumano: Novela sociológica original*. Madrid: F. G. Pérez, 1894.

Schyfter, Sara. *The Jew in the Novels of Benito Pérez Galdós*. London: Tamesis, 1978.

Sue, Eugène. *Le Juif errant*. Brussels: Société Typographique, 1844.

Toussenel, A. *Les Juifs, rois de l'époque: Histoire de la féodalité financière*. Paris: Paul Renouard, 1845.

Tresserra, Ceferino. *La judía errante*. Barcelona: Salvador Manero, 1862–1863.

Zavala, Iris. *Masones, comuneros y carbonarios*. Madrid: Siglo XXI, 1971.

Žižek, Slavoj. *Interrogating the Real*. Ed. Rex Butler and Scott Stephens. London: Continuum, 2005.

CHAPTER 6

"You will have observed that I am not mad"
Emotional Writings inside the Asylum
RAFAEL HUERTAS

"The writings of the mad," Roy Porter claimed at the end of the 1980s, "can be read not just as symptoms of diseases or syndromes, but as coherent communications in their own right" (*A Social History* 12). In so doing, Porter was drawing attention to the need to undertake research into sources that till then had barely been explored by the history of psychiatry, from a sociocultural perspective that took into account the subjectivity of the patient and not just the use of such writings in the context of expert clinical practice. This was an approach directly related to the proposal, theoretical and methodological, to write a history of medicine from the patient's perspective (Schipperges; Stolberg; Porter, "The Patient's View").

It is well known, as Philippe Artières demonstrated at the end of the 1990s, that from the mid-nineteenth century doctors promoted the clinical use of writing for diagnostic and therapeutic purposes in the case of the mentally ill (Artières, *Clinique*) and of those whose behavior was perceived as criminal or deviant (Artières, *Le Livre*).[1] These were, of course, clinical practices; nonetheless they paid close attention to the patient's innermost subjective and emotional experience. Reading madness, knowing how to interpret what mental patients were trying to express, became a priority for alienism—as the study and treatment of the mentally ill was called—from its beginnings (Rigolí 60–71). In France, writers like Brierre de Boismont or Marcé, among others, saw the writings of the mad as having a key importance for the exploration of their subjectivity, for the construction of a specific psychological semiology (Huertas, "Subjectivity").

In addition to the consideration of writing in the context of psychopathological practice—whether conceived in symptomatic terms, in terms of the metaphor of reading, as a self-reparative activity, as part of the therapeutic process, or as the very essence of psychosis (Colina)—the writing of the insane can also be seen as an expression of the experience of internment, as forming part of an emotional scenario.[2] Tales of captivity, narratives that may be eccentric, explosive, or impoverished, sometimes are manipulated but always are outpourings of an inner self, articulations of that self's personal experience, and capable of transmitting feelings, emotions, or states of mind.

In what follows I will briefly analyze some of the emotional features present in writings authored by patients interned in the former mental asylum of Leganés, outside Madrid, between 1860 and 1936. From its foundation in 1852, the Casa de Santa Isabel de Leganés (Santa Isabel Madhouse, Leganés) took in a substantial number of patients from all over the country (Villasante). The institution has a clinical archive in a fair state of conservation, thanks to which I have been able to locate, together with their clinical history, the diaries, unsent letters, and other texts written by patients interned there.[3] These writings contrast with the very different narratives of the psychiatrists who classify and diagnose with alleged "scientific" objectivity, but who are themselves not devoid of emotions when it comes to managing the madness and suffering of other human beings. This "polyphony of clinical reports"—to cite Andrés Ríos's phrase (23)—needs to be taken into account when dealing with this kind of source material, especially if the aim is to undertake a cultural historical analysis (Huertas, "Las historias clínicas" 25; Huertas, *Historia cultural* 149–59).

It should be clarified at the outset that the percentage of writings by patients in the archive at Leganés is slight (roughly 2 percent) and that the vast majority are letters that never reached their destination, were never dispatched by the institution's authorities, and were filed with the writer's clinical history, perhaps as supplementary material that might illustrate or confirm the patient's distinct pathology, or perhaps as additional information permitting assessment of the patient's "resistance" to internment. In general, these are missives that seek, in vain, a concrete, recognizable but inaccessible interlocutor (relatives, friends, occasionally those responsible for running the institution), letters without a destination or reply that effectively make writing into a dead letter—purveyors of loneliness and absence.[4]

If writing is the language of the absent, as Freud explained in *Civilization and Its Discontents*,[5] if "una carta de amor no es el amor sino un informe de la ausencia" (a love letter is not love but a report on absence) as the poet Mario Benedetti has put it (305) then the person who gives form to that absence, who suffers it, who doubts, who fears rejection, is the one who yearns for a reply, the one who waits. This anxious emotional state of waiting, which Roland Barthes associates with love letters, is implicit in practically all the written texts authored by the asylum's patients. A wait that can be prolonged for years of supposedly therapeutic isolation in a space of exclusion that, for the internees, is a kind of *paratopia*, that is, a paradoxical location, a place of alterity, a place that is not theirs, to which they are not linked by any sense of belonging, an "impossible" place in which they have no reason or need to be.[6] This sense of paratopia can be traced in a good number of the texts I have studied: "Este no es mi sitio" (This is not my place); "Yo no tendría que estar aquí" (I shouldn't be here); "Me dijiste que saldría de esta casa" (You told me I'd leave this institution); "Sácame pronto" (Get me out soon); "No puedo seguir aquí ni un día más" (I can't stay here one day more); "A ver si vienes a buscarme que yo no puedo estar aquí" (When are you going to come and fetch me as I can't be here?); "Usted habrá observado que yo no estoy loca" (You will have observed that I am not mad).

If the insane person is, as classical antiquity put it, a "stranger unto himself" (Huertas, *El siglo* 33), if the psychotic is an exile from language, if depersonalization or dissociative processes provoke sensations of anxiety, distancing, or dissociation of the self from the body, but, above all, if the madman or madwoman is socially excluded and denied civil rights, he or she becomes a nonperson. The mental asylum thus becomes a nonplace, in Marc Augé's sense of the term; a space of nonbelonging, of transit (since, in another paradox, the inmates expect to leave immediately); a place of confinement and exclusion in which the sense of not belonging is compounded by the negation of identity, the lack of linguistic reciprocity, solitude, silence—in a word, alienation.

Alienation—in its medical sense—has many faces or, at least, many different terms to describe or label it. By contrast with the schizophrenic's emotional blockage or the psychopath's coldness, and together with the obvious emotionality present in hysteria or obsessive neurosis, the two major psychiatric categories that can most clearly be linked to passional or emotional characteristics are melancholia and paranoia. And it is precisely the melancholics and the paranoiacs who write, who need to communicate their feelings, whether to explain the "truth" as they see it or to denounce the conditions of their internment. Practically all the texts authored by inmates that are conserved in the archive of the former Leganés mental asylum derive from patients diagnosed as suffering from one of these two ailments. The contents and style of their texts are very different in each case: the writing of those suffering from melancholia (almost all of them women) is intimate and autobiographical: "Encontrándome sola y a oscuras" (Finding myself alone and in the dark); "estoy muy angustiada" (I am very distressed); sometimes with contents verging on the mystical: "a un calvario muy sombrío subí con la cruz a cuestas" (I climbed up to a Calvary that was very dark, bearing a cross on my shoulders). These are texts, written forms of self-expression, that seem to want to recover the signs of the world, to neutralize its indifference or pressure, that is, an emotional writing, which implies an effort at self-interpretation, at self-knowledge, an attempt to construct some kind of individuality and to produce catharsis.

The paranoiac's writing has a very different emotional configuration. Paranoiacs do not doubt, and, bent on fending off the intentions of the "other," they erect a parapet behind which to dwell and protect themselves. Their writing is ingenuous—ingenuous because it is irreversible, incontestable. At times they seek to apportion blame and identify enemies: "yo no consentí . . . se aprovechó" (I didn't give my consent . . . he took advantage); "[él] se apoderó de mi persona, me encerró en esta casa" (he took hold of my person and shut me up in this institution); "[él] oscureció mi porvenir" (he darkened my future); sometimes obsessively: "La influencia del enemigo de quien te hablé en mi última sigue afectándome, en términos de no pensar casi en otra cosa" (The influence of the enemy I told you about in my last letter is still affecting me, to the extent that I barely think of anything else). At other times the paranoiac assumes the role of victim: "¿qué mal he hecho yo a usted para que así me mortifique?" (what wrong have I done you for you to mortify me like this?); "¿qué especie de tenacidad es esa de dejarme a merced de mis enemigos?" (why are you so determined to leave me at the mercy of my enemies?); "parece que se divierten a mi costa" (you seem to be amusing yourselves at my expense). The sufferer from paranoia comes to feel totally helpless: "la justicia no me oye" (the law does not hear me); finally turning on those responsible for his misfortunes and moving to threats and a thirst for revenge: "La justicia es la que debe juzgar y no las pasiones, y que por mucho que sea el odio que me tienes debes posponerlo a la necesidad de cumplir tu oferta de sacarme de esta casa de Santa Isabel, donde me han herido como sabes, donde me agitan diariamente y donde no sé si podrán conmigo. . . . Mira que después mis descargos serán contigo; mira que no me paso a tu bando conspirador, y tendré una seguridad de vencerte y de hacerte más desgraciado que yo" (The law should judge me and not passions, and no matter how much you hate me, you should subordinate your hatred to your obligation to fulfil your offer to get me out of the Santa Isabel Madhouse, where I've been ill-treated as you know, where they manhandle me all the time and I don't know if I'll be able to stand up to them. . . . Don't forget that I'll take it out on you later; don't forget that I'll never join your band of conspirators, and I'll be certain to defeat you and make you more wretched than I am).

Mistrust, jealousy, and resentment are other emotions typical of the paranoid makeup that are reflected in certain letters of reproach directed to a loved one: "yo no puedo estar aquí con tus compañeras las monjas porque yo creo que las monjas y los frailes es una cosa parecida . . . estoy herida y arañada por tus compañeras . . . y tú a lo mejor te vistes de seglar y te diviertes con la Dolores y yo en la higuera aquí, pasando toda clase de tormentos" (I can't be here with your friends the nuns because I think nuns and friars are much the same thing . . . I'm maltreated and mauled by your nun friends . . . and you're probably wearing civilian clothes and enjoying yourself with Dolores and me here with my imaginings, going through all manner of torments).

This last paragraph is interesting because it suggests several of the features we have noted. First, the sense of not belonging, of paratopia: "I can't be here"; second, the state of helplessness and maltreatment of the patients inside the asylum; third, the power of the nuns and their coercive role as carers-controllers within it: "I'm maltreated and mauled by your nun friends . . . going through all manner of torments"; and finally, reproach, jealousy, and a sense of abandonment: "and you're probably wearing civilian clothes and enjoying yourself with Dolores and me here with my imaginings."

As can be seen in the passages above, the writings of the paranoiac have an evident emotional force, but they also have the internal logic that defines paranoid delusion: systematized, coherent, with no loss of mental faculties and showing a clear and ordered awareness, reasoning, and behavior. That is why, in this kind of writing, with no evidence to go on other than that supplied by the source text, there always remains a degree of uncertainty about the "truth" proclaimed by the subject. In a period for which the existence of arbitrary internments has been demonstrated—some of them famous as in the case of Juana Sagrera,[7] or that of Vega Armentero—we cannot help but retain a margin of doubt when we analyze written utterances such as "I can't be here with your friends the nuns because I think nuns and friars are much the same thing . . . I'm maltreated and mauled by your nun friends . . . and you're probably wearing civilian clothes and enjoying yourself with Dolores and me here with my imaginings, going through all manner of torments."

The extent to which the writings of psychiatric patients can be understood as an emotional cipher is clear from the above. These emotions sometimes coincide with those that have been identified in other spaces of confinement, but they have the unavoidable hallmark of psychopathological disturbance or the suspicion of its existence. "Letters under suspicion," we might call them, borrowing the title of the important collective volume edited by Antonio Castillo and Verónica Sierra—under suspicion, among other reasons, because they leave open a number of questions that need to be articulated and tackled.[8]

The motivations for writing inside the mental asylum can be varied: to proclaim one's own "truth," to denounce an abusive confinement, or to demonstrate that one is mentally sound; alternatively, the aim can be to relate experiences lived or suffered, or to search for some kind of personal identity, among other things. It involves a strenuous effort, under conditions that make communication extremely difficult—but conditions under which even individuals with a low level of education were able to elaborate a written discourse.

What other meanings, then, may we attribute to these letters that never reached their destination? Did all of them, or only some of them, fail to reach their destination? There is no way of knowing. Nor it is easy to guess why they were not sent. A possible explanation is the authorities' desire to avoid denunciations of the conditions or treatment to which the patients were subjected reaching relatives or even public opinion, though another possible reason may be a wish to keep the patients isolated, without contact with the outside world, as a form of therapy or punishment.

It seems telling that these writings were filed together with the patients' clinical records, suggesting that a certain level of importance was attached to them as additional information that had at least some use for the inmate's treatment. However, contrary to the situation in other psychiatric institutions in the nineteenth and early twentieth centuries, we have no evidence that the doctors in the Leganés asylum encouraged their patients to write, or that they used that writing as a clinical resource for diagnostic or therapeutic purposes. The letters found in the clinical histories of a number of patients played no part in the justification given for the diagnosis of melancholia or paranoia.

According to Augusta Molinari's study of an Italian mental asylum, when patients are aware that their writings are going to be subject to analysis by psychiatric experts, they resort to textual formulas such as supplication or bureaucratic corroboration, addressed to the authorities, as part of a kind of ritual of subordination (395). No such thing happens in the sources from Leganés studied, where the letters do make use of codified epistolary formulas but do not go beyond mere formalities and do not constrain the outpouring of emotions. Most of the letters seems to be addressed to relatives or individuals not connected with the institution, showing the importance, in many of the cases analyzed, of the role played by the family in the decision to opt for confinement in a psychiatric asylum.[9] There are also letters addressed to the asylum's director, respectful but assertive, as if seeking complicity and understanding, and deferring to the clinical wisdom of the medical personnel: "you will have observed that I am not mad." The phrase I have taken for my title, written by a female patient, represents in itself, and above all else, an attempt at negotiation. It communicates with particular eloquence the anxiety of the victim, of the person who is being judged; it transmits the emotion of bewilderment, of waiting; it supposes a rejection of the subject's presumed state of madness, a hesitant, tentative resistance to madness as a destiny; it suggests, definitively, the inner agitation of the subject who feels helpless not only with regard to the authority of the expert who will decide on her fate, but also with regard to herself. "You will have observed that I am not mad." It is an assertion that does not necessarily express conviction, since it asks for a reply while succumbing to doubt and desire.

However we interpret such statements, we cannot, in the case of Leganés, talk of a doctor-patient pact, of a prior agreement between writer and reader similar to the "autobiographical pact" that has been defined and analyzed by Philippe Lejeune in relation to the literary genre of autobiography. In the context of the mental asylum, the existence of a tacit pact between writer and reader has been identified in certain cases (Molinari 380), whose findings do not coincide with mine in this respect, since, as previously mentioned, the medical personnel at Leganés showed no particular interest in the patients' writings. The act of reading is what generates the space inhabited by the biographical pact (Pozuelo 30), but that pact also implies recognition that the text being read is a "document of the real" (Alberca 69) that can be confirmed, thus becoming a "truth pact." However, the truth or reality of the delirious (or those presumed to be delirious) is not always accepted—and indeed is often ignored—by its potential readers. Thus in this case there is no two-way commitment, not even a tacit one, but rather a unilateral statement. In the letters written by inmates at Leganés, the writer seeks to explain a personal "truth," to assert rights, to seek recognition from the reader, but the reader, who is not necessarily the addressee, limits himself to "filing" the letter without replying to the writer's suffering or expectations. In conclusion, these are writings that, as we have seen, transmit a range of emotions, but above all suffering—fragments of, and variations on, a suffering clumsily expressed but which, in at least some cases, could be channeled through writing.

NOTES

1. For Spain, see Campos, "Leer el crimen"; also Campos, *El caso Morillo*.
2. In this respect, epistolary sources have been used chiefly for the study of everyday life inside the institution (Bartfoot and Beveridge; Beveridge).
3. The texts discussed and cited in this chapter are conserved in the Archivo Histórico del Instituto Psiquiátrico—Servicios de Salud Mental José Germain (Leganés). Uncatalogued.
4. I take the term "dead letter" from Jacques Derrida, although he uses it in a more general sense: "L'écriture au sens courant est lettre morte, elle est porteuse de mort" (Writing in its standard sense is a dead letter, a purveyor of death; 29).

5. Freud's original *Die Unbehagen in der Kultur* was published in 1930. The edition used here is the 1970 Spanish translation. The complete quote is "la escritura es, originalmente, el lenguaje del ausente" (writing is, in origin, the language of the absent; 34).
6. This sensation of paratopia has been analyzed in relation to other closed institutions, such as prisons, and can be found in varied forms of writing: letters, diaries, appeals, or even graffiti on the walls of inmates' cells or of the institution's courtyard (Gándara 251).
7. This case has been the object of several studies from different and more or less complementary historiographical perspectives, whose common denominator has been their discussion of the arbitrariness of Juana Sagrera's internment or her debatable mental state (Rey and Plumed), or alternatively gender analysis that associates madness and the female condition (Cuñat, *El enigma*). Especially interesting in this case is the presence of epistolary sources similar to those analyzed here (Cuñat, "Las cartas locas"), as well as their importance in the institutionalization of the study and treatment of mental illness in Spain (Huertas and Novella).
8. In Castillo and Sierra's book, the expression "letters under suspicion" refers to writing practiced not just inside mental asylums but in other closed institutions—prisons, concentration camps, orphanages, etc.—which are considered as "writing machines" that generate writing by the individual inmate and by the institution itself (Castillo and Sierra 13).
9. The huge influence that the family's decision could have not only on internment in an asylum but also on the conceptualization of the subject's madness has been studied in other social and geographical contexts (Prestwich).

WORKS CITED

Alberca, Manuel. *El pacto ambiguo: De la novela autobiográfica a la autoficción*. Madrid: Biblioteca Nueva, 2007.

Artières, Philippe. *Clinique de l'écriture: Une histoire du regard médical sur l'écriture*. Paris: Institut Synthélabo, 1998.

———. *Le Livre des vies coupables: Autobiographies de criminels (1896–1909)*. Paris: Albin Michel, 2000.

Augé, Marc. *Les Non-lieux: Introduction à une anthropologie de la surmodernité*. Paris: Seuil, 1992.

Bartfoot, Michael, and Allan W. Beveridge. "Madness at the Crossroads: John Home's Letters from the Royal Edinburgh Asylum, 1886–1887." *Psychological Medicine* 20.2 (1990): 263–84.

Barthes, Roland. *Fragments d'un discours amoureux*. Paris: Seul, 1977.

Benedetti, Mario. "Sobre cartas de amor." *Antología poética: Selección del autor*. Madrid: Alianza Editorial, 2011. 304–5.

Beveridge, Allan W. "Life in the Asylum: Patients' Letters from Morningside, 1873–1908." *History of Psychiatry* 9 (1998): 431–69.

Brierre de Boismont, Alexandre Jacques François. "Du caractère de l'écriture et de la nature des écrits chez les aliénés au point de vue du diagnostique et de la médecine légale." *Union Médicale* 16 February 1864: 289–97.

———. "Des écrits des aliénés." *Annales Médico-psychologiques* 1 (1864): 257–63.
Campos, Ricardo. *El caso Morillo: Crimen, locura y subjetividad en la España de la Restauración.* Madrid: Frenia, 2012.
———. "Leer el crimen: Violencia, escritura y subjetividad en el proceso Morillo (1882–1884)." *Frenia* 10 (2010): 95–122.
Castillo, Antonio, and Verónica Sierra. "Prólogo: Entre la represión y la libertad." *Letras bajo sospecha: Escritura y lectura en centros de internamiento.* Ed. Antonio Castillo and Verónica Sierra. Gijón: Trea, 2005. 11–14.
Colina, Fernando. "Locas letras (variaciones sobre la locura de escribir)." *Frenia* 7.1 (2007): 25–59.
Cuñat, Marta. "Las cartas locas de Juana Sagrera." *Frenia* 7.1 (2007): 89–107.
———. *El enigma de Doña Juana Sagrera: Feminidad y enfermedad mental en la España de la era isabelina.* Almería: Instituto de Estudios Almerienses, 2007.
Derrida, Jacques. *De la grammatologie.* Paris: Minuit, 1967.
Freud, Sigmund. *El malestar en la cultura.* Trans. Ramón Rey Ardid. Madrid: Alianza, 1970.
Gándara, Lelia. "Voces en cautiverio: Un estudio discursivo del graffiti carcelario." *Letras bajo sospecha: Escritura y lectura en centros de internamiento.* Ed. Antonio Castillo and Verónica Sierra. Gijón: Trea, 2005. 237–55.
Huertas, Rafael. *Historia cultural de la psiquiatría.* Madrid: La Catarata, 2012
———. "Las historias clínicas como fuente para la historia de la psiquiatría: Posibles acercamientos metodológicos." *Frenia* 1.2 (2001): 7–37.
———. *El siglo de la clínica: Para una teoría de la práctica psiquiátrica.* Madrid: Frenia, 2005.
———. "Subjectivity in Clinical Practice: On the Origins of Psychiatric Semiology in Early French Alienism." *History of Psychiatry* 25.4 (2014): 459–67.
Huertas, Rafael, and Enric Novella. "L'Aliénisme français et l'institutionnalisation du savoir psychiatrique en Espagne: L'affaire Sagrera (1863–1864)." *L'Évolution Psychiatrique* 76.3 (2011): 537–47.
Lejeune, Philippe. *Le Pacte autobiographique.* Paris: Seuil, 1975.
Marcé, Louis-Victor. "De la valeur des écrits des aliénés au point de vue de la sémiologie et de la médecine." *Annales d'Hygiène Publique et de Médecine Légale* 2nd ser. 21 (1864): 379–408.
Molinari, Augusta. "Autobiografías de mujeres en un manicomio italiano a principios del siglo XX." *Letras bajo sospecha: Escritura y lectura en centros de internamiento.* Ed. Antonio Castillo and Verónica Sierra. Gijón: Trea, 2005. 379–400.
Porter, Roy. "The Patient's View: Doing Medical History from Below." *Theory and Society* 14.2 (1985): 175–98.
———. *A Social History of Madness: Stories of the Insane.* London: Weidenfeld and Nicholson, 1987.
Pozuelo, José María. *De la autobiografía: Teoría y estilos.* Barcelona: Crítica, 2006.
Prestwich, Patricia. "Family Strategies and Medical Power: 'Voluntary' Committal in a Parisian Asylum, 1876–1914." *Journal of Social History* 27.4 (1994): 799–818.
Reaume, Geoffrey. *Remembrance of Patients Past: Patients' Life at the Toronto Hospital for the Insane, 1870–1940.* Toronto: Toronto UP, 2009.
Rey, Antonio, and Javier Plumed. "La verdad sobre el caso Sagrera." *Crimen y locura.* Ed. José María Álvarez and Ramón Esteban. Madrid: Asociación Española de Neuropsiquiatría, 2004. 85–132.

Rigolí, Juan. *Lire le délire: Aliénisme, rhétorique et littérature en France au XIXe siècle*. Paris: Fayard, 2001.

Ríos, Andrés. "Locos letrados frente a la psiquiatría mexicana a inicios del siglo XX." *Frenia* 4.2 (2004): 17–35.

Schipperges, Heinrich. *Homo patiens: Zur Geschichte des kranken Menschen*. Munich: Piper Verlag, 1985.

Stolberg Michael. *Homo patiens: Krankheits- und Körpererfahrung in der Frühen Neuzeit*. Cologne: Böhlau Verlag, 2003.

Vega Armentero, Remigio. *¿Loco o delincuente? Novela social contemporánea (1890)*. Ed. and introd. Pura Fernández. Madrid: Celeste Ediciones, 2001.

Villasante, Olga. "The Unfullfilled Project of the Model Mental Hospital in Spain: Fifty Years of the Santa Isabel Madhouse, Leganés (1851–1900)." *History of Psychiatry* 14.1 (2003): 3–23.

CHAPTER 7

A Sentient Landscape
Cinematic Experience in 1920s Spain

JULI HIGHFILL

In a decade when cinema as mass spectacle was relatively new and not yet naturalized, the writers of the Spanish avant-garde launched a wide-ranging inquiry into cinematic experience. They were preoccupied with precisely what happens in the intimate yet public space of the movie theater. How do moving pictures "move" the immobilized bodies seated before the screen? Fully admitting their susceptibility to cinematic seduction, the vanguardists engaged in a spirited dialogue on the "seventh art" in their *tertulias*, in their literary magazines, and in the cinema clubs where they gathered to view both popular and experimental films. In their writing, they forged a new poetic language, infused with audacious metaphors that could capture the sensorial effects of cinema—those affective flows that bind viewers to the images on-screen.

Salvador Dalí, for example, in "Film-arte, film-anti-artístico" ("Art-Film, Anti-art Film," 1927), evoked a "pájaro del *film*" (bird of film), imprisoned within the camera obscura, then let loose to fly invisibly through the electrical *vía lactea* of the projector (224–25).[1] Lit by the lens and launched by the reel, this bird is a creature of light and of air, at once spiritual and physical: it represents a "tan sutil y perfecto mimetismo que permanece invisible en sus vuelos por entre la desnuda objetividad" (such a subtle and perfect mimeticism that it remains invisible in its flights through naked objectivity; 224). The bird of cinema, Dalí concludes, is "aún el aire de un ventilador" (even the air of an electric fan), implicitly likening its spinning blades to a film reel (225). This evocative metaphor thus posits the essential paradox of cinematic experience: how can something so insubstantial as a wind of photons wield bodily effects—touching the skin of viewers and eliciting an emotional response?

While Dalí seizes on aerial metaphors to convey these affective flows, other writers turn to aquatics. Francisco Ayala, in *Indagación del cinema* (*Inquiry into Cinema*), describes the film experience as a "ducha de voltíos [y] chorro de luz" (high-voltage shower [and] torrent of light; 15). The peoples of the world, enthused with the new medium, "se han apresurado a recibir sobre sus cabezas el agua del cinema" (have rushed to experience the water of cinema pouring over their heads; 39–40). Using similar aquatic imagery, Lucía Sánchez-Saornil, in her poem "Cines" ("Cinemas"), projects an ongoing liquiform exchange between actors and audience. Light becomes water that flows through a movie screen, reconfigured here as window and mirror, and inundates viewers with emotion: "La calle llena el cuarto / Los espejos acuarios / fluyen sus aguas turbias" (The street fills the room / Through aqueous mirrors / flow cloudy waters; 98). Light and water, words and emotions, poetic and cinematic experience—all freely flow and converge: "A toda luz mis palabras-reflectores / proyectan en tus ojos / un film sentimental" (From every viewpoint my reflector-words / project in your eyes / an emotional film; 98). In these verses poetic language itself becomes cinematic, with "reflector-words" projecting in "your" (and "my") eyes an "emotional film." Notably, the term *film* connotes a movie and a malleable, skin-like substance, either transparent or porous, thus bringing touch as well as sight into the equation.

In more hyperbolic terms, Guillermo de Torre depicts the theater as a high-voltage, electromagnetic machine in his poem "En el cinema" ("At the Cinema"). We the spectators, enveloped in darkness, "sentimos agujereadas nuestras carnes / por la inyección vivificante de los films" (feel our flesh punctured / by the vivifying injection of the films; 104). It is above all the physicality of the experience that comes to the fore, as Torre mimics the torrent of images that assault the audience. Along with the names of Hollywood actors, he cites "Constelaciones de aviones / Sierpes de automóviles / Ramilletes de hélices" (Constellations of planes / Serpents of automobiles / Bouquets of propellers)—all emblems of modern life—followed by violent scenes of cavalry charges, gunshots, and fires. Finally, in a wry joke, he asserts that "el lazo del 'cow-boy' / estrangula la intriga sentimental" (the cowboy's lasso / strangles the emotional intrigue; 105). As movie watchers, we are in state of emotional capture, at the mercy of a rope of filmic images flung from the projector.

Across the vanguardist discourse on cinematic spectacle, the desire to embrace its sensory and emotional effects far outweighed any concerns with the vicariousness of viewers' experience. The spectacle of cinema, Miriam Hansen observes, "produced and globalized a new sensorium"; it "opened up hitherto unperceived modes of sensory perception and experience," offering "new models of identification for being modern" (71–72). In the modernist fascination with popular cinema, Hansen finds the expression of a potentiality—"the fantasy of a cinema that could help its viewers negotiate . . . the possibilities, anxieties, and costs of an expanded sensory and experiential horizon—the fantasy, in other words of a mass-mediated public sphere capable of responding to modernity and its failed promises" (72). It is precisely such a negotiation of the potentialities and pitfalls of cinematic experience that I find expressed in three striking "fantasies" from the 1920s, which I go on to examine in depth: Pedro Salinas's poem "Far West"; Francisco Ayala's short story "Polar, estrella" ("Polar, star"); and Francisco Elías Riquelme's film *El misterio de la Puerta del Sol* (*The Mystery of the Puerta del Sol*).

While these works foreground the physicality of cinematic experience—that "bodily intensity" that for Brian Massumi defines "affect" (15)—they also explore the entire spectrum of sensory and emotional responses. They attempt to understand the "affective practices" that were emerging within the new sensorium of the 1920s, and, in so doing, they express an intoxication with feelings aroused and a preoccupation with feelings denied. I draw here from Margaret Wetherell, who posits the notion of "affective practice"—a relational figuration wherein bodily intensities become "recruited or entangled together with meaning making and with other social and material figurations" (19). Throughout my discussion of these texts, I will likewise work across the broad spectrum of "affective practices," declining to separate affect, feeling, emotion—all of which become inextricably enmeshed in common usage, in poetic language, and in human experience.

A Wind of Images

It may be difficult for audiences today, so accustomed to sophisticated special effects, to imagine the thrilling expansion of the visible that occurred in the first decades of the twentieth century. Not only were remote, exotic locales now accessible on local screens, but many aspects of everyday life, heretofore unseen, were now *seeable* thanks to technological advances. Both mobility and spatiality underwent an extraordinary development, creating new sensory experiences for film audiences. As Antonio Espina observed in "Reflexiones sobre cinematografía" ("Reflections on Cinema," 1927), images could stream with near-infinite slowness, allowing viewers to dwell on the most subtle of gestures. Or they could accelerate to dizzying speeds: "lo hiperveloz del dinamismo maquinista y lo hipoveloz de lo semiestático" (the hypervelocity of mechanical dynamism and the hypovelocity of the semistatic; 41). In like manner, the content of those images could reveal both "el hipoespacio y el hiperespacio" (hypospace and hyperspace; 42)—an extreme close-up of a face or hand, or a vast panorama unfolding from the air. Such vistas enabled an unprecedented expansion in protagonism; the forces of nature—the sea, a forest, the wind—moving across the screen, now acquired agency. What was impossible in theater became possible in cinema, for audiences could now be riveted by the sight of "un león *de veras*," "una ciudad *de veras*" (a *real* lion, a *real* city), and I might add, a *real* landscape, like the Great Plains of the American West (43).

In Pedro Salinas's poem "Far West" (1929), the poetic "I" is watching a Hollywood western. Awestruck by images of the powerful winds of the American West, he utters an exclamation, followed by a series of questions:

> ¡Qué viento a ocho mil kilómetros!
> ¿No ves cómo vuela todo?
> ¿No ves los cabellos sueltos
> de Mabel, la caballista
> que entorna los ojos limpios
> ella, viento, contra el viento?

¿No ves
la cortina estremecida,
ese papel revolado
y la soledad frustrada
entre ella y tú por el viento? (67–68)
(What a wind at eight thousand kilometers!
Don't you see how everything flies?
Don't you see the loosened hair
of Mabel, on horseback
her clear eyes half-closed
Mabel, wind, against the wind?
Don't you see/the quaking curtain
the paper whirling about
and the frustrated solitude
between her and you, through the wind?)

This exclamation—"What a wind at eight thousand kilometers!"—has the ironic effect of misleading the reader, for initially, it appears to be a measure of wind speed, albeit an absurd velocity.[2] But as the poem goes on to disclose, this wind is located eight thousand kilometers away, the approximate distance from Madrid to West Texas. This is a faraway wind blowing across the wide-open spaces of the far West. And indeed, the poem may have been inspired by Victor Sjöström's film *The Wind* (1928), set in Texas and depicting a rancher's wife driven mad by the incessant wind.[3] In the repetition—"Don't you see? Don't you see how everything flies?"—the speaker calls for the reader's complicity in pondering a paradox. He is pointing to the invisibility and immateriality of wind, which can be "seen" only by virtue of the material objects it tosses about, in this case Mabel's long flowing hair, the quaking curtains, the fluttering paper, and the frustrated loneliness between Mabel and "you." The wind now appears to blow outward from the screen, producing a further material effect on the viewer, touching his skin, and arousing *feelings* of desire and frustration across the unbridgeable distance that divides them.

Yet the poetic speaker claims he cannot feel the particular wind portrayed onscreen, for it was filmed in another hemisphere and brought here by the film apparatus. In an interior dialogue, he goes on to answer the questions he posited earlier: "Sí, lo veo / Y nada más que lo veo" (Yes, I see it / and nothing more than see it; 68). While he sees the wind, he cannot feel it, since it is blowing on a remote stretch of land far away. He then reflects on the enigmas of wind and cinema, suggesting that they share the same ambiguous ontological status. The wind is touching people and things—tossing branches in some unknown place and kissing the lips of an unknowable being. Yet that particular wind no longer exists: "No es ya viento, es el retrato / de un viento que se murió / sin que yo le conociera" (It is no longer wind, it is the portrait / of a wind that died / without my ever knowing it; 68). In asserting that he sees only the *picture* of a wind that died before he encountered it, he is layering irony upon irony, for of course he cannot *see* the wind, but only its material effects. In three enjambed lines, at once ponderous and humorous, he laments that the wind "está enterrado en el ancho / cementerio de los aires / viejos, de los aires muertos" (is buried in the vast / cemetery of old / air, of dead air; 68)—thus expressing the eerie sense of loss, of "petrified unrest," produced by all photography (Benjamin, *Arcades* 325). The speaker concludes by repeating that he *sees* the wind, but he cannot *feel* it: "Sí le veo, sin sentirle. / Está allí, en el mundo suyo, / viento de cine, ese viento" (Yes, I see it, without feeling it. / It is there, in its own world, / wind of cinema, that wind; 68). Whereas before he said, "*lo* veo," now he uses the personal pronoun *le*, suggesting a more intimate relationship with the wind on-screen. But again, he emphasizes its remoteness, its inaccessibility—over there, in its own world, while calling it a "wind of cinema."

We recall that earlier in the poem, the speaker depicted Mabel on horseback with windblown hair, as she rides against the wind. He went on to suggest that she, too, is wind; she is an image that flies through the air: "wind against wind." By the logic set in motion here, cinema itself becomes figured as wind, for it consists of images propelled by the spinning reel, flung onto the screen, and "touching" the audience as well. Hence, the ironic predicament posited in the poem: the corporeal beings and things that are (or were) photographed, while tossed about by an invisible wind, come to serve as an embedded, mirror image of the cinematic apparatus and the effects it wields on viewers.

This playful poem thus tries to unravel a complex set of paradoxes—how to apprehend the swirling interplay of the material and immaterial, tangible and intangible, actual and virtual elements that make up the cinematic experience. Despite the speaker's claim that he sees but does not feel the wind blowing on-screen, he clearly feels the onslaught of images. But he also feels acutely deprived, overcome with a sense of loss and longing, for he can experience those scenes only across a distance of time and space. His access to the expanse of land unfolding before him is mediated—hence the "frustrated solitude" he senses between himself and the cowgirl on-screen.

As Béla Balázs observed in *Visible Man* (1924), every film has an atmosphere: "It is the air and aroma that pervade every work of art, and that lend distinctiveness to a medium and a world. This atmosphere is like the nebulous primal matter that condenses into individual shapes" (22). Even the most simpleminded and vacuous of films can "grip us from start to finish," Balázs asserts. "This is the effect of their living atmosphere, the dense, aromatic fluidity they possess of a living life that only the very greatest writers can manage on rare occasions to convey in words. . . . Every halfway decent American director knows how to create an atmosphere so vivid that you feel you can almost smell and taste it" (22). The atmosphere created in a film—that "dense aromatic fluidity"—flows outward toward viewers; it pervades the atmosphere of the theater, invades the collective sensorium of the audience. This apparently intangible, "nebulous primal matter" is tangibly felt and is this central paradox that Salinas ponders in his poem.

But how, precisely, do we define an atmosphere? That is the question that Ross Chambers poses in his study of atmospherics in the poetry of Baudelaire. To be sure, the term can be defined scientifically as "the invisible layer of breathable air that swathes the planet, sustaining life, and exerting the variable pressure we register as weather" (Chambers 1). But of course, in both a meteorological and derived sense, atmosphere is intimately bound to place; a given swath of air emanates from a given swath of land. To speak of the atmosphere of a city, a room, a landscape—whether directly perceived or represented in a work of art—is to invoke a "certain dimension of particularity, otherness or strangeness that attaches to objects, places or situations," Chambers observes (2). "This is the sense of there being an ungraspable or even uncanny hinterland of things, a dimension that defies definition or analysis, because it lies just beyond the domain of the intelligible and endows them with significance" (1–2).

The mise-en-scène in "Far West," as we have seen, offers a poetic reflection on the intimacy of atmosphere and hinterland by foregrounding how a rush of air (and of images) *touches* the bodies of people and things. In "Cinematógrafo" ("Cinema Theater," 1929), Salinas's earlier poem on cinema, these ephemeral flows take material form.[4] The poem stages a contest between *creación* and *re-creación*—between the creation story of Genesis and a cinematic representation: "Al principio nada fue. / Sólo la tela blanca" (In the beginning there was nothing. / Only the white screen; 77). But an expectant audience awaits: "Por todo el aire clamaba, / muda, enorme, la ansiedad de la mirada" (through the air clamored, / the mute, immense / anxiousness of the gaze; 77). Suddenly, the projectionist switches on "las máquinas maravillosas / para correr, para volar, / para amar, para aborrecer" (the marvelous machines / for running, for flying, / for loving, for hating)—an apparatus clearly able to create actions and emotions. As a vast inhabited world pours onto the screen, the personified first day of creation retreats to a corner to cry, humiliated by the superiority of cinematic re-creation. However, an instinctual spark leads to a reconciliation:

> Pero ya el instinto acechaba
> en los ojos de la mujer
> —la cabellera suelta al viento—
> y en el tejer y destejer de la tela del sentimiento. (78)
> (But instinct lay waiting
> in the eyes of the woman
> —her hair loosened in the wind—
> and in the weaving and unweaving of the fabric of emotion.)

Here the "instinct," or affective impulse, that resides in the eyes of the woman with the windblown hair, as well in the weaving and unraveling of the fabric of feeling, will draw the downcast "first day of creation" onto the screen in a synthesis of divine creation and artistic re-creation. The screen thus becomes what Giuliana Bruno calls an "affective map," a "tender geography"—ever being woven and unwoven by flows of feeling (8).

Fernando Vela, Salinas's contemporary, might have called this synesthetic melding of sensations "palpar ocularmente"—to visually touch (209). In "Desde la ribera oscura" ("From the Dark Side of the River," 1925), Vela argued that much of what was invisible to us in daily life, hidden beneath concepts and words, has now become visible, thanks to the apprenticeship of cinema (209). Drawing from Balász, Vela asserts, "El cine nos enseña a ver, y con su gran lupa y su reflector nos lleva los ojos como de la mano y nos obliga a palpar ocularmente el contorno de las cosas, a fijarnos en los mil movimientos de una mano que abre una puerta, nos sitúa a la vez en distintos puntos de vista, a la derecha, a la izquierda, cerca, lejos, arriba, abajo" (Cinema teaches us to see, and with its great magnifying glass and reflector it summons not only our eyes but also our hands, and it obliges us to *ocularly touch* the surface of things, to focus on the thousand subtle movements of a hand that opens a door; it simultaneously offers us different viewpoints—on the right, on the left, nearby, faraway, up and down; 209, emphasis mine). Movie-watching involves much more than passive vision; it demands an "ocular touch," it makes us see from multiple viewpoints, and it engages our bodies and transports us through space. Vela further emphasizes the opportunity for travel by likening the ribbon of film to a "una acera *roulante*" (a moving sidewalk; 214) and the screen to a "tapiz volador" (flying carpet; 223).

Vela's notion of "ocular touch" coincides with what film scholars today call the "haptic gaze." Starting in the late 1980s, a group of scholars turned their attention to the embodied viewer and developed theories of hapticity as a corrective to the reigning notion of the disembodied gaze.[5] As Steven Shaviro explains, the semiotic and psychoanalytic approaches had posited "a disincarnate eye and ear whose data are immediately objectified in the form of self-conscious awareness," ignoring "the primordial forms of raw sensation—affect, excitation, stimulation and repression, pleasure and pain, shock and habit" (27). The emerging discourse on hapticity brings sensation and synesthesia back into film studies and in so doing reconnects with a rich vein of early theory that was cut short once cinematic codes became standardized and the cinematic experience became naturalized. The film theorists of the 1920s—Balázs, Vertov, Kracauer, and Benjamin—were, like the writers of the Spanish avant-garde, acutely concerned with the sensorial, bodily effects of cinema, with what Benjamin called "collective innervation" (Benjamin, "Surrealism" 190–92).

Benjamin, so often the touchstone for cultural theory at large, brought hapticity to cinematic vision in "The Work of Art in the Age of Its Technological Reproducibility." The distracting, shocking element in film, Benjamin argues, "is primarily tactile, being based on successive changes of scene and focus which have a percussive effect on the spectator" (267). As an analogy for film reception, Benjamin turns to architecture, remarking: "Buildings are received in a twofold manner: by use and by perception. Or, better: tactilely and optically" (268). "Tactile reception," he adds, "comes about not so much by way of attention as by way of habit" (268). At historical turning points, when the human apparatus of perception faces new challenges, the tasks at hand "cannot be performed solely by optical means—that is, by way of contemplation"; rather, "they are mastered gradually—taking their cue from tactile reception—through habit" (268).

The film theorist Giuliana Bruno extends Benjamin's reflections by observing that habit is inscribed in habitation, and that by extension "haptic implies habitable": "As a house of moving pictures, film is as habitable as the house we live in" (250–51). Its "architexture" designs a mobile, emotional map that amplifies and extends space (251). When we view a film, Bruno suggests, even as its images inhabit our bodies, we simultaneously step into a habitable space and become "sightseers," thus partaking in what Burch calls "film's motionless voyage" (quoted in Bruno 250). And while the haptic gaze is typically associated with close-range viewing, the flat surface of the screen may give way, as it does for the sightseer in Salinas's poem, to a "far West," a vast sentient landscape.

Astral Bodies

The sentient geography of the film screen extends to the bodies of movie stars as well. The movie camera—in zooming in and out, or panning across the surface of the skin—provides unprecedented views of the human body. As Susan Buck-Morss observes, "Hollywood's new mass-being, the movie star, could only exist in the 'super-space' of the cinematic screen. Often, and increasingly female, the star was a sublime and simulated corporeality. Close-ups of parts of her/his body—mouth, eyes, legs, heaving breast—filled the screen in monstrous proportions. S/he was an awesome aesthetic spectacle, like a massive church icon" (52–53). The most emblematic of these stars of the 1920s was perhaps Greta Garbo, with her languid movements, luminous skin, and shimmering gowns.

Francisco Ayala's short story "Polar, estrella" offers a satiric case study of a film fan who is consumed with bodily desire for an ephemeral body on-screen:[6] "estaba enamorado como todo el mundo, de una estrella de cine" (he was, like everyone else, in love with a movie star; 286)—presumably Garbo since, although she is never named, she is later referred to as an "estrella escandinava" (Scandinavian star; 287). The protagonist, known only as "el amante" (the lover), is a pure spectator, susceptible to seduction, just like everyone else in his social world. Meanwhile, the astral body he calls "Polar" remains omnipresent—on-screen, on posters, and in his mind's eye—yet inaccessible in the flesh. Hence, the ironic inversion in the title: this is not the "Estrella Polar" (the North Star), the guiding light of sailors, but rather the Nordic actress, "Polar, estrella."

And insofar as she serves as the protagonist's *norte* (lodestar), she will lead him over the edge, to a suicidal plunge.

From the beginning, it is evident that life on-screen is becoming coextensive with the protagonist's everyday life. Yet the sensory onslaught of urban spectacle can still divert him from his obsessive desire for Polar:

> Al borde de un paseo, tuvo la intención de ahogar su sentimiento en una curva de aquel río—ondulante, invariable y gris—de asfalto.
>
> Pero le detuvo un paisaje de melenas y bicicletas que se le echaba encima, compacto: niñas de muslos rosa, alternos, y pechos divergentes, de victoria, punzando los jerseis. Las gomas circulares borraron al pasar su intención, y el tropel de flores ligeras—acero, carne, viento—le sacudió como un ventilador la tristeza. (286)

> (Along the street, he had the intention of drowning his feelings in the curve of that river of asphalt—undulating, invariable, and gray.
>
> But he stopped before a landscape of bobbed hair and bicycles that bore down on him, a compact throng: girls with pink, alternating thighs, their divergent, triumphant breasts piercing their sweaters. The circular rubber tires, as they passed, erased his original intention, and the rush of light flowers—metal, flesh, wind—shook him like an electric fan of sadness.)

These swirling images of modern life work as a metaphoric assemblage, a cipher for the film apparatus. The undulating river of pavement, the bicycle wheels, and the electric fan together suggest film stock rolling from the reels of the projector. In a further metaphoric turn, the bicycle wheels are likened to twin typewriter erasers (those small rubber wheels, topped by brushes) which, when passing by, erase the memory of his plans for the day. This opening passage reveals just how far filmic experience has impinged on the protagonist's life. It also sets up a contest, given that cinematic life and street life are competing over his body. The erotic appeal of those cyclists with bobbed hair and firm breasts can still halt and temporarily overcome the affective onslaught of cinema.

The contest between actual and virtual experience will continue to unfold through a narration that mimics the structure of film. In alternating scenes—quick cuts with no transitions—the narrator's camera-like eye zooms in and out, following the protagonist as he moves from the street to his study, to the cinema and back again, while intermittently focalizing through his gaze. In an early scene, he sits in his study and gazes at a wall map—"un sueño inserto en geometría" (a dream inserted into geometry)—which suggests a kinship between the map and movie screen. Spread across the table is a "bandada" (flock) of open books, described as "gaviotas de alas trémulas" (seagulls with tremulous wings; 286). All are travel narratives, tales of ancient and modern explorations of Africa and the Arctic. Above him, like a star, a personified armillary sphere "sleeps" on the bookcase. The protagonist allows his imagination to roam, to oscillate indecisively, as he contemplates possible itineraries. His thoughts, after a long period of "cabotaje" (coastal sailing), suddenly cast anchor with a jolt, as he remembers that today is the premiere of Polar's latest film (287).

By inserting these images of wanderlust in his story, Ayala establishes a close affinity between geographic and cinematic space. The protagonist's study—with the map, the travel narratives, and celestial model—clearly serves as an *antesala* (anteroom) for the *sala de cine* (cinema auditorium), in which the protagonist will feel himself transported by the images on-screen. The scene thus corroborates Bruno's argument that cinema was "born of a topographical 'sense'" (8). With roots in the spectacles of nineteenth-century travel culture—map rooms, scenic wallpaper, *tableaux vivants*, dioramas, panoramas, and train travel—cinema developed a "haptic way of picturing and experiencing space" (172). This moving, haptic space simultaneously produced the modern spectator—a "seeker after sensations," a "passenger" in an "emotion picture" (Bruno 172–73, 8).

The seeker of sensual pleasure in Ayala's story, while still in his study anticipating the premiere, is suddenly filled with haptic desire. He reaches into the drawer where he keeps his collection of film stock in order to *touch* an image of Polar, allowing his fingers to relish "la delicia táctil de un trozo de film cinematográfico—rizo suelto, curvado como una calcomanía—en cuyo borde acariciaron seco pespunte de telegrama" (the tactile delight of a piece of film stock—a loose curl, curved like a decal—as they caressed the telegram-like stitches along the edge; 288). He moves to the window and holds the film against the light to peruse Polar's face, "gustando matices insignificantes en la escala micrométrica de su sonrisa" (taking pleasure in the minute gradations of the micrometrical scale of her smile; 288). In this act of caressing the film strip and gazing at a photogram, Vela's notion of "ocular touch" becomes fully (albeit ironically) realized. The protagonist studies a close-up of Polar—a visage that on-screen would be colossal but here is miniscule—an irony that calls attention to the cinematic enhancement of space on a macro and a micro scale. He is overcome with excitement—*¡qué emoción!*—and the ribbon of film breaks loose in a spiral descent. But of course, herein lies the character's predicament; his "tactile delight" remains privative. Whereas he can touch the skin of the film, he can never touch the skin of the remote Nordic star herself.

Once the protagonist arrives at the theater, he waits to enter until the lights are turned off and the "viento cosmopolita" (cosmopolitan wind) of the newsreel blows across the screen, thus enabling him to "zambullirse en la emoción confluyente de los cuatro puntos cardinales" (plunge into the flows of emotion converging from four cardinal points; 288). Enticing images of travel once more come into play, as scenes from around the world flow across the screen—yachts sailing in a regatta, warships disembarking troops, and snowy landscapes that suggest a woman's curved shoulders, thus signaling the imminent appearance of the Scandinavian star. When Polar erupts onto the *écran*, wearing a dress of light, the protagonist feels himself "conmovido por un cataclismo visceral; el diafragma le redujo el tórax, mientras brotaba en su ánimo la evidencia difícil de lo astral, de lo inasible" (moved by a visceral cataclysm; his diaphragm contracted and halted his breath, while the hard evidence of the astral, of the ungraspable, invaded his soul; 288–89). While subject to this bodily assault, he is also struck by a painful truth—the star's ultimate inaccessibility, her ontological status as phantasm. When her intense gaze fixes on him, it feels like "disparo ineludible"—a gunshot that he cannot dodge; yet he is inundated with a current of absence, akin to the frustrated solitude acutely felt by the viewer in "Far West" (289). Both story and poem thus posit the same paradox—the powerful bodily feelings provoked by ephemeral figures of light and shadow.

The protagonist is jolted from this sensory trance when an accident occurs in the projection booth. The ribbon comes loose from the sprockets, and for a nightmarish moment Polar appears cut into fragments, upside down (289). While this accident exposes the machinic origins of the ghostly images, it sets the stage for another, more cruel interruption to come. Once the film ribbon reseats itself and the enchantment resumes, Polar begins disrobing for her bath. The protagonist trembles with impatience, his frustration growing, as the landscape of her body gradually comes into view: the curvature of her back and her serpentine legs, "surcadas, como el mapa, de venillas azules" (streaked with blue veins, like rivers on a map; 289). When Polar disappears in a quick cut to another scene, the protagonist is left resentful and angry, as if the door to her bedroom were suddenly locked "con una llave del agua fría" (with a faucet of cold water; 289). Once again, it is touch denied that nevertheless wields tactile force; his sexual desire is aroused by the Nordic star and then doused by icy water.

This excruciating irony marks a turning point, as the protagonist acquires the "resolución súbita de amante desdeñado" (sudden resolution of a scorned lover; 291). Yet despite his new resolve, he curiously renounces his own protagonism; for the narrator's camera eye now focalizes not through the protagonist but through the material objects around him, which come to life and assume agency. The *room* watches him as he enters the door, pale and trembling while fumbling for the light switch. Under its own volition, a *drawer* opens with a loud cry, offering an abundant pile of quivering celluloid curls, revealed in close-up. A lighted *match* draws near, and "el montón de celuloide quedó convertido en su propio olor tentacular, que no podría olvidarse nunca" (the pile of celluloid was transformed into its own tentacular odor, which he would never be able to forget; 291). The protagonist's cherished collection of film stock—his only means, however mediated, of *touching* his beloved Polar—has evaporated in a flash.

This ironic interplay of touch granted and touch denied—inherent in the cinematic experience—thus culminates in the denouement, as if the story itself were a fond and satiric response to Vela's notion of "ocular touch." While the protagonist can no longer caress Polar's image on the ribbons of film, a synesthetic "tentacular odor" remains in the room; and her memory sticks to his skin "como una película de grasa" (like a film of grease; 291). He tries to run her film backward in his mind in order to detach, point by point, the palpable impressions it has left on him, but to no avail (291). In desperation, he resolves to commit suicide by leaping from the bridge. As he walks to the river, the city "le iba cuajando paisajes de cine en planos superpuestos" (unfolded before him, a cinematic landscape of superimposed planes; 292), palpitating like flickering film. Meanwhile, the colors gradually fade away, becoming shades of black and white. The city has effectively turned into film; the contest between cinematic life and street life has ended. When he launches himself into space, he floats downward, *au ralenti*, upheld by the atmosphere, descending in a slow, spiral motion like the strip of film that he had earlier let fall from his fingers. Like the city, he has become filmic, but only at the moment of his expiration:

> Su último pensamiento y su última mirada fueron dirigidos a Polar. Le hablaba. La sentía presente, ángel ¡por fin! apiadado. Maniquí de cera, para los demás, invisible.
> Ella secó la firma de sus palabras con un paño blanco y una blanca sonrisa.
> (Eso fue todo.) (292)

> (His last thought and final gaze were directed to Polar. He spoke to her. He felt her present, an angel, showing pity at last! A wax mannequin, invisible to others.
> She dried the signature of his words with a white cloth and a blank smile.
> [That was all.])

As the angel of death, Polar fully actualizes her role as the femme fatale who guided this star-struck fan to his demise. As wax mannequin, she is a graven image, the false idol who led him astray. The stylistic descent into bathos is no doubt intentional here; for indeed, the story ends with an ironic wink. By concluding with the phrase—"she dried the signature of his words," followed by a parenthetical "That was all"—the story points to itself as artifice, as a mute thing made of words, akin to the voiceless images of silent film that nevertheless wield palpable power on the bodies of spectators (292). This suicide scene, while narrated with tongue in cheek, clearly calls attention to the transformative physical effects of cinema on the protagonist's body and on the city at large.

Like Salinas's "Far West," this text is concerned throughout with the complex interactions between the material and immaterial components of the film apparatus—between the *intangible* images it generates and its *tangible* effects on viewers. While telling a playful, satiric tale of a besotted fan, unable to touch his object of desire, the story also delves seriously into the paradoxes of cinematic experience. The flow of rich sensorial language reproduces the affective onslaught of cinematic images, casting spectatorship as an all-enveloping sensorial experience, which complicates and arguably belies the divide between virtual and actual experience. Moreover, the repeated geographical references—to travel, exploration, navigation—clearly cast viewers as passengers, as seekers of sensation, who are transported into the sentient expanses of heretofore unseen worlds.

Deranged by Celluloid

With the advent of cinema, as citizens avidly sought out new sensations, they found themselves immersed in a vast mediasphere—comprising the popular press, professional sports, advertising, radio, and cinema—all of which were engaged in the manufacture of public feeling for commercial gain. Modernity, as Justus Nieland points out, "is a sensational affair, bringing in its wake new sensory and perceptual regimes, new structures of feeling and modes of embodied knowledge, new technologies for the emotional organization of everyday life" (7). The film *El misterio de la Puerta del Sol* (1929), directed by Francisco Elías, offers a satiric spoof of this sensational mediasphere and of two Quixotic film fans who fabricate a cinematic crime.

This, the first sound film produced in Spain (albeit partially sonorized), opens to the deafening racket of a newspaper pressroom, as a linotypist sleeps before his machine, oblivious to the din around him.[7] An intertitle introduces the character: Pompeyo Pimpollo (Juan de Orduña), "chico simpático, fotogénico y algo linotipista. Su ambición es ir a Hollywood y hacer que la Greta Garbo pierda por él hasta el acento sueco" (a photogenic, amiable young man, and something of a linotypist. His ambition is to go to Hollywood and have Greta Garbo fall so hard for him that she loses her Swedish accent).[8] The camera pulls back to show the morning edition of the *Heraldo de Madrid*, flowing through the giant rollers of the press, like film stock in a projector (see Fig. 7.1). A second intertitle introduces a pressman, Rodolfo Bambolino (Antonio Barber), as "otro perturbado de celuloide, un chico sujeto a pesadillas" (another fellow deranged by celluloid, a young man subject to nightmares). As Rodolfo lifts piles of

Figure 7.1. Rotary printing press in *El misterio de la Puerta del Sol*, filmed in the press room of *El Heraldo de Madrid*.

newspapers from the conveyor belt, he is transfixed by a headline about the celebrated director Edward S. Carawa and the star Lia de Golfi, who have arrived in Madrid to shoot a film. The director is giving screen tests to young *madrileños* who dream of becoming the new Rudolph Valentino and Greta Garbo. Rodolfo (aptly named) and Pompeyo excitedly plan to audition for a part.

The scene cuts to the friends' shared room, with portraits of movie stars pegged to the wall, as they dress in formal attire, preparing for their screen tests. When Pompeyo mocks his friend as he struggles to fasten his collar, Rodolfo protests, "¡Maldito sea el verdugo que inventó el cuello de pajarito" (A curse on the executioner who invented the wing collar!). Later, when Rodolfo returns home and takes off the collar, he utters a more explicit curse: "¡Maldito sea el gachó que inventó el celuloide!" (A curse on the bloke who invented celluloid!). The incident thus serves as the opening gambit, with the celluloid collar serving as metaphor and motif in the thematics and events that unfold. And in so doing, the image gestures toward hapticity, calling attention to the materiality of the film apparatus and its bodily effects on viewers.

Equally significant are two lengthy shots of the Puerta del Sol, filmed from a stationary camera and recorded at midday—a cacophony of blaring car horns, backfiring engines, and rattling trolleys. A stream of advertisements, painted on trucks and perched atop trolleys, flow by like photograms of film (see Fig. 7.2). When the two youths pass through the plaza, dodging traffic as they cross the street, we can barely pick them out amid the urban chaos. They are immersed, as are we, in an all-encompassing mediasphere, in which the sensational press, the Hollywood star system, the advertising

Figure 7.2. Trolley advertisements in *El misterio de la Puerta del Sol*, filmed in the Puerta del Sol.

industry, and urban spectacle at large—all work in concert to bedazzle and potentially derange the more susceptible of citizens.

As we follow the trajectory of these two obsessed film fans, we are treated to satiric jokes on popular film and celebrity culture. When they approach the studio "Super-Carawa Productions," an automobile drops off passengers: two of them in medieval dress, two in flamenco garb, and one in leather breeches and a coonskin hat. Pompeyo exclaims that he feels *emocionado* (overwhelmed by emotion): "Me parece que estoy en Los Ángeles" (I feel like I'm in Los Angeles). Here Pompeyo and Rodolfo first glimpse Lía de Golfi, scantily dressed as Salomé, who although born in Torrejón, near Madrid, passes herself off as a Muscovite. As Andrew Ginger suggests, the two men are as seduced by Lía as by cinematic spectacle at large, and they yearn "to step from the vicarious position of spectators [to] a virtual location on the screen" (72).

Rodolfo and Pompeyo fail their "celluloid baptisms" (screen tests) for not sufficiently conforming to the *tipos populares* that the director Carawa requires for his *españoladas*. Disappointed, they resolve to become "popular" by making their own movie—which will appear not on-screen but in the press. They go on to fake a sensational crime by planting a skeleton in a suitcase and leaving it in a storeroom that opens to the Puerta del Sol. The lurid details of the crime—the body dismembered and burned to hinder identification—indeed play out in the pages of the newspapers. Intermittently throughout the film, we see the screaming headlines of newspapers, whether held in the hands of readers or hot off the press. Rodolfo is arrested, convicted, and sentenced to die by the garrote—the official mode of execution in Spain. The plan the two friends had hatched to save him by revealing the "truth" of the false crime goes awry. In a last-minute attempt to save Rodolfo, Carawa and Lía rush to Madrid.

A remarkable seven-minute sequence displays aerial shots from the plane, its engines loudly whining, as it carries Carawa and Lía from Barcelona to Madrid. Crosscut with these aerial scenes are shots of Rodolfo in his cell, as he hears the loud hammering of workers building the scaffold. After circling over the Puerta del Sol, the plane lands on the outskirts. Carawa and Lia race into the city in an automobile, but they are blocked by a train, then the engine breaks down, and it appears they will arrive too late. Just as the executioner is about to tighten the garrote around Rodolfo's neck, the condemned man awakens—he is still in the studio awaiting his screen test; he had dozed off and had a bad dream. Tugging at his neck, he swears that this is the last time he will ever wear a celluloid collar.

A corny plotline, to be sure, and even allowing for the limitations of early sound technology, a tight budget, and actors untrained for talkies, the film remains poorly executed. It consists of an incoherent pastiche of genres—farce, melodrama, suspense, interspersed with variety show numbers and magic tricks—and many of the satiric jokes were already well-worn clichés. Yet, however amateurish its execution, the film offers an astute metacommentary on a burgeoning culture industry in which cinema, print media, and publicity collude in manufacturing the sensorium of modern life.

Recurring throughout the film are shots of newspapers rolling off the press, with close-ups of headlines that work as pivot points for the action. The rotary press is cast as "el coloso de hierro que escupe crímenes por su colmillo" (the colossus of iron that spits crimes through its jaws), feeding public demand for shocking and thrilling news. When Rodolfo and Pompeyo dream up their convoluted crime, they count on its projection on the pages of the popular press. The overriding theme of the "dream factory" hinges on the film's central joke—that set of analogies that connect the celluloid collar, the *garrote vil*, and celluloid nitrate. Clearly, the gag points to the physical choke hold that spectacle had on its audience, especially those more susceptible to "celluloid derangement." But however corny, its presence in a film intended for a mass audience suggests a reflexive awareness that an embodied film experience had pervaded the culture at large.

The aerial sequence was surely designed to thrill audiences in that early age of aviation. As metacommentary, it pointedly calls attention to the expansion of space opened up by film technology. Cinema and aviation, after all, emerged at the turn of the century and developed almost in tandem. By 1914, Paul Virilio observes, "aviation was ceasing to be strictly a means of flying and breaking records; . . . it was becoming one way, or perhaps even the ultimate way of *seeing*" (22). But aerial vision also offered an unprecedented way of *feeling*, of sensing the vast expansion of the visible in the modern age. The dramatic aerial sequence thus works as another embedded "replicant" of the film apparatus—along with the rotary press, the truck and trolley advertisements, and the celluloid collar. Viewed through the windows of the plane, the landscape and cityscape—the sentient skin of Earth—flow across the screen like film stock itself, calling out for a haptic response (see Fig. 7.3a and Fig. 7.3b). As the plane lands, the dirt of the runway appears as a rough blur below the shadow of the wing, a tactile image rendered abstract.

In its own clumsy way, *El misterio de la Puerta del Sol* thus offers a thoughtful metacommentary on the complexities of spectatorship in cinema and in the mediasphere at large.[9] It attempts to decipher the same conundrum presented in "Far West" and in "Polar, estrella." How do we account for the intense bodily feelings produced by ephemeral images? As Steven Shaviro succinctly puts it: "How can cinema have so powerful a 'reality effect' when it is so manifestly unreal?" (25). And indeed a preoccupation with the falsity of cinematic spectacle, with the inaccessibility of its beguiling images, pervades the three works discussed here and sponsors their gestures toward tactility.

On the face of things, "Far West," "Polar, estrella," and *El misterio de la Puerta del Sol* could all be read as mere satire, as cautionary tales about the perils of confusing illusion and reality. However, the mockery remains mild, infused with affectionate humor, and authored by subjects who admit their own enchantment with filmic images. On a more profound level, these works expose the complex dynamic at play between worldly life and screen life and, in so doing, move us beyond the simple binary of actual and virtual experience.[10] What emerges more powerfully than presence lost is the presence

Figure 7.3a and b. Aerial shots of (a) the countryside and (b) the Puerta del Sol in *El misterio de la Puerta del Sol*.

of something new—a synesthetic spectatorial experience that adds more than it subtracts from reality. Without reaching resolution, these works suggest that virtual and actual experience coexist—not in opposition, not as two poles on a continuum—but rather as two experiential modes wrapped together in a complex circuitry of ongoing exchange, about which much remains to be understood. As representative of a rich vein of thought that emerged amid mass spectacle in the 1920s, these texts disclose the inadequacy of the actual/virtual binary for understanding the complex affective content of cinematic experience, an inadequacy ever more acute today as thinkers ponder the complexities of media experience in the digital age.

NOTES

1. This and all other translations are mine.
2. Few critics offer readings of this poem; for brief discussions see Morris (77–79) and Cirre (74–75).
3. Salinas could have seen *The Wind*, given that it appears in the movie listings of *ABC* in May 1929 at the Cine Royalty. But because countless westerns featured scenes of "tumbling tumbleweeds," without further evidence we cannot pin down the source. Note that Lillian Gish's character in the film is not "Mabel," but rather Letty. The name Mabel may be have been inspired by the comic actress Mabel Normand, although she made few westerns. I suspect that Salinas's choice of the name rested on the interior syllabic rhyme produced by *Mabel, caballista, cabellos*.
4. For commentaries on this poem, see Morris (75–77), Stixrude (124–26), and Palley (39–40).
5. These scholars include Barker, Burch, Lant, Marks, del Rio, Sobchack, and Shaviro. Deleuze has wielded enormous influence on theorists of the haptic; see his discussions in *Cinema 2*, and *Francis Bacon*, and in Deleuze and Guattari, *A Thousand Plateaus*. Deleuze credits the art historian Alois Riegl for originating the notion of hapticity.
6. "Polar, estrella" first appeared in Ayala's collection of stories *El boxeador y un angel* (1929). For critical commentaries refer to García Montero, "El cine"; Gubern, "Francisco Ayala"; Morris 147–51; Navarro Durán, "Ironía" and "Las prosas"; also, Nieto Nuño. In addition, see García Montero's invaluable study of Ayala's stance toward cinema in the 1920s, *Francisco Ayala*, which accompanies the facsimile edition of *Indagación del cinema*, reissued by Visor.
7. Like *The Jazz Singer*, this film retains many elements of silent film (intertitles, for example) and indeed was made to be shown as well in theaters not equipped for sound. For accounts of the film's production and the development of sound film in Spain, see Arce; Fernández Colorado, "El 'phonofilm'"; and Sánchez Oliveira. Scholars who offer brief accounts of the film's historical significance include Gubern, *El cine sonoro* 17–18, "The Transition" 370–76, and in Gubern et al. 125; Benet 80–81; and Fernández Colorado, "*El misterio*." See Ginger for an illuminating close reading of the film.
8. Quotations are drawn from the restored version of *El misterio de la Puerta del Sol*, available for viewing on the RTVE/Filmoteca website: *www.rtve.es/alacarta/videos/filmoteca/misterio-puerta-del-sol-ultimo-dia-pompeyo/1623253/* (accessed 30 September 2014).
9. Metacommentaries on cinematic experience and the Hollywood star system were pervasive in popular culture in the 1920s. Hansen argues that "modernization inevitably provokes the need for reflexivity"; and in classical Hollywood cinema she finds "ample evidence" of "vernacular reflexivity" (70). For examples from the Madrid newspaper *El Sol*, see "La cinematografía americana"; Armenta, "Para ellas"; and "¿Por qué son populares?" I thank Emily Thomas for bringing these articles to my attention.
10. I am using the virtual/actual terminology based on the more prosaic usage of these terms. However, the Bergsonian/Deleuzian concept has resonance here as well; see Deleuze, *Cinema 2* 68–97, 270–80, and his brief exposition "The Actual and the Virtual" (*Dialogues II* 148–52). In this speculative conclusion, I am indebted to Shaviro's argument in *The Cinematic Body*.

WORKS CITED

Arce, Julio. "Del Kinetófono a *El misterio de la Puerta del Sol*. Los comienzos del cine sonoro en España." *Revista de Musicología* 32.2 (2009): 623–43.

Armenta, Antonio. "Para ellas: La 'Estrellomanía.'" *El Sol* 3 March 1921: 6.

Ayala, Francisco. *Indagación del cinema*. Madrid: Mundo Latino, 1929.

———. "Polar, estrella." *Narrativa completa*. Madrid: Alianza, 1993. 286–92.

Balázs, Béla. *Early Film Theory:* Visible Man *and* The Spirit of Film. Ed. Erica Carter. Trans. Rodney Livingstone. New York: Berghahn Books, 2010.

Barker, Jennifer M. *The Tactile Eye: Touch and the Cinematic Experience*. Berkeley: U of California P, 2009.

Benet, Vicente J. *El cine español: Una historia cultural*. Barcelona: Paidós, 2012.

Benjamin, Walter. *The Arcades Project*. Ed. Rolf Tiedemann. Trans. Howard Eiland and Kevin McLaughlin. Cambridge, MA: Belknap–Harvard UP, 1999.

———. "Surrealism, the Last Snapshot of the European Intelligentsia." *Reflections: Essays, Aphorisms, Autobiographical Writings*. Ed. Peter Demetz. Trans. Edmund Jephcott. New York: Schocken, 1978. 177–92.

———. "The Work of Art in the Age of Its Technological Reproducibility." Trans. Harry Zohn and Edmund Jephcott. *Selected Writings (1938–1940)*. Ed. Howard Eiland and Michael W. Jennings. Vol. 4. Cambridge, MA: Belknap–Harvard UP, 2006. 251–83.

Bruno, Giuliana. *Atlas of Emotion: Journeys in Art, Architecture, and Film*. New York: Verso, 2002.

Buck-Morss, Susan. "The Cinema Screen as Prosthesis of Perception." *The Senses Still: Perception and Memory as Material Culture in Modernity*. Ed. C. Nadia Seremetakis. Boulder, CO: Westview, 1994. 45–62.

Burch, Noël. "Life to Those Shadows." Ed. and trans. Ben Brewster. Berkeley: U of California P, 1990.

Chambers, Ross. *An Atmospherics of the City: Baudelaire and the Poetics of Noise*. New York: Fordham UP, 2015.

"La cinematografía americana." *El Sol* 15 September 1919: 4.

Cirre, José Francisco. *El mundo lírico de Pedro Salinas*. Granada: Editorial Don Quijote, 1982.

Dalí, Salvador. "Film-arte, film-anti-artístico." *Los vanguardistas españoles (1925–1935)*. Ed. Ramón Buckley and John Crispin. Madrid: Alianza, 1973. 224–29.

Deleuze, Gilles. *Cinema 2: The Time-Image*. Trans. Hugh Tomlinson and Robert Galeta. Minneapolis: U of Minnesota P, 1989. Rpt. 2003.

———. *Francis Bacon: The Logic of Sensation*. Trans. Daniel W. Smith. New York: Continuum, 2005.

Deleuze, Gilles, and Félix Guattari. *A Thousand Plateaus: Capitalism and Schizophrenia*. Trans. Brian Massumi. Minneapolis: U of Minnesota P, 1987.

Deleuze, Gilles, and Claire Parnet. *Dialogues II*. New York: Columbia UP, 2007.

del Río, Elena. *Deleuze and the Cinemas of Performance: Powers of Affection*. Edinburgh: Edinburgh UP, 2008.

Espina, Antonio. "Reflexiones sobre cinematografía." *Revista de Occidente* 43 (1927): 36–46.

Fernández Colorado, Luis. "*El misterio de la Puerta del Sol*." *Antología crítica del cine español, 1906–1995: Flor en la sombra*. Ed. Julio Pérez Perucha. Madrid: Cátedra; Filmoteca, 1997. 80–82.

———. "El 'phonofilm': Un sistema ambulante de cine sonoro." *Actas del V Congreso de la Asociación Española de Historiadores del Cine*. A Coruña: Centro Galego de Artes da Imaxe, 1995. 107–15.

García Montero, Luis. "El cine y la mirada moderna." *El universo plural de Francisco Ayala*. Ed. Manuel Ángel Vásquez Medel. Seville: Alvar, 1995. 51–67.

———. *Francisco Ayala y el cine*. Madrid: Visor, 2006.

Ginger, Andrew. "Space, Time, Desire, and the Atlantic in Three Spanish Films of the 1920s." *Hispanic Research Journal* 8.1 (2007): 69–78.

Gubern, Román. *El cine sonoro en la II República, 1929–1936*. Barcelona: Lumen, 1977.

———. "Francisco Ayala y el cine." *Francisco Ayala: El escritor en su siglo*. Ed. Susana Martínez-Garrido. Granada: Fundación Francisco Ayala, 2006. 371–81.

———. *Proyector de luna: La generación del 27 y el cine*. Barcelona: Anagrama, 1999.

———. "The Transition from Silent to Sound Cinema." *A Companion to Spanish Cinema*. Ed. Jo Labanyi and Tatjana Pavlović. Malden, MA: Wiley-Blackwell, 2013. 370–76.

Gubern, Román, et al. *Historia del cine español*. Madrid: Cátedra, 1995.

Hansen, Miriam Bratu. "The Mass Production of the Senses: Classical Cinema as Vernacular Modernism." *Modernism/Modernity* 6.2 (1999): 59–77.

Lant, Antonia. "Haptical Cinema." *October* 74 (1995): 45–73.

Marks, Laura U. *Touch: Sensuous Theory and Multisensory Media*. Minneapolis: U of Minnesota P, 2002.

———. "Video Haptics and Erotics." *Screen* 39.4 (1998): 331–48.

Massumi, Brian. *Parables for the Virtual: Movement, Affect, Sensation*. Durham, NC: Duke UP, 2002.

Morris, C. B. *This Loving Darkness: The Cinema and Spanish Writers 1920–1936*. Oxford: Oxford UP, 1980.

Navarro Durán, Rosa. "Ironía y belleza en *El boxeador y un ángel*." *Francisco Ayala y las vanguardias*. Ed. Manuel Ángel Vásquez-Medel. Seville: Alfar, 1998. 57–71.

———. "Las prosas vanguardistas de Francisco Ayala: Una ventana abierta a la belleza y al ingenio." *Francisco Ayala: El escritor en su siglo*. Ed. Susana Martínez-Garrido. Granada: Fundación Francisco Ayala, 2006. 393–404.

Nieland, Justus. *Feeling Modern: The Eccentricities of Public Life*. Urbana: U of Illinois P, 2008.

Nieto Nuño, Miguel. "La imagen en la prosa vanguardista de Francisco Ayala." *El universo plural de Francisco Ayala*. Ed. Manuel Ángel Vásquez Medel. Seville: Alvar, 1995. 45–55.

Palley, Julián. *La luz no usada: La poesía de Pedro Salinas*. Mexico City: Ediciones de Andrea, 1966.

"¿Por qué son populares las estrellas?" *El Sol* 16 October 1921: 8.

Salinas, Pedro. *Poesías completas*. Vol. 1. *Fabula y signo, Seguro azar, Presagios*. Ed. Soledad Salinas de Marichal. Madrid: Alianza, 1997.

Sánchez Oliveira, Enrique. *Aproximación histórica al cineasta Francisco Elías Riquelme (1890–1977)*. Seville: U de Sevilla, 2003.

Sánchez Saornil, Lucía. *Poesía*. Ed. Rosa María Martín Casamitjana. Valencia: Pre-textos, 1996.

Shaviro, Steven. *The Cinematic Body*. Minneapolis: U of Minnesota P, 1993.

Sobchack, Vivian. *The Address of the Eye: A Phenomenology of Film Experience*. Princeton, NJ: Princeton UP, 1992.

———. *Carnal Thoughts: Embodiment and Moving Image Culture*. Berkeley: U of California P, 2004.

Stixrude, David L. *The Early Poetry of Pedro Salinas*. Princeton, NJ: Princeton UP, 1975.

Torre, Guillermo de. *Hélices*. Madrid: Editorial Mundo Latino, 1923.

Vásquez-Medel, Manuel Ángel, ed. *El universo plural de Francisco Ayala*. Seville: Alvar, 1995.

———, ed. *Francisco Ayala y las vanguardias*. Seville: Alfar, 1998.

Vela, Fernando. "Desde la ribera oscura (Sobre una estética del cine)." *Revista de Occidente* 23 (1925): 202–27.

Virilio, Paul. *War and Cinema: The Logistics of Perception*. Trans. Patrick Camiller. London: Verso, 1989.

Wetherell, Margaret. *Affect and Emotion: A New Social Science Understanding*. London: Sage, 2012.

CHAPTER 8

The Battle for Emotional Hegemony in Republican Spain (1931–1936)

JAVIER KRAUEL

> No one thought of wars, of revolutions, or revolts. All that was radical,
> all violence, seemed impossible in an age of reason.
> —STEFAN ZWEIG, *THE WORLD OF YESTERDAY*

How can someone come to imagine that violence is impossible? How can someone lead his or her political life without thinking about the possibility of wars, revolutions, or revolts? And, more significantly, what roles do reason and emotion play in ensuring such a secure world? For Austrian writer Stefan Zweig (1881–1942), it was painfully clear that the secure world he describes was the product of nineteenth-century "liberal idealism" (3) as it developed in the Austro-Hungarian empire, a state where before the Great War many thought that "the last vestige of evil and violence would finally be conquered" (3). Only in a world dominated by universal reason and free of emotions, a world "saturated with confidence in the unfailing and binding power of tolerance and conciliation" (4), can one think that violence is impossible and thus lead one's political life according to this idea. Following the horrors of the First World War, this world of reason and liberal ideology more generally came under attack wherever they had once existed.

In the political sphere, the problem was not only that war, revolutions, and revolts returned, nor that they returned with a vengeance, but that the experience accumulated in the world of reason and of parliamentary democracy suddenly became useless. This is what Walter Benjamin identified as "the poverty of experience" in an essay he wrote following his departure from Nazi Germany in 1933: "experience has fallen in value, amid a generation which from 1914 to 1918 had to experience some of the most monstrous events in the history of the world. . . . Wasn't it noticed at the time how many people returned from the front in silence? Not richer but poorer in communicable experience?" (731). The task that lay ahead was to "start from scratch; to make a new start; to make a little go a long way" (732). To make this fresh start, to think and to act politically in the ruins of reason, emotions became an indispensable tool. In other words, it is at the precise moment when parliamentary liberalism struggled for legitimacy, and when both the revolutionary left and the radical right questioned the core values of rationality, dialogue, and deliberation, that intellectuals and political theorists engaged emotions as an essential dimension of modern political life. Certainly, political theory had engaged emotions prior to World War I: Plato, Aristotle, and Seneca; Descartes and Hobbes; Rousseau and Smith are obvious examples. However, when emotions returned to the center of both political theory and political practice during the troubled times of interwar Europe, they did so because reason could no longer serve as the foundation of a stable political order.

Consider, for instance, the appeal that the theory of myth had for both the radical right and the revolutionary left at the time. Carl Schmitt famously uncovered this revolutionary use of myth in the closing pages of *The Crisis of Parliamentary Democracy* (1923). According to Schmitt, who derives his theory from revolutionary syndicalist Georges Sorel and his *Réflexions sur la violence* (1908), myth is essentially an emotional construct, one that provides "the most powerful symptom of the decline of the relative rationalism of parliamentary thought" (76). After showing that liberal beliefs in openness and discussion are outdated principles in modern mass democracy, he argues that in contemporary politics myth somehow fills the void left by reason, emerging as an irresistible force and as "a new evaluation of rational thought, a new belief in instinct and intuition" (66). The logical consequence of Schmitt's narrative is a conception of politics determined by the confrontation of two myths, the Marxist myth of class conflict and the Fascist national myth—the latter being stronger than the former because, for Schmitt, it evokes "more powerful emotions" (75).

This does not mean, however, that emotions were circumscribed to the politics of antiparliamentary, revolutionary movements of the right and the left. In fact, they played a significant role within political concepts that can be said to emerge from within the liberal tradition. I will cite four very different examples. The first, and most fundamental, is Max Weber's concept of charisma. Much like myth, charisma is essentially an emotional concept.[1] This is so not only because charismatic figures appear in situations where people feel "enthusiasm . . . despair and hope" (242), but also because charisma "*may* effect a subjective or *internal* reorientation born out of suffering, conflicts, or enthusiasm" (245) that ends up determining—much like an emotion—the orientation of action. Whereas Schmitt used the emotions unleashed by myth to attack the legitimacy of parliamentary government, Weber devised the concept of charisma to arrive at the formulation of a liberal, presidential constitutionalism. In short, the emotional thrust explicit in Weber's notion of charisma does not seek to destroy parliamentary liberalism but rather to reform it.

A second example would be José Ortega y Gasset's *España invertebrada* (*Invertebrate Spain*, 1922), a pessimistic, reactionary essay that laments what Ortega called Spain's disintegration owing to, among other factors, Spanish society's tendency toward *particularismo*, a kind of emotional selfishness where "cada grupo deja de sentirse a sí mismo como parte y, en consecuencia, deja de compartir los sentimientos de los demás" (each group stops feeling that it is part of something bigger and, consequently, stops sharing other people's feelings; 130). Ortega here relates emotion to groups rather than individuals, and he decries rather than encourages its central role in politics.

A third example can be found in Julien Benda, an intellectual entrenched in more or less conservative liberal positions who, like Ortega, decried the new centrality of emotions in politics. In *La Trahison des clercs* (*The Treason of the Intellectuals*, 1927), Benda denounced fin de siècle intellectuals for adopting the "political passions" of the masses, specifically the "national passion" and the "class passion" (33–34). To remedy this "treason"—that is, the betrayal of the (eternal) principles of truth, justice, and reason—Benda sought to recover the tradition of the liberal intellectual as someone who judges political passions with indifference because he is either attached to "the purely disinterested activity of the mind" or preaches "in the name of humanity or justice, the adoption of an abstract principle superior to and directly opposed to these passions" (44).

My fourth example is María Zambrano's proposal for a reformed liberalism in *Horizonte del liberalismo* (*Horizon of Liberalism*, 1930). Arguing from a philosophical position, Zambrano identified an emotional paradox in liberal morality: "la moral humana del liberalismo elude al hombre verdadero, a sus problemas efectivos de sentimiento" (liberalism's human morality evades the real man, ignoring the actual problems created by his feelings; 241). Because liberal morality requires us to sacrifice "los instintos, las emociones, las pasiones" (instincts, emotions, passions; 243), Zambrano calls for a new liberalism whose core commitment would be "[la] libertad fundada, más que en la razón, en la fe, en el amor" (liberty founded not so much on reason but on faith, on love; 269).

While many more examples could be cited, the four offered here are sufficient to show that, after the First World War, efforts to reform or do away with liberalism and its institutions contained numerous references to specific emotions (despair, hope, enthusiasm, love) or considered emotional life (instinct, intuition, passions) a sphere of prime political importance. My claim in this chapter is that the connection between emotions and liberal institutions proved decisive for the Spanish Second Republic (1931–1936). More specifically, the chapter attends to the ways in which a number of Spanish intellectuals used the press as a platform for the elaboration of emotional norms during the early 1930s. A time of accelerated political change and generalized social unrest, the Second Republic was characterized by the gap that existed between the existential realities of a sizable part of the population and the legal institutions sanctioned by the 1931 Constitution (Villacañas Berlanga, *Historia* 501–37). This gap, which was particularly evident in divisive issues such as the status of the Catholic Church, Catalonia's aspirations to self-government, and the dire situation of the agrarian proletariat (as evidenced, for example, in the anarchist uprising in Casas Viejas in January 1933), was the object of much public discussion in the press.

Taking the idea of "emotional discourse as a form of social action that creates effects in the world" (Abu-Lughod and Lutz 107) as my premise, I examine the newspaper and magazine articles written about these issues by Josep Maria de Sagarra in *Mirador*, by Manuel Chaves Nogales in *Ahora*, and by Francisco Ayala in *Diario de Alicante*, *Luz*, and *El Sol* in an attempt to understand why these journalists, all liberal intellectuals committed to the Republican reforms of 1931–1933, considered the emotional conduct of Spaniards a political problem and how they encouraged their readers to control and moderate their emotions. First, I argue that such recommendations of emotional control attempted to create what Alison Jaggar calls "emotional hegemony" (60–61), that is, that they were trying to establish a legal-rational legitimacy (Weber) for the Republic by defining what conventionally acceptable emotions were with regard to Republican reforms and institutions. Second, in a brief concluding section, I propose that this legitimacy failed in part because of the intervention of other intellectuals who attacked the model of emotional self-control by stirring powerful emotions in their readers, often for different political ends. These voices, which I label "charismatic" following Weber, included those of the revolutionary left, but also those of intellectuals such as Miguel de Unamuno, José Ortega y Gasset, and José Antonio Primo de Rivera, the leader of the Falange Española (the Spanish Fascist party founded in 1933).

To appreciate the political, economic, and social difficulties that besieged the Second Spanish Republic, it is helpful to distinguish between the international and the domestic problems it had to face. On the international front, Spain established a parliamentary government when most European countries, as has been suggested, were either questioning or rejecting parliamentary democracy. The news coming from Europe—notably from Fascist Italy and the Weimar Republic, and after 1933, Nazi Germany—cast a long shadow over the future prospects of Republican institutions and reforms, the development of which was further complicated by the devastating effects of the Great Depression.[2] On the domestic front, the great enthusiasm and hope that surrounded the proclamation of the Republic on 14 April 1931 soon gave way to mounting discontent and increased social unrest.

Historical accounts of the period echo the memories many Spaniards have of the time: the advent of the Republic was by and large saluted with an explosion of joy. Crowds took to streets and squares all over Spain, singing the "Marseillaise," the "Internationale," the "Himno de Riego" (the Republican anthem) and waving the tricolor—purple, yellow, and red—flag (Vincent 118–19). "Republicans hailed the turning toward a progressive and successful modern Spain, free of the contradictions and limitations of the nineteenth century," writes Stanley Payne (34). And although the Catholic Church "was not at all happy with the arrival of the Republic" (Casanova, *The Spanish Republic* 19), a feeling shared by the privileged classes, it initially accepted the new political reality. Recalling the sentiments during the weeks leading up to the proclamation of the Republic, Francisco Ayala noted that it was "un ambiente de alegre expectación" (an atmosphere of joyous expectation) that on 14 April turned into a moment of "general euforia" (general euphoria; *Obras* 2: 194).

Two concepts can help us understand the emotional energies collectively available during the coming of the Republic: Raymond Williams's "structure of feeling" and Martin Heidegger's *Stimmung*, a term that is often translated as "mood." While the first concept refers to "meanings and values as they are actively lived and felt" (132), the second, as explained by Jonathan Flatley, denotes "a kind of affective atmosphere . . . in which intentions are formed, projects pursued, and particular affects can attach to particular objects" (19). We thus can say that the coming of the Republic created a joyful structure of feeling for lower- and middle-class Spaniards, and that there was a joyous mood that made the Republican project a hopeful one in the spring of 1931. While this is certainly true, it is important to note that both concepts are historically variable, allowing for the possibility of change within a determinate "structure of feeling" or *Stimmung*. If "structures of feeling" are primarily related to "emergent formations" (Williams 134), and if moods provide "a way to articulate the shaping and structuring effect of historical context on our affective attachments" (Flatley 19), then it should not come as a surprise that the consolidation of the Republic into a political regime with specific legislation and institutions transformed the initial joy that abounded into other structures of feeling and moods. When the Republican project ceased to be emergent and became dominant (to use Williams's terminology), and when it became determined by a historical context that included not only the end of General Miguel Primo de Rivera's dictatorship, the departure of the king and queen, and the prospect of new liberties, but also a fair amount of social disturbances and insurrections, a new set of emotions was produced—one that included fear, anxiety, and hatred.

The key to this emotional transformation resides in the Republic's first biennium.[3] This was a period of intense legislative activity and of sweeping reforms. A general election to the Constituent Cortes was held on 28 June 1931. The ensuing provisional government, under leftist republican Manuel Azaña, commissioned a draft Constitution that was passed on 9 December 1931 after a three-month-long debate. The next day, the Cortes elected Niceto Alcalá Zamora, a conservative republican and a man of strong Catholic convictions, as president of the Republic. And, finally, an ambitious program of social reform was implemented by the Republican-Socialist coalition in power. Many of these sweeping changes, which originated, at least in part, in the accelerated modernization undergone by Spanish society since the early 1900s, were certainly democratic, but they were also highly divisive. Particularly contentious were the reforms relating to the separation of church and state, to political autonomy and devolution, and to land reform and distribution.

I will address these particularly contentious reforms shortly, but first I would like to emphasize that the problem encountered by Republican reforms was one of legitimacy. "Almost from the first moment of its existence, the legitimacy of the new regime began to decay" (127), writes Mary Vincent. One possible explanation for this deficit in legitimacy resides in how the Constitution and the office of the president took shape. The Constitution, which has recently been labeled by one commentator as "la última de las constituciones excluyentes del siglo XIX" (the last of the nineteenth-century discriminatory constitutions), contained explicitly leftist and anticlerical content that rendered it unpalatable to the right (Villacañas Berlanga, *Historia* 525). Furthermore, the presidency of the Republic had "una rara legitimidad, que no era popular ni parlamentaria" (a strange legitimacy that was neither popular nor parliamentary), and its executive powers were almost exclusively restricted to veto power, something that considerably weakened Republican governments (Villacañas Berlanga, *Historia* 523).

A second possible explanation for the Republic's loss of legitimacy is provided by Mary Vincent's observation that "the new Republican nation was, in a sense, to be legislated into existence" (122). This intense focus on legislation produced expectations from the law that were not only unrealistic but also misguided. Because the aim of the reforming legislation was "the transformation of Spanish society rather than of the institutions of the state . . . the shape and function of the state—its crystallization—remained, invisible, yet impervious" (124). The weakness of institutional reform at the state level only aggravated the problem of legitimacy, for it prevented the state from effectively implementing and consolidating its reformist agenda. Vincent notes, for instance, how the Republican program of reforms was not supported by taxation measures, how political participation still relied on clientelist networks that overwhelmingly favored the Confederación Española de Derechas Autónomas (CEDA)—a party that questioned the regime's legitimacy—and how the Republic's reliance on violence and military power to maintain public order alienated many on the revolutionary left (124–29).

Republican Reforms and Emotional Self-Control

How did intellectuals committed to the Republican project attempt to remedy this loss of legitimacy? Through what means did they seek to convince the Spanish public of the validity of the Republican regime? And, what role did emotions play in their endeavors to boost the Republic's legitimacy? To provide a partial answer to these questions, I turn to the writings of three intellectuals who, despite all their differences, used the periodical press to strengthen the regime's legitimacy by advocating emotional self-control. To be sure, Sagarra (1894–1961), Chaves Nogales (1897–1944), and Ayala (1906–2009) had clearly contrasting biographies and somewhat divergent political commitments—particularly with regard to Catalonia's status within Spain. In the early 1930s, Sagarra was a widely popular Catalan author who wrote regularly for the weekly magazine *Mirador* (1929–1936), where he had a column titled "L'aperitiu" ("Appetizer") devoted to a variety of cultural, social, and political topics; Chaves Nogales was a prestigious journalist and seasoned reporter who presided over the newsroom of *Ahora* (1930–1937), a newspaper clearly identified with the Republican project; and Ayala was an avant-garde writer who had put his literary career on hold to teach constitutional law, furnish legal advice to the Cortes, and write opinion pieces for newspapers such as *Diario de Alicante* (1907–1935), *Luz* (1932), and *El Sol* (1917–1939).[4] From a political viewpoint, Sagarra was a clear supporter of political Catalanism—in his youth he had been part of the Joventuts Nacionalistes of the conservative Lliga Regionalista and had briefly participated in the left-leaning Acció Catalana in 1934—whereas Chaves Nogales and Ayala were members of Acción Republicana, the moderate, left-wing republican party founded by Manuel Azaña, the main republican leader—Azaña often confided in Chaves Nogales and was an acquaintance of Ayala's.[5]

Despite these differences, all three intellectuals shared a number of basic beliefs that are essential to understand why and how they supported the Republican cause. For example, they shared the view that politics is an activity regulated by laws and mediated by institutions, a belief that put them at odds with the street politics of both left and right and the theory of direct action on which it relied—two features of Spanish political culture that had been condemned by Ortega y Gasset in his essay *España invertebrada*. Furthermore, they were equally convinced of the necessity of state power and aware that the exercise of such power often required a certain degree of violence. And, finally, their journalistic output was characterized by a steady concern with the emotional conduct of their readers, which they attempted to regulate by instilling a sense of civic duty in them. In the early days of the Republic, when "new meanings and values, new practices, new relationships . . . [were] continually being created" (Williams 123), they formulated opinions and advice on how to behave as ethical subjects of a democratic nation. More specifically, they identified emotions as a crucial dimension of their readers' conduct and thought that such emotions required moral reflection, seemingly aware of Azaña's insight that "únicamente como un resultado o un reflejo de la sumisión al deber moral nace la respetabilidad y el prestigio de quien gobierna" (only as a result or reflection of compliance with moral duty do governments enjoy respectability and prestige; Chaves Nogales 2: 1032). Guided by a shared sense of Republican moral duty, all three intellectuals encouraged their readers to control and moderate their emotions vis-à-vis Republican institutions and initiatives by invoking the virtues of reason. In general terms, they followed the positivist tradition that conceived of reason as a purely instrumental faculty, "as the ability to make valid inferences from premises established elsewhere, the ability to calculate means but not to determine ends" (Jaggar 51). And they conceived of emotions as "nonrational and often irrational urges that regularly swept the body, rather as a storm sweeps over the land" (Jaggar 51). Accordingly, they associated reason with "the mental, the cultural, the universal, the public, and the male," and emotion with "the irrational, the physical, the natural, the particular, the private, and, of course, the female" (Jaggar 50). In sum, all three contrasted the rational with the emotional and considered that there was an unbridgeable gap between reason and emotion.[6]

Another way to think about this connection between the rational control of emotions and political authority is to relate it to Weber's concept of legal-rational legitimacy, which he defines as resting on "a belief in the legality of enacted rules and the right of those elevated to authority under such rules to issue commands" (215). Although in Weber the concept lacks an explicit reference to emotions, this type of legitimacy, as we shall see, implies a certain dose of emotional self-control, especially when contrasted with charismatic legitimacy, which rests "on devotion to the exceptional sanctity, heroism or exemplary character of an individual person" (215). While the ascription of charismatic legitimacy to a social order is based on "affectual, especially emotional, faith" (36), and while charismatic figures, as noted above, emerge in extreme situations where people feel "enthusiasm . . . despair and hope" (242), the ascription of legal-rational legitimacy, as its name indicates, is an eminently rational operation. As such, it is based on beliefs that refer to enactments that are considered to be legal because either they derive "from a voluntary agreement of the interested parties" or they are imposed "by an authority which is held to be legitimate" (36). To put it schematically: the attribution of legal-rational legitimacy to a political order requires that emotions be held in check, whereas the establishment of a new, charismatic order calls for the mobilization of emotions.[7]

This was clearly understood by Sagarra, Chaves Nogales, and Ayala, who thought that controlling their readers' emotions was a necessary step in order to build trust in the Republic's legality and thus boost the political order's legal-rational authority. If, as Eva Illouz has observed, "much of social arrangements are also emotional arrangements" (3), the new social relations instituted by the Second Republic needed a rather balanced emotional culture to consolidate and stabilize its institutions. Concerned by the excessive emotions circulating among voters in the general election to the Constituent Cortes in June 1931, Sagarra advised his readers to moderate and control their emotions. This was not an easy task in the jubilant early days of the Republic, least of all for Sagarra himself, who confessed that "hi ha moments que fins m'esvero, en sentir el to de la meva veu en una discussió [política], un to de veu lúgubre, humit i tremolós, exactament igual que el d'un predicador que s'està dalt de la trona, amb els ulls en blanc i el cor ple de papallones inflamades" (there are moments in which I am alarmed by the tone of my voice in a [political] discussion, a lugubrious, humid, trembling tone, just like that of a preacher in his pulpit rolling his eyes, his heart inflamed; "Sobre les eleccions" [2 July 1931], in *El perfum* 183). But emotional control remained nonetheless a necessary task, one that Sagarra encouraged by welcoming the routinization of political life in the partial elections that took place a few months later in October 1931. Against those who decried the Catalan people's lack of excitement for those elections, he observed that "una bullida constant és un perjudici per tot; per consolidar les coses, fins per consolidar la República, fins per consolidar la felicitat, es necessita un ritme normal; el contrari és patologia o simple follia" (constant excitement only causes harm; to consolidate things, to consolidate the Republic, to consolidate happiness, it is necessary to get back into a normal rhythm; the contrary is pathological, is pure madness; "La tardor normal" [8 October 1931], in *El perfum* 213).

Much like Sagarra, Chaves Nogales and Ayala were aware of the importance of creating a sense of normalcy for Republican politics. After their own initial joy at the proclamation of the Republic, they immediately sought to manage the enthusiasm created by the new institutions and freedoms. In this regard, they were acutely conscious that, as Stephen Frosh writes, "a key element in social processes is how one is made to feel by them, and how much feeling infuses them" (77). As Frosh elaborates: "Social and institutional structures are contexts in which feeling is managed more or less well, in which people are prompted and provoked, encouraged and silenced, and as a consequence express in their feelings the dynamics of the social order itself" (83).

One year after the proclamation of the Republic, Chaves Nogales observed that the dynamics of the social order had continually fostered such intense enthusiasm that he thought it necessary to placate it. This is evident, for instance, in the series of chronicles he devoted to Alcalá Zamora's presidential visit to the eastern part of the country (Murcia, Cartagena, the Balearic Islands, and Valencia) to commemorate the Republic's first anniversary—all published in *Ahora* between 29 March and 7 April 1932. On the one hand, Chaves Nogales repeatedly registers, and at times seems to partake in, the enthusiasm of the people. He describes how Alcalá Zamora's arrival in Albacete is punctuated by "las manifestaciones de entusiasmo y los vítores [que] no cesan" (interminable manifestations of enthusiasm and cheers; 1: 286), how in Palma de Mallorca a multitude surrounded the presidential carriage "aclamando frenéticamente a Su Excelencia" (feverishly acclaiming His Excellency; 1: 315), and how in Valencia the public "pretendía entrarle en hombros en el Ayuntamiento" (wanted to carry him into City Hall on their shoulders; 1: 348). Chaves Nogales admits to being perplexed at the exhilaration provoked by Alcalá Zamora, attributing it to the fact that the president is "el símbolo de un régimen largos años anhelado" (the symbol of a long-yearned-for regime; 1: 291); most important, he seeks to placate the euphoria by anticipating its decline. "Todo está ahora en que la República no les defraude más que lo puramente indispensable; en la defraudación que fatalmente existe al hacerse realidad la ilusión" (The key now is that disappointment with the Republic be kept to a minimum, given that disappointment inevitably sets in when hope hits reality; 2: 292).

In much the same temperate vein, Ayala managed the emotions created by Republican institutions and legislation by suppressing them in a series of opinion pieces published in *Diario de Alicante* between September 1931 and April 1932. The display of calm, cool-headed rationality that characterizes these pieces is evident in the first article of the series devoted to the new parliament, which Ayala contrasts favorably with the old parliament of the monarchy. According to Ayala, the new parliament is a forum where its members, by employing authentic arguments "ajustados a la realidad" (that conform to reality), have the possibility of persuading each other "no precisamente por la oratoria, sino por la razón" (precisely not through oratory but through reason; "Viejo y nuevo Parlamento"). In Ayala's disapproval of oratory there is certainly a condemnation of the rhetorical emptiness of the old parliament—epitomized in the notorious oratorical flourishes of the late nineteenth-century republican politician Emilio Castelar (1832–1899)—but there is also an exaltation of rationality that requires the suppression of emotion. Although ever since Aristotle's *On Rhetoric* emotions have been known to shape and partially constitute persuasion, Ayala characterizes the Republican parliament as the house of reason, not emotions. For Ayala, the Republican Cortes is the place where persuasion is exclusively achieved through Aristotelian *logos*, not *pathos*, and where "la aceptación del argumento adversario, su examen, su honrado justiprecio" (to accept the adversary's argument, to examine it, and to evaluate it with honesty) is common practice.[8]

This serene view of parliamentary debates, no doubt the product of an enthusiastic idealization, has an important consequence: it attempts to manage the emotions created by Republican laws and institutions by dismissing or ignoring them. For instance, in a brief comment on the growing unrest experienced by the Republic in the summer and fall of 1931, Ayala ignores the uproar created by the Law of the Defense of the Republic passed on 21 October 1931, a law that was hardly democratic and was intensely protested by anarchists (Casanova, *Anarchism* 31), and simply states that "una vez promulgada ha restablecido automáticamente el orden público" (once promulgated, it has automatically restored public order; "La cuestión económica"), an assertion that would soon be refuted.

Sagarra's call to emotional moderation, Chaves Nogales's dampening of Republican enthusiasm, and Ayala's suppression of emotions inimical to the established order attempted to create what Alison Jaggar calls "emotional hegemony." The hegemony that a given society exercises over its people's "emotional constitution" is based, for Jaggar, on the fact that "within the very language of emotion, in our basic definitions and explanations of what it is to feel pride or embarrassment, resentment or contempt, cultural norms and expectations are embedded" (60). As Sagarra, Chaves Nogales, and Ayala knew well, the definition of cultural norms and expectations was a crucial arena for shaping the emotional constitution of their readers in the early days of the Republic. It is for this reason that the above interventions by these intellectuals can be seen as elaborations of two specific cultural standards: the ideal of emotional moderation and restraint (Sagarra and Chaves Nogales) and the view of the legislative process as a purely rational endeavor devoid of emotion (Ayala). What these cultural standards had in common is that they defined "perceptions and values" (Jaggar 61) that served the interests of the Republican order. Moreover, they contributed to the creation of an emotional culture based on two elements: the encouragement of practices of emotional self-control and the suppression of what Jaggar calls "outlaw" or "conventionally unacceptable" emotions (60). According to these authors, to be a good citizen of the Republic one needed either to be in control of one's emotions (so as to avoid acting them out) or to eliminate those emotions inimical to Republican legislation and institutions. When citizens were aware of their emotions and moderated them (Sagarra), when they reeducated their enthusiasm by accepting its demise (Chaves Nogales), and when they saw the legislative process as a purely rational procedure uncontaminated by negative emotions (Ayala), then the belief in the legality of rules enacted by the Republic was reinforced, and consequently its deficit in legitimacy was reduced. In short, the emotional hegemony designed by Sagarra, Chaves Nogales, and Ayala had a somewhat paradoxical quality: instead of imposing certain emotions beneficial to the political order, it sought to limit the positive emotions elicited by that order while at the same time suppressing those inimical to it.

As suggested above, the significance of emotions as a terrain of hegemonic struggle is most clearly appreciated when one considers the most controversial, emotionally charged issues on the Republican agenda: the religious question, Catalonia's political autonomy, and agrarian reform. With regard to the religious question, Ayala suppressed the intense emotions created by Republican legislation in his discussion of the religious clauses in the Constitution. These secularizing clauses were so saturated with emotion that many deputies refused to participate in the parliamentary debates, 233 deputies left the Chambers in the early hours of 14 October before the vote (Casanova, *The Spanish Republic* 33), and two prominent figures in the provisional Republican government resigned (the prime minister who later became president, Niceto Alcalá Zamora, and the interior minister, Miguel Maura). This was hardly a debate presided over by reason, but one would be hard-pressed to perceive an inkling of the storm caused by the secularizing clauses in Ayala's chronicle of these parliamentary sessions. Indeed, Ayala notes in a matter-of-fact tone the absence of deputies "de representación católica" (representing Catholic convictions) and the resignation of both Alcalá Zamora and Maura, but he quickly adds that parliament considered the religious question with a "criterio transigente" (tolerant outlook) and "reflexiones de templanza" (moderate thoughts; "Anales de quince días"). Ayala's article lacks any trace of emotion and thus makes the religious question look as dispassionate and ordinary as the reform of the judicial system that he discusses a few weeks later (see his "La reforma de la Magistratura").

Ayala's treatment of the parliamentary debates on the religious clauses in the Constitution smoothed over the sharp emotional edges to the point of suppressing them. He would later pursue the same strategy in an article titled "Política nacional de la República" ("The Republic's National Policy") published on 14 April 1933, to commemorate the Republic's second anniversary. There he insists that the new, diminished legal status of the Catholic Church simply seeks to "liberar al estado de la tutela y servicio de la Iglesia, relegando la religión al terreno 'privado'" (free the state from the Church's tutelage and service, confining religion to the "private" sphere). And he adds that this new status "no supone, como falazmente se ha dicho, persecución ninguna" (does not imply, as has been falsely stated, persecution of any kind whatsoever). Of course, the ecclesiastical hierarchy and many Catholics differed with Ayala's interpretation. Because they were unable to experience secularizing legislation as the outcome of an exclusively rational process, they perceived it as an attack on their beliefs, and they felt a growing hatred toward the Republic. The situation was so explosive that a leader of political Catholicism urged Catholics "to defend themselves from all these attacks, 'even with their blood'" (Casanova, *The Spanish Republic* 71). Faced with this contentious situation, Sagarra also attempted to negotiate the powerful emotions elicited by the church's diminished role in public life. Here, Sagarra once again advocated for a balanced emotional regime. Thus, in an article on the political debate on the Barcelona City Council's expulsion of the Jesuits, he advised his readers to master their emotions according to "el criteri liberal més moderat . . . [i] el més modest esperit de comprensió" (the most moderate liberal standard . . . [and] the most modest spirit of understanding) so as to avoid falling into the emotional excesses displayed by both anticlerical literature and Catholic propaganda ("Sobre els 'padres'" [28 May 1931], in *El perfum* 170–71).

Another Republican reform that elicited powerful emotions was the restoration of the Catalan executive and legislative branches (the Generalitat and the Parlament) and the granting of a statute of autonomy to Catalonia in 1932. Antonio Zugazagoitia y Frías's *Panfleto antiseparatista* (*Antiseparatist Pamphlet*), a text that was published when the Cortes was discussing Catalonia's statute of autonomy, is proof of the deep-seated hatred evoked by Catalonia's political demands in some leftist quarters. Hate, an emotion "involved in the very negotiation of boundaries between selves and others, and between communities, where 'others' are brought into the sphere of my or our existence as a threat" (Ahmed 257), is the driving force behind this rather unimaginative and repetitive diatribe against so-called separatists, "minorías despreciables y minúsculas, alimañas microscópicas, que, traicionando vilmente su historia y su raza, afrentan sus respectivos lugares con las más bajunas calumnias" (despicable and minuscule minorities, microscopic vermin that, after vilely betraying their history and race, crudely slander their respective territories; Zugazagoitia y Frías 48). Ayala, who like Chaves Nogales was supportive of the Republic's policies but was not enthusiastic about Catalonia's political demands, wrote a review of Zugazagoitia y Frías's *Panfleto antiseparatista* in March 1932. In that review, he sought to temper the author's hatred of Catalonia by noting that the intense emotions displayed "desde un punto de vista objetivo . . . carecen de razón de ser y responden a un prejuicio" (from an objective viewpoint . . . lack a raison d'être and are the product of prejudice). According to Ayala, Zugazagoitia y Frías's text is an unwelcome "muestra típica de actitud extrema" (typical example of an extreme attitude; "Problemas políticos"). In sharp contrast to Zugazagoitia y Frías, Sagarra described the new opportunities for cultural and political participation afforded by the Republic in terms of highly positive emotions. Writing from a clearly Catalanist perspective but much in line with Ayala's call for emotional moderation, he depicted the presentation of the statute of autonomy to the Spanish Cortes as an event that elicited a special kind of joy in him and in his fellow citizens, one that nonetheless did not overstep the limits imposed by serenity and self-mastery: "la nostra alegria va creixent; una mena de satisfacció d'ordre indefinible, un goig més perdurable, més líric, més serè que tots els espasmes" (our joy keeps growing; it is a kind of indefinable satisfaction, a joy that is more lasting, more lyrical, more serene than any spasm; "L'alegria més forta" [21 April 1932], in *El perfum* 256).

The last example of a highly emotional issue I would like to address concerns the disenchantment with the Republic's program of agrarian reform, a disenchantment that fueled one of the most tragic episodes of anarchist radicalism that subverted the Republic's public order: the armed insurrection that took place in Casas Viejas (Cádiz) in January 1933 and that was brutally crushed by Civil and Assault Guards in what has been described as a true massacre (see Casanova, *Anarchism* 70–72). In keeping with their creation of a balanced emotional culture, Chaves Nogales and Ayala treated these episodes as another occasion to suppress emotions against the Republican order and to encourage practices of emotional self-control. Chaves Nogales not only dismissed the intense emotions underlying anarcho-syndicalist revolts as "la bravata impresionante de los que . . . son incapaces de una reacción inteligente" (the striking bravado of those who . . . are incapable of an intelligent reaction; 3: 1433), but he also ended up laying blame for the events on anarcho-syndicalist propagandists and, significantly, on those who did not dare "alzar frente a ellos la voz de su razón" (raise the voice of reason against the anarchists) through democratic counter propaganda (3: 1438). Much as in Ayala, the invocation of reason serves to reinforce existing institutions by suppressing negative emotions. For his part, Ayala advised his readers to moderate their emotions with regard to both the revolutionaries and the Republican institutions. With respect to the former, he wrote, "Una conciencia republicana no puede sentir odio ni repugnancia contra esos campesinos exaltados, sino tan sólo el dolor de su aberración" (a Republican conscience cannot feel hatred nor revulsion for those irate peasants but only sorrow at their aberration); with respect to the latter, he urged his readers to curb their enthusiasm and their expectations of change, adding that their Republican fervor "se integra de esperanzas, de promesas, que comienzan sólo a tomar cuerpo de realidad" (is made of hopes and promises that are only beginning to take shape as reality; "La conciencia republicana").

Conclusion: The Irruption of Charismatic Forces

To be sure, the creation of this balanced emotional culture was a gender-specific and class-specific political project that operated within the assumptions of bourgeois culture. The gendered nature of the balanced emotional regime advocated by Sagarra, Chaves Nogales, and Ayala is clearly seen not only in their association of the practices of emotional self-control with a markedly masculinist sense of pride, but also in their views on the Republican legislative efforts to promote gender equality. Sagarra, for instance, lamented the passing of a law by the Catalan Parliament in June 1934 that entitled women to freely manage their properties on the grounds that "de disposar dels béns i d'administrar el capital en sabem molt més els homes que les dones" (men know much more than women about how to transfer property and manage capital; "El dret de les dones" [28 June 1934], in *El perfum* 387). In a similar vein, Chaves Nogales's newspaper *Ahora* weighed in on the debate on women's suffrage in the Constituent Cortes affirming that "la mujer española no está preparada para intervenir en la vida pública" (Spanish women are not ready to participate in public life; quoted in Campoamor 150). And finally Ayala, also commenting on the social debates on female suffrage, acknowledged that it was an issue that "en su día apasionó a la opinión pública" (in its day, was passionately discussed by the public). Thereafter he quickly—and predictably—suppressed any trace of emotion when touching on the parliamentary debates on this matter, simply noting, "Triunfó en la Cámara el criterio favorable [al voto femenino]" (The opinion favorable to women's suffrage triumphed in Parliament; "Anales de quince días").

Given Ayala's rational, cool-headed treatment of the parliamentary debates on women's suffrage, it may prove useful to contrast it with that of Clara Campoamor. Unlike Ayala, Campoamor (1888–1972), who was a member of the Radical Party and a crucial figure in securing political equality for women, did not see parliament as the house of reason and of dispassionate argumentation. In fact, her fascinating account of the parliamentary debate that took place on women's suffrage in the fall of 1931 is rich with references to emotions. For instance, she notes that "el primero de octubre fue el gran día del *histerismo masculino*, dentro y fuera del Parlamento" (the first of October was the great day of *masculine hysteria* both inside and outside of Parliament; 113), and she goes on to argue that this "nerviosidad e irritación masculinas" (masculine nervousness and irritability; 113) are based on men's fear of women, which she labels as "un miedo ancestral, subconsciente, casi biológico" (an ancestral, subconscious, quasi-biological fear; 125). In sharp contrast to Ayala's view of the legislative process as a purely rational endeavor, Campoamor uncovered its emotional dimension and, in doing so, contested the masculinist emotional hegemony designed by Ayala.

In terms of class, the balanced emotional regime advocated by Sagarra, Chaves Nogales, and Ayala revealed its bourgeois affiliation in, for example, the political positions taken by Chaves Nogales and Ayala with regard to the episodes of anarchist insurrection (see above). Having such an affiliation, this emotional regime was a fragile endeavor that was bound to be questioned by both the revolutionary left and right, two movements that had worked relentlessly to undermine the cultural principles of the bourgeoisie since at least the end of the Great War. As César Arconada, a former avant-garde writer turned Communist, succinctly put it: "el esplendor de la burguesía acaba con la guerra, que fue la zarabanda codiciosa de la burguesía mundial" (the bourgeoisie's splendor came to an end with the war, which was the rapacious free-for-all of the worldwide bourgeoisie; 117).

The climate of uncertainty, radicalization, and insurrection that took over Spanish politics after 1933 clearly shows that Sagarra's, Chaves Nogales's, and Ayala's endeavors ultimately failed. Their attempt to create an emotional hegemony that would consolidate the Republic's legal-rational legitimacy proved unsuccessful. At that point in time, as Vincent writes, the "fashionable doctrine" was that "legitimacy, the popular will, could be demonstrated, on the streets rather than in the polling booth" (134). The reasons for this failure are certainly manifold. But it can be argued that the collapse of the Republic's legitimacy lies, at least in part, in the irruption of what Weber called charismatic forces, unleashing and mobilizing powerful affects that, combined with the social discontent and fear dominating Spanish politics, crippled the Republic's legitimacy.[9]

As we already have seen, these forces included revolutionary syndicalism, which for Weber was a charismatic movement in that it sought "to change the value system and ethical attitudes of its followers and supporters, to delegitimate the symbolic and normative foundation of the established political authority, to generate a new legitimation discourse, and to form a new collective will" (Kalyvas 65). They also incorporated prestigious intellectuals such as Miguel de Unamuno and José Ortega y Gasset, two figures who originally lent their support to the Republican project but shortly thereafter deserted it. Much like a heroic, plebiscitary political leader that demands "a highly emotional type of devotion to and trust in" his leadership (Weber 269), Ortega y Gasset famously urged Spaniards to rectify the course of the Republic as early as December 1931 (*Obras* 837–55). These charismatic forces also encompassed figures like José Antonio Primo de Rivera, the leader of Falange Española, a party adept at brandishing a Fascist-inspired emotional rhetoric against the rationalism of parliamentary democracy. With the Falange's use of Fascist national myth, my argument comes full circle back to Carl Schmitt and his contention that the national myth evokes "more powerful emotions" (75) than the Marxist myth of class conflict. It certainly did for Falange doctrine, which was imbued with both the myth of national unity and the myth of empire. While the former was rooted in José Antonio Primo de Rivera's assertion that "the nation is a transcendental synthesis, an indivisible synthesis with a finality of its own" (54), the latter originated in the convictions of figures such as Ramiro Ledesma Ramos and Onésimo Redondo, for whom the myth of empire was necessary for Spain "to rule over itself as well as over other countries and thus become a unified territory and an authoritarian state" (Santiáñez 172). As Schmitt had predicted, the political horizon was now determined by the confrontation of two myths. In this battle between two essentially emotional forces, the establishment of a legal-rational legitimacy for the Republic through a balanced emotional regime appeared as an optimistic delusion, the remnant of an age in which emotions had perhaps never been dominated by reason but had somehow been directed, moderated, and channeled by it.

NOTES

1. Barbalet offers a fascinating account of the role of emotions in Weber's sociology, particularly their importance for Weber's later treatment of the concept of *Beruf* or vocation.
2. Although there are many Spanish testimonies of the political situation in Italy and Germany, those of Chabás and Xammar stand out.
3. My very brief description of the Republic's first biennium relies on Casanova, *The Spanish Republic* 27–48. Although I cannot here address other crucial reforms such as those relating to the reorganization of the army, the educational system, and labor legislation, my argument about the creation of emotional hegemony applies to them too.
4. The newspaper articles published by Ayala are also available in his *Obras completas*, vol. 7, issued in late October 2014 after this essay was written. For Sagarra's life, see Permanyer; for that of Chaves Nogales, see Cintas Guillén; for that of Ayala, see García Montero.
5. Chaves Nogales published an interview with Azaña in *Ahora* (2: 1024–50) and Ayala a laudatory review of his book *Una política (1930–1932)* in *Luz* ("El libro").
6. The contrast between reason and emotion was also understood at the time in terms of a contrast between the individual and the masses—exemplary of this is Ortega's 1922

allusion to "la rebelión sentimental de las masas" (the sentimental rebellion of the masses) in *España invertebrada* (208), a theme he would later pursue in *La rebelión de las masas* (1930); or Romain Rolland's assertion, in the spring of 1914, that "we live in a time of mass emotion, mass hysteria" (quoted in Zweig 211). For an alternative account of reason and emotion as they relate to epistemology, see Jaggar.

7. I am well aware that legal-rational, charismatic, and traditional legitimacy are what Weber called "ideal types." In other words, they are conceptual tools with which to approach concrete forms of authority, which often contain a mixture of the three types of legitimacy—including traditional legitimacy, which I do not discuss here given the radical novelty of Republican institutions.

8. According to Aristotle, *pathos* alludes to persuasion that takes place "through the hearers when they are led to feel emotion . . . by the speech" (39, 1356a), and *logos* concerns persuasion through "the arguments [*logoi*] when we show the truth or the apparent truth from whatever is persuasive in each case" (39, 1356a).

9. Here I have benefited greatly from Villacañas Berlanga's reflections on the charisma of intellectuals ("El carisma").

WORKS CITED

Abu-Lughod, Lila, and Catherine A. Lutz. "Emotion, Discourse, and the Politics of Everyday Life." *Emotions: A Cultural Studies Reader*. Ed. Jennifer Harding and E. Deirdre Pribram. London: Routledge, 2009. 100–12.

Ahmed, Sara. "The Organisation of Hate." *Emotions: A Cultural Studies Reader*. Ed. Jennifer Harding and E. Deirdre Pribram. London: Routledge, 2009. 251–66.

Arconada, César M. "Quince años de literatura española." *Los novelistas sociales españoles (1928–1936)*. Ed. José Esteban and Gonzalo Santonja. Barcelona: Anthropos, 1988. 114–22.

Aristotle. *On Rhetoric: A Theory of Civic Discourse*. New York: Oxford UP, 2007.

Ayala, Francisco. "Anales de quince días." *Diario de Alicante* 23 October 1931: 2.

———. "La conciencia republicana ante las perturbaciones sociales." *Luz* 13 January 1933: 1.

———. "La cuestión económica." *Diario de Alicante* 11 November 1931: 2.

———. "El libro de Azaña: *Una política (1930–1932)*." *Luz* 5 December 1932: 2.

———. *Obras completas*. Vol. 2. *Autobiografía(s)*. Ed. Carolyn Richmond. Barcelona: Galaxia Gutenberg; Círculo de Lectores, 2010.

———. *Obras completas*. Vol. 7. *Confrontaciones y otros escritos (1923–2006)*. Ed. Carolyn Richmond. Barcelona: Galaxia Gutenberg; Círculo de Lectores, 2014.

———. "Política nacional de la República." *El Sol* 14 April 1933: 6.

———. "Problemas políticos." *Luz* 25 March 1932: 1.

———. "La reforma de la Magistratura." *Diario de Alicante* 8 December 1931: 2.

———. "Viejo y nuevo Parlamento." *Diario de Alicante* 9 September 1931: 1.

Barbalet, J. M. "*Beruf*, Rationality and Emotion in Max Weber's Sociology." *Archives Européennes de Sociologie* 41 (2000): 329–50.

Benda, Julien. *The Treason of the Intellectuals*. Trans. Richard Aldington. New York: Norton, 1969.

Benjamin, Walter. *Selected Writings*. Vol. 2. *1927–1934*. Ed. Michael W. Jennings, Howard Eiland, and Gary Smith. Trans. Rodney Livingstone et al. Cambridge, MA: Harvard UP, 1999.

Campoamor, Clara. *Mi pecado mortal: El voto femenino y yo*. Seville: Instituto Andaluz de la Mujer, 2001.

Casanova, Julián. *Anarchism, the Republic and Civil War in Spain, 1931–1939*. Trans. Andrew Dowling and Graham Pollok. London: Routledge, 2005.

———. *The Spanish Republic and Civil War*. Trans. Martin Douch. Cambridge: Cambridge UP, 2010.

Chabás, Juan. *Italia fascista (política y literatura)*. Ed. José Luis Villacañas Berlanga. Valencia: Biblioteca Valenciana, 2002.

Chaves Nogales, Manuel. *Obra periodística*. Ed. María Isabel Cintas Guillén. 3 vols. Seville: Diputación de Sevilla, 2013.

Cintas Guillén, María Isabel. *Chaves Nogales: El oficio de contar*. Seville: Fundación José Manuel Lara, 2011.

Flatley, Jonathan. *Affective Mapping: Melancholia and the Politics of Modernism*. Cambridge, MA: Harvard UP, 2008.

Frosh, Stephen. *Feelings*. London: Routledge, 2011.

García Montero, Luis. *Francisco Ayala: El escritor en su siglo*. Granada: Publicaciones Diputación de Granada, 2009.

Illouz, Eva. *Cold Intimacies: The Making of Emotional Capitalism*. Cambridge: Polity, 2007.

Jaggar, Alison M. "Love and Knowledge." *Emotions: A Cultural Studies Reader*. Ed. Jennifer Harding and E. Deirdre Pribram. London: Routledge, 2009. 50–68.

Juliá, Santos, ed. *Violencia política en la España del siglo XX*. Madrid: Taurus, 2000.

Kalyvas, Andreas. *Democracy and the Politics of the Extraordinary: Max Weber, Carl Schmitt, and Hannah Arendt*. Cambridge: Cambridge UP, 2008.

Ortega y Gasset, José. *España invertebrada: Bosquejos de algunos pensamientos históricos*. Ed. Francisco José Martín. Madrid: Biblioteca Nueva, 2002.

———. *Obras completas*. Vol. 4. *1926–1931*. Madrid: Taurus, 2005.

Payne, Stanley G. *Spain's First Democracy: The Second Republic, 1931–1936*. Madison: U of Wisconsin P, 1993.

Permanyer, Lluís. *Sagarra, vist pels seus íntims*. Barcelona: La Campana, 1991.

Primo de Rivera, José Antonio. *Selected Writings*. Ed. Hugh Thomas. Trans. Gudie Lawaetz. London: Jonathan Cape, 1972.

Sagarra, Josep Maria de. *El perfum dels dies: Articles a Mirador (1929–1936)*. Ed. Narcís Garolera. Barcelona: Quaderns Crema, 2004.

Santiáñez, Nil. *Topographies of Fascism: Habitus, Space, and Writing in Twentieth-Century Spain*. Toronto: U of Toronto P, 2013.

Schmitt, Carl. *The Crisis of Parliamentary Democracy*. Trans. Ellen Kennedy. Cambridge, MA: MIT P, 1988.

Villacañas Berlanga, José Luis. "El carisma imposible: Una crítica de los intelectuales españoles de primeros de siglo." *Pensar lo público: Reflexiones políticas desde la España contemporánea*. Ed. Francisco Colom González. Medellín: U Pontificia Bolivariana, 2005. 125–51.

———. *Historia del poder político en España*. Barcelona: RBA, 2014.

Vincent, Mary. *Spain 1833–2002: People and State.* Oxford: Oxford UP, 2007.
Weber, Max. *Economy and Society: An Outline of Interpretive Sociology.* Ed. Guenther Roth and Claus Wittich. Trans. Ephraim Fischoff et al. Vol. 1. Berkeley: U of California P, 2013.
Williams, Raymond. *Marxism and Literature.* Oxford: Oxford UP, 1977.
Xammar, Eugenio. *Crónicas desde Berlín (1930–1936).* Ed. Charo González Prada. Barcelona: Acantilado, 2005.
Zambrano, María. *Horizonte del liberalismo.* Ed. Jesús Moreno Sanz. Madrid: Morata, 1996.
Zugazagoitia y Frías, Antonio. *Panfleto antiseparatista en defensa de España.* Madrid: Compañía General de Artes Gráficas, 1932.
Zweig, Stefan. *The World of Yesterday: An Autobiography.* Lincoln: U of Nebraska P, 1964.

CHAPTER 9

Love in Times of War
Female Frigidity and Libertarian Revolution in the Work of Anarchist Doctor Félix Martí Ibáñez

MAITE ZUBIAURRE

Critics have written extensively about Iberian anarchism and sexuality, in particular about the eugenics movement and the strong prejudice against homosexuality common among libertarian thinkers.[1] However, other aspects of sexuality pertaining to the female libido (or lack thereof) have barely been touched on in the context of anarchist thought. This chapter looks at female frigidity as represented in a selection of writings by anarchist doctor and thinker Félix Martí Ibáñez, including essays from the years 1936 and 1937 and his "Consultorio Psíquico-Sexual" ("Psycho-Sexual Advice Column"), which was published from 1936 to 1937 in the Valencian anarchist and eugenicist magazine *Estudios*.[2] This libertarian advice column sought to remedy a series of sexual ailments, female anaphrodisia figuring prominently among them. The majority of the texts I will discuss were published after the start of the Spanish Civil War (1936–1939), with some appearing in the months of violent unrest that preceded it. As the pages that follow try to show, the specific historical context of violent conflict not only influenced Martí Ibáñez's theories on the workings (and failings) of the female libido but, more important, hampered his efforts at acknowledging the right of women to erotic emotion.

One of Spain's most prominent anarchist intellectuals, Martí Ibáñez graduated as a psychiatrist from the University of Barcelona in 1934. In October 1936, after the Civil War's outbreak in July, he was named deputy secretary for health and social welfare in the Catalan government (Generalitat) at a time when the city was effectively under anarchist control. During his ten-month period in office, he was able to put forward many important health reforms, among them the legalization of abortion.[3] The ultimate goal of Martí Ibáñez's highly popular and unprecedented "Consultorio Psíquico-Sexual" in *Estudios* was to alleviate "sexual problems" (such as female frigidity, onanism, sexual superstitions, lesbianism, and, to a lesser extent, male homosexuality) within the context of the Revolution, as a means to invigorate libertarian ideals through sexual health. As Vidal explains (18–19), each issue of *Estudios* had fifty-six pages, of which four to five were devoted to the counseling section. The section addressed sex and sexuality clearly and directly. The format used by Martí Ibáñez was almost always the same: first, his abridged and edited version of the question (most of the letter writers were women), followed by his answer, structured as follows: introduction to the subject, offering a "scientific" explanation; development of the ideas; and a provisional conclusion since a definitive conclusion depended on the coming of the Revolution. Martí Ibáñez noted that the first step was to make sure patients explained the problem well in their letters, setting out the individual details; these individualized cases were then integrated into a far-reaching scientific, pedagogic, and political project. As he specified: "La educación sexual de la nueva generación comprende dos facetas: la estrictamente médico-higiénica, la enseñanza eugénica que se recibe en las obras científicas escritas al efecto, y la preparación psicosexual, el aprendizaje de la espontaneidad amorosa y la sinceridad sexual" (The sexual education of the new generation comprises two aspects: the strictly medical-hygienic aspect, the eugenic teachings provided by scientific works on the subject, and psycho-sexual training, which teaches how to love with spontaneity and sexual sincerity; "Las actitudes" 12).

"Love" is a prevalent subject in anarchist thought, with topics such as eugenics, sexual education, and free (heterosexual) attachments as an alternative to institutional marriage copiously filling the pages of libertarian books and magazines. But "love" is also a tenacious euphemism that more often than not stands for unabashed sexual desire, or plain (and dangerous) "lust." Sexual desire is anything but simple or unproblematically celebrated in the context of anarchism. Libertarians, Martí Ibáñez included, frown on "lust," and specifically the female sexual impulse, as an "emotion" or "passion" that systematically defies control. With alarming ease it becomes either "too much" (in which case, in consonance with the sexological wisdom of the time, it systematically "degenerates" into compulsive onanism, lesbianism, hysteria, nymphomania, and prostitution) or "too little," turning women into frigid ice blocks. In his 1937 essay "Una nueva moral sexual como base de las conquistas revolucionarias" ("A New Sexual Morality as a Basis for Revolutionary Conquests"), Martí Ibáñez defined the ideal of sexuality as understood and defended by anarchist thought. Equally repelled by the two extremes of love—"un libertinaje doloroso, o un seco ascetismo" (a painful debauchery or a dry ascetism; 126)—he proclaimed: "Ni libertinaje ni monaquismo. El sexo ha de surgir del crisol revolucionario purificado y límpido. Con alas para volar libremente, pero con una aguja náutica que marque un rumbo determinado" (We say no to sexual licentiousness, but no also to monasticism. Sex must emerge purified and cleansed from the crucible of [anarchist] revolution. It needs wings to fly freely, but also a compass able to set a specific course; 128).

The insistent reference to "purified" love and to the (oxymoronic) ideal of sexuality as both "free" and "controlled" anxiously permeates Martí Ibáñez's writings. Among all the "passions," the only one Martí Ibáñez holds dear is "revolutionary passion" ("Una nueva moral" 128). But "revolutionary emotion," as he also calls it, suffers the continuous assault of yet another "passion" or "emotion": "Sobre la red de incertidumbre y preocupación colectivas, flota pavoroso el nubarrón sexual, cargado de inquietudes y plasmando uno de los eternos e insoluble enigmas de la Humanidad" (Above the tissue of collective uncertainty and concern, there hovers the menacing sexual cloud, laden with anxieties and forming one of the eternal, insoluble enigmas of Humanity; "Una nueva moral" 126). "Sexual emotion" is thus the ill-fitting piece—the terrifying enigma defying reason—that systematically distorts the anarchist utopia of "clean" bodies and "limpid" minds working together as well-oiled machines. *Mens sana in corpore sano* (A healthy mind in a healthy body), Martí Ibáñez consistently acknowledges in his writings, needs the complement of *"animus sanus"* (a healthy spirit) since an ailing emotional state or an unruly sexuality will unavoidably compromise the well-being of body and mind in the service of libertarian revolution.

Needless to say, Martí Ibáñez's musings on the female sexual drive (or lack thereof) and its "emotional" complications (or "psychic" ailments, as he prefers to call them, for the sake of "scientific" rigor) are by no means unique. A long Western tradition has complicated or demonized the erotic impulse, seen as an often destructive passion. Within that frame and in early twentieth-century Spain, Martí Ibáñez's reflections on female desire are notably similar to those of nonlibertarian thinkers such the philosopher José Ortega y Gasset or the writer and cultural critic Luis Torres del Hoyo. For example, Ortega y Gasset's *Estudios sobre el amor* (*Studies on Love*), whose core essays were published in the newspaper *El Sol* from 1926 to 1927, establishes a clear distinction between "el amor espiritualista" (spiritualist love), and its lesser cousin, "el enamoramiento" (falling in love or infatuation). The former favors distance, both spatial and temporal: it is the type of love that permeates the platonic idealism typical of chivalric literature. By contrast the latter—which Ortega also calls "amor corporalista" (corporalist, or bodily, love)—is incapable of intellectual *froideur*: intensely emotional, it favors irrational manifestations of love and often diverts into the orgiastic (Zubiaurre 93–94). Torres del Hoyo's widely read volume *La emoción erótica* (*Erotic Emotion*, 1927) similarly distinguishes between different types of emotions that come under the heading of "love." Thus his introduction lists "erotic emotion" alongside "mystical emotion" (*emoción mística*), "patriotic emotion" (*emoción patriótica*), and "artistic emotion" (*emoción artística*). Like Martí Ibáñez, Torres del Hoyo finds erotic emotion an inscrutable enigma, of which only one aspect—falling in love or infatuation (*enamoramiento*)—has been sufficiently explored. But love, which Torres del Hoyo writes in capital letters, is much more than "merely" falling in love. For him, "AMOR" (LOVE) is the ultimate emotion, to be distinguished from "en segundo término una forma rudimentaria aún, el deseo, y otra borrosa y despreciable por frívola en exceso, el *flirt*" (at a secondary level a still rudimentary form, desire, and another form that is vague and despicable because of its excessive frivolity, flirtation; Torres del Hoyo 12). In regarding sexual desire as a "lesser" form of love, Ortega and Torres del Hoyo position it at a lower point on a hierarchical emotional scale. The same view of sexual desire as a "lower" emotion is found in Martí Ibáñez.

Like other anarchist thinkers, Martí Ibáñez shares with his contemporaries Ortega and Torres del Hoyo a revulsion toward the "lesser" aspects of "Love"—namely, amorous frivolity in the form of flirtation, crass sensuality, mercenary concupiscence, and even naïve sentimentalism and (pseudo) romanticism. This revulsion is particularly strong when the flirtatious subject is female. In his 1936 article "Mensaje eugénico a la mujer" ("Eugenic Message for Women"), Martí Ibáñez is quick to condemn female flirtatiousness. Addressing a group of *milicianas* (militiawomen), he admonishes:

> No podéis . . . iniciar flirteos en apariencia sin consecuencias, pero que dejan en ambos labios la sed de agua que tan sólo [los humedeció]. Biológicamente, el flirteo es un defraudamiento y una mutilación; socialmente una odiosa frivolidad; sexualmente un prólogo vacío de sentido. Pero en época de guerra, el encender ansias que ya no se apagarán y dejarán al hombre luchando con un tiránico enemigo interno es además una traición. (10)

> (You cannot . . . initiate supposedly harmless and inconsequential flirtation for it will make the lips of both parties all the more thirsty for the water that merely moistened them. From a biological point of view, flirtation is a fraud and a mutilation; from a social perspective, it is frivolity of the most odious kind; and from the angle of sexuality, a mere prologue empty of any real meaning. But in times of war, to kindle desires that will not be quenched and will set men fighting against a tyrannical interior enemy is treason, on top of everything else.)

Throughout the article and not only in the paragraph quoted above, Martí Ibáñez uses war as an "excuse" to carefully dissect female sexual emotions and behaviors, flirtation being the more benign and less harmful among them. Or, rather, he uses women's sexual "debauchery" as a pretext to reclaim war as a scenario solely apt for men. "Mensaje eugénico a la mujer" was first published in the December 1936 issue of *Estudios*, two months after its author was named deputy secretary for health and social welfare in revolutionary Catalonia. It not only clearly depicts Martí Ibáñez's political and ideological conviction that, ultimately, women were a health hazard to revolutionaries and therefore had to be removed from the front, but also foreshadows what would occur later, in May 1937, when the pressures to integrate independent militias (many of them anarchist) into the regular army grew, and milicianas were forced to relinquish their weapons for good. In 1937, this article became part of a slim volume *Tres mensajes para la mujer* (*Three Messages for Women*) that included two more essays by Martí Ibáñez: "Mensaje a la mujer obrera" ("Message to Proletarian Women"), and "La mujer en la Revolución" ("Women in the Revolution"). All three articles glorify "la emoción revolucionaria" (revolutionary emotion) as an essentially virile emotion superior to female libidinous longings. Martí Ibáñez's premise is that war exacerbates the latter, and that women become "¡víctimas de la acre emanación sensual de la guerra, del erotismo exacerbado que la muerte despierta! . . . La compensación de la muerte la busca la Biología exacerbando los instintos genésicos, lo cual, unido a la ausencia de responsabilidad en los amenazados por el peligro, provoca ese frenético abrazo voluptuoso de hombres y mujeres durante la guerra, en cuyo fondo late la ansiedad de crear más vida que compense la que se marcha" (victims of the acrid sensuality emanating from war and of the exacerbated eroticism aroused by death! . . . Biology exacerbates the sexual instinct to compensate for the loss of life. This, coupled with the lack of responsibility typical in situations of danger, is what provokes the frantic, voluptuous embrace of men and women in times of war, driven by the urge to create new life to make up for the lives destroyed; "Mensaje eugénico a la mujer" 10).

This observation, presented as historically and scientifically "proven," allows Martí Ibáñez to highlight women's sexual shortcomings and their penchant for erotic excess. Against the violent, lawless backdrop of military conflict, female sexuality shows its true colors, with sudden, shocking vividness. We learn that, on the battleground, women do what they always do, supposedly, but with far less restraint: they flirt and seduce; they fall prey to over-the-top sentimentalism and romantic longings; they become victims of unchecked sensuality; and they openly sell their bodies ostensibly for the sake of Revolution and in reality to satisfy their own mercenary needs.

Indeed, Martí Ibáñez deems it useful to construct a "typology" of the miliciana along these lines. "True" milicianas are few, according to him, with the overwhelming majority falling within one of the following categories of female combatant: the romantic (who mistakenly believes that "war is a novel" and buys into the romanticized depictions of violence to be found routinely in bourgeois high letters); the sensual (who, under the potent spell of a misguided sexual instinct, robs the male soldier of the energy he needs to fight and survive); and the mercenary (who turns the battleground, drenched in proletarian blood, into a love bed). And for all these types of miliciana—the romantic, the sensual, and the mercenary—Martí Ibáñez has the same advice, given with a sense of urgency and even impertinent exasperation: "¡Retornad a la Retaguardia! La guerra es cosa de hombres. . . . La enfermedad venérea debe ser extirpada del frente, y para ello, hay que eliminar previamente a las mujeres. ¡Id voluntariamente a retaguardia! Aquí os aguardan las máquinas de coser, los talleres, las fábricas, todos aquellos sitios donde antes trabajó el miliciano, y que hoy deben ser ocupados por las mujeres. . . . ¡¡A trabajar todas!! . . . ¡La Revolución os lo exige!" (Go back to the rearguard! War is for men only. . . . Venereal diseases need to be extirpated from the frontline, and for this to happen, women must be eliminated first. Go back to the rearguard voluntarily! Here, sewing machines, workshops, and factories are waiting for you, all those places where militiamen used to work but that now need to be occupied by women. . . . Go back to work, all of you!! . . . The Revolution demands it!; "Mensaje eugénico a la mujer" 11)

Martí Ibáñez starts this December 1936 article by emphasizing the need for women to relinquish the "individual" heroism of the first milicianas and to engage in collective action: "A la heroína, a la sacerdotisa, a la mística agitadora, a la indomable guerrillera, han de reemplazar ya ejércitos silenciosos y anónimos, pero entusiastas y fecundos, de mujeres ... dispuestas a aceptar el sino de trabajo y sacrificio que el Destino les marca" (Female heroes, priestesses, mystical agitators, indomitable guerrilla fighters need to be replaced with armies—silent and anonymous, but nonetheless enthusiastic and fecund—of women ... willing to accept the work and sacrifice that Destiny has in store for them; "Mensaje eugénico a la mujer" 7–8). Revolution thus demands of women that the collective replace the individual; anonymity, the heroic; and the drudgery of industrial work, the excitement of battle.

An outspoken and successful defender of (some) women's sexual rights—one should not forget that Martí Ibáñez was responsible for legalizing abortion in Catalonia, and a tireless listener to and dissector of female erotic emotions in his essayistic work and sexual advice column—in the above article he nonetheless fails to support or even acknowledge such emotions. Female erotic emotions, in Martí Ibáñez's essays, and particularly in "Mensaje eugénico a la mujer," appear as flat and lifeless, with women reduced once again to dim-witted romantics and flirtatious flappers, at best, and to dangerous seducers (who spread venereal diseases) and vampiric predators (sucking much-needed energy out of heroic revolutionaries), at worst. In fact, women ultimately are reduced to "de-eroticized" and "de-emotionalized" entities, an anonymous mass that should retreat to the exploitative and remarkably un-erotic drudgery of factory work, and leave behind the heavily sensualized battle/play ground. We should remember here that it was a commonplace in the early twentieth century, even in countries like Spain that did not fight in World War I, to regard the battlefield as an intensely sexualized locus, where emotions of a homoerotic nature effectively enhanced war's intrinsic and vigorous sensuality—see, for example, renowned writer Rafael Cansinos Assens's *Estética y erotismo de la guerra* (*Aesthetics and Eroticism of War*, 1916) or the less well known sexologist Ángel Martín de Lucenay's *El erotismo en la guerra y en la revolución* (*Eroticism in War and Revolution*, 1934). Martí Ibáñez's anxiety about, and sexualization of, women's role in war suggests that his enthusiasm for "revolutionary emotion" shares something of the contemporary fascination with war as the supreme incarnation of an eroticized virility.

As often happens with male "pseudo" feminists, Martí Ibáñez was able to rationally grasp misogyny, and even openly challenge sexist misconceptions, but he could not "feel" for women, nor could he refrain from trying to control what he, and the great majority of his male fellow anarchists, feared, and perceived as the disorderly and unpredictable (sexual) emotions of females. It is important to note that the contradictory combination of rational acknowledgment of women's rights and lack of a true understanding of female emotion was present not only in the works of Martí Ibáñez, but also in those of intellectuals not necessarily tied to anarchist thought, among them, illustrious endocrinologist and liberal thinker Gregorio Marañón. Not unlike Martí Ibáñez, the latter defended the rights of women, some of them at least, such as the right to receive education (although not for the sake of the mother but for that of the offspring) or the right to work (although only for single women, or during exceptional circumstances such as war; *Tres ensayos*). And no less than Martí Ibáñez, Marañón also tried anxiously to control the emotional and sexual lives of women by emphasizing maternal instinct and downplaying female erotic pleasure. For both Marañón and Martí Ibáñez, "excessive" sexual emotionality was an indicator of pathology, and women "suffering" from it were invariably reduced to a clinical case in need of urgent cure. For Marañón the "cure" was motherhood as the imprint of radical sexual differentiation, while for Martí Ibáñez it was deep commitment to the anarchist cause.

Thus in accordance with the Zeitgeist, both Marañón and Martí Ibáñez anxiously puzzled over the extreme erotic "emotionality" of women and were always on the watch for a conciliatory—and occasionally (pseudo) feminist—"solution." In the case of Martí Ibáñez, any such "solution" was inextricably tied to the goals of the Revolution and its propagandistic apparatus. In fact, Martí Ibáñez believed that, in order to "prevent" and "cure" sexual and emotional extremes, vociferous propaganda that approached females as an "abstract" and depersonalized collective identity (in the style of "Mensaje eugénico a la mujer") was required but not enough. Instead, what was needed, in addition to incendiary public discourses, was the more soft-spoken discussion and "scientific" dissection of "individual" cases extracted from (sexual) quotidian experience, following the lead of the "clinical histories" so abundantly collected (or invented) by popular sexology, foreign and national. As Javier Navarro Navarro aptly points out,

> uno de los aspectos que definían la originalidad de los planteamientos libertarios . . . era la creencia en la posibilidad de abordar la transformación de la sociedad desde lo cotidiano. Es en ese énfasis en lo personal, en la praxis diaria, en lo que hay que enmarcar la insistencia ácrata en el cambio de actitudes en ámbitos como la sexualidad . . . , el papel de la mujer en la sociedad . . . , y la asimilación y divulgación de conocimientos médicos y científicos. ("Anarquismo, revolución" 178)

> (one of the aspects that defined the originality of libertarian thought . . . was the belief that it could transform society by transforming quotidian existence. The emphasis on the personal and on daily praxis is one of the characteristics of anarchist thought, always keen to change attitudes in areas such as sexuality . . . , women's role in society . . . , and the assimilation and divulgation of scientific and medical knowledge.)

Thus guided by the principle of subjecting a sexual "slice of life" to scientific inquiry for the sake of advancement of the libertarian ideal, Martí Ibáñez decided to exemplify one of the "truths" of his "Mensaje eugénico a la mujer" (namely, that the experience of war exacerbates sexual desire) with a "real" case, published in his "Consultorio Psíquico-Sexual" in the same December 1936 issue of *Estudios*. The letter explaining the case reads as follows:

> Doctor Martí Ibáñez: En estos días de guerra y de angustia me ha sucedido un hecho que me tiene altamente intrigado y para cuya explicación recurro a sus conocimientos psicológicos y sociológicos. Hace dos años que voy detrás de una mujer, a la cual

amaba locamente, tanto sexual como espiritualmente, sin conseguir de ella más que una amistad cordial, pero viéndola completamente fría en el terreno sexual. Esa mujer tiene fama en el pueblo de frialdad y de ser indiferente al amor. Me he consumido por ella sin conseguir ser correspondido. Ella tan sólo aprecia sus libros, su carrera de maestra y sus tareas literarias (escribe en varios periódicos de la provincia), y yo creía que siendo un trabajador manual era la razón por la que no le interesaba. Hace una semana hubo un bombardeo de los aviones fascistas y todos tuvimos que escondernos en diversos refugios subterráneos. En aquella hora de pánico, ella permaneció tres horas escondida debajo de unos puentecillos de la carretera junto a algunos labradores. Pasó el peligro y entonces (después lo contaron ellos mismos) ella cayó en brazos de uno que ni siquiera la conocía y se entregó a él, después de lo cual huyó atropelladamente y vino a encontrarme hecha un mar de lágrimas y diciéndome que no se lo explicaba cómo le había pasado. Al afearle yo su conducta y decirle lo que pensaba de ella, arreció en su llanto y dijo que ahora comprendía que me amaba y que se sentía ligada a mí, que la perdonase y que viviésemos felices. Sin oírla casi la eché a la fuerza de mi casa y la he vuelto a echar tres veces más que ha acudido con la misma historia. Pero estoy sufriendo mucho, y aunque creo que todo es una comedia de esta mala mujer, deseo de su bondad que me saque de esa duda espantosa en que vivo y me diga cuál debe ser mi conducta.—Un anarquista madrileño. ("Consultorio" [December 1936] 28).

(Doctor Martí Ibáñez: During these days of war and anguish something has happened to me that really intrigues me. I resort to you and your psychological and sociological knowledge in order to gain some insight. For two years I have been courting a woman whom I love profoundly, both spiritually and sexually. A cordial friendship unites us, but sexually speaking she remains cold and unresponsive. People from the village see this woman as cold and perfectly indifferent to love. I have done everything I could, but she will simply not react to my feelings. She cares only about her books, her career as a teacher, and her literary activities (she writes for several local newspapers). I thought that the reason for her indifference was that I am a manual worker. A week ago, there was a bombing by the fascist air force, and we all had to hide in various underground air raid shelters. During that time of panic, for three hours she remained hidden under a small bridge in the company of several farm workers. When the danger was over (they told the story afterward) she fell into the arms of one of them, whom she did not even know, and gave herself to him. Later, she ran away precipitously and came to me, all in tears, and told me that she did not know how it could have happened. When I criticized her behavior and told her what I thought of her, she started crying even more and told me that now she understood that she loved me, that she felt linked to me, that I should forgive her, and that we should live happily together. Without even listening to her I threw her out of my house, and I have done the same on the three occasions she has come to me with the same story.

But I am suffering horribly, and, although I believe this is all playacting on the part of that bad woman, I appeal to your kindness to rescue me from the terrible doubts that are plaguing me and tell me what to do.—An anarchist from Madrid)

According to Martí Ibáñez's ready diagnosis, the teacher is not frigid, as the village gossip likes to have it, but a "latent lover." In the teacher's soul, he reflects, the hours spent squatting under the bridge with death literally pending over her head, unleashed dormant forces. Her sexuality, which remained compressed by her idealism, "[de pronto] se estira como un muelle a presión" (suddenly expands like a spring; 29). The circumstance is unfortunate but not tragic, as Martí Ibáñez explains to the desperate letter writer: in fact, this tumultuous and sudden sexual experience is beneficial, since it provided a much-needed sexual awakening. The Revolution gives women the gift of sex, and the freedom to dismiss "la odiosa virginidad" (hateful virginity) as yet another bourgeois prejudice. But the Revolution has its demands also: now that she is a perfected female human being, newly born to (hetero)sexual experience and erotic bliss, Martí Ibáñez urges the now "active" lover to happily join her suitor in the enthusiastic pursuit of anarchist ideals.

Here again, Martí Ibáñez's "solution" to the "problem" very much coincides with Marañón's approach. Sexual promiscuity, be it male or female, is as reprehensible as homosexuality; in fact, the former is often a sign of the latter. The promiscuous Don Juan, according to Marañón's highly influential "scientific" hypothesis (*Don Juan*), is a latent homosexual, and the promiscuous female, a woman that dangerously toys with other erotic excesses, easily falls prey to tribadic longings. Marañón explicitly and insistently proclaimed the need for radical sexual differentiation, and the erasure of any bisexual mark or homosexual inclination: "Diferenciación sexual. Ser hombres y ser mujeres en toda su plenitud. En esto debe estribar fundamentalmente el progreso sexual de la Humanidad que . . . vale tanto como decir su progreso moral. . . . Matad al fantasma del otro sexo que cada cual lleva dentro; sed hombres, sed mujeres" (Sexual differentiation. Being a man or a woman to the full. That must be the ultimate goal of the sexual progress of Humanity, which is to say its moral progress. Kill the phantom of the other sex that each carries within; be men, be women; *Tres ensayos* 221–22). Martí Ibáñez followed Marañón's lead by equally abhorring homosexuality ("Consideraciones") and paying a no less persistent homage to the radically heterosexual and painstakingly monogamous anarchist couple.

Love is a carefully engineered affair in libertarian thought, as it is in Marañón's writings, and there is not much room left for the genuine expression or sincere exploration of female erotic emotion. Libertarian women "fall" and "sin" (through emotional excess or emotional lack) as often and as gravely as devout Catholic bourgeois and need equal amounts of generous redemption and regeneration. No matter how "individualized" the case, the female characters in the "real-life" letters published in Martí Ibáñez's advice column are exactly that: "characters," artificial constructs, no less artificial than the caricaturesque collective of milicianas in "Mensaje eugénico a la mujer." That is, they are rigid female prototypes who routinely err, until Revolution rescues (and enslaves) them all—flirtatious libertarians, naïve sentimentalists, calculating prostitutes, or "freaks" in the guise of frigid teachers on heat.

In Martí Ibáñez's writings, sexual pathologies and emotional ailments are carefully tailored to fit the model of female redemption and rescue—a model ironically dear to both libertarian and Catholic thought. And among the pathologies and unorthodox sexual behaviors and emotions that populate Martí Ibáñez's "Consultorio Psíquico-Sexual"—namely, female sexual promiscuity as a liberating experience among urban workers, sexual superstitions, male erotomania among the working classes, precocious menopause and its sexual consequences, female and male homosexuality, and female anaphrodisia—the last is the most prevalent. Martí Ibáñez's sex advice column appeared for the first time in January 1936, with the whole section—two letters from anonymous patients and his responses—devoted to female frigidity. Moreover, the same magazine issue included one of Martí Ibáñez's articles on anaphrodisia, "Las que no saben amar y las que no pueden amar: Esquema psicológico de la frigidez sexual femenina" ("Women Who Don't Know How to Love, or Can't: A Psychological Outline of Female Sexual Frigidity"). The next issue, published in February, also contained one letter on female anaphrodisia, and so did the June issue of the same year, in the midst of increasing political unrest. In September 1936, with full-blown civil war as a backdrop, Martí Ibáñez published a second article on female frigidity in *Estudios*: "La incapacidad de amar: Esquema psicológico de la frigidez sexual femenina" ("The Inability to Love: A Psychological Outline of Female Sexual Frigidity"). Incidentally, and for unknown reasons, the September issue appeared without the by then widely popular sex advice column. In December 1936, the "Consultorio" once again included a letter on frigidity (the case reproduced above), and in January 1937 yet another letter on female anaphrodisia became the sole protagonist of the "Consultorio," written by what Martí Ibáñez termed "una paciente levemente frígida" (a slightly frigid female patient). The same *Estudios* issue published a column on Sigmund Freud's reflections on female anaphrodisia. The "Consultorio" appeared for its last time four months later, in May 1937, with a letter from an ardent young wife, whose aging husband could not satisfy her healthy sexual appetite.

Female frigidity is the only sexual "dysfunction" that merits so many letters (six out of a total of twenty-two) and painstakingly detailed responses in Martí Ibáñez's sex advice column. Two additional letters present cases of male impotence, two more discuss (latent) male homosexuality, and (latent) lesbianism also comes up twice. Somewhat capricious and isolated issues are the subject of the remaining letters, such as marriage among cousins, menstrual pain, male philandering or "donjuanismo," and sexual repulsion. To add even more relevance to the subject, a steady string of articles in *Estudios* on female frigidity by Spanish anarchist intellectuals and foreign medical experts gave "scientific rigor" to the anecdotal evidence presented in the letters. Martí Ibáñez too supported his advice column with more rigorous argumentation in the two aforementioned articles that set out his approach to female frigidity: "Las que no saben amar y las que no pueden amar" and "La incapacidad de amar," published in *Estudios* in February and September 1936 respectively. In both these articles, Martí Ibáñez presents female frigidity as an emotional problem: an inability to love.

A firm believer that female "inferiority" is not innate but learned, Martí Ibáñez starts the first of these articles by comparing the medical office of a psychologist to a sanctuary, and the psychologist himself to a priest. Both are privy to painful secrets, and both learn about the traumatic experience of female frigidity—an experience, Martí Ibáñez adds, "que hasta hace poco monopolizó la literatura . . . [ya que] durante largos años la frigidez sexual femenina ha sido un tema silenciado, tapiz de amargura que tejieron el egoismo masculino y el callado sacrificio de la mujer" (that has been mostly monopolized by literature until very recently . . . [since] for many years, female sexual frigidity has been consistently silenced, a tapestry of suffering woven by male egotism and female sacrifice; "Las que no saben" 5). Now, however, modern sexology comes to the rescue and "proyecta la luz sobre los dramas de esa cámara nupcial, que es más veces celda de tortura que dosel áureo de la felicidad" (sheds light on the dramas occurring in the nuptial bedroom, which more often than not morphs into a torture chamber; "Las que no saben" 5).

Martí Ibáñez then mentions prominent doctors and sexologists interested in studying female sexual frigidity, notably Austrian physician and psychologist Wilhelm Stekel and American doctor and scholar Phyllis Blanchard. He puts particular emphasis on Blanchard's Freudian reflections on the three phases of sexual maturation in the human female: the narcissistic phase, the phase of parental projection (which includes the Oedipus complex and the Electra complex), and the phase of erotic specificity ("Las que no saben" 6). If there is an abrupt interruption of "normal" sexual development—something that, according to Martí Ibáñez, happens with alarming frequency—then an "abnormal type of woman" ensues. Some of these women remain stuck in the narcissistic phase, in love with their own bodies and souls, and tied forever to a mirror; others feel prey to incestuous longings ("Las que no saben" 6). But, whatever the phase they are in, matrimony will happen soon enough to most women. And, for Spanish females in particular, "que viven aún en un infierno de oscurantismos" (who grow up surrounded by hellish obscurantisms; "Las que no saben" 6), marriage is looked on as "un astro de luz en el caos tenebroso de su vida erótica de soltera" (a bright star in the midst of the murky chaos of their erotic lives as single women; "Las que no saben" 6). Supposedly, "casarse es para ella poder al fin dar vía libre y legal a su reprimida sexualidad" (for her, to marry is to give free and legal rein finally to her repressed sexuality; "Las que no saben" 6). Martí Ibáñez is quick to point out, however, that this only happens in novels. Reality will often contradict literature, and newlywed women will soon find out that they either can't love, or don't know how to love ("Las que no saben" 7). Frigidity has dire consequences. Women take refuge in numbing resignation and sacrifice, or they fall prey to adultery and neurosis.

Martí Ibáñez's second article on female anaphrodisia (a sequel to the first), "La incapacidad de amar," leaves out the exogenous or "extra-feminine" reasons (as he calls them) mentioned in the first article, such as male frigidity due to impotence ("La incapacidad" 19), and concentrates exclusively on the psychological causes of endogenous female frigidity. While acknowledging that the latter can have genital neuro-vegetative, hormonal, or spinal-cerebral causes, he concludes that in all these cases psychological components nonetheless play a crucial role ("La incapcidad" 20). The emphasis on psychological causes over organic ones (in other words, on "psychologism" over "biologism"), and the belief that "scientific psychology," combined with sexual education can effectively cure endocrinological "anomalies," had already been a recurrent motif in Martí Ibáñez's reflections on "homosexualism." In fact, the approach adopted in these essays does not differ in any substantial way from what was commonly thought by sexologists and anarchists alike. Both international and Spanish sexology and libertarian dogma were rotund defenders of sexual moderation and restraint and demanded from female sexuality in particular that it be intimately linked to amorous feelings, and that these be heterosexual in nature. Both anxiously sought to cure frigidity, and both agreed on a series of "proven" endogenous and psychological causes of the latter, such as unconscious taboo, lack of love and sexual attraction, fear of committing a sin, and a series of factors related to fear of childbirth and possessive motherhood.

Martí Ibáñez strongly disagreed with Marañón's widely disseminated "scientific" hypothesis (the subject of two of Marañón's articles in *Estudios*) that women are "naturally" frigid because the female libido focuses obsessively on motherhood and leaves no room for sexual pleasure ("Nuevas ideas . . . [Conclusión]" 26). In this Martí Ibáñez agreed with Juan Lazarte, author of a 1935 article in *Estudios* entitled "La atrofia de la sensibilidad en las mujeres" ("The Atrophy of Sensibility in Women") and with the hugely popular writer of erotic novels, Felipe Trigo. Trigo's book-length essay *El amor en la vida y en los libros* (*Love in Life and in Books*, 1908), which enjoyed multiple editions and was read well into the mid-1930s, presents a compelling defense of the right of women to sexual bliss, and their ability, superior to that of men, to experience intense erotic arousal (Zubiaurre 296–300). Martí Ibáñez conceded, however, that pregnancy and childbirth could adversely affect female erotic emotion. This becomes particularly apparent in his response to the first of the two letters on female frigidity published in the inaugural issue of his "Consultorio" in *Estudios* (January 1936). When a despairing epistolary male "victim" brings up female frigidity (for eight years it has been very difficult for him to make his wife experience an orgasm, a situation that has worsened since the birth of their second, one-year-old son), Martí Ibáñez suspects motherhood is to blame, at least in part. Among the "endogenous" causes, due to "sexual anesthetics provoked by childbirth," he mentions first the trauma produced by birth and second the fear of another pregnancy. Finally, certain mothers gear all their affective energy to the newborn and become insensitive to sexual stimulus ("Consultorio" January 1936; 62). Male sexual incapacity or impotence, on the other hand, is seen as one of the main "exogenous" causes of female frigidity by Martí Ibáñez, who also blames it on the lack of erotic dexterity and skill so alarmingly common among males. Therefore, in this same "Consultorio," he first wants to rule out the possibility that "la eyaculación precoz, la impotencia relativa o una técnica sexual inadecuada" (premature ejaculation, relative impotence, or inadequate sexual technique) might be the cause, before moving on to the female sexual partner ("Consultorio" January 1936; 62).

However, in his second essay "La incapacidad de amar," to male impotence and sexual clumsiness Martí Ibáñez adds a crucial, albeit largely overlooked, factor to the list of psychological causes that hamper female pleasure; namely, the ingrained sense, among many women, of their social and sexual inferiority. In an effort to move away from sexual oppression, and from the secondary role women are forced to play when it comes to sexuality and heterosexual intercourse, many "choose" frigidity as a tool for overcoming male domination. Not to feel—not to let the male be the source of sexual pleasure—gives them power over men and (partially) frees them from victimhood ("La incapacidad de amar" 21). As often happens in Martí Ibáñez's writings, always pedagogically infused and keen to illustrate theoretical insights with empirical examples, in this instance too a "real-life" example supports the hypothesis of female empowerment via frigidity. Martí Ibáñez offers the case of an extremely beautiful woman, intelligent and highly cultured, who is madly in love with a mutilated writer ill with tuberculosis. "Le amo," she explains, "porque él agradece mi amor casi como una limosna y nunca ha hecho sentirme humillada bajo los despotismos propios del varón" (I love him because he is grateful for my affection, almost as if it were an act of charity. He has never humiliated me, or treated me with the despotism so characteristic of the male"; "La incapacidad de amar" 21). The woman, who previously suffered from frigidity, is now "cured" and able to experience "erotic ecstasy." Martí Ibáñez's explanation is that, aware that she is stronger than her male lover, she can lower her defenses and give herself to him both physically and emotionally, knowing that, in his vulnerable position, he will not crush her spirit or exacerbate her insecurities ("La incapacidad de amar" 21).

Martí Ibáñez's (pseudo) feminist insights, alas, tend to be patchy. In his answer to the second letter on frigidity in his January 1936 advice column (61–63), this time by a (childless) female patient, the Valencian doctor, after ruling out a series of possible triggers such as "lesión anatómica, trastorno nervioso de las vías de conducción de la sensibilidad erótica . . . , temor al embarazo, o, al contrario, deseo exagerado de un hijo" (anatomical injury, damage of the nerves responsible for erotic sensitivity. . . , fear of pregnancy, or, conversely, exaggerated longing for a child), suspects that masturbation is probably the underlying cause, thus fully embracing sexology's revulsion toward women who "dare" to seek, and find, pleasure without the assistance of the male. According to Martí Ibáñez, onanist practices during adolescence, fueled by erotic fantasies, can have very dangerous consequences. Many women create for themselves "una sexualidad romántica de cuentos de hadas" (a fairy-tale-like romantic sexuality), while others concoct "imágenes monstruosas de aberración sexual" (monstrous images of sexual aberration). Once married and sexually active, none of these two extremes—bland erotic sentimentalism or over-the-top sexual frenzy and erotic "deviation"—matches the rather prosaic reality of (heterosexual) intercourse, and yet another frigid woman is born ("Consultorio" January 1936; 63). Thus masturbation, and the extremely sensitive organ from which it extracts so much pleasure, the clitoris, are strangely oxymoronic entities, for they bring into being the monster of "too much" (hysteria, nymphomania, tribadism, and prostitution, among other "perversions" and sexual "excesses") or the monster of "too little" or even nothing (frigidity). As Alison Moore cogently puts it,

> The clitoris became the site of a curious contradiction in which perversion and lack were made to meet—the frigid woman and the nymphomaniac became as one and the same. One could become frigid as a result of masturbation or as a result of developing a taste for other perverse pleasures. . . . excess pleasure causes the absence of pleasure. . . . Clitoral stimulation would desensitize the genitals of a woman [frigidity] causing her to veer off into rampant sexual perversions [tribadism, prostitution, nymphomania] in search of new forms of stimulation. (188, 190)

The question remains as to why Martí Ibáñez—although he spoke of "excess" in his "Mensaje eugénico a la mujer" and pictured milicianas turned into monsters of sensuality—chose to devote so much attention to frigidity in his "Consultorio Psíquico-Sexual." We cannot be naïve at this point and have to acknowledge that Martí Ibáñez, more likely than not, was the ghostwriter of the letters "sent" to the "Consultorio Psíquico-Sexual." We certainly suspect that, in the best of cases, he selected them very carefully, and we know for a fact that he personally edited the letters before submitting them for publication. The frequency of cases relating to female frigidity in his advice column is therefore likely to be the result of a strategic choice. First, it is important to remember that Martí Ibáñez was not as interested in women and their sexual lives and emotions as he was in the Revolution; that is, he was interested in women as crucial pieces within the libertarian movement. Hence the females portrayed in the letters to his advice column, and extensively dissected in his replies, have to be made exemplary in some fashion—no matter how "real," quotidian, and "individualized" the case may be or sound—in order to serve the anarchist cause. A "frigid" woman can more easily be made "exemplary" and, crucially, can more easily be "redeemed" than a nymphomaniac. It is not by chance that Martí Ibáñez prefers to identify supposedly frigid females as "latent lovers." Four equally relevant reasons can be suggested for this, in no particular order of importance. First, "latent lovers" are less threatening and less "degenerate" than "patent lovers" given up to debauchery: there is a certain virginal flair and "proletarian" purity in the dormant lover that contrasts with the bourgeois perversity of an excessively awake "lady of the night." Second, a "latent" lover who innocently awakes to the erotic stimulus and sheds her coldness to enthusiastically join young anarchist love at its purest vigorously contributes to the libertarian dream of a world coming to life afresh (as opposed to the "active" lover who would drag along the soiled baggage of her unruly life). Third, a "latent" and thus utterly inexperienced (quasi-virginal) lover provides a boost to the anarchist male ego, cast in the role of the prince who will awaken the sleeping beauty with his kiss, restoring warmth to her frigid limbs (preferable to becoming the toy of a harlot whose sexual experience is greater than his). And fourth, "strong" emotions remain within the exclusive purview of the male libertarian, who puts them in the service of the Revolution. Masculine sexuality sublimates into fighting power, and only there is emotion allowed to erupt and even to overflow. "True" emotion comes from men and is for men, and it is called "revolutionary emotion."

NOTES

1. See, for example, works by Álvarez Peláez; Amezúa; Amezúa and Cleminson; Cleminson; Cleminson and Vázquez García; Díez; Nash; Navarro Navarro; Vázquez García and Moreno Mengíbar.
2. *Estudios: Revista Ecléctica* (1923–1937) was one of the most influential, widely distributed, and long-standing anarchist reviews in early twentieth-century Spain. With a strong focus on sexual education, anarchist sexology, and eugenics, its primary goal was to reach out to the working class, particularly to factory workers and the peasant population. Initially entitled *Generación consciente*, the magazine changed its name to *Estudios* in 1928, for reasons of censorship. It appeared regularly every two months, at one point reaching a circulation of seventy thousand copies, despite high illiteracy rates. Renowned anarchist writers (such as Joaquín Juan Pastor and Antonio García Birlán), medical doctors and sexologists (among them, Isaac Puente Amestoy, Roberto Remartínez Gallego, and, even more frequently and prominently, Félix Martí Ibáñez), and visual artists (Josep Renau and Félix Monleón) were regular contributors.
3. For important articles written by Martí Ibáñez in the mid-1930s on topics other than female frigidity, see "El sexo," "Consideraciones," and "Ensayos." After the Civil War, Martí Ibáñez went into exile in New York, were he worked as professor and chair of the Department of the History of Medicine at New York Medical College, and as the founder of *MD Publications Inc*. In 1957 he became editor in chief of the prestigious and internationally distributed medical journal *MD*. An extremely prolific writer and scholar of wide-reaching interests, Martí Ibáñez published dozens of volumes on medicine, the history of medicine, and anarchist thought in Spanish and in English. His early books and essays, published during the Spanish Second Republic and the Civil War, were primarily devoted to sexology, eugenics, and sexual education.

WORKS CITED

Álvarez Peláez, Raquel. "Eugenesia y control social." *Asclepio* 40.2 (1988): 29–80.
———. "Eugenesia y fascismo en la España de los años treinta." *Ciencia y Fascismo*. Ed. Rafael Huertas and Carmen Ortiz. Aranjuez: Doce Calles, 1998. 77–95.
———. "Penetración y difusión de la eugenesia en España." *Ciencia en expansión: Estudios sobre la difusión de las ideas científicas y médicas en España (Siglos XVIII–XX)*. Ed. Elvira Arquiola and José Martínez Pérez. Madrid: U Complutense, 1995. 211–31.
———. "Prólogo." *Francis Galton: Herencia y eugenesia*. Madrid: Alianza, 1988. 9–29.
Amezúa, Efigenio. *Cien años de temática sexual en España: 1850–1950; Repertorio y Análisis*. Monographic issue of *Revista de Sexología* 48 (1991).
———. *Los hijos de don Santiago: Paseo por el casco antiguo de nuestra sexología*. Monographic issue of *Revista Española de Sexología* 59–60 (1993).

Amezúa, Efigenio, and Richard M. Cleminson. "Spain: The Political and Social Context of Sex Reform in the Late Nineteenth and Early Twentieth Centuries." *Sexual Cultures in Europe: National Histories*. Ed. Franz X. Eder, Lesley A. Hall, and Gert Hekma. Manchester: Manchester UP, 1999. 173–96.

Cansinos Assens, Rafael. *Estética y erotismo de la pena de muerte: Estética y erotismo de la guerra*. Madrid: Renacimiento, 1916.

Cleminson, Richard. "En las negruras de su horizonte vital un rayo de esperanza: El doctor Martí Ibáñez, la ciencia y la homosexualidad." *Actas del I Simposium Internacional Félix Martí Ibáñez: Medicina, historia e ideología*. Ed. José Vicente Martí Boscá and Antonio Rey González. Valencia: Generalitat Valenciana, 2004. 39–56.

Cleminson, Richard, and Francisco Vázquez García, eds. *"Los Invisibles": A History of Male Homosexuality in Spain, 1850–1939*. Cardiff: U of Wales P, 2007.

Díez, Xavier. *Utopia sexual a la premsa anarquista de Catalunya: La revista Ética-Iniciales (1927–1937)*. Lérida: Pagès, 2001.

Lazarte, Juan. "La atrofia de la sensibilidad en las mujeres." *Estudios* 141 (May 1935): 30–32.

Marañón, Gregorio. *Don Juan: Ensayos sobre el origen de su leyenda*. Madrid: Espasa-Calpe, 1940.

———. "Nuevas ideas sobre el problema de la intersexualidad y sobre la cronología de los sexos." *Estudios* 70 (June 1929): 19–25.

———. "Nuevas ideas sobre el problema de la intersexualidad y sobre la cronología de los sexos. (Conclusión)." *Estudios* 71 (July 1929): 26–33.

———. *Tres ensayos sobre la vida sexual*. Madrid: Biblioteca Nueva, 1928.

Martí Ibáñez, Félix. "Las actitudes ante el problema sexual en la literatura." *Estudios* 163 (April 1937): 11–13.

———. "Consideraciones sobre el homosexualismo." *Estudios* 145 (September 1935): 3–6.

———. "Consultorio Psíquico-Sexual: Dr. Félix Martí Ibáñez." *Estudios* 149 (January 1936): 61–63.

———. "Consultorio Psíquico-Sexual: Dr. Félix Martí Ibáñez." *Estudios* 159 (December 1936): 28–30.

———. "Ensayos sobre el amor." *El sentido de la vida*. Valencia: Estudios, 1937. 95–163.

———. "La incapacidad de amar: Esquema psicológico de la frigidez sexual femenina." *Estudios* 156 (September 1936): 19–22.

———. "Mensaje eugénico a la mujer." *Tres mensajes a la mujer*. Barcelona: Ediciones y reportajes, 1937. 7–12. Rpt. from *Estudios* 159 (December 1936): 4–7.

———. "Una nueva moral sexual como base de las conquistas revolucionarias." *Tiempos Nuevos* 4.2 (1937): 34–36. Rpt. *Antología de textos de Félix Martí Ibáñez*. Ed. José Vicente Martí and Antonio Rey. Valencia: Generalitat Valenciana, 2005. 125–29.

———. "Las que no saben amar y las que no pueden amar: Esquema psicológico de la frigidez sexual femenina." *Estudios* 150 (February 1936): 5–7.

———. "El sexo en la historia." *Estudios* 137 (January 1935): 18–22.

Martín de Lucenay, Ángel. *El erotismo en la guerra y en la revolución*. Colección "Temas Sexuales." Madrid: Fénix, 1934.

Moore, Alison. "The Invention of the Unsexual: Situating Frigidity in the History of Sexuality and in Feminist Thought." *French History and Civilization: Papers from the George Rudé Seminar*. Vol. 2. Ed. Vesna Drapac and André Lambelet. 2009. 181–92. *www.h-france.net/rude/rude%20volume%20ii/Moore%20Final%20Version.pdf* (accessed 28 August 2014).

Nash, Mary. "Social Eugenics and Nationalist Race Hygiene in Early Twentieth Century Spain." *History of European Ideas* 15.4–6 (1992): 741–48.

Navarro Navarro, Javier. "Anarquismo, revolución y vida cotidiana: La revista *Estudios* (1928–1937)." *Actas del I Simposium Internacional Félix Martí Ibáñez: Medicina, historia e ideología*. Ed. José Vicente Martí Boscá and Antonio Rey González. Valencia: Generalitat Valenciana, 2004: 175–90.

———. "Anarquismo y neomalthusianismo: La revista *Generación Consciente* (1923–1928)." *Arbor* 156 (1997): 9–32.

Ortega y Gasset, José. *Estudios sobre el amor*. Buenos Aires, 1939. Rpt. Barcelona: Círculo de Lectores, 1966.

Torres del Hoyo, Luis. *La emoción erótica*. Madrid: Renacimiento, 1927.

Trigo, Felipe. *El amor en la vida y en los libros: Mi ética y mi estética*. Madrid: Pueyo, 1920.

Vázquez García, Francisco, and Andrés Moreno Mengíbar. *Sexo y razón: Una genealogía de la moral sexual en España (Siglos XVI–XX)*. Madrid: Akal, 1997.

Vidal, Ignacio, ed. *Consultorio Psíquico-Sexual: Dr. Félix Martí Ibáñez*. Barcelona: Tusquets, 1975.

Zubiaurre, Maite. *Cultures of the Erotic in Spain, 1898–1939*. Nashville: Vanderbilt UP, 2012.

CHAPTER 10

From the History of Emotions to the History of Experience
A Republican Sailor's Sketchbook in the Civil War

JAVIER MOSCOSO

In a short text on Nietzsche's philosophy of history, the philosopher Michel Foucault defended a form of genealogy that would allow us to locate the singularity of events and find them in what seems to lack a history—such as sentiments, emotions, or instincts. Rephrasing Nietzsche's *The Gay Science*, Foucault claimed that feelings also have their own story (139–40). Genealogy, in his view, called into question not only the history of origins but, more important, the origins of history, the means by which a singular experience, even a trivial experience "without appearance [of truth]," including an emotional experience, could be turned into a story.

Since Foucault wrote this short text in 1971, the history of emotions has flourished as an academic discipline. Albeit still timidly, emotional experiences have become a topic of discussion in the new humanities of the twenty-first century, with a number of cultural historians writing about fear, compassion, anger, boredom, sensitivity, or love.[1] Specialist journals, research centers, and graduate schools have also proliferated in Europe, Australia, and the United States. Although we generally speak of the "history of emotions," many scholars include other subjective experiences under this heading, such as affects, feelings, impulses, or instincts.[2] Most of these approaches understand that to disregard desire, aversion, happiness, mourning, hope, fear, modesty, shame, revenge, anger, hatred, or love in the study of culture would imply replacing the history of humanity with a rational reconstruction in which human actions would, against all evidence, be stripped of spiritual emotions and corporeal passions. "Beneath the known history of Europe," wrote Horkheimer and Adorno in a little-quoted passage of *Dialectic of Enlightenment*, "there runs a subterranean one. It consists of the fate of human instincts and passions repressed and distorted by civilization" (192). This new historiographical trend has also given rise to new theoretical and methodological concerns that historians classify in different ways depending on their professional background and cultural milieu. In this essay, I will attempt to explain how the study of emotions of the past is concerned not with those objects traditionally associated with internal psychic mechanisms, but with the cultural forms that make them possible. In fact, emotions, far from being "objects," are colorations or intensifications of experience through which the latter takes on a cultural meaning that can be shared collectively. From this point of view, the history of emotions involves a form of archaeology: an unveiling of the culturally mediated conditions that may configure, say, courtly and romantic love, Enlightenment humanitarianism, or expressions of wrath in classical antiquity. To illustrate this point, I will make use of a privileged source of information: the drawings and notes left by a member of the Republican armed forces during the Spanish Civil War. These documents will allow me to examine the interplay between experiences and expressions using a rich, though limited, source of information. I will argue that research on the cultural forms of emotional experience involves the study of poetic, rhetorical, and political factors. My perspective, in this sense, differs from that proposed by Barbara Rosenwein ("Problems and Methods"), since the unit of analysis is not determined by the configuration of human groups that adhere to a set of rules of conduct or emotional values, but by those circumstances that enable the formation of culturally meaningful experiences.

The Poetics of Experience

The reason the history of emotions has until recently been widely ignored lies, at least partially, in the historiographical or conceptual problems that it has always raised (Matt and Stearns 1–14, 17–40; Frevert). According to English historian Peter Burke, cultural history should clarify what is included under the heading "history of the emotions," especially given that the words used to describe subjective states of consciousness, like *affections*, *sentiments*, or *emotions*, are not interchangeable. At the beginning of this century, Thomas Dixon sought to identify the guidelines governing the psychologization of the passions in the nineteenth century and the first uses of the word "emotion" in the context of early twentieth-century biomedical research. In a similar vein, other scholars have traced the passionate elements of all mental illnesses studied by the new psychiatric experts (Goldstein, *Console and Classify*, *The Post-revolutionary Self*). Though this is a fundamentally historical matter, the choice of vocabulary has been dependent on national preferences and disciplinary variations. Many North American scholars, for example, influenced by the history of psychology, talk about "affects" and the "affective turn." While French academics are inclined to speak about "sensibilities," the rest of Europe and other parts of the world, like Australia or Latin America, favor "emotions" as a general term to designate all subjective experiences related to feelings and passions, but also to sensations, perceptions, and gut reactions.[3]

To this terminological difficulty we must add the philosophical problem of how we gain access to the emotions and feelings of our fellow human beings. This difficulty becomes even more pressing in the case of passions from the past, where testimonies are limited or nonexistent and evidence can be obtained only by indirect means. According to Brian Massumi, affects, defined as physiological but not necessarily conscious appraisals, are followed by conscious feelings and emotional recognition (26–28). In this sense, Massumi's book suggested, first, that the terminology issue was indebted to prior ontological considerations and, second, that emotional states could not be understood as mere objects of the world, even if we refer here to the world of the inner psyche. In her article "Doing Things," Jo Labanyi has gone further. From her point of view, we must follow the path of what emotions *do* instead of attempting to understand what they *are*; a performative view of emotionality that is further supported by the materiality of experience.

To these terminological, cognitive, and ontological difficulties, we should add three further important issues. The first concerns the potential dissolution of our subject matter in its cultural manifestations. After all, if emotional experiences are historically determined, as many cultural historians seem to imply, why should we still believe that we are dealing in different instances with one and the same emotion? Are we not forced to distinguish the existence of as many different emotions as there are cultures or, ultimately, human beings? The second danger is that of writing a teleological narration, inscribed, for example, in the context of a progressive civilizing process or any other goal-oriented dynamics. This has been especially clear in the case of the history of pain. For its protagonists, the appearance of new pain medicine in the mid-twentieth century always seemed to be the last chapter in a sequence that had led human beings from the logic of resignation to the technology of resistance. Surgeons and neurologists have unfailingly interpreted their history in this way: as the necessary culmination of a broader historical process involving the attainment of a humanitarian perspective on pain and death (Moscoso).

The third difficulty depends on the conscious or unconscious nature of emotions, and the relation between emotional states and the corresponding social awareness. The undeniable reality of emotions that can at the same time be (privately) conscious and (socially) unnoticed explains why history must also bring unnoticed experiences into the field of memory (LaCapra, *Writing History*; *History in Transit*). This may be what Febvre had in mind when he argued for a "vast collective inquiry" into the fundamental feelings of humanity ("Sensibility" 26). For him, as for many others after him, history was not something that could be separated from life or distanced from the present.

Some of these difficulties may be solved, or dissolved, when the history of emotions is replaced with the history of experience.[4] The choice of words truly matters here because the dichotomies of modern philosophy do not quite fit under the new heading. For one thing, the idea of a "private experience," from which many of the philosophical problems related to the history of emotions seem to stem, seems truly unacceptable. It was the German philosopher Reinhart Koselleck who explained how the forms of writing and understanding history were related to different forms and layers of experience. For him, as previously for Foucault, the problem was never how experiences of different kinds could justify universal statements about the world, but how the flow of life could become a self-referential expression of meaning. That is partly the reason cultural history always found its source of inspiration in anthropology. Johan Huizinga's *The Autumn of the Middle Ages*, a book that dealt with the cultural forms of medieval life, is perhaps the most famous, but not the only, example. Marc Bloch's *The Royal Touch* or Lucien Febvre's *The Problem of Unbelief in the Sixteenth Century* could also be added to this list. In the case of French analysts, from the first generation to Alain Corbin, we can see the influence of Émile Durkheim's understanding of collective experiences. The history of the senses and sensibilities, smell or sound, present in Corbin, but also in the Bologna historiographical school of Piero Camporesi for example, was fashioned through reference to a cluster of sources that were never intended to explain the mechanisms of community formation but rather the emergence of private experiences from collective experiences (Corbin; Demartini and Kalifa; Bernabéu and Langue). Although many historians believe that the history of subjective experience is tantamount to the history of private life and that, consequently, the best sources to unravel this story are those that might be considered more intimate, what makes the understanding of diaries, autobiographies, and confessions possible is the desire to transcend one's own perspective, to find comfort in each other's company, or to find the *me* in the *us*.

The use of the word "experience" has been subjected to sharp and intelligent critiques by proponents of the so-called linguistic turn. This is partly natural, since defenders of Rortyan contextualism have claimed that experiences are always propositional. The history of experience, however, has nothing to do with empirical foundationalism, pragmatism's real enemy, or with the theory of truth as correspondence.[5] The problem that concerns us here is not knowledge but history. Thus the emphasis should not be placed on the referentiality of subjective experiences but on their narrativity. This is partly the reason why, when dealing with emotions of the past, it will be always more interesting to refer to the philosophy of history than to the philosophy of language. Understood within the framework of the history of experiences, the history of emotions does not deal with the process of knowledge formation, nor with the truth value of linguistic (or visual) representations of the world. Neither is it concerned with the transformation of sensations into language, as Elaine Scarry attempted to prove in her influential book on pain, but with the cultural circumstances that allow the configuration of a singularity, even a singularity without the appearance of truth, into a story.

The Dramatic Form of a War Experience

In order to explore some of these difficulties, I will consider a set of drawings, "En el puerto: Apuntes de un movilizado en la Marina Roja" ("In the Port: Notes of a Recruit in the Red Navy"), made by a Spanish sailor, Luis Sarabia, during the Spanish Civil

War. From 1937 to the end of the conflict in April 1939, this young sailor mobilized by the Republic produced around fifty drawings, which he accompanied with short texts explaining the events represented in the respective image. More than captions, these phrases and paragraphs contain inner reflections and value judgments on the experiences he had to endure. The first drawing in the series (Fig. 10.1) is a self-portrait upon arriving at the military port of Cartagena. Sarabia wrote underneath: "Cuando llegué, después de 37 horas de viaje para recorrer 300 kilómetros, aun seguían los incendios producidos por los bombardeos de la aviación. Todos mis pensamientos fueron para vosotras" (When I arrived after a 37 hour journey covering 300 kilometers . . . the fires caused by the air raids were still burning. All my thoughts went out to you). For the duration of the war, this city port in the southeast of Spain, which received military supplies for the Republic, was the scene of terrible bombing and armed conflicts. This first drawing however, could not foresee the unfolding of future events. It refers merely to a moment of separation and distancing between the artist and his wife and newborn daughter. It is a full body portrait, in pencil and sanguine, with the soldier standing with his campaign bedroll in one hand, expressing a truncated life in a way that is simultaneously pictorial and narrative. In the course of the following years, Sarabia sketched further images of the conflict, including some other self-portraits. This set of illustrations depicts pain, sorrow, indignation, madness, hunger, love, misery, the absurdity of the military commanders, the unjustified violence of the battles, fear, death, or the helplessness of children wandering through Cartagena's streets. Though his experience is saturated with emotions, the narrative is not only emotional in nature. Many of the descriptions involve sensorial experiences. Sight, of course, but also hearing or taste play an important role in the configuration of his universe. In one instance he writes: "Giraban los proyectores. ¡Qué larga era la noche! El menor ruido parecía un aviso del más allá" (The searchlights kept revolving. How long the night was! The slightest noise seemed a warning from the other world). And then he adds in relation to another drawing (Fig. 10.2): "¡Zafarrancho de combate! El silbido de las bombas se clavaba en los sentidos. En breves momentos surgían atropelladamente todos los recuerdos de nuestra infancia . . . Nerviosismo, carreras precipitadas por cubierta. Después, un sabor agridulce, como si tuviéramos sangre en la boca" (Call to arms! The whistle of the bombs stabbed into the senses. For a few seconds, all our childhood memories flashed past us in a jumble. Nervousness, rushing around the deck. Then, a bittersweet taste, as if we had blood in our mouths).

From the point of view of their content, the drawings provide information on the day-to-day activities of a military port during the Spanish Civil War. They make clear reference to many bloody events, but they are not simply concerned with depicting the crudest scenarios. On the contrary, the images also represent the daily activities of sailors and marines, their interaction with the civilian population, and their fears, hopes, and expectations. As well as giving a physical description of his fellow sailors and the officers, Sarabia seems well aware of their emotional regimes. He describes not just what he sees but what he knows. The representation of his lived experience is

Figure 10.1. Luis Sarabia, *Apuntes.* "When I Arrived."

Figure 10.2. Luis Sarabia, *Apuntes.* "Call to Arms."

fully determined by other forms of information and background knowledge. As an eyewitness, he gives a detailed account of the observed behavior of many people, but also of the inner feelings of his comrades and fellow sailors. On many occasions, the visual depiction is strengthened by the power of the text accompanying the image, and by his value judgments and remarks. If the drawings provide information about activities in the military port, they also create a story, a form of organization of lived experience that can be simultaneously descriptive and emotional, visual and literary, private and public, sensorial and material. This overall narrative takes the poetic form of what the anthropology of experience calls a "social drama" (Turner, *From Ritual*). In this dramatic form, the tragedy of war is rendered comprehensible by the use of rhetorical elements and tools of persuasion. As in any other case, these rhetorical forms are firmly embedded in social values and cultural conventions.

Many of the most emotive scenes include detailed topographical indications: "Al filo de la medianoche, un ciego que tocaba el violín y una niña pedían limosna cerca del Arco de la Caridad. Las limosnas eran vales de la Defensa Pasiva o sellos de correos. A la derecha estaban las ruinas de un colegio y al fondo el Molinete, un barrio de mala nota. El caudal de lágrimas de la humanidad tenía aquí un magnífico afluente" (On the cusp of midnight, a blind violinist and a young girl were begging next to the Arch of

Figure 10.3. Luis Sarabia, *Apuntes*. "The 'Gato Negro.'"

Charity. The alms they received were Civilian Defense vouchers or postage stamps. To their right were the ruins of a school and in the background El Molinete, a district of ill repute. The river of tears of humankind had here a magnificent tributary). In some other cases, Sarabia saw fit to refer to the weather conditions or to specific historical or referential facts. The attention to detail generates conviction, for the verisimilitude of affects and feelings depends also on the descriptive precision of peoples and places. Though some of the drawings clearly relate to the bombings and other catastrophes of war, they also portray minor details of the "here and the now," that is, "small singularities without appearance," as in Figure 10.3, which depicts the Gato Negro nightclub. The caption explains this lighthearted scene in the context of what happened subsequently: "La proximidad de la muerte desarrollaba el deseo de vivir. La vida pasaba rápido. No había que perder el tiempo. Una bomba cayó en el "Gato negro" y entre los escombros aparecieron abrazados dos hombres a una misma mujer" (The proximity of death triggered a wish to live. Life went by very fast. There was no time to waste. A bomb hit the "Gato Negro" and in the debris were found the bodies of two men embracing the same woman).

The same poetic strategy allows, at one and the same time, a sense of detachment and involvement. Some of the drawings deal with conditions at the military port, but there are plenty of other stories reported in different ways. Sometimes Sarabia's autobiographical narrative is told in the third person, as if by a distant onlooker. The impression of detachment can be perceived throughout the series. After all, it is that ability to assume a detached perspective that holds the whole story together. This is especially clear in the description of the most common activities related to the military life of both sailors and marines. Sarabia does not take part in the rivalry between these two bodies or in many other circumstances relating to his military experience.[6] He seems to be at the same time fully involved and emotionally detached. In the midst of the tragedy, his privileged position allows him to provide eye-witness reports and accurate information, but he may also be placed backstage, looking at events from an imaginary remoteness: "Éramos peones de ajedrez con plato, manta y cuchara" (We were chess pawns with plate, blanket, and spoon). His narrative repertoire includes impersonal forms, but also use of the first and second person. On rare occasions, he addresses acquaintances in direct speech. "¿Alguna cosa más camarada? Nada más, gracias, señorita. Tú me miraste entre irónica y perpleja. Eras entonces dependienta de una tienda en la calle mayor. Meses más tarde acabó la guerra, y cuando nos volvimos a ver te miré yo, como tú me habías mirado aquel día" (Anything else, comrade? No, that's all, thank you, señorita. You stared at me half ironically, half perplexed. At the time you were a sales assistant in a high street store. Months later, when the war was over and we met again, I looked at you in the same way you had looked at me that day).

The correspondence between the tough conditions of everyday life and the expectations of those involved in the military actions is counter-balanced by the presence of special characters, particularly children. Their miserable living conditions become a matter of concern in a remarkable number of instances. "Siempre se encontraban niños al extremo de la plancha, que famélicos exclaman: ¡Marino, dame pan!" (There were always children at the end of the gangplank, in a starving chorus: "Sailor, give me some bread!"). The presence of these victims of war, with their pitiful gestures and unhappy lives, forms part of a wider rhetorical strategy. On the one hand, the sobriety and bravery of the military life may be replaced here by an emotional regime in which certain expressions are permitted. The reference to crying or tears, for example, absent in the crudest episodes, seems acceptable here: "En los tristes ojos del niño veíamos reflejados otros niños que levantando al aire sus manos parecían retenernos. Llanto sin lágrimas y en silencio. La máquina de la guerra había cogido a todos entre sus engranajes. ¿Por qué?" (In the boy's sad eyes we saw the many other children who seemed to retain us with their outstretched hands. Silent sobs without tears. The war machine had swept them all up in its cog wheels. Why?). On the other hand, the presence of children also suggests a correlation between the life force and the way that expectations and hopes had been shattered: "La ballenera trajo varias víctimas del bombardeo. Entre ellas estaba un niño. En sus dedos aún tenía el sedal con el que estaba pescando en el espigón del muelle" (The whaler brought back some victims of the air raid. Among them there was a boy. In his hand, he still had the line he was fishing with on the wharf). In the midst of tragedy children play the role of those who are ill prepared to understand the unfolding of events or the fragility of life. Their attitude is comparable only to the role played by those who became deranged as a result of battle: "Un marinero se volvió loco en un bombardeo. Días más tarde hubo que desembarcarlo, pues sin previo aviso gritaba en el sollado: ¡Cubrid antiaereos! Ya caen, nos matan!" (A sailor went crazy during an air raid. A few days later he had to be taken off the ship, since for no reason at all he'd start to shout on the lower deck: Man the anti-aircraft guns! The bombs are falling, they're killing us!).

Like children, women also play an important role. Interestingly, they are sometimes depicted as military officers, but their most important role is through their occasional encounters with the artist, who nonetheless portrays himself as a devoted father and husband. In one of the most intriguing drawings in the series, he seems to have abandoned his post to meet his one-year-old daughter in Valencia, on her birthday (Fig. 10.4). In another, perhaps the most tender of all, he stands smoking while his wife, with their daughter in her arms, waits to be evacuated. He describes his encounters with other women mainly as the result of fortuitous encounters in Cartagena's air-raid shelters or as a logical consequence of his wandering around the city. At the same time, he claims that these meetings were not the outcome of fortune. As in many other circumstances, war mixes freedom and necessity, fortune and inevitability.

> Leyes imperiosas nos unían. No era la casualidad. De la Facultad de Filosofía y Letras la guerra te había traído hasta aquí. A veces sin darte cuenta pensabas en alta voz con la parda tierra de tu castilla: Burgos. Yo te hablaba de los pazos y maizales, del arrullo amoroso de las rías. . . . Después tú y yo, arrepentidos de habernos dicho tanto, volvíamos a "nosotros mismos." Tú eras una mujer hermosa, yo . . . un hombre que la guerra había arrojado a la cubierta de un destructor.

> (Ineluctable laws united us. It was not sheer coincidence. From the Faculty of Arts, war had brought you here. Sometimes you spoke aloud unconsciously about the dark earth of your Castilian Burgos. And I talked to you about Galician country mansions and cornfields, about the gentle babble of coastal inlets. . . . Afterward, you and I, ashamed of having spoken so much, came back to "ourselves." You were a beautiful woman, and I . . . I was a man thrown by war onto a destroyer's deck).

Finally, the theatricality of experience also allows reflection on the traces and wounds that war has inflicted on different objects endowed with evocative properties: "Colgados de una plancha, bajo un sol abrasador se picaban y pintaban las amuras. La pintura no era suficiente para borrar la tragedia" (Dangling from a metal platform, under a scorching sun, they scraped and painted the ship's bows. But paint was not enough to erase the tragedy). In this as in many other instances, objects were the raw material from which to craft a memory: "¡Hambre, miedo, frío! En la calle Gisbert estaban los refugios más sólidos. Una muñeca en el barro ponía una nota sentimental" (Hunger, fear, cold! The most solidly built air-raid shelters were in Calle Gisbert. A doll

Figure 10.4. Luis Sarabia, *Apuntes*. "My Daughter's Birthday."

in the mud added a sentimental note). The theatrical nature of the narrative involves games of presence and absence, expression and repression. In some instances, Sarabia encounters people who he clearly would have loved to see again.[7] In others, he wishes he could have said something but could not. The need to give an account remains pressing, not just with regard to what affects him personally, but also with regard to other people's lives and stories. His way of acting, thinking, and feeling is configured by a moral economy of hopes and expectations, by a mixture of what he feels and what he knows. On some occasions, his descriptions are based on his knowledge of poetry, as in the following reference to Gabriela Mistral's poem "Ruth": "Fue cerca de santa Lucía. En un refugio en construcción aguantamos el bombardeo. ¡Cómo sentía palpitar aceleradamente su corazón! Su voluntad la había abandonado. Inconscientemente iba recordando el poema de Ruth en el desierto" (It was near Santa Lucía. We sat out the bombing in an air-raid shelter still under construction. How I felt her heart pounding! Her will had left her. Unconsciously, I began to remember the poem about Ruth in the desert).[8] On many other occasions, he seems overwhelmed by feelings of nostalgia and melancholia.[9] From a visual point of view, his drawings share aesthetic features with the murals and posters used in the Republic's propaganda campaigns. Their lines recall, especially in the depiction of women, the stylized bodies of Rafael de Penagos,

Figure 10.5. Luis Sarabia, *Apuntes.* "Victory."

then Professor of Drawing at Valencia's Instituto Obrero (Worker's Institute). The value of Sarabia's work, however, depends not so much on its artistic quality as on its will and determination to construct a narrative: to produce a story that could at the same time lay the groundwork for memory. Stronger than the will to live is the will to order the heterogeneous elements of lived experience so that the unconnected, the illogical, and the disproportionate may take on the meaningful qualities of a coherent narrative. Although these images do not constitute a military chronicle or a political history, they offer experience in its temporary delimitation and collective significance. In their particular way, they reflect the tension between the flow of life and the need to endow that flow with order, stability, coherence, and meaning.

In May 1939, just over a month after Franco's victory on 1 April 1939, Sarabia did one of the last drawings in the series. He wrote: "Amanecía. . . . Las horas de espera y de frío nos habían entumecido. Ansías de llegar otra vez, de encontrarnos a nosotros mismos, de sonar despiertos. . . . En un trozo de manta de marinero, envuelta y dormida en aquel áspero amanecer, yacía la ilusión e inquietud de nuestra existencia" (Day was breaking. . . . The hours of waiting and cold had numbed us. Eager to arrive, to find ourselves, to daydream. In a piece of sailor's blanket, wrapped round us as we slept in that rough dawn, lay the hope and anxiety of our existence). The next two drawings depict starving beggars and children watching the military victory parades (Fig. 10.5). The journey through the real and imaginary space of the armed conflict, as a result of which no one would ever again be what they had been before, uses ritualized forms and cultural frames (Simmel). The terminology issue to which we referred above is not relevant here. Sarabia's experiences are permeated with sensations, feelings, and emotions. The fictional constitution of a dramatic form in which war could be both experienced and expressed implies the mobilization of cultural constructs and rhetorical tools.

The drawings, which remained hidden during the postwar period, were unearthed in the late years of Francoism. Around 1960, their author portrayed himself for the last time. Alone again, not numb with cold now but daydreaming of events lived in the past in the half-light of his sitting room, he wrote: "Han pasado los años, pero a veces, cuando surgen atropellados los recuerdos de aquellos días, nos preguntamos si hemos vuelto a ser los mismos de aquel ayer" (The years have passed, but sometimes, when the memories of those days flood back chaotically, I ask myself if I've reverted to being the person I was then). His work, which remains unpublished, represents an example of culture understood, as Nietzsche claimed, as a symptom of the body, and of how experience is materialized, as Wilhelm Dilthey suggested, in legal, literary, scientific, or artistic forms (Dilthey, *Selected Works* 153–74). The fifty or so images that make up the series share the narrative structure of what the anthropologist Victor Turner thought to be the constitutive elements of experience (*From Ritual*). Rupture, separation, and reconciliation meet in this form of living and understanding the inner nature of war.

The anthropologist Clifford Geertz, following the philosopher Dilthey, distinguished between a mere experience, an experience, and an exemplary experience. For our purposes, it is enough to distinguish between the mere experience and its public or intersubjective expressions (Bruner 5). Sarabia's drawings do not exhaust what he may have seen and lived after being mobilized. His sketchbook configures only one possible formula for structuring and giving sense to what he endured. The relationship between his experience of war and his drawings is not simply *causal*, in the sense that the former (the experience) determined the form of the latter (the expression). On the contrary, it is the already articulated experience, infected with his knowledge, expectations, and values, that modulates the moment and disposition in which he decided which representations would be produced and in what way they might also be accurate and meaningful.

The Anthropology of Experience

Cultural historians have noted that images are not transparent and that, consequently, they cannot be interpreted as mere representations of states of things or states of mind. This is tantamount to saying that pictorial expressions can be understood not as literal accounts of experiences, but rather as indications of the evaluative, intellectual, and emotional factors that modulate different forms of life. From this point of view, the cultural history of emotions can then consist not of knowing how we can access the private contents of another person's consciousness, but rather of knowing how an articulate experience may be constructed. Conversely, it will be necessary to clarify the extent to which that material repository, those culturally embedded expressions, determine how people feel and make sense of their world. The anthropology of experience has given us some suggestions for how we might untangle this Gordian knot. Experiences, it claims, have a dramatic form, which means that they are interpreted and staged (Turner, "Dewey, Dilthey"; Kubiak). As in the case of Sarabia, whose imaginary existence is determined by its constant staging, emotions have their actors, their plots, their audiences, their costumes, their props, their scenery, and, of course, their audience (Rancière). Far from lacking a voice or challenging language, the literary form of the emotions is theater, the dramatic manifestation of their iconic character (Enders). Their cultural expression is not merely demonstrative, just as those who express their emotions, even to themselves, do not wish to prevail but to persuade. They want to share them via a repertoire of learned rhetorical rules. Their cries, their words, their actions attempt to turn certainties into truths through the mediation of persuasive elements. In the emotional drama of experience, feelings and emotions always materialize via the strict observance of rules of persuasion. Thus, the history of emotions should focus on the conditions that make possible the cultural and historical modulations of experience or, more precisely, on the material and discursive forms that allow the emotionality of the experience. The content of these cultural forms, to use the terminology of the sociologist Georg Simmel, not only represents a material expression of lived experiences; it also brings into the arena of public awareness undetected or forgotten pasts.

NOTES

This text has benefited from a research grant from the Spanish Ministry of Economic Affairs (FFI2013-46361-R). It was written while I was visiting professor at the Center for the Humanities of Washington University in St. Louis, Missouri; I am grateful to the center's director, Jean Allman, and all those who made that visit possible.

1. Scholars generally quote a 1941 text by Lucien Febvre as the starting point of this new discipline. See Febvre, "Sensibility and History." For a general review of the history of the emotions since the 1940s, see Rosenwein "Worrying about Emotions," in which she defended "emotional communities" or "affective systems" as heuristic tools, an idea developed in her later influential *Emotional Communities*. Particularly valuable work has been done by Bourke (*Fear*; "Fear and Anxiety"); Dinzelbacher; Gay (*Education of the Senses*; *The Tender Passion*; *The Cultivation of Hatred*); Paster, Rowe, and Floyd-Wilson; Reddy; Spacks; Stearns and Stearns; Stearns; Bouwsma.
2. By "other subjective experiences" that cannot simply be considered "emotions," I mean, for example, the inner narrative of any illness, or the set of subjective states related to complex emotional, volitive, and intellectual experiences, like the experience of war, for example. Generally speaking, the term "affect" has come to signify the conscious or unconscious property of being influenced or acted on by something (Charland 9).

3. Despite many efforts to distinguish clearly between "affects" and "emotions," the latter being the conscious and evaluative version of the former, the distinction remains rather blurred. For a general overview, see Moors.
4. For an intellectual history of the word "experience," see Jay. I use a notion of experience close to that of Dilthey (*Introduction* 245–353).
5. See Rorty: "The crucial premise of this argument is that there is no such thing as a justified belief which is non-propositional, and no such thing as justification which is not a relation between propositions" (*Philosophy and the Mirror* 183). See also Rorty, *The Linguistic Turn*, especially his postscript to the Spanish edition "Veinte años después" (159–67).
6. "La rivalidad con los marinos eran ancestral. Hasta la piedad parecía detenerse ante el color del uniforme. Al fondo, las palmeras parecían querer hablarnos de las islas paradisíacas de los mares del Sur" (The rivalry with the marines was ancestral. Even pity seemed to be blocked by the color of the uniform. In the background, the palm trees seemed to speak of the idyllic islands of the southern seas).
7. "Rodó vertiginosamente el camión durante muchas horas. Al llegar, con palabras entrecortadas, me agradeciste la ayuda que os presté. Por primera y última vez nos vimos" (The truck hurtled on for hours. When we got there, you thanked me breathlessly for my help. It was the first and last time we saw each other).
8. Mistral's poem reads: "Ruth moabita a espigar va a las eras, / aunque no tiene ni un campo mezquino. / Piensa que es Dios dueño de las praderas / y que ella espiga en un predio divino" (Ruth the Moabite goes to glean at the threshing floor, / though she owns no land of her own. / She thinks that God is the owner of the fields / and that she is gleaning on divine ground).
9. "¿Un marino? ¡Un héroe! Decían unos carteles de propaganda. ¿Tres? Una borrachera, apuntaba la gente. Y es que en el fondo de cada vaso de vino siempre quedaba una canción, que hablaba de la paz serena de las rías. Canciones alegres cantadas por gentes tristes" (A marine? A hero! said the propaganda posters. Three marines? A booze-up, people added. At the bottom of every wine glass there was always a song that evoked the peace of the coastal inlets. Happy songs sung by sad people).

WORKS CITED

Bernabéu, Salvador, and Frédérique Langue, eds. *Fronteras y sensibilidades en las Américas*. Madrid: Doce Calles, 2011.

Bloch, Marc. *The Royal Touch*. 1924. London: Routledge and Kegan Paul, 1973.

Bourke, Joanna. *Fear: A Cultural History*. London: Virago, 2005.

———. "Fear and Anxiety: Writing about Emotion in Modern History." *History Workshop Journal* 55 (2003): 111–33.

Bouwsma, William James. "Anxiety and the Formation of Early Modern Culture." *A Usable Past: Essays in European Cultural History*. Ed. William James Bouwsma. Berkeley: U of California P, 1990. 157–90.

Bruner, Edward M. "Experience and Its Expressions." *The Anthropology of Experience*. Ed. Victor W. Turner and Edward M. Bruner. Chicago: U of Chicago P, 1986.

Burke, Peter. "Is There a Cultural History of the Emotions?" *Representing Emotions: New Connections in the Histories of Art, Music and Medicine*. Ed. Penelope Gouk and Helen Hills. Aldershot: Ashgate, 2005. 35–48.

Charland, Louis C. "Affect." *The Oxford Companion to Emotion and Affective Sciences*. Ed. David Sander and Klaus R. Schreder. Oxford: Oxford UP, 2014. 9–10.

Corbin, Alain. *Les Cloches de la terre: Paysage sonore et culture sensible dans les campagnes au XIXème siècle*. Paris: Albin Michel, 1997.

Demartini, Anna Emmanuelle, and Dominique Kalifa, eds. *Imaginaire et sensibilités au XIXème siècle: Études pour Alain Corbin*. Paris: Creaphis, 2005.

Dilthey, Wilhelm. *Selected Works*. Vol. 3. *The Formation of the Historical World in the Human Sciences*. Princeton, NJ: Princeton UP, 2002.

———. *Introduction to the Human Sciences*. Vol. 1, book 4. *Foundations of Knowledge*. Trans. Jeffrey Barnow and Franz Schreiner. Princeton, NJ: Princeton UP, 1989.

Dinzelbacher, Peter. *Angst in Mittelalter: Teufels-, Todes- und Gotteserfahrung; Mentalitätsgeschichte und Ikonographie*. Munich: Schningh, 1996.

Dixon, Thomas. *From Passions to Emotions: The Creation of a Secular Psychological Category*. Cambridge: Cambridge UP, 2003.

Enders, Jody. *The Medieval Theater of Cruelty: Rhetoric, Memory, Violence*. Ithaca, NY: Cornell UP, 1999.

Febvre, Lucien. *The Problem of Unbelief in the Sixteenth Century*. 1942. Trans. Beatrice Gottlieb. Cambridge, MA: Harvard UP, 1983.

———. "Sensibility and History: How to Reconstitute the Emotional Life of the Past." *A New Kind of History and Other Essays*. Ed. Peter Burke. Trans. K. Folca. New York: Routledge and Kegan Paul, 1973. 12–27.

Foucault, Michel. "Nietzsche, Genealogy, History." *Language, Counter-memory, Practice: Selected Essays and Interviews by Michel Foucault*. Ed. D. F. Bouchard. Ithaca, NY: Cornell UP, 1977. 139–64.

Frevert, Ute. "Defining Emotions: Concepts and Debates over Three Centuries." *Emotional Lexicons: Continuity and Change in the Vocabulary of Feeling 1700–2000*. Ed. Ute Frevert et al. Oxford: Oxford UP, 2014. 1–31.

Gay, Peter. *The Cultivation of Hatred*. New York: W. W. Norton, 1993.

———. *Education of the Senses*. New York: Oxford UP, 1984.

———. *The Tender Passion*. New York: Oxford UP, 1986.

Geertz, Clifford. *The Interpretation of Cultures*. London: Basic Books, 1975.

Goldstein, Jan. *Console and Classify: The French Psychiatric Profession in the Nineteenth Century*. Cambridge: Cambridge UP, 1987.

———. *The Post-revolutionary Self*. Cambridge, MA: Harvard UP, 2005.

Horkheimer, Max, and Theodor W. Adorno. *Dialectic of Enlightenment: Philosophical Fragments*. Ed. Gunzelin Schmidt Noerr. Trans. Edmund Jephcott. Stanford, CA: Stanford UP, 2002.

Huizinga, Johan. *The Autumn of the Middle Ages*. Trans. Rodney J. Payton. Chicago: U of Chicago P, 1966.

Jay, Martin. *Songs of Experience: Modern American and European Variations on a Universal Theme*. Berkeley: U of California P, 2006.

Koselleck, Reinhart. "Transformation of Experience and Methodological Change: A Historical-Anthropological Essay." *The Practice of Conceptual History*. Trans. Todd Samuel Presner et al. Stanford, CA: Stanford UP, 2002. 45–83.

Kubiak, Anthony. *Stages of Terror: Terrorism, Ideology, and Coercion as Theatre History*. Bloomington: Indiana UP, 1991.

Labanyi, Jo. "Doing Things: Emotions, Affect, and Materiality." *Journal of Spanish Cultural Studies* 11.3 (2010): 223–33.
LaCapra, Dominick. *History in Transit: Experience, Identity, Critical Theory*. Ithaca, NY: Cornell UP, 2004.
———. *Writing History, Writing Trauma*. Baltimore: Johns Hopkins UP, 2001.
Massumi, Brian. *Parables for the Virtual: Movement, Affect, Sensation*. Durham, NC: Duke UP, 2002.
Matt, Susan, and Peter N. Stearns. *Doing Emotions History*. Urbana: U of Illinois P, 2014.
Moors, A. "Theories of Emotion Causation: A Review." *Cognition and Emotion* 23 (2009): 209–37.
Moscoso, Javier. *Pain: A Cultural History*. Trans. Sarah Thomas. London: Palgrave Macmillan, 2012.
Paster, Gail K., Katherine Rowe, and Mary Floyd-Wilson, eds. *Reading the Early Modern Passions: Essays in the Cultural History of Emotion*. Philadelphia: U of Pennsylvania P, 2004.
Rancière, Jacques. *The Emancipated Spectator*. Trans. Gregory Elliot. London: Verso, 2009.
Reddy, William M. *The Navigation of Feeling: A Framework for the History of Emotions*. Cambridge: Cambridge UP, 2001.
Rorty, Richard. *The Linguistic Turn: Recent Essays in Philosophical Method*. Chicago: U of Chicago P, 1975. Rpt. in Spanish as *El giro lingüístico*. Trans. Gabriel Bello. Barcelona: Paidós, 1998
———. *Philosophy and the Mirror of Nature*. Princeton, NJ: Princeton UP, 1979.
Rosenwein, Barbara H. *Emotional Communities in the Early Middle Ages*. Ithaca, NY: Cornell UP, 2006.
———. "Problems and Methods in the History of Emotions." *Passions in Context* 1.1 (2010): 1–32. www.passionsincontext.de/index.php?id=557 (accessed 5 December 2013).
———. "Worrying about Emotions in History." *American Historical Review* 107 (2002): 821–45.
Sarabia, Luis. "En el puerto: Apuntes de un movilizado en la Marina Roja." Unpublished. Private collection, Madrid.
Scarry, Elaine. *The Body in Pain: The Making and the Unmaking of the World*. New York: Oxford UP, 1985.
Simmel, Georg. "Subjective Culture." *On Individuality and Social Forms*. Ed. Donald N. Levine. Chicago: U of Chicago P, 1972. 227–34.
Spacks, Patricia M. *Boredom: The Literary History of a State of Mind*. Chicago: U of Chicago P, 1995.
Stearns, Carol Z., and Peter N. Stearns. *Anger: The Struggle for Emotional Control in America's History*. Chicago: U of Chicago P, 1986.
Stearns, Peter N. *Jealousy: The Evolution of an Emotion in American History*. New York: New York UP, 1989.
Turner, Victor W. "Dewey, Dilthey, and Drama: An Essay in the Anthropology of Experience." *The Anthropology of Experience*. Ed. Victor W. Turner and Edward M. Bruner. Urbana: U of Illinois P, 1986. 33–44.
———. *From Ritual to Theatre: The Human Seriousness of Play*. New York: PAJ Publications, 1982.

CHAPTER 11

Affective Variations
Queering Hispanidad in Luis Cernuda's Mexico

ENRIQUE ÁLVAREZ

In spite of the emotionality so characteristic of his writing, Luis Cernuda's first impressions of exile in a Spanish-speaking country have been studied in terms of their political implications. But, as Nigel Thrift argues, "political concepts and beliefs can never be reduced to 'disembodied tokens of argumentation'" ("Intensities" 71). Instead, Thrift proposes a "geology of thinking" that takes into account a multilayered notion of culture in which identity and difference "operate on several registers, each with their own organizations and complexities" ("Intensities" 71–72). In what follows, I will apply Thrift's argument to Cernuda's writing on Mexico from the critical perspective afforded by affective encounters and relationships. I am mainly concerned with the affective in the sense of pertaining to feeling, that is, as an emotional attachment produced through the relationship to another. I will also identify certain moments in Cernuda's Mexican texts in which he seems to describe a preconscious impact of the external world on the body, approximating to what, in recent scholarship, has been theorized as affect (Massumi; Clough and Halley; Thrift, *Non-representational Theory*). From this angle, I would like to reflect on the semantic effects of precognitive impulses on the Cernudian creative process. In both cases, my intention is to explore the different ways whereby Cernuda's literary representation of Mexico engages with the affective by offering "forms of embodied knowledge" (Labanyi 230).

Critics have emphasized the semantic contradiction of the placing side by side of Hispanic and indigenous motifs in Cernuda's major 1952 collection of prose poetry *Variaciones sobre tema mexicano* (*Variations on a Mexican Theme*) (*Obra completa* 1: 617–58). James Valender, for example, rightly points out that Cernuda's vision of Mexico reproduces the ahistorical tendency, so characteristic of the Generation of 98, to affirm spirituality as the ideological basis of the Hispanic collective consciousness. In Valender's perceptive argument, Cernuda's vision of the Mexican *Volksgeist* has a dual basis,

> por una parte, la indolencia asociada con su Andalucía nativa . . . y por otra, el fervor contrarreformista identificado con la Castilla imperial. . . . De ahí el gran atractivo de México, en cuanto le permitía crearse la ilusión de tener el conflicto resuelto; en

la interpenetración de las dos tradiciones culturales—la hispánica y la indígena—Cernuda pensaba haber encontrado una imagen perfecta del equilibrio entre Castilla y Andalucía que él reclamaba como base de su identidad. (*Cernuda* 118–19).

(on the one hand, the indolence associated with his native Andalusia, . . . and, on the other, the Counter-Reformation fervor identified with imperial Castile. . . . That was for him Mexico's greatest attraction, insofar as it allowed him to create the illusion of having resolved the conflict; in the interpenetration of the two cultural traditions—the Hispanic and the indigenous—Cernuda thought he had found the perfect image of the balance between Castile and Andalusia that he claimed as the basis of his identity).

Following Valender's critical line, Bernard Sicot speaks of a "síntesis geográfica" (geographical synthesis; *Exilio* 171), arguing that Cernuda's difficult attempt at a geographical compromise "lleva al poeta a repetir, a veces palabra por palabra, el discurso dominante que, desde principios de la guerra civil, el franquismo imponía en España" (leads the poet to repeat, sometimes verbatim, the dominant discourse that the Franco regime imposed in Spain from the start of the Civil War; *Exilio* 172). Noting the poor reception of Cernuda's book in Mexico, Sicot asks, "¿Cómo imaginar . . . que se acogiera favorablemente un libro que, publicado en semejante colección, ignora el rico pasado prehispánico de México y glorifica a aquellos que lo destruyeron?" (How could we expect . . . a book published in such a collection, but which ignores the rich past of prehispanic Mexico and glorifies those who destroyed it, to be received favorably?; *Exilio* 191–92). Indeed, ironically, *Variaciones* was first published by a Mexican press in a series devoted to "México y lo mexicano" ("Mexico and Mexicanness"), coinciding with nationalistic discourses prevalent in Mexico in the 1950s.

While Cernuda's use of the discourse of *Hispanidad* to understand the Mexican context is undeniable, I would like to argue that there is another crucial element of his exile poetry that unsettles what could otherwise be perceived as a rather traditional view of Latin America. Cernuda's open display of a queer desire and sensibility conflicted head-on with the hyperbolic notion of heterosexual masculinity prevalent not only in Mexican understandings of national identity, but also within the bureaucratic logic of the Francoist state. As is well known, the dictatorship's vindictive politics of national regeneration, based on the demonization of its Republican adversaries, invoked crude versions of machismo alongside the fierce repression of male homosexuality.[1] Within this historical context, Cernuda's account of his emotional attachment to Mexico works against the gender politics implicit, and often explicit, in twentieth-century Spanish discourses of national identity. In this respect, Cernuda contributes to what Mabel Moraña has called the shift from "the illusion of the existence of fixed and ahistorical identities" to "a much more volatile, porous, temporary experience of *the social*, where *otherness*, heterogeneity, and diversity are the conspicuous protagonists of cultural exchanges and epistemological explorations" (xvii). My goal is to show how Cernuda's Mexican reimagining of Spain builds on a queer affective narrative that replicates but at the same time undermines the Spanish nationalist principles it ostensibly articulates. The anchoring of Cernuda's Mexican imaginary in queer desire disturbs the homophobic rhetoric of official Hispanidad.

In *The Homoerotics of Orientalism*, Joseph Allen Boone questions the binaries (subject/object, self/other) that are often taken for granted in the critical analysis of colonial texts. According to Boone's insightful argument, "within the Western fantasies of the 'Orient' lies the potential for unexpected eruptions of sex between men that, however temporarily, disrupt European norms of masculinity and heterosexual priority" (xviii). Boone urges us "to attend to nuance, suggestion, indirection and contradiction" and "to imagine the interpretative possibilities that exist between the lines" (xxiv). Considering the undisputable presence of an Orientalist poetics in Cernuda's Mexican writing, I propose that his ambiguous, paradoxical self-inscription in these texts has to be read cross-culturally as an affective map of the three incompatible themes that characterize it: Hispanidad, *indigenismo*, and male homoerotic desire.

Spanish Exile Writing and Textual Emotionality

In a discussion of the role that emotions play in Spanish exile writing, Noël Valis notes that "you cannot separate the historic-political fact of exile from the feelings which emerge from it" (117). Valis reads these feelings as historically specific, nostalgic yearnings for the lost home. Indeed, Cernuda's unapologetic praise of Spanish colonial history in his Mexican writing needs to be studied as a nostalgic structure of feeling that bonds the emotional experience of exile to the cultural imaginary of the nation, thereby determining its relevance at a specific juncture of twentieth-century Spanish history. I follow here Raymond Williams's definition of structure of feeling as "a particular quality of social experience and relationship, historically distinct from other particular qualities, which gives the sense of a generation or a period" (131). As Williams further explains, "we are talking about characteristic elements of impulse, restraint, and tone; specifically affective elements of consciousness and relationship: not feeling against thought, but thought as felt and feeling as thought" (132). Feelings such as shame, pride, anger, sympathy, and love are also present in Cernuda's Mexican writing, complicating the melancholic attachment to the past that Mari Paz Balibrea has analyzed in Republican exile texts. On the one hand, Balibrea notes that the nostalgia of these attachments seems to make them "useless to the forward-looking nation" (15). On the other hand, she asks whether these texts might be approached differently as counter-readings that interrupt the temporalities of modernity, or, alternatively, be read as signs of memory's new political and critical role (15). She notes that colonialism is one of these modern temporalities (Balibrea 14). This invites a counterreading of Cernuda's Mexico that would potentially destabilize the rigid ideological boundaries of colonial Spain, while showing the flimsy contingency of masculinized, heteronormative understandings of Spain as a nation.

My alternative reading of Cernuda's Mexico will address the question of textual emotionality from two main theoretical angles. First, my claim rests on Sara Ahmed's influential take on the "emotionality of texts" (12) as "the way in which texts name or perform different emotions" (13). Following Ahmed's contention, "feeling does not simply exist before the utterance, but becomes 'real' as an effect, shaping *different kinds of actions and operations*" (13; emphasis added). In addition, my understanding of textual emotionality is further grounded in Cernuda's poetic language as an anxious juxtaposition of affective and ideological impressions. In line with Stanley Fish's teaching on "affective stylistics," I will identify several moments in the reading experience "when attention is compelled because an expectation has been disappointed by the appearance of an unpredicted element" (155). Although Fish's work is not necessarily concerned with textual emotionality, he does talk about textual incoherence and the role of the reader in semantic reconstruction. In my analysis of Cernuda's Mexico, I understand textual emotionality in a similar way; that is, as a moment of stylistic uncertainty that somehow affects the reading experience.

Untimely Love and Depersonalized Bodies

In 1950s Spain, Cernuda was a writer particularly despised by the Franco regime; consequently, during the dictatorship his work was met with silence. After Franco's death, in an introductory essay to his 1977 edition of Cernuda's prose poetry, Jaime Gil de Biedma indicated the particular relevance of affective relationships between men as the emotional drive of Cernuda's writing on Mexico: "en México se enamoraría por última vez . . . y uno casi se siente tentado de sospechar, que ese enamoramiento no fue sino la concreción final, en un cuerpo y en una persona, del deslumbramiento instantáneo, del inesperado brote de felicidad sensual que aquella tierra propició en él, cuando en su edad madura apenas ya nada esperaba" (in Mexico he would fall in love for the last time . . . and one is almost tempted to suspect that this falling in love was nothing less than the final materialization, in a body and a person, of the immediate, overwhelming, unexpected rush of sensual happiness that Mexico induced in him, when in his maturity he had hardly any expectations left; Cernuda, *Ocnos* xvii). As Gil de Biedma suggests, same-sex emotional attachments are at the core of Cernuda's Mexican writing. However, most critics who have discussed the issue have dematerialized it, subscribing to an ideal sexual fantasy of the Cernudian poetic subject as "un cuerpo despersonalizado" (a depersonalized body; Valender, *Cernuda* 103).

As has been amply explained in biographical accounts of Cernuda's life in Mexico, the body that concretized the homoerotic experience for Cernuda had a proper name, Salvador Alighieri, who occupies a key place within Cernuda's exile writing. Most critics agree that Alighieri was the object of the speaker's affection in "Poemas para un cuerpo" ("Poems for a Body"), the series of sixteen love poems dated between 1951 and 1952, published later as a colophon to *Con las horas contadas* (*With Numbered Hours*,

1950–1956) (Valender, "Luis" 40; Teruel 148, 152). In his own recollection of the emotional thrust behind these poems, Cernuda explained: "Creo que ninguna otra vez estuve, si no tan enamorado, tan bien enamorado, como acaso pueda entreverse en los versos antes citados, que dieron expresión a dicha experiencia tardía. Mas al llamarla tardía debo añadir que jamás en mi juventud me sentí tan joven como en aquellos días en México; cuántos años habían debido pasar, y venir al otro extremo del mundo, para vivir esos momentos felices." (I think that no other time was I, if not so much in love, so well in love, as perhaps can be glimpsed in the previously cited verses that gave expression to that late experience. But, having called it 'late,' I should add that in my youth I never felt so young as in those days in Mexico; how many years had to pass, not to mention having to come to the other end of the world, to be able to live those happy moments; P 2: 656).[2]

José Teruel suggests that homophobia is at stake in the moral panic so pervasive in critical approaches to Cernuda's Mexican love object: "la reducción del amor a un cuerpo, de la identidad a una 'x' y la exclusión del deseo del amado, que queda barrido y fuera de la historia, han sido apreciadas como referencias que pudieran 'estropear' su poesía" (The reduction of love to a body, of an identity to an 'x' and the exclusion of the desire of the beloved, which is swept out of history, have been perceived as references that might 'spoil' his poetry; 152). Teruel further explains that the depersonalization of the beloved in Cernuda's Mexican writing should be considered not so much as a conscious attempt to erase the particularity of the love object, but rather as motivated by *pudor* (embarrassment; 152). As we will see, in Cernuda's affective "variations," queer *pudor* is inextricably intertwined with a proud, Hispanocentric colonial discourse at the very foundation of his Mexican writing.

Queer Performativity: Hispanidad and the Love of Shame

A certain feeling of national shame can be detected at the very opening of *Variaciones*. "El tema" ("The Theme"), which functions as an introduction to the entire collection, laments Spanish intellectuals' lack of historical responsibility toward Latin America, citing the oft-quoted examples of Larra and Galdós. According to Cernuda, the national vision of Larra and Galdós is incomplete because they showed no concern for the independence process of the Spanish American nations: "Ni Larra ni Galdós, quienes, aunque tan diferentes, tenían una conciencia igualmente clara, se preocuparon nunca por estas otras tierras de raigambre española. Ante su desgarramiento peninsular, Larra, contemporáneo, Galdós, casi contemporáneo, guardan silencio" (Neither Larra nor Galdós, who, though so different, were equally clear-sighted, ever showed any interest in these other lands with Spanish roots. Faced with their severance from the peninsula, Larra, a contemporary, Galdós, almost a contemporary, keep silent; PC 621). Although he does not specifically talk of "shame" in this passage, this lack of interest is clearly felt by Cernuda to be somewhat shameful. Using Sara Ahmed's apt characterization of national shame in a different context, we could say that Cernuda's vicarious sense of national shame expresses the failure of the Spanish nineteenth-century intellectuals "to live up to an ideal as a mode of identification with the nation" (Ahmed 108). This initial feeling of shame conflicts with, and seems to intensify, Cernuda's explicit pride in the magnitude of the Spanish colonial enterprise in the Americas, which he refers to as "el acontecer maravilloso, obra de un puñado de hombres cuyo igual no parece haberse visto antes o después" (that wonderful achievement, the work of a handful of men, whose equal has not been seen before or since"; PC 622), a rhetoric very consistent with Francoist views on the subject of colonization.

Confronted with a new American reality, Cernuda initiates *Variaciones* with a process of affective restitution toward Latin America that moves between a renewed attention to the Spanish colonial past, and an interest, sympathy, and love for Mexico's territory and its inhabitants, which explicitly produces in him an emotional response of pudor: "Esa curiosidad fue la vida con sus azares quien mucho más tarde la provocó en ti, al ponerte frente a la realidad americana. Y tras la curiosidad vino el interés; tras el interés la simpatía, tras la simpatía el amor. Mas un pudor extraño le dificulta su expresión a ese amor tardío. ¿Reconocimiento de su inutilidad? Pudor es, en todo caso, lo que en este punto, callándote ahora, te lleva a soslayar el tema" (That curiosity was life with its vicissitudes, a curiosity aroused in you much later on when life presented you with America. And after curiosity came interest; after interest, sympathy; after sympathy, love. But a strange embarrassment makes it difficult to express that late love. Recognition of its uselessness? Embarrassment is, in any case, what keeps you quiet now in this respect, making you sidestep the issue; PC 622). Although not automatically equated with *vergüenza* (shame) in the sense of having done something wrong, *pudor* summons in Spanish a feeling of modesty, shyness, and sexual embarrassment related to the body, all of which produce in Cernuda's text a new, self-conscious awareness of shame.[3]

It has been argued that shame manifests a desire for the reconstitution of individual and collective subjectivities. Ahmed, for example, maintains that "the individuation of shame—the way it turns the self against and towards the self—can be linked precisely to the inter-corporeality and sociality of shame experiences" (105). For Ahmed, the experience of shame "requires an identification with the other who, as witness, returns the subject to itself" (106). Similarly, Eve Kosofsky Sedgwick understands shame as "a form of communication" that manifests "a desire to reconstitute the interpersonal bridge" (36). Sedgwick also notes that shame is "transformational" (38), constantly attaching itself to other feelings such as pride and dignity, self-display and exhibitionism, all of which can be readily applied to Cernuda's emotional plea in the previously quoted text.

Taking into account Sedgwick's argument about shame as a transformational impulse, Michael D. Snediker has coined the concept of "the love of shame." As he explains: "The love of shame . . . occurs in the disruption of what otherwise might be seen as a continuous self. The love of shame does not 'merge,' does not synthesize, but flourishes in the space of personal fissure" (18). In *Variaciones*, this "personal fissure" materializes in the dialogic form ubiquitous in Cernuda's texts; that is, in the textual dialogue established between the speaker and the "you" he addresses at the moment of writing. This idiosyncratic stylistic feature of Cernuda's poetry allows him to counter his own argument with an opposing statement, making it difficult for the reader to adhere straightforwardly to either view. However, Cernuda's personal fissure emerges first and foremost in his reticence to fully engage the true nature of his Mexican love object. As we have seen, in this inaugural Mexican text, the shift from shame to pride; from pride to sympathy and love; and from all these feelings to some sort of sexual embarrassment, brings into relief a textual performance of emotion that shows Cernuda's ambivalence toward "El tema" that he is about to tackle. What undoubtedly becomes clear is that, in Cernuda's Mexico, "love is shown to occur both in spite of shame and, more remarkably, through it" (Sedgwick 40). Consequently, Cernuda's final display of pudor in "El tema" can be read as an example of what Sedgwick calls "queer performativity," namely, "a strategy for the production of meaning and being, in relation to the affect shame and to the later and related fact of stigma" (61). We cannot forget that, as Didier Eribon has argued, the stigma associated with insult can be found at the core of gay and lesbian shaming, which also plays a part in Cernuda's pudor.

We should note that the "unashamed" reproduction in *Variaciones* of the discourse of Hispanidad includes Cernuda's pride in the imposition onto the Americas of the Spanish language. For instance, in "La lengua" ("Language") Cernuda describes his emotion on hearing Spanish spoken as he crossed the US-Mexican border in the following terms: "qué gratitud no puede sentir el artesano oscuro, vivo en ti, de esta lengua hoy tuya, a quien cuatro siglos atrás, con la pluma y la espada, ganaron para ella destino universal. Porque el poeta no puede conseguir para su lengua ese destino si no le asiste el héroe, ni éste si no le asiste el poeta" (how can the obscure craftsman alive in you not feel gratitude to those who, four centuries ago, with pen and sword, won a universal destiny for this language that is yours today? For the poet cannot achieve that destiny for his language without the aid of the hero, nor the hero without the aid of the poet; PC 626). Cernuda, so harsh in his appraisal of what it means to be Spanish—"soy español sin ganas" (I am reluctantly Spanish; PC 503)—seems to have no problem with the colonial imaginary.[4] Sebastiaan Faber explains the coincidence of Republican intellectuals' and Francoist accounts of Spanish national identity as a struggle for "cultural hegemony." Within the context of post–Civil War international relations, prestige became a pressing issue for the Republican exiles as they disputed the Francoist appropriation of the cultural symbols of the nation. According to Faber's argument, "[Spanish] exiles set on maintaining their national identity have to make do with cultural symbols [of traditional Spanishness]" in order to "ground" the imagined community (Faber, *Exile* 41).

By describing himself as an obscure craftsman ("artesano oscuro") of the Spanish language, Cernuda is both perpetuating the imposition of Spanish and distancing himself from the triumphalism of the conquistadors for whom he professes admiration. The term "oscuro" can also be read as having connotations of nonnormative sexuality. Since the belated publication in 1984 of Federico García Lorca's highly emotional *Sonetos del amor oscuro* (*Sonnets of Dark Love*, 1935), the adjective "oscuro" has become a troublesome metaphor for male homosexual love within the poetics of the Generation of 27, as Daniel Eisenberg and Patrick Garlinger have noted. Although several references to darkness and shadows can be found in Cernuda's work before 1935, the use of "oscuro" to qualify the male body as the object of homoerotic desire features prominently in "A un muchacho andaluz" ("To an Andalusian Lad"; PC 221) and "El joven marino" ("The Young Sailor"; PC 239), written in August 1934 and June 1935 respectively (PC 789, 791). In Cernuda's ambiguous poetics of exile, "oscuro" also establishes a meaningful relationship between sexual and geographical dislocation, making it impossible to disentangle one from the other. For example, in "El ruiseñor sobre la piedra" ("The Nightingale on the Stone"), Cernuda's poetic tribute to El Escorial in *Las Nubes* (*The Clouds*, 1943), the speaker claims: "Mucho enseña el destierro de nuestra propia tierra / . . . / De ella también somos los hijos / Oscuros" (Exile teaches much about our own land / . . . / We are also its dark / Offspring"; PC 313–14). The abrupt enjambment in the last line has been read as signaling Cernuda's refusal of the Francoist victorious politics of exclusion (Sicot, *Exilio* 113); it can also be read as signaling an inner displacement already experienced within the political borders of the nation. Therefore, coming back to "La lengua," Cernuda's shift from triumphant Hispanidad to obscurity—whether understood as the humble craft of the artisan, or as sexual and political displacement—can perhaps be read as an indication of his interest in exploring emotional ambivalence, that which refuses clear definition. The juxtaposition in *Variaciones* of seemingly incompatible imaginaries—the nationalistic and the intimate—can be criticized for inconsistency, but it can also be read as a rejection of the clarity that underwrites oppositional and necessary exclusionary thinking. In what follows, we will see that the word "oscuro" is also in Cernuda's writing associated in a very literal sense with nonwhite bodies.

The Sympathetic Gaze: Cernuda's Indigenismo

Critical studies of Cernuda have persistently argued that his writing of Mexico subjects Mexican space, people, and culture to a totalizing Hispanocentric gaze (Márquez Aguayo 354, 355; Sicot, *Exilio* 188, 191). This argument has viewed the act of seeing as a seamless intellectual operation in which objects are automatically apprehended and made comprehensible by the gaze of the subject (Mázquez Aguayo 352). However, the affective dimension of vision—present even when not conscious—needs to be taken into account. Cernuda's explicit sympathy for racially marked others significantly modifies the doctrinal approaches to indigenous peoples as "'criaturas miserables'" (wretched creatures) reproduced in the discourse of Hispanidad (Maeztu 202). Indeed, Cernuda's sympathy for indigenous Mexicans reaches a convoluted moment in which the speaker literally expresses a desire to take the place of the other: "lástima que el azar no te hiciera nacer uno entre los suyos" (too bad that chance didn't allow you to be born as one of them; PC 651). In fact, Cernuda's affective gaze determines the overall authorial intention of this collection, as he explicitly affirms in the book's postscript: "lo que yo quería, insisto, era simpatizar. Qué ocurra luego con el don de esa simpatía no me concierne" (what I wanted, I stress, was to sympathize. What happens to the gift of sympathy afterward is not my concern; PC 658). In these lines Cernuda anticipates the ideological debate his Mexican book was to provoke.

Despite the multiple connections that *Variaciones* establishes between Spain and Mexico, the indigenous are presented as an ethnic other that denies any possibility of cultural affinity with the Spanish. Furthermore, as Valender has seen, "al reconocer, a pesar de la larga dominación española, la vigorosa continuidad de las tradiciones indígenas, Cernuda decide abandonar la visión histórica, sustituyéndola con la idea de un paralelismo cultural (México como tierra indolente andaluza)" (on recognizing the vigorous continuity of the indigenous traditions, in spite of the lengthy Spanish domination, Cernuda decides to abandon a historical vision, replacing it with the idea of a cultural parallel [Mexico as indolent Andalusia]). Valender adds: "En México existen ciertos elementos que rehúsan ser acomodados dentro del marco de Sansueña, sea esta histórica o indolente" (Certain elements of Mexico refuse to be accommodated within the framework of Sansueña, whether represented as historical or as indolent; *Cernuda* 106).[5] The presence of an irreducible indigenous otherness in Cernuda's Mexican poems can be detected in "La gruta mágica" ("The Magic Cavern") (Valender, *Cernuda* 106). In this poem, an anxious speaker finds himself at a loss and begs for "sosiego" (quietude) having noticed the lasting endurance of pre-Hispanic art in colonial architecture (PC 462). This realization not only challenges suggestions that Cernuda shows outright disregard for pre-Cortesian Mexicans, as previously claimed (Sicot, *Exilio* 193); it also acknowledges cultural continuity and resistance, rather than Hispanocentric schemes of domination.

Cernuda's sympathetic gaze toward the indigenous is best understood as a structure of feeling that he had previously experienced in Spain as an orientation of the self toward class others through education. The conflation of class and race can be related to Cernuda's own involvement in 1935 with the Misiones Pedagógicas (Pedagogical Missions), the Spanish Republic's controversial program of cultural politics.[6] In "El pueblo" ("The People"), for example, it is the vision of some "indios taciturnos" (taciturn Indians; PC 634) that prompts Cernuda's self-reflection about sympathy toward the lower classes. This affective affinity is first understood in terms of personal vulnerability: "el insistente sentimiento de diferencia no pudo impedir en ti la percepción, entre el pueblo y tú, de una equivalencia en fortuna. Porque al fin y al cabo tú, igual que el pueblo, carecías de ella" (the insistent feeling of difference [from the people] could not prevent your perception of an equivalence in fortune, between you and the people. For, after all, fortune eluded you, as it did the people; PC 634). However, the Indians return the gaze and the speaker recognizes that there are insurmountable differences between them: "entre el pueblo y tú, no te engañes, percibes un espacio difícil del salvar" (don't kid yourself, between you and the people you are aware of a gap that can't be bridged; PC 634). The poem ends with a surprising statement regarding the pre-eminence of the affective impulse in the creative process, thus questioning the overall control of mind over body characteristic of the Cartesian subject:

> Esto que en ti simpatiza con la gente del pueblo es lo que de animal hay en ti: el cuerpo, el elemento titánico de la vida, que ya tarde tanto poder alcanzó sobre ti, y según el cual muchas veces te sentiste, no solo igual, sino inferior al pueblo. Porque el espíritu, excepto en cuanto el cuerpo puede arrastrarlo (y en ti puede mucho), apenas tiene ahí parte. En ti, cuando el cuerpo, lo titánico, habla, tu espíritu, lo dionisíaco, si no otorga, lo que más puede hacer es callar.
> Verdad es que la poesía también se escribe con el cuerpo. (PC 635)

> (The part of you that sympathizes with the people is the animal in you: the body, the titanic element of life, that later in life exerted so much power over you, and which often made you feel, not just like, but inferior to the people. For the spirit, except when it succumbs to the pull of the body (which can easily happen in your case), has little to do with it. In your case, when the body, the titanic, speaks, the best thing your spirit, the Dionysian, can do, if it does not consent, is remain silent.
> The truth is that poetry is also written with the body.)

In this text, sympathy for the indigenous Mexican as "pueblo" transforms into the emotional catalyst of the conceptual struggle between spirit and matter that characterized Hispanic thought at the turn of the nineteenth century (Faber, "Contradictions" 167–69). Using this debate as a cultural pretext, Cernuda's final dictum contradicts his own uncritical alignment to the spiritual character of the Spanish collective subject as expressed in poems such as "Lo nuestro" ("That Which Is Ours"; PC 629) and "La imagen" ('The Image'; PC 633). In "El pueblo," the acknowledgement of the (preconscious) affective response—"The part of you that . . . is the animal in you"—becomes the condition of possibility of the creative mind, indeed, of poetry itself. But, more important, it implies that truth is always already written *in* and *with* the body.[7]

Cernuda's insistence that poetry is also written by the body "obscures"—that is, forces us to reconsider—the predominance of spirit over matter as the conceptual mark of Hispanic exceptionalism, which is characteristic of both liberal and ultraconservative discourses on Spanish national identity. As Faber explains, we should distinguish between *hispanismo* and Hispanidad in terms of the latter's Catholic, neoimperial and reactionary version of post-1898 Pan-Hispanic cultural nationalism. By contrast, liberal Hispanism "assumed a more equal relationship between Spain and Spanish America and did not see Catholicism as a defining characteristic" (Faber, "Contradictions" 170). But, as Faber also notes, both discourses turned spirituality into a diacritical mark of national identity opposed to the ideological and materialist ambitions of the Anglo-Saxon world ("Contradictions" 180). By invoking late nineteenth-century stereotypes in defense of the Hispanic character, "Hispanism . . . projects the [spirit-matter] dichotomy onto an even larger, international context, in which the body is represented by the materialist North and the spirit is assumed to have its principal residence in the Hispanic or Latin South" (Faber, "Contradictions" 180–81). Consequently, Cernuda's unmistakable emphasis on embodied knowledge shows his heterodoxy with regard to so many post–Spanish Civil War narratives that postulate spirituality as *the* structure of feeling defining the exceptionality of the Hispanic character. However unstable, Cernuda's writing of the body provides a safety net that prevents him from falling into the "ideological trap" into which most Spanish exiles fell because of their indiscriminating alignment with stock definitions of Spain as a spiritual nation (Faber, "Contradictions" 179). And most important, it also questions (and anticipates the blurring of) the reification of North/South relations in terms of a supposed dichotomy between materially and spiritually orientated forms of sociocultural behavior.

Rituals of Penetration: Dark Bodies, Homoerotic Desire, and the Undoing of the Colonial Subject

After his first visit to Mexico in the summer of 1949, Cernuda wrote a highly emotional letter from Mount Holyoke to the Mexican composer Salvador Moreno: "No quiero callarle que, cuando temprano en la mañana, miré el cielo sucio y el verde amarillento del norte, todo lo que perdí con la ausencia de México se me representó: el cielo limpio, el aire claro, las flores que no pasan, los cuerpos oscuros; y se me arrasaron con lágrimas los ojos" (I don't want to keep from you that when, early in the morning, I looked at the dirty sky and the yellow-green of the north, all that I lost with the absence of Mexico appeared before me: the cloudless sky, the clear air, the everlasting flowers, the dark bodies; and my eyes brimmed with tears; *Epistolario* 470). The following year, shortly before his second summer visit to the country, he wrote to Moreno again: "Mi único deseo es estar ahí, abrazado a un cuerpo oscuro y olvidar esta completa 'extrañeza' en que vengo viviendo" (my only desire is to be there, embracing a dark body and to forget about this whole feeling of "strangeness" in which I continue to live; *Epistolario* 492). Landscape and the love object appear so emotionally intertwined in Cernuda's Mexico that one cannot be understood completely without the other. But, what is the true nature of this love? And, most important, how does the love object contribute to the constitution of a speaking subject that in "Centro del hombre" ("At the Center of a Man") claims that "el sentimiento de ser un extraño, que durante tiempo atrás te perseguía por los lugares donde viviste, allí callaba, al fin dormido" (the feeling of being a stranger, which in the past pursued you as you moved from place to place, there fell silent, at last asleep; PC 652)? Taking into account Cernuda's unmistakable Orientalism in his poetic projection of his desires onto postcolonial landscapes and beings, the relevance of these questions should not be underestimated. The affective significance of the male homoerotic experience seems unquestionable, as the speaker of "Dúo" ("Duo") makes abundantly clear. In this vivid description of an intimate encounter with a preadolescent dark body, Cernuda says:

> A este cuerpecillo oscuro que, en el umbral de la adolescencia apenas ha dejado atrás la infancia, lo estrechan con transporte tus brazos. Penumbra en la penumbra de la habitación, delatado tan sólo por contraste con la blancura de las sábanas, parece un poco de sombra, tan ligero y tan moreno es; una sombra cálida, pero cuyo contacto refresca tus miembros y orea tu pensamiento. A tu ternura envolvente responde con su abandono, y no te cansas de acariciarle ni de besarle, sintiendo más que vislumbrando su cara, donde brillan los ojos con una chispa aún de travesura y ya de malicia. (PC 643)

(This little dark body that on the threshold of adolescence has hardly outgrown childhood, your arms embrace tenderly. Dimness in the dim room, betrayed only by the contrast with the whiteness of the sheets, so light and so dark it is that it seems a little like a shadow; a warm shadow, but whose contact refreshes your limbs and airs your thought. He abandons himself to your all-embracing tenderness, and you do not tire of stroking him or kissing him, feeling, rather than seeing his face, his eyes shining with a spark still of mischief and now of malice.)

"Dúo" was significantly suppressed from the 1952 Mexican edition of *Variaciones*, and, surely, Cernuda's pudor played into his decision not to expose it to hostile eyes. As Sicot points out, "era quizás obvio que no podía tener cabida en una colección dedicada a 'lo mexicano'" (it was perhaps obvious that it could have no place in a collection devoted to "Mexicanness"; *Exilio* 192). However, the self-conscious rapport between emotion and cognition developed in this poem is important. First, the speaker claims that he *feels* rather than *sees* a certain expression of resistance in the boy's face, which seems to excite him even more. Then, in the midst of the lovemaking scene, he recalls a few lines of an anonymous English sixteenth-century poem: "*(Western wind, when will thou blow/ The small rain down can rain?/Christ, if my love were in my arms/And I in my bed again!)*" (PC 643; italics in original). Initially bothered by literature's impertinent entry into what he regards as "un trance de animalidad pura" (an instance of pure animality), the speaker continues: "quieres desechar, olvidar los versos. Sin pensar que en ti los había hecho nacer, grito del ser humano y de su afán idéntico, el mismo impulso que los creara desde la entraña de su autor anónimo, como tú, separado largos, interminables días, durante el invierno, de un cuerpo oscuro como este que acaricias y besas, del abrazo oscuro y cálido de otra misma sombra deseada" (you want to discard, forget those lines. Forgetting that the same gut impulse, a human cry and identical desire, had generated them in you as in their anonymous author, like you separated for long, endless, winter days from a dark body like the one that you are caressing and kissing, from the dark, warm embrace of another identical desired shadow; PC 643–44). The insistence on sameness at the core of poetry past and present (that of the anonymous,

English poet and that of Cernuda), establishes a semantic continuity between affective impulses—"afán *idéntico*, el *mismo* impulso"—and dark bodies—"otra *misma* sombra deseada"—that disrupts the coherence of the spatiotemporal framework of reading and writing. That is, the absence of the young dark body at the time of writing the poem creates a virtual present that has already passed.[8] Memory joins past and present, different sites of writing and reading, texts and bodies, providing a spatiotemporal setting that only makes sense when determined by sexual desire. Consequently, by identifying the preconscious affective impulse at the root of the creative process, Cernuda defies the unequal value attached to the terms in the hetero/homosexual binary.

In Cernuda's creative mind, sexual desire for dark bodies transforms cultural sameness into cultural diversity, the text itself becoming a plurality of texts in which historical and sexual inversions seem to inform each other. For example, "El mirador" ("The Mirador"), whose location has been identified as a quiet corner in the Convent of Tepotzotlan (Sicot, "Luis" 107, 114), establishes an epistemological link between colonial Spain and Cernuda's initial attraction to that specific place. However, the speaker also recognizes a feeling of profound sympathy and affectionate knowledge, *the source of which he is unable to specifically name or locate*: "Acodado luego en el muro, miras el paisaje, te dejas invadir por él, de tus ojos a tu imaginación y su memoria, donde algo anterior, no sabes qué imagen venida cómo o por dónde, parecía haberte preparado para esta simpatía profunda, este conocimiento entrañable que a su vista en ti despierta" (Then, leaning on the wall, you look at the landscape and let yourself be engulfed by it, from your eyes to your imagination and its memory, *where some prior image, you don't know what, or how or where*, seemed to have prepared you for this deep sympathy, this endearing knowledge that its sight awakens in you; PC 632, my emphasis). Within this visual framework, speaker and landscape become almost indistinguishable through this profound sympathy and "endearing knowledge" that, paradoxically, seem to have already occurred preconsciously within the bounded body. The speaker then adds: "En lo que ves, cierto, hay mucho que fue y es tuyo, por nacimiento, desde siempre: el fondo religioso y sensual de tu país está aquí; el sosiego remansado de las cosas es el mismo; la tierra, labrada igual, se tiende en iguales retazos tornasolados; los cuerpos esparcidos por ella, cada uno con su dignidad de ser único, apenas son más oscuros que los de tu raza, acaso más misteriosos, con un misterio que incita a ser penetrado" (In what you see, it's true, there is much that was and is yours by birth, from the beginning: the religious and sensual environment of your country is here; the tranquil quietude of things is the same; the land, plowed in the same way, is made up of the same iridescent patches; the bodies that dot it, each dignified in its uniqueness, are barely darker than those of your race, perhaps more mysterious, with a mystery that asks to be penetrated; PC 632). The bold force of the possessive "tuyo" ("yours"), nostalgically entangled with homely, indolent things found within the locative "aquí" ("here"), makes the reader aware of an opposing narrative: that of the unlawful apprehension and dispossession of indigenous lands carried out by the Spanish in Mexico. But then the poem continues: "Pero con todo eso hay otra cosa, algo exótico sutilmente aliado a cuanto es tuyo, que parecías presentir y se adueña de ti. Así debió también adueñarse de los viejos conquistadores, con el mismo dominio interior, como si ellos hubieran sido entonces, como tú lo eres hoy, los subyugados" (But in addition *there is something else*, something exotic subtly allied to all that is yours, that you seemed to sense and that takes possession of you. And so it must have taken possession of the earlier conquistadors, exerting the same power over their inner being as if they, like you today, had been the ones who were subjugated; PC 632, emphasis added).

In these ambiguous "rituals of penetration" (Sicot, "Luis" 114), the incorporation of the exotic into the self (into himself) poses difference as constitutive of identity, subjugates the subjugators, and distorts, at the very least, the powerful optics of the Orientalist gaze. Indeed, as Joseph Boone argues:

> The essence of any Orientalizing erotics lies in the projection of desires deemed unacceptable or forbidden at home onto a foreign terrain, in order to reencounter those desires . . . "at a safe distance" . . . Sometimes, as in the case of what seems "like" homosexuality, that distance proves not to be so safe after all, dissolving the boundary between self and other and reconfiguring both in the process—or, conversely, revealing the extent which that "other" *already exists within the self, haunting his self-definitions.* (5, emphasis added)

In the conclusion to "El mirador," geography maps out the continuity of self and other in the following terms: "Algo diferente de tu mundo mediterráneo y atlántico, que se asoma ya al otro lado de este continente, al otro mar por donde Asia se vislumbra, y tan admirablemente se empareja contigo y con lo tuyo, como si sólo ahora se completara al fin tu existencia" (Something different from your Mediterranean and Atlantic world, which emerges now on the other side of this continent, in another ocean facing Asia, and so admirably complements you and what is yours, as if only now were the goal of your existence finally realized; PC 632). Using an unmistakably Orientalist rhetoric, Cernuda's poetic voice reveals that otherness, this "otra cosa" he was unable (or unwilling) to specifically name or locate, constitutes, in fact, the condition of possibility of his own being.

The "cuerpos oscuros" of *Variaciones* finally become the means of fusion with Mexico and the Mexican in an emotional assemblage of space, words, and bodies that disrupts any pretension to a stable subject position, whether individual or a collective. Cernuda resorts to a highly controversial title, "La posesión" ("Possession"), to describe this process:

> Aquella tierra estaba frente a ti, y tú inerme frente a ella. Su atracción era precisamente del orden necesario a tu naturaleza: todo en ella se conformaba a tu deseo. Un instinto de fusión con ella, de absorción en ella, urgían tu ser, tanto más cuanto la precaria vislumbre sólo te era concedida por un momento. ¿Y cómo subsistir y hacer subsistir al cuerpo con memorias inmateriales?

> En un abrazo sentiste tu ser fundirse con aquella tierra; a través de un terso cuerpo oscuro, oscuro como penumbra, terso como fruto, alcanzaste la unión con aquella tierra que lo había creado. Y podrás olvidarlo todo, todo menos ese contacto de la mano sobre el cuerpo, memoria donde parece latir, secreto y profundo, el pulso mismo de la vida. (PC 650)

> (That land was facing you, and you defenseless facing it. Its attraction was precisely of an order necessary to your nature: everything in it conformed to your desire. An instinctive urge to fuse with it, to be absorbed by it, took you over, all the stronger for the brevity of the precarious vision. How then to survive and make the body survive with intangible memories?
>
> In an embrace you felt your being merge with that land; through a smooth dark body, dark as the half-light, smooth as fruit, you achieved union with the land that had created it. And you may forget everything, everything but that contact of a hand on a body, a memory in which the very pulse of life seems to beat, secret and deep.)

In the context of the colonial encounter, the sexual possession of the dark body constitutes a well-known trope for the presumed availability of foreign territory for possession by the colonizer. This territorial availability is normally figured by a passive, racially marked, sexualized female body, willing to be penetrated by an all-powerful Western, white, male, rational mind (McClintock 14; Boone 25). However, as Boone notes, "the implicit heterosexism of this model . . . only tells part of the story of the sexual politics of Orientalism" (25). As he explains, "the fluidity between cultures—however overshadowed by larger histories of opposition and antagonism—encourages us to keep in mind the contingencies, the unforeseen events, the accidental intersections, that challenge dualistic modes of seeing the world" (26). Cernuda's sexual and affective encounter with a Mexican otherness that proves inassimilable but rather engulfs him, in a blissful union that remains ephemeral, conflicts with the colonial imaginary and attests of his own journey of acceptance beyond shame. Cernuda's homoerotic gaze seems to operate "in- and outside the dominant structures of Orientalism" becoming "the potentially subversive element that calls the binaries [subject/object and self/other] supporting Orientalism's rhetoric of power into question" (Boone 26–27).

Conclusion

Cernuda's dissolving of the subject in the other describes a moment of individual *jouissance* that points to the negation of compulsory heterosexuality and heteronormative socialization. From this perspective, Cernuda's lyrical self-destruction through immersion in postcolonial landscapes and bodies points toward a different model of collectivity within the Hispanic "we." Male homoerotic emotional attachments transform Cernuda's Mexico into a utopian spatiotemporal setting that, nonetheless, unsettles naturalized schemes of national and sexual relations. Borrowing José Esteban Muñoz's words, I would like to conclude that "the affective tone of [Cernuda's Mexican texts] lights the way to the reparative" (15). Within Cernuda's poetic representation of Mexico and Mexicans, same-sex emotional attachments constitute a semantic component that forces us to reconsider colonial desire, while putting into perspective the desires of the other. In Cernuda's text, this other is national and racial as well as sexual. Anne McClintock forcefully argues that we should "explore the dynamics of gender as a critical aspect of the imperial project." In this respect, she emphasizes that "bogus universals such as 'the postcolonial woman,' or 'the postcolonial other' obscure relations not only between men and women but also among women" (14). Likewise, in the "postcolonial other" we should also recognize that the presence of male, same-sex relations modifies the gender bias of traditional schemes of imperial power. From this angle, Cernuda's Mexico constitutes an affective map of colonial and queer desires that upsets the structural hierarchy between Spain and Mexico, North and South, subject and object, self and other, mind and body. Cernuda's *Variaciones* are, in a literal sense, variations, that is, queer reworkings of Spain's colonial imaginary.

NOTES

All translations from the Spanish are my own. I am thankful to Michael Leeser and Roberto Fernández for proof reading my translations. I am also thankful to the editors of this volume for suggesting improvements to previous drafts of my work. Needless to say, any remaining errors are my sole responsibility.

1. For a comprehensive recollection of personal lives and histories of male homosexuality under Francoism, see Olmeda and Arnalde. Mira also provides useful information on the Francoist repression of homosexuality (291–300). For Francoist legislation on homosexuality, see Pérez-Cánovas (18–25).
2. Unless otherwise specified, my quotes from Cernuda's texts are taken from Harris and Maristany's edition of his *Obra completa*, with vol. 1, *Poesía completa*, referred to here as PC; and vols. 2 and 3, *Prosa*, referred to here as P 1 and P 2 respectively.
3. I follow here the definition of *pudor* given in María Moliner's *Diccionario de uso del español*: "vergüenza de exhibir el propio cuerpo desnudo, de la vista del de otros, de ser objeto en cualquier forma de interés sexual o de hablar de cosas sexuales" (shame at displaying one's naked body to others, at the sight of that of others, at being the object of any form of sexual interest, or at talking about sexual issues; 2428).
4. I am thankful to Luisa Elena Delgado for making this point.
5. "Sansueña" is the name given by Cernuda to his mythical representation of Andalusia in his exile writing.
6. On this involvement, see Dennis.
7. It is curious that Cernuda here equates the Dionysian with the spirit rather than the body.
8. Cernuda dates the composition of this poem between 14 and 20 October 1950 (PC 838). At the time, he had already returned to Mount Holyoke after his second visit to Mexico in the summer of the same year (Valender, *Entre la realidad* 166).

WORKS CITED

Ahmed, Sara. *The Cultural Politics of Emotion*. New York: Routledge, 2004.

Arnalde, Arturo. *Redada de violetas: La represión de los homosexuales durante el franquismo*. Madrid: La esfera de los libros, 2003.

Balibrea, Mari Paz. "Rethinking Spanish Republican Exile: An Introduction." *Journal of Spanish Cultural Studies* 6. 1 (2005): 3–24.

Boone, Joseph Allen. *The Homoerotics of Orientalism*. New York: Columbia UP, 2014.

Cernuda, Luis. *Epistolario 1924–1963*. Ed. James Valender. Madrid: Residencia de Estudiantes, 2003.

———. *Obra completa*. 3 vols. Ed. Derek Harris and Luis Maristany. Madrid: Siruela, 1993.

———. *Ocnos seguido de Variaciones sobre tema mexicano*. Ed. and intro. Jaime Gil de Biedma. Madrid: Taurus, 1979.

Clough, Patricia T., and Jean Halley, eds. *The Affective Turn: Theorizing the Social*. Durham, NC: Duke UP, 2007.

Dennis, Nigel. "Luis Cernuda, la II República y las misiones pedagógicas (1931–1936)." *Entre la realidad y el deseo: Luis Cernuda 1902–1963*. Ed. James Valender. Madrid: Residencia de Estudiantes, 2002. 235–52.

Eisenberg, Daniel. "Reaction to the Publication of the *Sonetos del amor oscuro*." *Bulletin of Hispanic Studies* 65 (1988): 261–71.

Eribon, Didier. *Insult and the Making of the Gay Self*. Trans. Michael Lucey. Durham, NC: Duke UP, 2004.

Faber, Sebastiaan. "Contradictions of Left-Wing Hispanismo: The Case of Spanish Republicans in Exile." *Journal of Spanish Cultural Studies* 3.2 (2002): 165–85.

———. *Exile and Cultural Hegemony: Spanish Intellectuals in Mexico, 1939–1975*. Nashville: Vanderbilt UP, 2002.

Fish, Stanley. "Literature in the Reader: Affective Stylistics." *New Literary History* 2.1 (1970): 123–62.

Garlinger, Patrick. "Voicing (Untold) Desires: Silence and Sexuality in Federico García Lorca's *Sonetos del amor oscuro*." *Bulletin of Spanish Studies* 79.6 (2002): 709–30.

Labanyi, Jo. "Doing Things: Emotion, Affect, and Materiality." *Journal of Spanish Cultural Studies* 11.3–4 (2010): 223–33.

Maeztu, Ramiro de. *Defensa de la Hispanidad*. Buenos Aires: Poblet, 1945.

Márquez Aguayo, César Alejandro. "La construcción del espacio, construcción del poema, en *Variaciones sobre tema mexicano*." *El exilio literario español de 1939: Actas del Primer Congreso Internacional (Bellaterra, 27 de noviembre–1 de diciembre de 1995)*. Vol. 2. Ed. Manuel Aznar Soler. Barcelona: GEXEL, 1998. 349–57.

Massumi, Brian. *Parables for the Virtual: Movement, Affect, Sensation*. Durham, NC: Duke UP, 2002.

McClintock, Anne. *Imperial Leather: Race, Gender and Sexuality in the Colonial Context*. New York: Routledge, 1995.

Mira, Alberto. *De Sodoma a Chueca: Una historia cultural de la homosexualidad en España en el siglo XX*. Barcelona: Egales, 2004.

Moliner, María. *Diccionario de uso del español*. Madrid: Gredos, 2007.

Moraña, Mabel. "Introduction: Mapping Hispanism." *Ideologies of Hispanism*. Ed. Mabel Moraña. Nashville: Vanderbilt UP, 2005. ix–xxi.

Muñoz, José Esteban. *Cruising Utopia: The Then and There of Queer Futurity*. New York: New York UP, 2009.

Olmeda, Fernando. *El látigo y la pluma: Homosexuales en la España de Franco*. Madrid: Oberon, 2004.

Pérez Cánovas, Nicolás. *Homosexualidad, homosexuales y uniones homosexuales en el derecho español*. Granada: Comares, 1996.

Sedgwick, Eve K. *Touching Feeling: Affect, Pedagogy, Performativity*. Durham, NC: Duke UP, 2003.

Sicot, Bernard. *Exilio, memoria e historia en la poesía de Luis Cernuda*. Trans. Tomás Onaindía. Madrid: Fondo de Cultura Económica de España, 2002.

———. "Luis Cernuda, *Variaciones sobre tema mexicano*: El espacio y el tiempo recobrados." *Luis Cernuda en México*. Ed. James Valender. Madrid: Fondo de Cultura Económica de España, 2002. 107–16.

Snediker, Michael D. *Queer Optimism: Lyric Personhood and Other Felicitous Persuasions*. Minneapolis: U of Minnesota P, 2009.

Teruel, José. *Los años norteamericanos de Luis Cernuda*. Valencia: Pre-textos, 2013.

Thrift, Nigel. "Intensities of Feeling: Towards a Spatial Politics of Affect." *Geografiska Annaler* ser. B 86.1 (2004): 57–78.

———. *Non-representational Theory: Space/Politics/Affect*. Abingdon: Routledge, 2008.

Valender, James. *Cernuda y el poema en prosa*. London: Tamesis, 1984.

———, ed. *Entre la realidad y el deseo: Luis Cernuda 1902–1963*. Madrid: Residencia de Estudiantes, 2002.

———. "Luis Cernuda en México." *Letras Libres* 56 (2003): 39–43.

Valis, Noël. "Nostalgia and Exile." *Journal of Spanish Cultural Studies* 1.2 (2000): 117–33.

Williams, Raymond. *Marxism and Literature*. Oxford: Oxford UP, 1977.

CHAPTER 12

Sentimentality as Consensus
Imagining Galicia in the Democratic Period

HELENA MIGUÉLEZ-CARBALLEIRA

A series of recent turns in the Spanish cultural and political map are pointing to the urgent need to give emotion and its political uses more sustained attention than has so far been the case in studies of contemporary Spain. A deliberate deployment of sentimental strategies appears to be accompanying the irruption of two political events seemingly with the capacity to destabilize the post-Transition paradigm for Spanish politics, namely, the gathering momentum of the Catalan process toward independence since the massive demonstration of July 2010, and the appearance on the Spanish political map of the new left-wing party Podemos (We Can), which, with a mostly crowd-funded electoral budget and patchy media coverage consisting mainly of the TV appearances of its leader, the university lecturer and activist Pablo Iglesias, won five seats in the European parliamentary elections of May 2014 and has since become a significant political force. An analysis of the campaign discourses used by both these political projects—from the different Catalan independence campaigns describing the nation as a matter of the heart, to the Podemos slogan "We are a factory of love," used by one of its charismatic leaders, Juan Carlos Monedero—reveals an overt capitalization of the political uses of emotion to enfranchise a new collective subject in Spain that is responsive to discourses based on the immediacy of subaltern experiences linked to life under Spanish-state rule—from mortgage-induced suicides to political repression and the silencing of historical trauma (see Delgado in this volume).[1]

Still, despite the undeniable presence of emotional discourses underpinning the above contemporary processes, work is only beginning to appear on the specific roles that emotion may have played in the forging and perpetuation of the culture of consensus that has been the pillar of post-Transition Spanish culture and politics until the widespread protests of 15 May 2011, which marked the beginning of an ongoing process of political redefinition in contemporary Spain. Luisa Elena Delgado's *La nación singular: Fantasías de la normalidad democrática española (1996–2011)* goes a long way toward explaining the role that an "uncritical sentimentalism" has played in the fastening together of the Francoist imaginary of a pacified Spain and contemporary de-ideologized conceptions of a virtuous Spanish society united in hardship (Delgado 284). Looking back at cultural policies during the Spanish Transition (1976–1986),

Giulia Quaggio has emphasized, as Mari Paz Balibrea had done before her, how certain symbolic events in the process of Spanish political reconciliation, such as the orchestrated return from political exile of writers Jorge Guillén, Rafael Alberti, and María Zambrano, were emptied of historical significance and packaged as highly emotive representations of migrants' return to their beloved homeland (Quaggio 238–44).

Among the recent explosion of monographic studies of Spanish culture during the Transition, however, one book stands out for its extraordinary propagation as an overarching explanatory formula with which to refer to the discourses and products corresponding to this period, as well as their possible links with the political uses of sentimentality.[2] I am referring to the book *CT o la Cultura de la Transición: Crítica a 35 años de cultura española* (2012), edited and with an introduction by the journalist and TV scriptwriter Guillem Martínez, who had already written extensively on the many faces and facets of the "Culture of the Transition" in his opinion articles, interviews, and personal blog (*www.guillemmartinez.com*). In this multiauthored anthology, the term *CT* is used to refer to the particular cultural paradigm arising from the process of Spanish Transition to democracy, which was premised on the obliteration from public discourse of political and social conflict. In this sense, the umbrella term *CT* subsumes all forms of cultural production and dissemination contributing to the Spanish political culture of consensus, from the weekly cultural supplements of mainstream newspapers reviewing perfectly unproblematic literary novelties, to heavily subsidized historical dictionaries where the memories of war violence are pushed out of view, or the filmic representation of internal armed territorial struggles through the conventions of a romantic comedy.

Taken as a whole the essays included in the volume *CT* provide a serviceable starting point for a critical analysis of how the cultural products of Spanish political consensus often resort to emotion as a tool for its program of "representation," "classification," and "depoliticization" (Fernández-Savater 48, my translation). In the view of the volume's authors, CT products can be recognized by the way they empty out the materiality of the sociopolitical conditions from which they emerge, filling the resulting vacuum with a conventional wisdom based on the erasure of history and an inflated recourse to crass humor and sentimentality. Gonzalo Torné, for example, explains the limited scope available for (self-)criticism under the CT paradigm as delineated by the parameters of what he calls the permitted "'lenguaje patrimonial': (nacionalismo, ETA, lucha superficial de partidos, supremacía acrítica de los sentimientos, relevancia de lo sentimental)" ("inherited language": [nationalism, ETA, the superficial disputes between parties, the acritical predominance of feelings and the relevance of sentimentality]; 57).

In this chapter, I would like to argue that sentimentality has not only been one of the recognizable traits of the Spanish CT toolkit but that, in certain enclaves, it has become the foundation of a particular political culture. In Galicia, for example, as I explained in *Galicia, a Sentimental Nation: Gender, Culture and Politics* (2013), discourses of sentimentality have formed the very tissue of the region's political, cultural, and intellectual history since the mid-nineteenth century, for historical reasons rooted in the unequal power relations between Galicia and Spain. In line with the values of sexual difference already operative in the late nineteenth century, representations of Galicia as sentimental and feminine served the paradoxical double function of facilitating the management of peripheral alterity from a Spanish centralist perspective and securing a narrative of national difference for an emerging nationalist movement in Galicia. The deployment of such discursive modes was seldom clear-cut or polarized, with leading figures of Galician nationalism such as the historian Manuel Murguía contradictorily conceding that Galician is a somewhat feminine language in his only known Galician-language public address, delivered at the 1891 Floral Games (Murguía 84), or the Spanish writer Azorín, who has gone down in Galician cultural history as an eminent *galegófilo*, resorting with paternalistic compassion to the stereotype of Galician sentimentality in his travel writing about the region ("Su sonrisa triste" 59). Descriptions of Galicians as naturally averse to radical political action would become a staple in the repertoire of centralist representations of Galicia during the twentieth century, with Victoriano García Martí's books on the Galician lyrical character (*Una punta de Europa, Galicia: La esquina verde*) and Manuel Fraga's political vision (as laid out in his publications and praxis) perhaps forming the most compact examples. The effect of this discursive corpus has been the propagation at a Spanish level, but also in Galicia, of an image of the region as entirely conflict-free, even when there is evidence suggesting otherwise.[3]

In this chapter I will examine the durability of such tropes in Spanish and Galician cultures, immersed as they have been in a particular cultural paradigm from the Transition to the present. My aim here will be to show just how integral to the discourses of political consensus has been the image of a sentimental, feminized, and politically sedate Galicia. Following Stephen Ahern's pointed remark that processes of sentimentalization for political purposes tend to create the illusion of a power void where there is, in fact, a veritable "psychology of dominance and submission" at work (11), I will argue that the field of Spanish-Galician cultural relations provides us with an important case study for how emotion-related discourses (their circulation and repetition) can fuel a culture of political consensus that denies those operating at its fringes the ability to create collective meanings. However, it is through the parodic mimicking of those very mechanisms of political consensus—their recognizable tropes, their monotonous outlines—that cultural creators in Galicia are starting to produce powerfully subversive critiques of the mirage of post-Transition political and cultural cohesion.

From Hotel to Home: Domestic Figurations of Galician Culture

In 1985 the Spanish poet and playwright Antonio Gala returned to the kind of historical theater that he had successfully essayed in 1973 with the play *Anillos para una dama* (*Rings for a Lady*), based on the figure of Jimena Díaz, El Cid's widow. If Jimena's life story in a city of Valencia under siege and not at liberty to pursue love with the Castilian military leader Álvar Fáñez can be interpreted as an allegory of Spain two years before Franco's death, Gala's play *El hotelito* (premiered at Albacete's Teatro Carlos III on 6 December 1985 and on show again in September 2013 at Madrid's Teatro Fernán Gómez) would be no less in sync with the historical debates of its time.[4] On the brink of Spain's entry into the European Union in 1986 and seven years after the passing of the Spanish Constitution that divided the country's administrative map into seventeen autonomous communities, *El hotelito* offers a brazen look at the enduring challenges of Spanish territorial cohesion and at how these may stand in the way of the country's capacity to package itself for internationalization. The overriding metaphor is that of the *hotelito* (where the use of the diminutive points to the idea of a modern outlook, as opposed to traditional or historic, but also of coziness and affordability) functioning as post-Transition Spain. The rich symbolic potential of this image is deployed as follows: the play starts with the view onstage of the hall of a poorly maintained mansion that has seen better times. Elements of modern décor can be seen alongside the ragged remnants of an illustrious past (crooked paintings on the walls, a frayed flag, an old chest). Five women live in this house: Carmiña, Rocío, Monserrat, Begoña, and Paloma, representing respectively the four regions granted historical status in the 1978 Spanish Constitution (Galicia, Andalusia, Catalonia, and the Basque Country) and the Castilian region containing the capital, Madrid. It is intimated in the course of the conversations among these women that Paloma/Madrid represents the voice of "las primas que faltan" (our cousins who are not here; Gala 119), these being "las de las Islas" (those of the islands; referring to the Canaries and the Balearics), "las de la Huerta" (those of the Mediterranean Orchard; referring to Valencia and Murcia), "Lupe de la Dehesa" (Lupe of the Grassland; representing Extremadura), "las del Castillo" (those of the Castle; representing Castile-León and Castile-La Mancha), "la de la Bodega" (that of the Winery; representing La Rioja), "la prima Aparecida" (the cousin that just turned up; representing the autonomous region of Cantabria, often described as a purely administrative demarcation), "la prima Covadonga" (our cousin Covadonga: referring to Asturias), and "la prima Pilar" (our cousin Pilar; referring to Aragón).

The debate providing the play with its constituting drama revolves around Paloma/Madrid's proposal to repackage the house and advertise it as a boutique hotel, which would force each of the occupants with a say in the process (again, only Spain's historic communities) to raise money to find "un apartamentito postmoderno con su calefacción, su horno empotrado y su nevera" (a nice little postmodern apartment, with central heating, a built-in oven, and fridge; 119). The challenge of modernization, here presented as a corollary of Spain's opening up to European integration and investment, is therefore an opportunity for new sources of funding but also a directive to abandon home as one knew it, a challenge that each historical community will have to ponder according to its characteristics and needs—although never losing sight of the fact that, as Paloma/Madrid warns them: "yo tengo trece votos. De modo que se hará lo que yo quiera" (I have thirteen votes. So we'll do as I say; 119–20).

The women's initial reticence and conflicting standpoints (organized around their different views on whether they should let or sell part of the house so as to make a profit) evolve into a final consensus that they are simply better off not leaving the house at all. Unanimity on this matter is reached only through the softening effect of a series of dramatic elements. First, we see how, while they await the arrival of the "extranjera" (foreign woman) impersonating Europe, the five women's "last supper" comprises the typical gastronomic specialties of their regions, which each of them brings to the table with pride and generosity. Here, for the first time in the play, there is a sense of harmonious unity against the values of a foreign female visitor who, in a colloquial twist, is described as a vegetarian that "con una naranjita y un par de aceitunas va que arde" (can have an orange and a couple of olives, and count herself lucky; 172). The soft folkloristic matter reconciling the once quarrelling nations on the basis of their gastronomic richness—which is all the more magnificent when brought together on the same table—is enhanced by the play's final scene. Here the group's harmony while awaiting the arrival of foreign interest in the hotelito is represented by their spontaneous dancing of their respective regional dances: "Cada una baila su baile: una muiñeira, una sardana, unos tanguillos, un schotiss [sic], un txortzico" (*Each one of them dances her dance: a muiñeira, a sardana, a tanguillo, a schotiss, a txortzico*; 183, emphasis in the original). It is at this moment that their epiphany of well-being in unity takes place: when they hear the noise of change approaching from the outside, Monserrat/Catalonia cries: "Quinientos años esperándola, tú, y se le ocurre llegar cuando menos hace falta" (Five hundred years waiting for her, and she turns up when she's least needed; 183). Suddenly a bomb threat is announced from the outside, requiring the house occupants to vacate immediately, a directive that is immediately questioned by Paloma, in what is perhaps the play's only overt moment of transcendence: "Estamos entre la oscuridad de fuera y la esperanza. ¿Cabe duda sobre lo que hemos de elegir?" (We're pitted between the darkness outside and hope. Does anyone have any doubts about what to choose?; 184). Ignoring the calls by police and the fire brigade, and even Begoña/the Basque Country's intimation that the bomb may have been placed by her lover Josetxu as a "broma" (prank; 184), all five women choose to continue with their regional dances. In a final solution to the threat of imminent, traumatic change, Spain's four historical nations and central state embrace a sense of unity that is fragilely constructed by the merging together of regionalist difference into one final soft metaphor of harmony: the dancing together of the quintessentially "Spanish" dance, the *sevillana* "que bailan y cantan TODAS" (which they ALL sing and dance; 186, capitals in the original). As the curtain comes down, placing the final scene out of sight, a bomb explosion is heard as a closing reminder that the materialities of history do not make ready material for public spectacle in Spain.

How is Galicia represented in this play of Spanish cultural identity in (tender) conflict? It is worth noting, first and foremost, that the character of Carmiña in Gala's *El hotelito* was played by the Madrid-born actress Beatriz Carvajal, who by 1985 was already known to Spanish TV audiences for incarnating the eponymous character of

"Carmiña" in the third season of the popular TV contest *Un, dos, tres . . . responda otra vez* ("One, Two, Three . . . Answers Please!), running from 1982 to 1984. The immediate comic effect of Beatriz Carvajal's Carmiñas relied on her use of an overplayed Galician accent and the constant references to rurality and remoteness. This apparently infallible humorous strategy was also deployed in the episode "Las novias autonómicas" ("Autonomic Sweethearts") of the popular TV series *Farmacia de guardia* (*All-Night Chemist's*), aired on 25 May 1992, where Beatriz Carvajal played a Galician character also named Carmiña who came to announce to the chemist's owner, Lourdes Cano, that she was her ex-husband's girlfriend, only to find a Catalan and an Andalusian woman had also done the same. The theme of Spain's "autonomies" then, was not an infrequent humorous device in Spanish mass culture products during the 1980s and 1990s, where the source of comicity was provided by acting out a set of recognizable "regional" stereotypes, linguistic recourse to non-Castilian accents, and the recurrent representation of Spain's territorial autonomies as a bunch of bickering women.

The Carmiña/Galicia of *El hotelito* is presented from the outset as fanciful and infantile. The play opens with her skipping an imaginary rope while singing the opening lines of Rosalía de Castro's poem "Miña Santiña, miña Santasa" ("Dear Little Saint, Dear Wicked Saint"; Gala 109). While the Catalan Monserrat and the Basque Begoña plunge immediately into a conversation about their different native tongues, Carmiña is depicted as staring restlessly out of the window to see if one of her sailor lovers has arrived (111). This differentiation between a Catalan and Basque focus on hard politics as opposed to a Galician state of sentimental longing is strengthened by the ensuing conversation between Monserrat/Catalonia and Begoña/the Basque Country, where the former states a preference for intellectual activity and reading books on accounting, while the latter announces that she is more prone to action when the circumstances require it—"cuando llegue el momento, actuaré" (when the time comes I will act; 115)— thus leaving in the air a hardly veiled reference to Basque armed struggle in a period (the early 1980s) when ETA killings had been through a historical high. Outside this logic of political action, Galicia is described as "[viviendo] en un ay" (living in a state of lament; 116). Its inherent sentimental qualities are embodied in Carmiña's incorporeal longings (her references to her sailor sweethearts, who of course never arrive, point to the Atlantic dimension of Galician sentimental attachments owing to emigration), but also in her explicit remark that she is incapable of violent action: "Mi futuro es la marina. Pero mercante, no de guerra. Yo con la Armada, nada. ¡Un verso!" (My future lies with the navy. But the merchant navy, not the Armed Forces. I don't want anything to do with the military. A poem!; 117). Toward the end of the play, when all the women are getting ready for the arrival of "the foreigner," Carmiña reminisces about her childhood in a tone of heightened sentimentality that sets her apart from the rest: "Yo siempre fui dulciña. Me encantaba bailar en las campas de las ermitas, los días de fiesta, con los rapaciños. Ya no distinguía si era el pandeiro lo que sonaba o era mi corazón" (I was always a sweet little girl. I loved to dance around the chapel fields with the children. I could never tell whether it was the tambourine or my heart pounding; 167). It is important to note that Carmiña/Galicia's pacifying sentimentality is represented as compatible with her awareness of her own subaltern position with regard to the others: while the women are thinking of how to get the house ready for the arrival of "la extranjera," Carmiña/Galicia and Rocío/Andalusia scoff at the fact that "somos ésta y yo las que limpiamos" (she and I are the ones who end up doing the cleaning; 131). When it dawns on her that modernization will mean getting rid of her cow, she pronounces herself unable to do the killing and asks whether "alguna quiere hacer de matarife . . . tengo tanta costumbre de darlo todo, todo" (anyone wants to play butcher . . . I always tend to give away everything, everything; 169). Begoña/the Basque Country takes Carmiña's cow willingly, in what is one of the play's lucid predictions of just how uneven (and ultimately decimating) the effects of European agricultural policy would be for the Galician milk industries. Subtly throughout the play, then, the relationship between sentimentality and Galicia's status plays out the double function of eliciting sympathy while allowing difference, thus turning Galicia into one of the grateful martyrs of post-Transition Spanish politics.

I would like to dwell further on the notion of gratefulness, for it provides an interesting angle from which to assess another dimension of the power/representation struggles of this period. I am referring here to the new institutional politics arising from the post-Transition "Spain of the autonomies." As the different nonstate voices of Spanish politics anticipate the arrival of homogenizing modernity, Carmiña/Galicia says melancholically: "Todas íbamos a ser reinas" (We were all meant to be queens; 168), to which Rocío/Andalusia responds: "Bueno, ahora seremos presidentas" (Well, now we can be presidents; 168). Their dialogue is suggestive of what has been described as the "café para todos" (coffee for everyone) principle of post-Transition territorial politics, whereby the Catalan, Galician, and Basque claims for home rule were diluted in the state's decision to create seventeen autonomous communities with their own elected parliaments and devolved competencies. The creation of the necessary institutional and bureaucratic structures for the maintenance of this decentralized formula for Spanish territorial politics went hand in hand with the flow into each of the regions of significant funding from the state. Part of this funding went into the creation of autonomous institutions that would enable Spain's nonstate nations to promote their differentiated cultures both at home and internationally: the Consello da Cultura Galega (whose creation was embedded in the Galician Statute of Autonomy passed in 1980 and which today holds a budget of over two million euros) is a good example of the sort of cultural institutions that were specifically enabled by the cultural politics of the Spanish Transition in Galicia. Arguably, the Casa de Galicia en Madrid, opened in February 1992 by Manuel Fraga's administration in a mansion located just behind the Prado Museum, is another example of such institutions. It interests me here because, unlike the Consello da Cultura Galega, Madrid's Casa de Galicia has the double function of acting as an administrative representation of the Xunta de Galicia government in the state capital and simultaneously representing Galician culture *in* and *for* Madrid. Its history, contents, and functions over the years can therefore prove useful for an understanding of what images of Galician culture and identity can be granted circulation without imperiling the grand narratives of the Spanish Culture of the Transition (including its emphasis on political consensus, manageable difference, and acritical, dehistoricized cultural production).

A recent event in relation to the Casa de Galicia en Madrid may help us identify how a certain packaging of *regional* differences went hand in hand with the institutional cultures of consensus of the Spanish Transition. In February 2014 the news was published in the crowd-funded online Galician newspaper *Praza Pública* that the Casa de Galicia en Madrid had held an evening event with B-list Spanish celebrity Carmen Lomana ("A delegación da Xunta en Madrid"). This episode brought to the fore two important questions for this essay's argument: first, what counts as "culture" under the paradigm of the Culture of the Transition? Secondly, what counts as "Galician culture" under such a paradigm? If, as David García Aristegui says, the defining feature of CT cultures is the "pura desarticulación del carácter problemático de la cultura" (the sheer deactivation of culture's problematic nature; 108), then the program of activities at the Casa de Galicia en Madrid and the discourse created around it provide more than one instance of what possible formats this type of culture may adopt. From the presentation of a book of conversations with Galicia-born artist Antón Lamazares presided over by a former press officer of the coalition party Alianza Popular—created in 1976 by former Francoist ministers and the antecedent of today's Popular Party—and the Ministry of Public Works and Highways, to a recital of Spanish poetry by the pharmacist and president of the Casino de Madrid (also formerly a deputy director of the Children's Programs Department of Francoist state television) and the above-mentioned roundtable on journalism led by the semiaristocratic socialite and TV show-biz commentator Carmen Lomana, many of the cultural activities held at the Casa de Galicia en Madrid have the air of being tailored specifically to the socializing needs of local power elites. That crowds such as these should converge around the celebration (in one way or another) of Galician culture—after all, a nonstate nation both politically and culturally in conflict with Spain—can partly be explained by the emphatically *soft* discourses about Galician culture and identity promoted at such events. Again, recourse to the language of emotions acts as the contouring agent for the particular definition of Galician culture promoted at these events, where the use of a language loaded with sentimental rhetoric—although notably not of the Galician language itself—is promoted as a marker of identity. Of the Spanish poetry recital by Mariano Turiel where some poems by Rosalía de Castro were declaimed, the director of the Casa de Galicia en Madrid since 2009, José Ramón Ónega, said that it was an "interpretación magistral que nos ha dejado a todos con el alma en vilo, por su proverbial sentimiento" (a masterful reading that has left us all on tenterhooks because of its proverbial sentiment; "El presidente del Casino").[5] With similar sentimental tones, the artist Antón Lamazares was described as a "constructor de espacios sublimes, que siembra emoción con su obra" (a creator of sublime spaces, who sows emotion with his work; "Presentada en la Casa de Galicia"). A look at the Casa de Galicia in Madrid's temporary art exhibitions reveals a similar thematic intention. In December 2013, for example, one could visit a sculpture exhibition by Madrid-based Galician artist Xosé Azar entitled *Saudade*, the quintessential metaphor of Galician-Portuguese sentimentality, often also referred to as "morriña" in the Galician context, although the differences between the two remain the subject of ongoing speculation (Soto, *O labirinto da saudade*). At the same time, another photographic exhibition was on display entitled *Os adeuses* (The Farewells), which focused on the representation of the most readily *sentimentalizable* dimension of Galician economic and political transatlantic emigration in the 1950s and 1960s, that is, the moment of painful separation from one's loved ones. Significantly too, the viewing of the Casa de Galicia en Madrid's permanent art exhibition starts with Fernando Álvarez de Sotomayor's painting *La gallega* (Galician Woman), an oil on canvas dating from the early twentieth century, which was part of the artist's program to paint Galician female portraits according to a purportedly Celtic stereotype, with a view to representing a modicum of regional difference that could still be perceived as "en absoluto ferinte[s] aos do '98 madrileños partidarios da rexeneración de España e practicantes, para iso, da estética rexionalista" (entirely harmless to the eyes of '98 Madridians who supported the regeneration of Spain and practiced, for this reason, a regionalist aesthetics; López Vázquez 44). The fact that this painting presides over the house's entrance hall can potentially be read as a curatorial decision that adds to a definition of Galician culture as melancholic, Celtic, and feminine, easily lending itself to sentimentalizing readings.

That this accumulation of emotional intensities may be the result of a specific political program to package Galician culture in this way for a Madrid-based public is borne out by the differently pitched discourses created for the Casa de Galicia en Madrid during the period of the Partido Socialista de Galicia-Bloque Nacionalista Galego (PSdG-BNG) coalition Xunta de Galicia government known as the *bipartito* (2005–2009). It was during this period that the book *A casa habitada: A colección da Casa de Galicia en Madrid* (*The Inhabited House: The Collection of the Casa de Galicia in Madrid*) was published, a lush color catalogue of the house's permanent art collection accompanied by five academic studies on the history of Galician art. The collection opens with a prologue by the then president of the Xunta de Galicia, Emilio Pérez Touriño, which briefly traces the history of the Casa de Galicia en Madrid and reiterates that its official function is both administrative and cultural. However, Pérez Touriño's prologue includes an eloquent remark about the projected use of the house in openly unsentimental terms: "A Casa de Galicia en Madrid non quere ser, porén, un espazo consagrado aos tortuosos praceres da morriña" (The Casa de Galicia en Madrid does not, however, aim to be a place dedicated to the tortuous pleasures of Galician homesickness; Pérez Touriño 11). By trying to distance the new image of the Casa de Galicia en Madrid from the deep-seated rhetoric of Galician sentimentality epitomized by the notion of *morriña*, Pérez Touriño's words pointed to the different institutional definition of Galician culture essayed by the PSdG-BNG coalition—where, it needs to be added, the Galician nationalist party had been assigned the Department of Culture. That the subsequent direction of the Casa de Galicia en Madrid, under conservative Popular Party government since 2009, has visibly returned to the public use of the rhetoric of Galician sentimentality points to the pivotal role that the politics of emotion play in the discursive dilution of Spanish-Galician conflict still today.

Enter Os da Ría: Repetition, Parody, and CT Simulacra

Recent explanations of the workings of Spanish CT seem to echo Judith Butler's theory of signification as was first laid out in *Gender Trouble* (1990). Understood not as a "founding act, but rather a regulated process of repetition" (144), signification works on the basis of quasi-invisible or naturalized processes, which are nevertheless assumed by communities as the canvas on which normativities are written. With regard to the mechanisms of Spanish CT, Gonzalo Torné has pointed out that, although total normative collapse is still far from sight, there are indicators that "La CT ha sido puesta algo más en evidencia, es más difícil ejercerla de manera automática, ha aumentado el número de usuarios que sienten algo de vergüenza ajena" (CT has been exposed; it is now more difficult to practice it unreflectively; the number of users who feel somewhat embarrassed by it has gone up; 62). However there is as yet no understanding or analysis of how this shift is taking place in the cultural field, beyond the repeated mention of the 15-M protests of 2011 as a watershed event in this regard. In what remains of this chapter, I will propose a first analysis of the Galician cultural project Os da Ría as an example of how the Spanish and Galician Cultures of the Transition are starting to be subverted on their own terms, that is, by the parodic repetition of the very discursive elements that construct them. My earlier reference to Judith Butler's work was not meant to be casual. Rather, my analysis here draws strongly on her concluding definition of subversive parody in *Gender Trouble* as the possibility of a "phantasmatic" repetition, a "failed copy, as it were," of the naturalized processes of signification, just at that vertiginous moment when agency happens (146).

Playing on an obvious parallel with the Andalusian duo Los del Río, Os da Ría is a Galician musical band formed by comedians Carlos Meixide and Tomás Lijó and the musicians Suso Alonso, Xabier Olite, Ramón Reynolds, and Roi Fernández, whose first performances appeared as sketches in the *Ultranoite* series of the today closed alternative music and theater venue Sala Nasa, in Santiago de Compostela. Going from a local Santiago-based orbit to Galicia-wide live performances, Os da Ría have capitalized on the use of social media to disseminate their interventions and increase their popularity, to the extent that they were able in 2012 to record their first album, *Disco Díscolo*, thanks to a crowd-funding campaign. Their humorous and creative potential relies heavily on their mimicking of the discourses of Galician autonomic institutional cultures, with their characteristic obliteration of linguistic conflict in Galicia and their promotion (through public funding) of bland, acritical, or unproblematic forms of culture, often through the constant recourse to sentimental rhetoric and values.

Their parodic use of the Galician language is perhaps the first element that catches the ear of Os da Ría's audiences. While perfectly understandable to Galician speakers, the language spoken by the comedic pair, which they call *galegueiro*, is not quite standard Galician but an overelaboration of its recognizable features, particularly after the publication of the 2003 reform of the Galician norm. The question of the Galician language norm has remained one of the sticking points of Galician postautonomic politics, which kick-started a process of linguistic normalization premised on the institutional invisibility of the previously coexisting *lusista* solution advocating a Portuguese spelling for Galician. Far from subsiding, the tension between these two options has stayed well embedded in Galician cultural politics—and political cultures—to this day. The language reform of 2003 constitutes one of the few attempts at a partial conciliation of the two factions, which finally agreed on the release of a new set of orthographic, grammatical, and lexical rules drawing standard Galician somewhat closer to Portuguese (adjective endings in "-ábel" were now admitted, for example, as well as the thanking word "grazas," nonexistent until then in spoken Galician but considered a happy medium between the Spanish "gracias" and the Portuguese "obrigada/o"). The result, however, was for many speakers an increased sense of language constructedness, as well as the perception that the Galician language was an artifact for power struggles, used—albeit deficiently—by politicians and Galician TV and radio channels, but removed from the "real" language of the people.[6] Os da Ría's galegueiro plays to such perceptions in a variety of ways. First, it parodies that sense of constructedness by creating a quasi-made-up language where a series of mechanisms are applied erratically. Typical Galician word endings (-eiro, -án, -olo) are added indiscriminately to nouns and adjectives, thus overgalicianizing them. The contractions between prepositions (en, con, de, a) and the definite articles are not observed, with the effect of either creating a strangely formal register or mimicking the language of speakers unfamiliar with spoken Galician (such as that of many high-profile politicians in Galicia attempting to speak it in public appearances). Iconic solutions of the 2003 norm such as "grazas" are turned into the even more hybrid "grazañas" (an alteration of the thanking formula one is more likely to hear in Galicia, "graciñas"). Taken as a whole, the Galician variant used by Os da Ría in their performances fulfills a multiplicity of parodic functions, aimed primarily at exposing the contemporary Galician language as one of the most highly intervened objects of Galician autonomic politics.

But the language of Os da Ría also raises important questions from the perspective of the politics of Galician sentimentality as consensus, which, as I have argued in this chapter, has been a core element of the Galician postautonomic period, posited as essentially nonconflictual. There is in the band's mode of expression a profusion of positively connoted yet banal adjectives that echo—and on occasions completely coincide with—the kind of sentimental expressions that early twentieth-century Galician nationalists had identified as typical of apolitical regionalists, with their "catro cousas hocas, valeiras, 'cursis'" (handful of vapid, shallow and "cursi" things; Varela) or the commonplace, repeated like a mantra, that Galician is a sweet, feminine, and musical language, "meiga e leda" (enchanting and chirpy; "Do meu feixe"). Os da Ría's excessive use of the adjective "senlleiro" (whose literal meaning is "unparalleled" or "peerless") acts also as an echoic device of the language of institutional cultural adulation in Galicia, with its blend of shallow interchangeability, ahistorical abstraction, and the kind of pandering to the official linguistic norm for which the gestural peppering of discourse with high-sounding Galician words is key.

One song in the album stands out for its parodic indictment of a Culture of the Transition in Galicia based on a politics of sentimental representation. I have explained elsewhere how discourses of Galician sentimentality have often gone hand in hand with the feminization of Galician identity or of Galicia itself. The recurrent image of Galicia as the "Terra Nai" (Motherland), or as the object of presidential conjugal love in the case of the Galician Popular Party's electoral campaign in 2009, where Núñez Feijóo's mother described her son as "married to Galicia," are two examples of how sentimental, feminizing metaphors have populated political discourses in Galicia (Miguélez-Carballeira 214–16). Os da Ría's song "Caramba que guapa estás!" ("Blimey, How Pretty You Are!"; track 5 in the album) plays precisely on this rhetoric to make the point that post-Transition Galicia became the sought-after "bride" of a particular political class, eager to navigate a new world of significant state subsidies and decentralized autonomic power. The song's central metaphor relies on the necessary ideation of Galicia as an attractive woman, whose newly acquired charms are sung by a chorus of increasingly aroused voices. References to Galicia's assets go from the charming ("¡caramba qué guapa estás!"; blimey, how pretty you are!; "que morena estás!"; you've got a tan!) to the lecherous ("que tetas sacaches!"; you've grown boobs!), yet always pointing to a process of self-amelioration that has made her a more attractive partner. Particularly, the chorus seems to be attracted to the institutional assets provided by Galicia's new status as a historical autonomous community ("as túas consellerías, os teus medios de comunicación"; your regional government departments, your media). For an understanding of the song's full metaphorical intention, it is important to add that the live performances of this song include the two lead singer-comedians imitating the physical movement of a sexual act from a male perspective, in a crescendo of moans and gasps that finally culminates in the quintessential expression of postcoital relaxation: one of the song's closing lines goes "botámoslle un pitilliño, Galicia?" (fancy a fag, Galicia?). The final message, therefore, is that an effectively feminized Galicia adapts itself quite well to being *fucked*, in the word's double meaning of enjoyment—at least on the part of the subject with agency—and destruction. Os da Ría's song "Caramba que guapa estás!" is, in this sense, one of the first and most acerbic parodic enactments of how the vocabularies of sentimentality embedded in the political feminization of Galicia have been instrumental for the easing in, during and after the Transition, of rampant institutional corruption, political repression, and cultural dismantling in the region. Put another way, if Judith Butler's framework for subversive parody is to be found in the "local possibilities of intervention [present in] those practices of repetition that constitute identity" (*Gender Trouble* 147), Os da Ría's project makes for a rich example of how, if identified and recontextualized outside of their original institutional uses, the discourses of sentimentality and bland consensus that have been embedded in the history of Galician identity can begin to point to the culture's otherwise seemingly hidden conflicts.

In conclusion, I would like to suggest that analyzing the discourses of sentimentality in contemporary Galician politics and culture can tell us a great deal about how an image of the region as politically nonconflictual, and therefore as ready ground for the practices of the Spanish Culture of the Transition, has been one of the anchors of the Spanish politics of consensus with regard to the country's peripheral nations. As Os da Ría's cultural interventions show, however, the parodic subversion of such discourses exposes not only their historical roots and political motives, but also the fact that a new generation of Galicians might be ready to recognize and ridicule them as a thing of the immediate past.

NOTES

1. In 2008, for example, a video campaign promoting the creation of a Catalan football team used the image of a boy not being allowed to play football with others owing to the fact that he was wearing a top that bore the word "Catalunya." When the boy decided to play bare chested, a close-up focuses on the left side of his chest, the place of his heart, as the phrase 'Una nació" (One nation) comes up on the screen. The video was banned from being aired ("Prohibeixen el lema"). For a reference to the Podemos slogan "We are a factory of love" and its function as part of their emotively charged electoral discourses, see de Francisco.
2. To Delgado and Quaggio's books, we may add the forthcoming monographs of Germán Labrador (*Culpables por la literatura*) and Duncan Wheeler (*Art, Power, Governance*).
3. For a historical account of the Galician proindependence struggle, its episodes of armed conflict, and violent repression from the Spanish state, see Rios Bergantinhos.
4. I am grateful to Marta Pérez Pereiro for bringing Antonio Gala's *El hotelito* to my attention. *El hotelito* is published together with Gala's play *Samarkanda*.
5. José Ramón Ónega is the brother of the journalist Fernando Ónega, who was codirector of the Falangist newspaper *Arriba* in the 1970s and is best known for having been press director in the first democratically elected government of the Spanish Transition, under Adolfo Suárez's presidency.
6. The idea that the Galician language is constantly mangled by power politics was widely disseminated in the Galician press in the years prior to the passing of the 2003 norm. The secretary of the Real Academia Galega from 1997 to 2001, Constantino García, said in an interview that the norm being debated contained "moreas de cousas sen sentido" (a whole load of nonsense), making explicit reference to the solution regarding noun endings in "-za" proposed by the "nationalists" ("Unha Academia" 4). I am grateful to Valentim R. Fagim for locating this reference for me.

WORKS CITED

"A delegación da Xunta en Madrid acolle a Carmen Lomana para debater sobre a prensa rosa." *Praza Pública* 19 February 2014. praza.gal/politica/6565/a-delegacion-da-xunta-en-madrid-acolle-a-carmen-lomana-para-debater-sobre-a-prensa-rosa/ (accessed 1 September 2014).

Ahern, Stephen, ed. *Affect and Abolition in the Anglo-Atlantic, 1770–1830*. Farnham, Surrey: Ashgate, 2013.

Azorín. "Su sonrisa triste: Evocación." *Galicia (Paisajes, gentes, carácter, costumbres, escritores . . .)*. Santiago de Compostela: Xunta de Galicia, 2008. 59–60.

Balibrea, Mari Paz. *Tiempo de exilio: Una mirada crítica a la modernidad española desde el pensamiento republicano en el exilio*. Barcelona: Montesinos, 2007.

Butler, Judith. *Gender Trouble: Feminism and the Subversion of Identity*. New York: Routledge, 1990.

Costa, Jordi. "CT y cine: La inclemencia intangible; Una primera aproximación a la obra crítica y cinematográfica de j.l.i." *CT o la Cultura de la Transición: Crítica a 35 años de cultura española*. Ed. Guillem Martínez. Barcelona: DeBolsillo, 2012. 125–40.

de Francisco, Andrés. "Podemos, el 15-M y la izquierda: Una primera reflexión." *Rebelión* 18 February 2014. *www.rebelion.org/noticia.php?id=180991* (accessed 22 August 2014).

Delgado, Luisa Elena. *La nación singular: Fantasías de la normalidad española (1996–2011)*. Madrid: Siglo XXI, 2014.

"Do meu feixe: Os cursis." *A Nosa Terra* 13 (1917): 4.

Fernández-Savater, Amador. "Emborronar la CT (del 'No a la guerra' al 15M)." *CT o la Cultura de la Transición: Crítica a 35 años de cultura española*. Ed. Guillem Martínez. Barcelona: DeBolsillo, 2012. 36–51.

Gala, Antonio. *Anillos para una dama*. Madrid: Júcar, 1974.

———. *Samarkanda. El hotelito*. Madrid: Espasa Calpe, 1985.

García Aristegui, David. "Un Ministerio de Cultura en la sombra: SGAE, propiedad intelectual y CT." *CT o la Cultura de la Transición: Crítica a 35 años de cultura española*. Ed. Guillem Martínez. Barcelona: DeBolsillo, 2012. 101–13.

García Martí, Victoriano. *Una punta de Europa: Ritmo y matices de la vida gallega*. Madrid: Editorial Mundo Latino, 1927.

———. *Galicia: La esquina verde (alma, historia, paisaje)*. Madrid: Editora Nacional, 1954.

Labrador, Germán. *Culpables por la literatura: Imaginación política y contracultura en la Transición española (1964–1984)*. Madrid: Siglo XXI, forthcoming.

López Vázquez, José Manuel. "A pintura galega nos dous primeiros terzos do século XX." *A casa habitada: A colección da Casa de Galicia en Madrid*. Santiago de Compostela: Xunta de Galicia, 2008. 31–65.

Martínez, Guillem, ed. *CT o la Cultura de la Transición: Crítica a 35 años de cultura española*. Barcelona: DeBolsillo, 2012.

Miguélez-Carballeira, Helena. *Galicia, a Sentimental Nation: Gender, Culture and Politics*. Cardiff: U of Wales P, 2013.

Murguía, Manuel. "Discurso de Manuel Murguía nos Xogos Froráis de Tui do 1891." *Grial* 43 (1974): 83–89.

Pérez Touriño, Emilio. "Limiar." *A casa habitada: A colección da Casa de Galicia en Madrid*. Santiago de Compostela: Xunta de Galicia, 2008. 11.

"Presentada en la Casa de Galicia en Madrid la segunda edición de *Lamazares. Viaje íntimo.*" *Xunta de Galicia* 22 January 2013. *www.emigracion.xunta.es/es/actualidad/noticia/presentada-la-casa-galicia-madrid-la-segunda-edicion-lamazares-viaje-intimo* (accessed 18 June 2014).

"El presidente del Casino de Madrid, Mariano Turiel de Castro, ofrece en la Casa de Galicia el recital 'Decir el verso,' con una cuidada selección, deteniéndose especialmente en la obra de Rosalía." *Xunta de Galicia* 22 January 2013. *www.emigracion.xunta.es/es/actualidad/noticia/presidente-del-casino-madrid-mariano-turiel-castro-ofrece-la-casa-galicia-recital* (accessed 18 June 2014).

"Prohibeixen el lema 'Una nació, una selecció.'" *E-notícies* 15 December 2008. *esports.e-noticies.cat/prohibeixen-el-lema-una-nacio-una-seleccio-23975.html* (accessed 26 June 2014).

Quaggio, Giulia. *La cultura en transición: Reconciliación y política cultural en España, 1976–1986.* Madrid: Alianza Editorial, 2014.

Rios Bergantinhos, Noa. "Contemporary Galician Politics: The End of a Cycle?" *A Companion to Galician Culture.* Ed. Helena Miguélez-Carballeira. Woodbridge, UK: Tamesis, 2014. 195–212.

Soto, Luís G. *O labirinto da saudade.* Brión: Laiovento, 2012.

Torné, Gonzalo. "Un mes en el que la CT enfermó." *CT o la Cultura de la Transición: Crítica a 35 años de cultura española.* Ed. Guillem Martínez. Barcelona: DeBolsillo, 2012. 53–64.

"Unha Academia para o século XXI: Entrevista con Constantino García." *O Correo Galego* 19 (2001): 4.

Varela, Bernardino. "O día de Galicia: 25 de xullo." *A Nosa Terra* 123 (1920): 4.

Wheeler, Duncan. *Art, Power, Governance: The Cultural Politics of Spain's Transition to Democracy.* London: Bloomsbury Academics, forthcoming.

CHAPTER 13

Emotional Competence and the Discourses of Suffering in the Television Series *Amar en tiempos revueltos*

JO LABANYI

Amar en tiempos revueltos (*Loving in Troubled Times*), set during the Civil War and early Franco dictatorship, proved an unexpected hit, averaging three million viewers, when screened on Spanish state television (TVE-1), its first episode appearing in September 2005.[1] Originally conceived as a one-season series, its success led to its indefinite prolongation until November 2012, when it moved to the private television channel Antena 3 with the banal title, stripped of any reference to history, *Amar es para siempre* (*Loving Is Forever*). I limit my discussion here to the first season of 2005–2006, whose 199 episodes—screened Monday through Friday in the prime-time *sobremesa* slot—cover the period from the Popular Front's election victory of February 1936, under the Second Republic, to the escape to France in August 1945 of its protagonists Andrea and Antonio.[2] The first season was broadcast at a time when the media debates on the proposed Historical Memory Law, then being drafted by the Socialist government, were becoming increasingly polarized; these debates peaked during *Amar*'s second and third seasons as the draft law was debated in Congress from 2006 to 2007 (Gálvez; Labanyi, "Memory," *The Politics*). My reasons for focusing on the first season are threefold. First, it covers the historical period—the Civil War and immediate postwar—whose contested memory was the object of the Historical Memory Law and related media debates. Second, it was scripted as a self-contained unit with a high degree of narrative coherence (by contrast with the following seasons' open-ended format). Third, political critique is more subdued in the later seasons, which, while retaining reference to political and especially sexual repression, focus more heavily on the minutiae of everyday life, thanks to the slower pace required by the move to an open-ended format, and to the fact that, from the mid-1940s, historical events were less dramatic.

It is well known that, during the Transition to democracy and under the Socialist governments of 1982–1996, Spanish state television used the production of TV series (in this case literary adaptations and biopics) to promote civic values (Palacio, *Historia* 152–64, *La televisión* 295–336). *Amar* was broadcast under the Socialist government of José Luis Rodríguez Zapatero and produced by a Barcelona commercial production company, Diagonal TV.[3] Its pedagogical aim is evident: the producers hired a researcher to produce digests of the press for the period covered, so that real-life events could be woven in by the team of scriptwriters.[4] Its characters represent a wide range of political orientations: from Republican activists to monarchists and Falangists (members of Spain's fascist party, Falange Española), and the gray middle zone of the politically uncommitted who were affected by historical circumstances nonetheless. Overall, there is a clear intent to educate viewers in the horrors of Francoism, including its penal regime, the children stolen from Republican mothers in prison, a corrupt police force, and particularly its reinforcement of a retrograde morality that had devastating repercussions for women.[5] In this sense, *Amar* contrasts with the nostalgic take on late Francoism of TVE-1's longest running and recently concluded historical series, *Cuéntame cómo pasó* (2001–2014), which covered the period 1968–1982, though we may note the problems inherent in *Amar*'s representation of political repression in terms of personal suffering—a point I shall return to at the end.

This chapter will explore the ways in which the first season of *Amar* invites Spanish viewers to evaluate a range of attitudes toward suffering. Suffering, of course, lies at the melodramatic heart of soap opera; in practice, however, soap opera, which deals with the everyday, is a mix of melodrama and realism. Paul Julian Smith has suggested that *Amar* is a mix of the typically melodramatic Latin American *telenovela* and more realist US and British soap opera.[6] I will argue that *Amar* engages in a pedagogy of spectatorship, not just by informing viewers about the level of suffering experienced during the Civil War and early postwar period, but, more subtly, by requiring them to assess different discourses of suffering enacted by its characters as they navigate their way through "troubled times."

I suggest that three discourses of suffering can be seen as operating in the series: that represented by the church, omnipresent in postwar Spain, with its particular inflection in Falangist discourse; that represented by the present-day historical memory debates in which the series can be seen as an intervention; and the discourse of emotional competence (the ability to work at and through emotions) that Eva Illouz has seen as a product of late capitalism, into which Spain was plunged by the neoliberal market policies of both Socialist and Popular Party governments from the early 1980s. I call these three discourses "suffering as redemption," "suffering as victimhood," and "suffering as work" respectively. There are areas of overlap between them, and indeed the characters move around different positions, forcing spectators to rethink their identifications—and the values that support them—in the process. This mobility allows the series to go beyond the black-and-white depiction of character associated with melodrama, despite the recourse to melodramatic plot twists and extreme emotions. I will argue that the series steers viewers away from the notion of suffering as redemption; engages partially but critically with the notion of suffering as victimhood; and ultimately encourages identification with the emotional competence that Eva Illouz analyzes as a trademark of the self-help and therapy cultures fostered by capitalism. The very fact that viewers have to process a number of attitudes toward suffering means that they inevitably internalize a notion of suffering as something that has to be worked at. My proposal is that *Amar* provides viewers with a training in emotional competence, both in its depiction of characters whose greater or lesser attractiveness at any one moment corresponds to their position on a sliding scale of greater or lesser emotional competence, and by requiring viewers themselves to work at processing different attitudes to suffering. The series' title uses the verb "amar" and not the noun "amor": love is presented as an activity, as something one has to work at.

In a country starting belatedly, at the time the series was broadcast, to work through its repressive past, the provision of tools that encouraged viewers to work at evaluating different attitudes to suffering—and, above all, to acknowledge the existence of suffering, the first step toward emotional competence—was an important intervention in the public sphere. By 2005, when *Amar* went on the air, Spain had experienced a boom in novels and films (fiction and documentary) resorting to realism to invite readers to empathize with the war's losers. The mix of melodrama and realism in *Amar* takes the focus on suffering further; what is novel in the series is the juxtaposition of different regimes of suffering. Television also has the advantage of reaching a wider audience than fiction and film. Its mode of reception, in the family sitting room, incorporates it into spectators' everyday life routines, particularly when, as in this case, the series is broadcast daily. The prime-time after-lunch slot allocated to *Amar* also meant that it was typically viewed with several family members gathered together, encouraging collective debate on the dilemmas posed in each episode.

Suffering as Redemption

As is well known, the Franco dictatorship relied on National-Catholicism to legitimize its illegal seizure of power with the Civil War of 1936–1939 (Raguer; Casanova). Its penal regime was based on the Catholic notion that sin must be purged though penance; thus "erring" Republican supporters must endure imprisonment and multiple forms of humiliation and hardship in order to be "redeemed" and made fit for incorporation into the New Spain. Prison sentences could be remitted through the system of "Redención de Penas por el Trabajo" (Redemption of Sentences through Labor), instituted in 1938, which made explicit the underlying religious ethos (Lafuente; Richards 79–95), hence the dictatorship's argument that its punishment of the defeated was an act of generosity, "saving" them from "damnation." It suited the Falange, despite its tensions with the church, to adopt the vocabulary of religious salvation to legitimize its implementation of a rule of terror. The Falange also borrowed from the church the vocabulary of martyrdom to refer to its own "fallen," creating the impression that Falangist militants or sympathizers, whether killed in battle or in reprisals in the Republican zone, had actively chosen to embrace suffering. This allowed them to be distinguished from the Republican defeated, who were to be stripped of all agency (exterminated or forcibly "redeemed"). The same religious discourse was thus used to create two contrasting regimes of suffering: bestowing agency in the case of the war's victors; obliterating agency in the case of its losers.

In *Amar*, the discourse of suffering as a purging of sin is articulated most explicitly by the vicious mother superior of the convent for "deviant" (i.e., Republican) women, where Andrea is transferred after her son with the Republican worker Antonio has been taken from her in Madrid's Ventas prison. This blatant example clearly aims to make viewers react against the Catholic stress on suffering as redemption but risks irritating devout or right-wing viewers likely to find it exaggerated.[7] A more subtle, and thus more persuasive, manipulation of viewer response is achieved through the evolution, in the course of the first season, of Padre José Enrique, the local priest who counsels Andrea's bourgeois family. José Enrique takes seriously his Christian mission to "ayudar a los que sufren" (help those who suffer); this leads him to try to arrange Andrea's religious marriage to Antonio in prison (their civil marriage under the Republic is void under Francoism). He is cut short by the prison director when his enthusiasm for the Christian message of love leads him to compare Antonio's death sentence to Christ's crucifixion. In a brilliant later scene, José Enrique's religious orthodoxy is challenged when his officiation at the anarchist Germán's funeral is interrupted by Germán's seminarist grandson Ángel, who sings the "International" to honor the memory of an atheist grandfather who had respected his religious beliefs—indeed, Germán had previously told Ángel that Christ was "el primer socialista" (the first socialist). Predictably, Ángel is arrested. José Enrique intercedes for Ángel, admitting that his atheist grandfather was a good man. José Enrique's orthodoxy will unravel near the first season's end, when he has to administer to the teenager Manuel the night before his execution for anti-Francoist sabotage. When Manuel rejects his Christian exhortation to go willingly to his death, the priest has no answer. We next see him in his parish church admonishing God: "Estamos del lado de los asesinos, ¿es que no te das cuenta? . . . y tú no dices nada, nada" (We're on the side of the murderers, don't you realize? . . . and you say nothing, nothing). He exits the series, transferred to the provinces for speaking of forgiveness at Manuel's funeral, protesting—in ironic agreement with the atheist Germán—that, if Christ were alive today, those in power would consider him a subversive.

Viewers are asked to question the Catholic notion of suffering as the purging of sin also through the evolution of the pious Loreto (Andrea's mother). Her self-sacrificial insistence on caring personally for her unfaithful husband Fabián when he is incapacitated by a stroke is shown to be a mask for her revenge on Fabián, reminded by her constantly that his paralysis is a punishment for his sins. She resists the possibility of brain surgery, preferring him to continue to suffer—a vindictiveness of which she subsequently repents. As will be discussed later, the series also seems to view Fabián's stroke as the result of moral error—not adultery but emotional cowardice: the discourse used is that of emotional competence, not religion.

The Falangist notion of martyrdom enters the series through Andrea's Falangist brother Rodrigo, seduced by the Falange's rhetoric of purification through violence. Before the war's outbreak Rodrigo guns down Republican supporters, regarded as "gentuza" (rabble), ironically killing the left-wing aristocrat Eduardo (Andrea's first boyfriend). The series will punish Rodrigo by having him sign up for the División Azul (Blue Division) of mostly Falangist volunteers who fought alongside Hitler's army on the Russian Front from 1941 to 1943, as a result of which he becomes a victim of what today is called post-traumatic stress disorder (PTSD). The discourse of martyrdom applied by the regime to the División Azul is undone by the narration of Rodrigo's sufferings on the Russian front in terms of the very different discourse of trauma. While the depiction of Rodrigo as trauma victim might appear to let him off the hook for his fascist thuggery by eliciting viewers' pity, in practice he scores badly when measured in terms of the discourse of emotional competence. Rodrigo is perhaps the series' most complex character because he invites consideration in terms of the three discourses of suffering discussed in this essay; I thus return to him below.

Suffering as Victimhood

The debates on historical memory that were contemporaneous with *Amar* changed the way the Civil War and its aftermath were remembered in Spain. After Franco's death in 1975, when it became possible to discuss the issue openly, historical studies and documentaries tended to focus on Republican protagonists, seen as heroes. A global shift occurred in the 1990s with the development in international law of the concept of transitional justice, based on the institution of Truth and Reconciliation Commissions such as had been held in Chile and Argentina—a process clinched by the creation in 1998 of the International Criminal Court. These legal developments produced a new emphasis on the rights of victims. The historian Santos Juliá's 1999 edited volume *Víctimas de la guerra civil* (*Victims of the Civil War*) was the first systematic attempt to compile statistics of Republican victims. The focus on victims was consolidated by the creation, in 2000, of the Asociación para la Recuperación de la Memoria Histórica (Association for the Recovery of Historical Memory), to assist families wanting to exhume and give proper burial to their Republican relatives shot and buried in mass graves (for the exhumation movement, see Ferrándiz in this volume). The media debates surrounding the exhumations have forced the Spanish public to recognize the extent of the extrajudicial killings in and after the war, and to acknowledge the bereaved relatives' suffering. However, the focus on victims—perpetrators remain a taboo subject—runs the risk of turning the war's losers into objects of violence rather than seeing them as historical agents. The consequent right-wing backlash has produced an ugly form of "competitive victimhood" (Judt's term), reviving Francoist claims that the right, who won the war, were the victims of the losers.[8]

It was in this context that, on its 2004 election victory, the incoming Socialist government announced the creation of a commission to draft a Law of Historical Memory. Despite bending over backward to avoid appearing partisan, the law was conceived within the framework of transitional justice culture as an act of reparation to the victims of the Francoist repression. In this climate, it was logical that *Amar* should use the melodramatic component of soap opera—melodrama has historically focused on victims (Elsaesser 64)—to depict the suffering of the war's losers. Victim discourse intrudes at numerous points, but the series focuses mostly on how the characters manage to survive. In hiding after Nationalist victory, Andrea's Republican husband Antonio declaims: "¿Es justo lo que está pasando, dime, es justo? . . . Tanta y tanta gente fusilada, enferma, desesperada . . . tanto sufrimiento, ¿para qué?" (Is what is happening just, tell me, is it just? . . . So many people shot, sick, desperate. . . . so much suffering for what?) But he prefaces and follows this outcry by expressing his desire to act, refusing the victim's helplessness. Ironically, his action—giving himself up on learning that a wartime comrade has been sentenced to death in his name—will make him an even greater victim. But this is not straightforward victimhood: the scene of his voluntary surrender to save another man's life cuts to the crucified Christ in the cemetery whose posture echoes that of Antonio on arrest. This places Antonio in the role of Christian martyr, normally reserved for Francoist victims—a role that, as noted above, confers agency. Antonio's depiction as martyr rather than helpless victim is reinforced when he refuses religious marriage to Andrea in prison, preferring Andrea to forget him and remake her life, rather than, after his execution, suffer as widow of a "red"; and similarly when he sacrifices himself so his cellmates can escape. The prison director accuses him of obduracy in refusing to play the role of the defeated.

When Antonio temporarily lapses into victimhood, resourceful women snap him out of it. After release, having discovered that Andrea has remarried (thanks to her pact with her Falangist brother Rodrigo that he will get Antonio reprieved if she marries the monarchist aristocrat Mario), he wonders whether it would after all be better to accept defeat. The shopkeeper Paloma retorts: "no hay que darles el gusto de vernos rendidos" (we mustn't allow them the pleasure of seeing us capitulate). When Antonio breaks off his relationship with Luisa, realizing he can't forget Andrea, he blames the historical circumstances that separated him from Andrea. Luisa insists that one can't blame circumstances since she and Antonio freely chose to get into a relationship. Antonio is indeed a victim of Nationalist victory, but, apart from brief lapses, he refuses to "play the victim," choosing antifascist activism—first as a British spy, later as a member of the anti-Franco resistance—because he would rather risk his life than accept helplessness. The greatest example of the refusal of victimhood is Antonio's mother Elpidia, the housekeeper of Andrea's bourgeois family (superbly played by veteran actor Pilar Bardem, whose Communist credentials are well known to Spanish audiences). After the war, Elpidia regally refuses the offer of help from Andrea's father Fabián, who has not lifted a finger to save her imprisoned husband, his most trusted worker, with the words "Mi hambre me la administro yo" (I'll manage my hunger myself).

Andrea is placed in impossible emotional double binds that make her a victim whichever option she chooses. If she refuses Rodrigo's pact, Antonio will be executed; if she accepts it and saves Antonio's life, she must marry Mario and lose Antonio. Similarly, being faithful to Mario means being unfaithful to her first husband, Antonio; being unfaithful to Mario means, under Francoist law, which penalizes adultery, risking imprisonment and loss of her child with Antonio (her legal husband, Mario, who has taken the child in on his reappearance, has paternal rights). The only solution is to break out of the system altogether: that is, to risk all by fleeing to France with Antonio and their child. Francoism is depicted not as turning the war's losers into helpless victims, but as causing immense suffering by placing them in situations whereby they can choose only between alternative kinds of misery.

Given the emphasis on victims in the memory debates in Spain since 2000, it is important that *Amar* stresses the personal suffering caused by Francoism while depicting characters who refuse to play the role of victim. In this respect, the series' use of trauma discourse in relation not to the war's losers but to the Falangist Rodrigo is especially interesting. Trauma discourse became institutionalized in the memory debates on the Holocaust that gained prominence internationally in the 1990s, contributing to the stress on victims in transitional justice legislation, where genocide was a key topic. While dating back to Freud's studies of shell shock in World War I, trauma theory became prominent during the Vietnam War when PTSD was recognized in the American Psychiatric Association's *Diagnostic and Statistical Manual of Mental Disorders* as a condition affecting war veterans. Trauma theory supposes that the traumatic event is not registered in consciousness but on the body, which suffers belated replays of the traumatic experience (Caruth; LaCapra). In treating sufferers as victims of unconscious psychic mechanisms, trauma theory risks eliding agency.

The psychology of perpetrators has not been investigated in Spain. We must therefore ask what is going on with the representation of Rodrigo as trauma victim. On return, wounded, from the Russian front, he gives his Falangist superior a contradictory account, accusing the División Azul of committing atrocities but saying they let themselves be massacred like rabbits: both positions undo the heroic view of war that had led Rodrigo to enlist. His account of the Russian front triggers a flashbulb memory of his shooting of Eduardo in early 1936, showing that both are connected in his mind. The traumatic experience undergone in Russia emerges when Rodrigo starts to tell his wife, Consuelo, how he was captured and tortured by the Russians: we cut to a representation of the scene, in which Rodrigo betrays his battalion's battle plans to the Russians. As Eduardo's voice-over comes in, calling him a coward, we cut to Eduardo's "ghost" saying he will forever remind Rodrigo how his military comrades died, cutting back to Rodrigo telling Consuelo he didn't betray them but they died anyway. Unable to admit his betrayal, Rodrigo projects his repressed conscience onto an imaginary persecutor in the form of his victim, Eduardo. Mark Levene has noted that the common characteristic of all historical cases of genocide is the perpetrators' insistence that they are being persecuted by their victims (196–202). In the mental hospital where Rodrigo is interned, the doctor names his illness as trauma. The doctor's attempts to probe his unconscious produce another flashbulb memory of the torture scene. But Rodrigo never admits to breaking under torture or to killing Eduardo, suffering continued hallucinations in which Eduardo's "ghost" now plays the double role of persecutor and ally, insisting that Rodrigo is a victim of betrayal by his wife and the Falange. This prompts Rodrigo, having tried to strangle Consuelo, to attempt to assassinate his Falangist superior (whose bodyguard will shoot Rodrigo dead). The series depicts Rodrigo as a trauma victim but, in stressing his refusal to acknowledge his guilt, suggests that trauma is an alibi for the failure to work through shame.

Suffering as Work

In her book *Cold Intimacies: The Making of Emotional Capitalism*, Illouz suggests that the capitalist market economy has produced a particular emotional regime that has come to permeate both the workplace and the home thanks to the culture of therapy and self-help that, since the 1920s, has advocated specific techniques of emotional management. The resulting advice literature has promoted the notion of emotional competence, which makes the individual responsible for managing the self. Illouz observes (12–16) that the concept of emotional competence emerged out of management theory, and that the first surveys conducted in the United States in the 1920s were based on women workers; the result was a feminization of workplace relationships, with communication skills (empathy) made central to effective interpersonal management. The resulting therapeutic culture is based on the notion of emotional rights: for feelings to be validated, it is enough that they be felt and articulated by the subject; productive relationships are based on recognition of the feelings of others (35–39).

Illouz notes that, as the liberal view of the right to self-development intensified in the 1960s thanks to the "sexual revolution" and the takeoff of consumer capitalism, American therapy culture became obsessed with the idea that the major obstacle to fulfillment was "fear of success" (44–45). Emotional competence thus required not only empathy with the emotions of others but also the ability to admit to one's own emotions, seen as the root of one's problems (45–47). Illouz analyzes the television talk show as the epitome of this therapeutic culture (50–57), whereby "identity is found and expressed in the experience of suffering and in the understanding of emotions gained by the telling of the story" (53). Soap opera, in which characters talk constantly about their sufferings, can be seen as having a similar function. Illouz relates this incessant talking about suffering to today's cult of victimhood and trauma (52–56) but notes that this is contradicted by the concept of emotional competence, which makes individuals responsible for managing their emotions (57, 62). She observes that, unlike religious discourses for dealing with suffering, therapy culture does not apportion blame (55). She also notes that the less educated, having less access to therapy culture, are less likely to develop emotional competence—reversing Freud's suggestion that the lower classes, being less emotionally inhibited, were less likely to develop neurosis than the bourgeoisie (Illouz 71–73). It seems to me, however, that therapy culture does apportion blame in the case of those members of the middle classes who, despite their educational and social advantages, fail to work at and through their emotions. *Amar* offers several examples.

We have already seen Rodrigo's failure to face his sense of shame. His emotional incompetence makes him a bad manager of his father's factory when he steps into that role after Fabián's stroke. It also makes him a failure as a husband: Consuelo will discover that his idea of sexual fulfillment is akin to rape. Curiously, Rodrigo admires his sister Andrea, despite their opposing political beliefs, for being true to her emotions; he thus champions her against their father, Fabián, who is the series' major emotional coward. A conservative but basically decent factory owner (he takes his Republican workers back on Nationalist victory), Fabián's class prejudice overrides his love for Andrea; after the war, he doesn't want to know about her marriage to his worker Antonio and her imprisonment. Once Andrea is out of jail, Fabián locates her child with Antonio, taken from her in prison, and puts him in an orphanage, lying that he has died, to stop her looking for him. Fabián tells Andrea at the time that, if one day she finds out that he did something "monstrous," she should know that he did it for her good. In fact Fabián maintains the child and visits him like a doting grandfather; his main failing is his inability to deal with his guilt at his "monstrous" lie.

When Fabián is blackmailed by the crooked policeman Rafael, who, having discovered Fabián's guilty secret, has kidnapped the child and returned him to Andrea, Fabián accepts Rafael's extortions rather than admit his lie to his family. (Rafael, the series' major villain, is also emotionally incompetent because of his inability to face his shame at the fact that his father, Fabián's business partner, drank and gambled away his share in the business.) This in turn makes Fabián a bad manager of his factory, which cannot prosper when he is handing Rafael half the profits. It is made clear that terror of Rafael revealing the truth is what causes his stroke. Before undergoing brain surgery, he writes a letter confessing his lie to Andrea and admitting his cowardice in not telling her in person and asks his youngest son, Sito, to give it to her if he dies under surgery, and to destroy it if he survives. Elpidia interrupts Sito trying to burn the letter, reads it, and burns it herself—a typically melodramatic case of bad timing since, immediately after, as Andrea sits with Fabián at the clinic, he has a nightmare in which she repudiates him on discovering the truth, which triggers his death from another stroke. Andrea discovers the truth only much later from the blackmailer Rafael, confirmed by Elpidia. There is poetic justice in the confirmation of the truth by Elpidia—the epitome of emotional honesty—since Fabián had shown his emotional cowardice earlier by avoiding the funeral of her husband, his foreman, because he could not face her when he had done nothing to get him out of prison. As Fabián's wife, Loreto, retorts at the time: "darle la espalda a los problemas no significa que éstos desaparezcan" (turning your back on problems won't make them go away).

The complicated emotional triangle formed by Antonio-Andrea-Mario requires viewers to work particularly hard at evaluating their positions, since Andrea and Mario oscillate between disavowal and recognition of their emotions, and since both Antonio and Mario are loving, tender, and handsome. Like Andrea, viewers are torn between Antonio and Mario; what decides their alignment is the working-class Antonio's superior emotional competence. Mario does everything he can to make Andrea happy, including searching for her missing son and taking him in when he reappears, but is unable to face the fact that she still loves Antonio. He has moments of lucidity with Consuelo, in love with him from the start, asking why do we fall in love with people who don't love us (Consuelo, unbeknown to him, has the same problem). But, after he and Consuelo make love, he denies that anything happened between them. Both he and Antonio are feminized men in that they are fully able to articulate their love for Andrea. What Mario cannot admit is the failure of their marriage, as Andrea points out when she snaps at him: "sé asumir mis fracasos, algo que tú no puedes" (I've learnt to accept my failures, unlike you). His response on discovering that Andrea married him to save Antonio's life is to get drunk. His inability to face up to his failed marriage—the failure of an institution that was the cornerstone of Francoist morality—is consonant with his social position as a lawyer who, despite his disaffection from the regime as a monarchist (he will come to see monarchism as a sham too), is caught up in the state apparatus. By the end, however, Mario comes to see that he had chosen failure by marrying a woman he knew was in love with another man. Having overcome his fear of success, he is able to recognize his feelings for Consuelo: "¿Por qué me empeño en renunciar a lo único bueno que hay en mi vida?" (Why do I insist on renouncing the only good thing in my life?) he asks rhetorically before kissing her. The end, as he wishes Andrea and Antonio luck on their escape to France and says goodbye to the child he has treated as his own, is a tearjerker because Mario has come to terms with his emotions but has lost nonetheless. The always emotionally competent working-class Antonio recognizes what Mario is feeling.

Andrea oscillates throughout between recognition and disavowal of her feelings for Antonio. She identifies with the Republic as the promise of freedom to love across class lines. This being soap opera, the Republic and the Franco dictatorship are evaluated in terms of their granting or denial of emotional rights. Francoism will make emotional honesty impossible for Andrea—a situation illustrated visually in the scene where she tells Antonio they must forget the past, in front of the slogan "Franco Franco Franco Arriba España" on the wall behind (Fig. 13.1). But when the past returns with their child's reappearance, she resists Mario's wish to give the child his name, not wanting to suppress Antonio's memory. While pretending to her parents that she is happy with Mario, she admits to Antonio that she can't live without him. But when Mario threatens her with loss of her child because of her infidelity, she submits, though giving up the pretense that she is happy with him. The working-class Antonio points out her bourgeois emotional dishonesty, insisting "lo único que puede obligarte a algo son tus sentimientos" (your only obligation is to your feelings). By the first season's end, she has

Figure 13.1. *Amar en tiempos revueltos*: Andrea and Antonio with image of Franco on the wall behind. Courtesy of RTVE.

asserted her emotional rights, is living separately from Mario, and is trying to get their marriage annulled. Her escape to France with Antonio and their son is an affirmation of freedom in the form of emotional rights: "¡Somos libres!" (We're free!), they exclaim as they embrace on crossing the border.

Antonio's steadfast emotional competence makes him a less complex but highly attractive character. There is a strong suggestion here of Freud's supposition, noted by Illouz, that the working classes are more emotionally competent than the bourgeoisie because they are less repressed: like his mother Elpidia, Antonio is always emotionally honest and not afraid to face difficult emotional situations. This is a class issue also in that, unlike the aristocratic lawyer Mario, Antonio is clearly outside the state apparatus; this makes it easier for him to act in accordance with his emotions. Even when Antonio tries to make a relationship with Luisa, he is honest to her about his feelings for Andrea. Antonio is frequently seen—with Andrea and with Luisa—on the roof terrace of Andrea's family home (he and Elpidia occupy the servants' quarters), which represents a space of emotional openness in a repressive society (Figs. 13.2a and 13.2b). Symbolically, it is the place where the sheets are hung out to dry (as opposed to the injunction not to expose one's dirty linen in public). Illouz notes that, in interwar management theory, the discourse of emotional competence was particularly aimed at factory foremen (15–16): Antonio is an efficient worker, promoted to foreman in Andrea's father's factory and previously promoted to sergeant in the war.

The other emotionally competent male in the first season is the very different Isidro, a comic character who not coincidentally is a fan of sentimental *radionovelas* (radio serials). He too forms part of an emotional triangle, in this case with Consuelo's petty-bourgeois mother Pura (also a radionovela fan) and her estranged husband, José. In this case, the triangle is a loving ménage-à-trois comprising the most unlikely

Figure 13.2a and b. The roof terrace in *Amar en tiempos revueltos*: (a) Antonio with Luisa; (b) Antonio with Andrea. Courtesy of RTVE.

characters. Isidro's chronic shyness conceals a heart of gold. Although his pending marriage to Pura, his landlady, is upset by the discovery that her public persona as a widow is a lie invented by her to cover up the shame of José having left her for another woman, he encourages her to visit José in hospital and, after José's common-law wife dies, insists they take him in. His emotional competence is shown not only in his loving care of José but also in enabling Pura to overcome her emotional dishonesty. José too is a man who listens to his heart, having preferred to break with his wife rather than adopt the standard hypocritical solution of having a mistress on the side, and forgiving Pura for having brought up their daughter Consuelo to think her father was dead. Before José dies, he tells Consuelo always to follow her heart, thus helping her overcome her

Figure 13.3. *Amar en tiempos revueltos*: Isidro (*right*), José (*left*), and Pura form an unorthodox "Holy Family." Courtesy of RTVE.

emotional dishonesty in pretending she is happily married to Rodrigo. In a wonderful scene, Isidro and José fall asleep on each other's shoulders; as Pura appears behind them, they form an unorthodox "Holy Family" (Fig. 13.3)—Isidro had previously said to José, "¿Te das cuenta de que somos una familia?" (Don't you realize we're a family?). This could not be further from the Francoist family ideal. When Pura gets pregnant by Isidro, José is as pleased as anyone; when José dies, Isidro is the one most upset, despite that fact that Pura is now free to marry him. Pura's gain in emotional competence is shown by her taking the initiative in proposing to Isidro. When the baby is born, Isidro acts as midwife. Both Isidro and José, as men who listen to their hearts, teach others (Pura and Consuelo) to recognize their emotions.

There are many other characters who are presented in terms of emotional competence or lack of it: Sito, who does not censure his father for his affair with Paloma but is unable to accept his own homosexuality; Mario's venomous mother, Eulalia, who refuses to see that her lover Arturo is using her; Mario's father, Javier, a playboy who nonetheless is completely honest about his promiscuity; Charles, the British International Brigadier and later spy, whose political integrity matches his emotional independence. I will end by discussing the three female characters who best represent emotional competence: Luisa, Paloma, and Beatriz—for the models are not all male. We have already seen Luisa's rejection of victim discourse. A self-possessed young woman who has come from the countryside to study to be a schoolteacher, Luisa believes in free love, rejecting marriage as a curtailment of her freedom (which it certainly was for women under Francoist legislation). After breaking up with Antonio, she not only gets on with her life but goes to tell Andrea that Antonio loves her, since she wants the best for him. She thus manages other people's emotions as well as her own.

Managing the emotions of others is Paloma's specialty. She can do this because she is in command of her own emotions. This is explicitly related to her business acumen. A shopkeeper and later, thanks to her practical savvy, owner of a nightclub, she is regularly shown doing her accounts. Equally good at managing her money and her emotions, she is generous in sharing her bed (with Antonio, Charles, and Fabián) in exchange for emotional honesty and conservation of her financial independence. When sleeping with Antonio at the series' start, she tells him he is in love with Andrea before he has realized it. When Fabián installs her in an apartment, she insists on keeping her grocery store so as not to be a kept woman—"soy una mujer libre" (I'm a free woman). Her nightclub becomes a place where all and sundry come to air their emotional problems, with Paloma presiding. Paloma is the only person Fabián feels able to tell about his shameful lie, because she listens without judging. She insists to Elpidia that, in the face of tragedy, one has to go on living: "Las mujeres sabemos más de esto que nadie" (Women know more about that than anyone). When Antonio asks Paloma what matters to her more, love or business, she replies: "El amor, siempre" (Love, always) but in the sense of "el amor a sí mismo" (self-respect)—adding that "el otro amor, ése que tú entiendes, sólo existe en las películas" (the other kind of love, the kind you mean, only exists in movies). The similarly independent and frank Javier falls for her, but she will not give up her financial independence to leave Madrid with him. In the penultimate scene, before Andrea and Antonio cross the French border, Charles returns to Paloma's nightclub. Their intermittent romance is clinched with a kiss, with the theme song "Amar en tiempos revueltos" playing over, but is indefinitely postponed as neither will give up their independent lives; he leaves, saying he'll be back. The openness of this love based on mutual respect and independence contrasts with Andrea's and Antonio's passionate romance, which ends with closure: viewers are left to evaluate the two models, both presented as positive.

The connection between espionage and emotional competence is explored with Beatriz, Mario's lesbian cousin who works for British Intelligence. Beatriz is admired by Andrea for putting emotional honesty before all else in deciding to leave Spain for the United States with her married female lover. It is, of course, easier for Beatriz to accept her lesbianism than for Sito to face his homosexuality since she is an aristocrat, the aristocracy having always had freer morals. When Beatriz recruits Antonio to work for British Intelligence during World War II (when Madrid was a hotbed of Allied and Axis espionage, as the series shows), she tells him that, for this work, you have to control your emotions completely. Antonio will make a good spy. But Beatriz is the supreme example of bravery: when captured by German spies the day before her planned escape to the United States, she takes a cyanide capsule to avoid betraying others under torture. The contrast with Rodrigo is evident.

Illouz's book is based on the United States, but the therapy culture she analyzes has been disseminated globally through television. The talk shows that she sees as its maximum expression are omnipresent on Spanish television. The mix of Latin American telenovela and English-language soap opera that Smith observes in *Amar* suggests that the series tempers the telenovela's generally fatalistic concept of suffering with a more Protestant notion of taking responsibility for one's emotions. Several of the most emotionally competent characters are associated with English-language culture: apart from Beatriz and Charles, Antonio—who will be recruited into British Intelligence—is shown to be studying English from the series' start out of a concern with self-improvement.

Illouz calls the ethos of emotional competence "emotional capitalism," since it is a product of the capitalist stress on individual initiative—a discourse very different from the various collectivist solutions, of both political left and right, that were being tried out under the Republic and that clashed in the Civil War. Jesús Izquierdo Martín and Pablo Sánchez León have critiqued today's memory movements in Spain for promoting identification with the victims of the Civil War and its aftermath, since Spaniards in the 1930s and early 1940s had very different belief systems and emotional regimes from Spaniards today (227–76). The discourse of emotional competence is a product of the neoliberal ideology that has triumphed in contemporary Spain. It must be recognized that, in privileging this discourse, *Amar* limits its analysis of Francoism to a matter of decisions taken by individuals about their personal conduct. While the political context of those decisions is made clear, it is mostly left offscreen—with the notable exceptions of Andrea's and Antonio's incarceration after the war, and the wonderful sequence that intercuts shots of Franco's Victory Parade with Antonio, on the run, taking advantage of the police's deployment at the parade to find and make love to Andrea. The most glaring example of the personalization of the political is the crooked policeman Rafael, portrayed as driven by personal hang-ups, thereby avoiding depiction of the systemic corruption and brutality of the Francoist state apparatus. I have noted above that the series evaluates the Republic and the Franco dictatorship in terms of their granting or denial of emotional—rather than social or political—rights. Thomas Elsaesser has criticized melodrama for presenting political issues in personal terms (46–47); soap opera by definition deals with personal emotions. There is a limit to what emotions can do as a tool of historical analysis, but they are an effective instrument for assessing the relative merits of different value systems. It is important that *Amar* confronts viewers with a range of discourses of suffering, requiring them to develop their own emotional competence in evaluating them. The fact that each of these discourses of suffering has its own historical and political baggage means that, in adjudicating between them, viewers are making decisions of more than personal importance.

NOTES

1. This audience figure does not include online viewers; *Amar* was TVE's first series to be made available online from the start. Its website, *www.rtve.es/television/.amarentiempos revueltos/*, contains detailed information (including its many awards), its 1,716 episodes, and a forum with many postings from overseas, especially Latin America. Its broadcast was accompanied by several commercial tie-ins (novels, history books, cookery book).

It flopped however as the first Spanish television series to be broadcast on US Spanish-language television (Telemundo, September–November 2009).
2. The *sobremesa* slot corresponds roughly to 4:00–5:00 p.m., when Spaniards are traditionally at home for the 2:00–5:00 p.m. lunch break. The second to seventh seasons of *Amar* covered the period 1945–1957. Antena 3's continuation has had low audience ratings, but at the time this book went to press (May 2015) it was still running.
3. The success of *Amar* led to two other Diagonal TV period productions for TVE-1: the series *La Señora* (2008–2010), which explores class conflict in the 1920s; and its spin-off *14 de abril: La República* (2011), whose second season, ending with the outbreak of the Civil War and scheduled for 2012, was put on hold by TVE under the new conservative Popular Party government. Since then, Diagonal TV's period productions for TVE have treated safer historical territory: *Isabel* (2012–2014), chronicling the life of Isabel la Católica (with Rodolfo Sancho, who played the Republican worker Antonio in *Amar*, improbably cast as Fernando el Católico), and the planned *Carlos V*. Diagonal TV's Catalan-language productions for Catalan Television (TV3) have also tended to take a critical attitude to Francoism: for example, the 2001–2002 series *Temps de silenci*, covering 1932–1998; and the miniseries *Les veus de Pamano* (2008), based on Jaume Cabré's novel. See *www.diagonaltv.es* and *www.formulatv.com/noticias/* (accessed 12 September 2014).
4. Conversation with Adolfo Puerta Martín, a member of the scriptwriting team and author of three novels based on the series (Madrid, 16 March 2010). I thank him for giving me his time.
5. The systematic stealing and selling for illegal adoption of babies of jailed Republican mothers was revealed in 2002 (Vinyes; Armengou and Belis). In 2009 it was discovered that the practice had continued, for financial gain, in Spanish hospitals till the 1990s.
6. The technical distinction between the terms "telenovela" and "soap opera" is that the former, running for a fixed period, works toward a conclusion, while soap opera, running for an indefinite period, is open-ended (Mazziotti 14; Lizaur 9–27). Strictly, the first season of *Amar* is a *telenovela* since it was conceived as a one-season serial culminating in its protagonists' escape to France, as shown in the trailer for the series (Episode 0 on TVE's website). The series' indefinite prolongation turned it into a soap opera. I will not dwell on this technical distinction, since no genres appear in "pure" form.
7. Of the three interviews I conducted in Madrid in June 2010 with fans of *Amar en tiempos revueltos* in their sixties or seventies, the one couple who expressed pro-Franco attitudes insisted that the series exaggerated the suffering of Republican prisoners. The conversation produced an argument with their daughter who disagreed. All three interviews confirmed that the series' main merit was that it led to discussion among those watching of how what was depicted on-screen did or did not correspond to the narratives they had imbibed from their upbringing—and in some cases to the airing of stories that had been kept silent in the family.
8. In his recent major study *The Spanish Holocaust*, Paul Preston's estimate for victims of the Francoist terror during the war is 150,000, with another twenty thousand shot and thirty thousand dying in prison after the war's end. His estimate for victims of wartime reprisals in the Republican zone is fifty thousand.

WORKS CITED

Armengou, Montse, and Ricard Belis. *Els nens perduts del franquisme*. Documentary. TV3, 2002.

Caruth, Cathy. *Unclaimed Experience: Trauma, Narrative, and History*. Baltimore: Johns Hopkins UP, 1996.

Casanova, Julián. *La iglesia de Franco*. Barcelona: Crítica, 2001.

Elsaesser, Thomas. "Tales of Sound and Fury: Observations on the Family Melodrama." *Home Is Where the Heart Is: Studies in Melodrama and the Women's Film*. Ed. Christine Gledhill. London: BFI Publishing, 1987. 43–69.

Gálvez, Sergio, ed. *Generaciones y memoria de la represión franquista: Un balance de los movimientos de la memoria*. Spec. issue of *Hispania Nova* 6–7 (2006–2007). hispanianova.rediris.es (accessed 3 August 2014).

Illouz, Eva. *Cold Intimacies: The Making of Emotional Capitalism*. Cambridge: Polity, 2007.

Izquierdo Martín, Jesús, and Pablo Sánchez León. *La guerra que nos han contado: 1936 y nosotros*. Madrid: Alianza Editorial, 2006.

Judt, Tony. "Epilogue: From the House of the Dead; An Essay on Modern European Memory." *Postwar: A History of Europe since 1945*. London: Pimlico, 2007. 803–31.

Juliá, Santos, ed. *Víctimas de la guerra civil*. Madrid: Temas de hoy, 1999.

Labanyi, Jo. "Memory and Modernity in Democratic Spain: The Difficulty of Coming to Terms with the Spanish Civil War." *Poetics Today* 28.1 (2007): 89–116.

———, ed. *The Politics of Memory in Contemporary Spain*. Spec. issue of *Journal of Spanish Cultural Studies* 9.2 (2008).

LaCapra, Dominick. *Writing History, Writing Trauma*. Baltimore: Johns Hopkins UP, 2001.

Lafuente, Isaías. *Esclavos por la patria: La explotación de los presos bajo el franquismo*. Madrid: Temas de hoy, 2002.

Levene, Mark. *The Meaning of Genocide*. London: I. B. Tauris, 2005.

Lizaur, María Blanca de. *La telenovela mexicana 1958–2002: Forma y contenido de un formato narrativo de ficción al alcance mayoritario*. Mexico City: UNAM, 2002.

Mazzioti, Nora. "Introducción: Acercamientos a las telenovelas latinoamericanas." *El espectáculo de la pasión: Las telenovelas latinoamericanas*. Ed. Nora Mazzioti. Buenos Aires: Ediciones Colihue, 1993. 11–27.

Palacio, Manuel. *Historia de la televisión en España*. Barcelona: Gedisa, 2001.

———. *La televisión durante la Transición española*. Madrid: Cátedra, 2012.

Preston, Paul. *The Spanish Holocaust: Inquisition and Extermination in Twentieth-Century Spain*. London: HarperPress, 2012.

Raguer, Hilari. *La pólvora y el incienso: La iglesia y la guerra civil española, 1936–1939*. Barcelona: Península, 2001.

Richards, Michael. *Un tiempo de silencio: La guerra civil y la cultura de la represión en la España de Franco, 1936–1945*. Barcelona: Crítica, 1999.

Smith, Paul Julian. "*Amar en tiempos revueltos* (Loving in Troubled Times, 2005)." *Spanish Screen Fiction: Between Cinema and Television*. Liverpool: Liverpool UP, 2009. 132–44.

Vinyes, Ricard. *Irredentas: Las presas políticas y sus hijos en las cárceles franquistas*. Madrid: Temas de hoy, 2002.

CHAPTER 14

From Tear to Pixel
Political Correctness and Digital Emotions in the Exhumation of Mass Graves from the Civil War

FRANCISCO FERRÁNDIZ

The exhumation of mass graves resulting from rearguard repression during the Civil War (1936–1939) is creating unprecedented political and emotional cartographies in contemporary Spain. These exhumations are taking place in a legal void since, according to Spanish penal law and the 1977 Amnesty Law, the statute of limitations on these crimes has expired and they cannot be prosecuted. As a result, the process of scientific investigation and social dignification of these radically anachronistic corpses—framed by the disorderly arrangement and display of burial pits and inscribed with explicit violence—has become part of a broad, internally diverse political culture linked to the memory of the defeated in the war, which claims these reemerging bodies and the ideals they are understood to represent as a key foundation for activism and public action. In turn, the exhumations in Spain are connected with similar developments elsewhere in the world, within the framework of global human rights discourses and practices (Ferrándiz and Robben).

On the ground, disagreements regarding the handling of these disturbing corpses between different "associations for the recovery of historical memory"—representing different identitarian and political sensibilities—have emerged in many areas, one of the most contentious being divergent attitudes to the emotional management of this potentially "moving" past. In this context, I will analyze two interrelated topics. First, I will show how the ability of exhumations to provoke strong feelings in relatives, sympathizers, and onlookers has given rise to conflicting views on how to emotionally relate to the dead in a meaningful way and on how these emotions ought to be played out in the private and public spheres. In this respect, there have been arguments over what is felt to be politically correct with respect to the emotional tone to be adopted as the bones emerge, the political symbolism that should trigger and accompany the surfacing of feelings, and the relationship between emotions and the politics of victimhood. Second, I will consider how the management and public display of these emotions, understood as social processes in continuous negotiation, and their iconic power as expressions of traumatic memories are increasingly bound up with the contemporary proliferation of affordable, easy-to-use digital devices and networks. This increasing digital profiling of emotions expressed at exhumations and related events raises several connected issues. I shall pay particular attention to the modes and styles in which emotions are performed—posed—for the new digital technologies (from video and still cameras to smartphones) and their dissemination networks in the new media (from Facebook to Twitter). Beyond this, we need to consider how this transformation of emotions into digital artifacts is affecting the construction of social memory in contemporary societies. The memories surfacing in Spain are linked with those arising from human rights violations elsewhere not just through the framework of global human rights discourses, but also thanks to their circulation and consumption via digital new media, leading to their homogenization with other transnational digitized displays of suffering and mourning.

Contemporary exhumations are mostly related to repressive violence against civilians behind the front lines. The Spanish Civil War, caused by a military rebellion against the democratically elected Republican government on 18 July 1936, lasted for almost three years, leaving around five hundred thousand Spaniards dead, with some three hundred thousand killed in combat and up to two hundred thousand civilians executed in the rearguard. These figures are estimates, and there are still some disagreements amongst historians. Regarding the execution of civilians, contemporary historiography places the numbers at around fifty-five thousand executed in the Republican zone, and as many as 150,000 in the rebel Nationalist zone during the war and in the Francoist repression of the early postwar years (Rodrigo; Ferrándiz, "Exhuming"). Paul Preston adds to this figure a further twenty thousand executions after the war, not counting those who died from hunger and disease in jails and concentration camps (17).

Contemporary exhumations in Spain are only the latest episode in successive waves of disinterment and reburial of Civil War corpses in Spain, each corresponding to rather different necropolitical regimes (Mbembe). Exhumations started immediately after the war, as part of the mourning for losses on the winning side, national reconstruction, and the organization of the new dictatorial state. This happened within a pervasive official narrative of military victory anchored in the concepts of religious crusade, heroism, and martyrdom—known in Spanish political history as National Catholicism (Aguilar; Box; see Fig. 14.1). Later, starting in the late 1950s, more than thirty thousand Civil War bodies were dug up and transferred to the Valley of the Fallen, a huge memorial planned by Franco to commemorate his victory for eternity, which became his burial place in 1975.

As for Republican mass graves, some were opened clandestinely by relatives during the dictatorship, and after Franco's death other exhumations took place with scarcely any institutional or technical support, within the framework of the emerging political cultures of the Transition to democracy. But it was sociologist and journalist Emilio Silva who, in October 2000, started the latest chapter in Civil War necropolitics in

Spain when organizing the exhumation of a Republican mass grave in Priaranza del Bierzo (in León) containing thirteen corpses, including that of his grandfather. This exhumation was the first to be conducted with the participation of technical experts (Silva and Macías).

A political and media storm regarding the appropriate management of these anachronistic bodies—or even questioning the need for their reappearance in a consolidated democratic state—hit Spain in the following decade, gaining international attention. The political right cried foul in the face of this emergent process of mourning in the public sphere, as it generally considered that Civil War suffering was a thing of the past and that reconciliation had been satisfactorily achieved during the Transition. The main developments in Spain since the Priaranza excavation can briefly be summarized as follows: the passing in 2007 of a Historical Memory Law ("Ley 52/2007") after high-voltage debates in parliament and more generally in the public sphere; the unsuccessful attempt in 2008 by internationally renowned judge Baltasar Garzón to link the Spanish case with international human rights law, and the 2011 government appointment of a Commission of Experts to decide on the fate of dictator Francisco Franco's tomb and the controversial monument housing it.

In the period 2005–2012, under the Socialist government of José Luis Rodríguez Zapatero, state funding was made available to support exhumations and other commemorative activities related to the defeated in the war ("Ley 52/2007," Article 11), in what I have labeled elsewhere a "human rights subcontracting system" whereby the state merely "facilitated" the demands by civil society, transferring responsibility to the associations and technical teams (Ferrándiz, "Exhuming"). After the right-wing Partido Popular assumed power in December 2011, state funding for exhumations ceased. In 2014, two UN Human Rights Council reports ("Report of the Working Group"; "Report of the Special Rapporteur") admonished the Spanish state for refusing to treat these reburials—and the bigger issue of crimes against humanity committed during the war and the dictatorship—as covered by international human rights legislation and transitional justice frameworks, to no avail. As of July 2014, 357 mass graves, containing 6,288 bodies, have been opened since 2000—a tiny fraction of the mass graves containing Republican victims largely left abandoned to their fate since the war, both executed civilians (almost 90 percent of the total) and prisoners who died while in jails and concentration camps (10 percent).[1]

Emotional Afterlives

My work on mass graves is part of a long-term ethnography of memory politics in contemporary Spain, undertaken from the perspective of social anthropology. It is based on "multi-sited" fieldwork (Marcus) over a period of almost fourteen years. This has been carried out in diverse contexts including excavations, reburial rituals, cemeteries, commemorative events, conferences on memory, book presentations, art exhibitions,

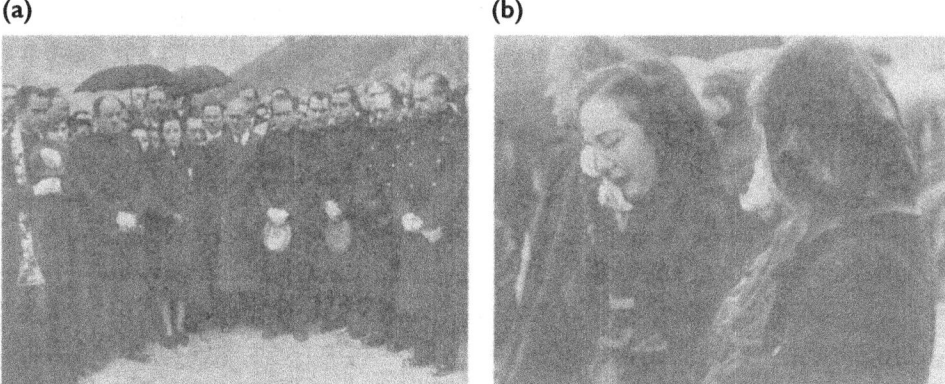

Figure 14.1a and b. Official commemoration and public mourning at Paracuellos del Jarama (Madrid), the site of the major Republican Civil War massacre, immediately after the war's end. The photographs were published in the *Semanario Gráfico Nacional Sindicalista* year 3, no. 143 (25 November 1939). **(a)** The "profoundly emotive" ceremony was presided over by top Francoist politicians (including Serrano Suñer, *far right*) and church authorities. Photographer: Santos Yubera. Courtesy of Archivo Regional de la Comunidad de Madrid. **(b)** The original caption read "A victim's daughter sobs uncontrollably while evoking that tragic episode in 1936." Photographer unknown. Private collection.

forensic laboratories, and NGOs devoted to the "recovery of historical memory." The research also includes the systematic compilation of press articles, news and television documentaries, and fieldwork carried out on the Internet, where a great deal of information (and disinformation) circulates about different aspects of the recovery of the historical memory of the Civil War, and where intense debates about exhumations and the circumstances surrounding them are posted (Ferrándiz, "Exhuming," *El pasado*).

When thinking about the management of politically sensitive dead bodies in contemporary societies, Katherine Verdery's *The Political Lives of Dead Bodies* (1999) is a crucial reference. In this seminal book, the author refers to the importance of researching the postmortem journey of exhumed or preserved bodies and contentious statues, and other forms of disquiet concerning the mortal remains left by the Soviet political past in Eastern Europe. To account for the Spanish case, I have elsewhere used and extended Verdery's discussion of the "corpse politic" to include the scientific, judicial, media, artistic, or associational afterlives linked to the reappearance of these exhumed bodies (Ferrándiz, "Exhuming"). In this chapter, I will elaborate specifically on their emotional afterlives; that is, their ability to mobilize feelings both privately and in the public sphere, this being one of the most unequivocal signs of their impact on the present. I will analyze how the appearance, circulation, and consumption of uncomfortable images of cadavers in public spaces has set in motion a controversial transference of empathy from the bodies shot decades ago to their descendants and supporters, an emotional flow from the murdered body to the mourning body. This anachronistic, deferred grieving is translated into and modulated by complex, unstable emotional expressions and experiences.

From the standpoint of social anthropology and in the wider context of the debate on emotions, I adhere to the social constructivist approach that considers emotions to be necessarily colored by cultural and political meanings in the specific contexts in which they are expressed. In this respect, they are not properties of the self or mere biological or psychological drives. Rather, they should be seen as complex spaces of historical, social, political, and culturally bound experience, intercorporeal and intersubjective, negotiated and controversial, continuously learned and recycled, and, most important, producers of knowledge, meaning, and subjectivities (Lutz and White; Lutz; Tarlow; Harding and Pribram). In their classic paper "The Mindful Body," Scheper-Hughes and Lock conceive of emotions as the "missing link capable of bridging mind and body, individual, society and body politic," questioning "whether any expression of human emotion and feelings is ever free of cultural shaping and cultural meaning" (28–29). Emotions are thus dynamic and should be viewed as productive ways of acquiring knowledge about the world. Furthermore, while arguing for the potential virtues of sentimental mobilization in contemporary societies, Daniel Innerarity has demonstrated the extent to which feelings are a form of political experience and social knowledge of considerable significance in the configuration of the public sphere, and how the politicization of emotions—not to be confused with populism—can improve the quality of democracy (*El nuevo*, "El gobierno").

That the mobilization of emotions in the public sphere is multifold and problematic—whether in democratization processes, in identity politics, or in relation to contemporary recreations of the past (in the case that concerns us here, a segment of a painful past irrupting into public space decades after the event)—goes without saying. Yet there is no clear template to understand this. It thus seems crucial to explore contextually and critically how these processes operate and in what modalities emotions express themselves. My argument here only scratches the surface of some of the more or less formalized regulatory codes, styles, and repertoires of emotions that are being revealed in these tense, unstable, spasmodic spaces of death and grieving. The aim is to decipher the sentimental order or orders articulated around a poignant past that reappears abruptly and overwhelmingly in certain political and technical scenarios, that is, "structures of feeling" that are both emergent and in transit, and in which restraining, feeling, or even giving free rein to emotion can be as controversial as it is unavoidable (Williams 128–35; Harding and Pribram 13). To all of this, I will add some reflections on the impact that new digital technologies are having on communication and knowledge with regard to the production, circulation, and consumption of emotions expressed, modulated, or repressed at gravesides or other events associated with exhumations and the recovery of historical memory.

The Politics of Emotion at Exhumations

To say that the exhumation of a mass grave is a setting of great emotional intensity is to state the obvious. However, the emotive textures are not always immediate and can be understood only in a framework of negotiation and controversy over the meaning and political and social reach of such excavations. To adopt a dynamic bodily metaphor, I follow Michael Taussig's suggestion that contemporary societies should be understood not so much as systems, but as nervous systems. We might therefore equate mass graves—crucial to the memory politics of the Civil War in contemporary Spain—with synaptic terminals with a capacity to jolt both private and public spaces of social experience, as would appear to happen in other historical and social contexts in which mass graves have become black holes for both present and past violence.

The processes of *dignification* of those considered by many to be "improperly buried" at roadsides or in pits, wells, or ditches is an integral part of a political culture undergoing a process of expansion and transformation, but also fragmented and with different groups involved in the "recovery of memory" and different autonomous communities taking different approaches. Indeed, there is no consensus on how to proceed, and major disputes have arisen between the various associations over their conception of the political, symbolic, and emotional handling of exhumations. From the moment when attention started to be given to the excavations and to public and media exposure of the remains, tensions began to surface over different ways of interpreting dignity when faced with a traumatic past (Ferrándiz, *El pasado* 61–68, 191–201).

The "appropriate" handling of emotions in particular was from the beginning part of the debate within and between the associations involved. Initially some associations, such as the Archivo Guerra y Exilio (War and Exile Archive; AGE) and the Asociación de Familiares y Amigos de la Fosa Común de Oviedo (Association of Relatives and Friends of the Mass Grave in Oviedo; AFAFC), considered exhumations without judicial mandate an erasure of genocide, since evidence of the crimes was destroyed. In their view the graves should remain intact, except in extreme situations. Using the example of the approach adopted at the mass grave in Oviedo, where disinterments were ruled out, these associations proposed a "dignification" of graves that provided an alternative to exhumation, by promoting their location, investigation, demarcation, institutional recognition, and commemoration, including the erection of monuments or other kinds of memorial, and the establishment of rituals to honor the victims and keep their memory alive. For the associations that took this line, exhumations would create uncertainty and decontextualized ossuaries, risking loss of dignity and dismantling for future generations sites that were crucial to the memory of the Francoist repression. Quite early on, this position lost out to those associations favoring exhumation, with the corpocentric regime of truth and reparation associated with the public exposure of bones in mass graves winning the day.

Nonetheless, this early antiexhumation sector made a significant intervention in the debate on the relationship between memory, dignification, and emotion. Its views were expressed in a 2002 communiqué issued by AGE, AFAFC, and others, which anticipated future lines of debate and emotive performance. This document argued that the exhumation and handling of disinterred remains necessarily make for a macabre spectacle promoting a televised pathos that tends to encourage a sentimental treatment of grief, undermining the gravitas with which, the document insisted, the suffering of the defeated should be treated. Its position was summed up as follows: "No queremos ver escenas patéticas sino escenas de dignidad, no queremos heroicidades utilitarias sino valores profundos y sentidos, no queremos que se saquen en las televisiones ancianitos que lloran, sino gentes que reclaman con dignidad y que saben llorar en silencio a sus muertos, presos y exiliados" (We don't want pathetic scenes but scenes of dignity; we don't want utilitarian heroics but profound, deeply felt values; we don't want television channels to show elderly people sobbing but people who make their demands with dignity and who are able to weep for their dead, imprisoned, and exiled relatives in silence). A distinction was established between the "private tear" and the dignified, silent, and proud "political tear," amid fears that melodrama would prevail over activist remembrance. Thus this early stage of the process showed an awareness of the potentially problematic display of emotions in the "media circus," which has remained present in the debate ever since. Although I cannot pursue the topic here, this reasoning regarding the appropriateness or not of the public, even transnational, visibility of exhumed remains, and the distrust some social stakeholders show toward the emotional life of these dead bodies, meshes with debates in journalism, humanitarian aid, and of course the humanities and social sciences on issues such as the limits that should be set when representing horror, the commercial manipulation of pain and shock, the pornography of violence, the effects of an excess of representation, or the cycles of saturation of empathy in the society of the spectacle.

Among the objections to emotional display, one of the most interesting is Ángel Loureiro's provocative article "Pathetic Arguments," which, speaking from a perspective sympathetic to the recovery of historical memory, criticizes the new global sense of "history as grievance" as expressed in contemporary Spain (227). While Loureiro shares with the AGE and AFAFC a distrust of the "easy tear," he does not acknowledge the internal debates on appropriate emotions within and between the associations concerned, nor the academic arguments on the crucial role of emotions in the regeneration of the public sphere, as discussed by Innerarity and others. Through analysis of specific contemporary documentaries on the exhumation process, Loureiro argues that historical memory movements are not so much interested in historical knowledge as in "the politics and affects mobilized in the personal discovery of horrors that in good measure were already in the public domain" (228). In his view, this emotional mobilization is undertaken by "injecting" mass graves and images of horror into the present, resulting in an abusive, obsessive use of mourning and melancholia as explanatory tools. The result of the sentimental rhetoric deriving from the contemporary boom in victimization accounts is, he argues, the replacement of "knowledge and reflection with easy sentimentality and moral admonitions" (233).

While Loureiro is right to highlight the potential misuse of emotion and of (actual or imagined) emotional links to the past as a privileged explanatory model, his argument is grounded in a problematic hierarchical approach to emotion and reason or, more specifically, to emotion and historical awareness: "a minimally rigorous history of the war will be infinitely more complex than any historical memory," he claims (226).

Emotions are seen by him as simplistic, melodramatic devices supplanting reflection and knowledge. My premise in this chapter is that, in both their private and public expression, emotions can create complex processes of signification and knowledge, which, far from being opposed to other forms of knowledge available in the information society (for example, historiography), intersect with them. As I hope to show, the debates on the ground over exhumations, the emotions they induce, and their political and reparative signification are more nuanced and diversified than Loureiro's otherwise inspiring text allows.

Indeed, the politics of emotion are clearly expressed in a dispute that has caused particular tension between associations that agree that the exhibition of executed bodies plays a crucial role in denouncing, and educating the public about, the atrocities that took place, and that it is part of an urgent dignification initiative. Despite this agreement, the associations differ in their choice of scenography and protocol. From the outset, many of them decided to develop and apply scientific protocols in their excavations, involving a range of academic specialists, including archaeologists, forensic and social anthropologists, psychologists, historians, and even lawyers. Whatever emotions may be expressed or repressed at exhumations, the latter are conducted according to these scientific protocols: data is systematically recorded, mainly by archaeologists and forensic experts who organize the excavation activities, generating professionalized forms of public presentation of cadavers, regulating access to bones, digitizing images of the remains and information about the social and political circumstances. This is done within a framework of differentiated professional cultures, using techniques of dissemination and analysis that are standard in their respective disciplines. Finally, after laboratory and desk research has been undertaken, the past violence is translated into bulky, profusely illustrated technical reports for relatives and sympathizers, generating what, expanding on Katherine Verdery's term, I call "the scientific life of dead bodies."

Regardless of the establishment of forensic exhumation protocols, discrepancies have arisen between the main proexhumation associations regarding the irruption of exhumation-induced emotions into the private and public spheres. This is a debate about the political correctness of emergent structures of feeling at exhumations. The key issues are the proper emotional tone or appropriate "victimization gradient" in the expression of emotion, and the political and private symbolism accompanying and modulating the emergence and display of emotion in the complex context of the politics of grieving. That is: how, where, and to what extent should emotion be expressed, and what are the boundaries of emotional dignity? Should such emotion be kept private or displayed in public? And what level of political denunciation can or should these feelings communicate?

The major orders of sensibility that have evolved in relation to the exhumations in Spain since 2000 can largely be attributed to the practice of the two major nationwide historical memory associations: the Asociación para la Recuperación de la Memoria Histórica (Association for the Recovery of Historical Memory; henceforth, ARMH) and the Foro por la Memoria (Forum for Memory; henceforth, Foro). There are, however, alternative approaches deployed by other associations and in Spanish regions with nationalist sensitivities, where the emotive configurations activated in the context of contemporary identity politics and even claims for independence from Spain—in, for example, Catalonia or the Basque Country—may vary quite substantially. For reasons of space, I will only mention here that memorial practices in these two regions, linked or not to exhumations, differ from each other and even more significantly from those in other parts of Spain, in that they are linked to the fostering and display of collective nationalist and proindependence feelings. In the Basque Country, for example, these ceremonies are mostly celebrated in *euskara* and colored by Basque-specific dance, music, hymns, and political paraphernalia. While some participants may long for the defeated Republic, the predominant political feelings expressed relate to the continuity of a fight for independence long predating the Civil War, and to the historical suffering of the Basque people.

The ARMH explicitly identifies itself as an association of victims' relatives and sympathizers with the losing side in the Civil War. While for the ARMH exhumations have many objectives—including the search for truth, forensic identification, denunciation of the shortcomings of the Transition and democracy in Spain, the establishment of further reparative practices to honor the war's losers, and the "dignified" reinterment of their bodies—a crucial tenet of their activism is the need to provoke chain reactions in the public sphere through visual and emotional impact—initially, even shock. The production of large scale empathy with victims of the Francoist repression through an alliance with particular media organizations and the public exposure of bones of the executed was decisive in order to break what the ARMH considers the shameful taboos surrounding, and silent complicity with, Francoist residues in a low-quality democracy.

This is clearly expressed in the style of political activism of its founder and leader, the sociologist and journalist Emilio Silva. In his well-known book coauthored with the ARMH's other founder, Santiago Macías, Silva affirmed the important role of emotion in connecting past with present, the individual with the social and the political. First, by describing his attempts to recreate the emotions of those who knew they were about to be executed: "más de una vez he cerrado los ojos y he tratado de ponerme en su lugar, de sentir la misma angustia, la misma impotencia, el mismo pánico" (more than once I have closed my eyes and tried to take their place, to feel the same anguish, the same powerlessness, the same panic; 47). And second, through his sense of having a moral duty to transfer to the public sphere the "immense emotion" and "anguish" he had felt in locating his grandfather's mass grave, in order to help other victims' relatives and secure recognition and justice (24–25).

Without denying a clear affinity with the left and the defeated in the Civil War, the ARMH as an organization is not directly connected to any specific political party. It sustains an increasingly elaborated discourse on human rights and transitional justice and, very important, considers victims' relatives to be the decisive agents in the management of affliction and of the commemorative rituals organized around exhumations. In shying away from imposing symbolic or emotional guidelines, the ARMH is open to all available approaches to private or public mourning, including religious counsel if that is the family's decision, but also more politically oriented performances. As Silva states, exhumations elicit multilayered political and emotional responses that represent contemporary Spain's diversity. In this context, the connection between the private and the political is important: even "una simple lágrima, setenta años después, puede tener un valor politico enorme" (a simple tear, seventy years after the event, can have a powerful political meaning; personal communication).

For this reason, the Foro has consistently accused the ARMH of having become the neoliberals of Spain's historical memory movement, of privatizing and depoliticizing mourning, or of practicing what has been called *abuelismo* (grandfatherism), that is, a sentimental and family-oriented approach to the past that elides the political nature of the killings. In its famous 23 January 2004 manifesto, *Apoyar a la ARMH es enterrar la memoria* (*To Support the ARMH Is to Bury Memory*), the Foro's long-standing president, José María Pedreño, claimed that prioritizing the recovery of the bones of grandfathers—caricatured in the emotive parody "¡mi abuelo, mi abuelo, mi abuelo!" (my grandpa! my grandpa! my grandpa!)—defuses the true nature of the repression, which was and is a political crime, turning it into a mere matter of private mourning and trivial media consumption.

Thus, in contrast to what we might dub the "open mourning" attitude of the ARMH, the Foro considers it essential that exhumations be openly politicized and that attributes of the left-wing circuit within which the Foro operates—specifically, that of the Communist Party—be incorporated into the memory process. Any emotion that surfaces at the excavations must necessarily be relevant to this political and ideological context. Here ideological kinship takes precedence over biological kinship. The Foro argues that this should occur irrespective of the feelings of the families concerned, since it is the presumed antifascist and Republican ideas of the dead that should be respected and given priority. According to their 2007 protocol, respect for the victims' ideals implies the use of political elements and rituals (flags, hymns, etc.) that are specific to the ideals they defended and for which they died, even when these differ from those of their relatives today. The Foro believes this issue to be fundamental to moral reparation, because recovering values and ideals is not "una cuestión nostálgica" (a nostalgic matter) but one that is instrumental "para las luchas de hoy en día" (for today's struggles). They conclude: "Siempre se ha dicho que el Foro por la Memoria es una combinación de amor, rigor y lucha. Amor a los ideales por los que combatieron al Fascismo antes que nosotros, rigor en el trabajo y, finalmente, lucha incansable" (It has always being said that the Foro is a combination of love, rigor, and struggle. Love of the ideals of the past fight against fascism, rigorous work, and tireless struggle).[2] Accordingly, the Foro provides precise, nonnegotiable instructions as to the appropriate emotional order for exhumations and related events—one that is unilaterally geared to the presumed political feelings of those who were killed—in a kind of postmortem ideological and emotional communion in which decades of repression and oblivion are collapsed into a shared political objective: the continuity of the fight (Smaoui). To the ARMH, this attitude amounts to the imposition of an emotional political commissariat akin to the Communist Party's activist sensibility, which mutilates and impoverishes the multiplicity of legitimate emotional responses available in Spanish society (Silva, personal communication).

Regardless of these programmatic stances, many exhumations actually involve a mix of approaches depending on the specific circumstances. Thus, in practice, private forms of mourning and emotional remembrance are mixed with more politicized modes, resulting in unstable emotional kaleidoscopes, the tone of which may vary from one exhumation to another. Referring back to Loureiro's argument: whatever the preferred emotional style and tone, in no case do they oppose or replace available forms of scientific knowledge of the past, whether forensic, historiographical, anthropological, or otherwise. Many activists read historical studies and promote local historical and archival research. Forensic reports and public presentations are part of funerary practices (Ferrándiz, *El pasado* 237–53). It is important to remember that, since most of the emotional display at exhumations occurs within forensic and archaeological frameworks, the emotions concerned are not only politically but also scientifically informed. A different issue is the more or less problematic way in which evolving academic knowledge about the past is recycled by associations, activists, or relatives.

Posing for Pixels: Digital Emotions

Against this background of controversy, I shall now move to discussion of the range of particular *emotional repertoires* that have taken shape around exhumations. Here I give another twist to the discussion by exploring the increasing importance of digital technologies in the configuration of the historical memory of these seventy-year-old crimes. Analysis of how new digital technologies, devices, and online platforms are profoundly affecting the production, circulation, and consumption of knowledge and images of past atrocities is a huge field, not only in the Spanish case, acknowledged by the growing interest in this issue in memory studies—as illustrated by the September 2014 special section of the journal *Media, Culture and Society*, entitled "Digital Media—Social Memory." In Spain, particularly in the last ten years, the arrival and increasing accessibility of digital technologies have radically changed and accelerated the memory-construction process with regard to the Civil War, projecting it into the global arena. The wide availability of digital devices that can be used on-site and the increasing preeminence of cyberspace in the transmission of memory also mean its reconfiguration as a social construct, with the digital reframing of social memory having drastic effects on the relationship between past and present, and with new technologies transforming social movements and their forms of activism.

The astonishing speed with which traditional black-and-white family photo albums and the associated social contexts of memory circulation have given way to the predominance of a mostly digital memoryscape in the memory movement in Spain is

Figure 14.2. The relative of a victim of Francoism takes a picture with his smartphone of an exhibition of images showing the exhumation process in Calera y Chozas (Toledo) on 10 February 2013, immediately preceding the reburial ceremony. Although the bodies were not identified, he was establishing a sort of "digital kinship" with this particular skeleton. Photo by the author.

one of its most salient features (Ferrándiz and Baer). After the first four or five years of exhumations, still recorded in analogic formats, pixels took over in a very short period of time. Images and information regarding exhumations started to become an integral part of blogs, PowerPoint presentations, websites, and social networks and platforms such as Facebook, Twitter, Flickr, and YouTube as this new "digital media ecology" took off and transformed "the temporality, spatiality, and indeed the mobility of memories" (Hoskins 93–94). This new media ecology can allow faster or even instant visual consumption of emerging memories; for example, when photos or video clips taken with mobile phones at exhumations or commemorative events are rapidly distributed within particular "memory recovery" networks via WhatsApp, Facebook, or, at closer range, Bluetooth. Although full discussion of this topic exceeds the scope of this chapter, it is evident that, as digital devices and social networking services proliferate, the new equipment and platforms are constructing new avenues for the production, circulation, and consumption of historical memory, as well as, more generally, new genres, iconographies, and styles of imaging, imagining, and recycling the past. The potentially instant accessibility of content and images in real time afforded by digital cultures also creates new forms of witnessing, new subjectivities, new political identities, and new sites for configuring multidimensional memories. It also brings memory processes closer to the global media spectacle (Rabinovitz and Geil; Torchin; see Fig. 14.2)

In this rapidly evolving digital memoryscape, to which many associations have very skillfully adjusted, one of the key phenomena that allows us to explore emotional encoding and decoding is that of what I call "emotive poses." Such performances are increasingly conditioned by what I label the "cyberspace consciousness" of social actors on the ground; that is, awareness of the potential global projection of the images recorded, and the modalities and frames (new social networks) of this open display. They are also affected by common knowledge of other salient features of the digital ecology: the multiplication of recording devices and registers, the speed of digital image taking, and the profusion of images recorded, whose only limit is the capacity of huge memory cards. In Hoskins's terms, "contemporary memory is thoroughly interpenetrated by a technological unconscious in that there occurs a 'co-evolution' of memory and technology" (96). With this growing savvyness with regard to the workings of new technologies and social networks, the different stakeholders present at exhumations and other related activities stage their emotions for cyberspace via their digital recording with still or video cameras and, more recently, smartphones.

If it is true that different modalities of emotive posing have been integral to exhumations since the year 2000, they have gained increasing relevance with the spread of digital recording. These dramatizations, relating to the above-mentioned debates on what constitutes "proper" emotions and to the emerging "cyberspace consciousness," take on a new dimension as they enter into global information flows. At this point, it should be noted that the Foro exercises particularly strict control of image taking at its exhumations, in line with its previously discussed political protocol. However, since the Foro's exhumations constitute only a small fraction of the 357 undertaken so far in Spain, most of what follows refers to exhumations carried out by the ARMH, the Sociedad de Ciencias Aranzadi (Aranzadi Scientific Society), and other organizations, necessarily colored by broader debates within the memory movement.

As described, this conjunction of emotion with the display and representation of emotion in digital formats increases the level of self-consciousness and control that social players have in the face of their own emotiveness, given the growing awareness of digital technologies, the types of visibility associated with social networks, and ultimately the uncontrollable circulation in cyberspace of the images taken. Such emotions could therefore be considered "emotions to the second degree," "posed emotions," or "digital emotions," expressed in public in the knowledge that they may be recorded by the different electronic devices always present at the excavations, whether by relatives, members of the technical team or the association, or just onlookers. I have organized these emotions into three main categories, though I am aware that they partially overlap. For the sake of coherence, I have structured them as a sequence, ranging from more contained and even stereotypical emotional experiences to other acts of—or experiments in—empathetic identification with those executed and subsequently recovered from mass graves.

The first category, which is the most general, includes what I call "digital album" poses. These include both private poses and more political poses of individuals or groups, which may then be used by families, associations, or even technical experts and academics in their reports and presentations. For instance, for victims' relatives the exhumation may be a culminating moment in family history and emotions overflow; what happens is photographed as freely and easily as digital memory cards of several gigabytes will allow. Photographs of people at gravesides or commemorative events linked to mass burial sites and exhumations sometimes represent a meeting of the analog and the digital, with analog family photographs included in the pose that will be photographed and circulated digitally. I use the concept "digital album" to refer to the many forms of digital recycling and organization of photographs, for example, in blogs, Powerpoint presentations, etcetera. By "digital album pose" I mean the particular kinds of pose adopted thanks to digital cameras' ability to take multiple photographs in rapid succession, in the knowledge that the photographs taken can be circulated in multiple digital platforms. A variant of the digital album pose are the poses of emotional communities governed by the construction, however ephemeral, of a photographable community of sufferers or celebrants involved in a tragic event, as expressed at exhumations and reburial ceremonies. These communities can be of many types, and they gather specifically and provisionally for the purpose of posing. The living and the dead are sometimes photographed together, creating in such cases an emotive iconographic bond or "digital kinship" with the executed that immortalizes for cyberspace a key moment in the exhumation process, before the bodies are removed from the grave by archaeologists and forensic experts. The Foro's preference is for visual displays that show the community of comrades posing with appropriate political paraphernalia and embodied expressions of their activism, such as the adoption of a solemn posture with fist raised or with Republican flags held aloft (Fig. 14.3).

A second category is represented by poses with photographs of executed persons. There are clear transnational precedents for these emotional performances at public demonstrations that render the disappeared visible, particularly in certain Latin American countries such as Argentina and Chile, where such practices have been at the heart of the political and judicial movement against the legacy of dictatorship. As Ariel Dorfman has observed, such poses have become repertoires of images of suffering that are "only conceivable in the context of present day globalization" (256). These poses, linking the living and the disappeared, have become "a widespread, almost epidemic, image of tragedy and defiance that is just as much a part of our planetary imagination as the brands and logos that pervade us with an opposite sort of message" (Dorfman 255). Given their iconographic power and their potential to counter official attempts to cover up political repression, such poses are an appropriate response to the disappearances, since they reverse the politics of invisibilization of the victims by meeting the needs of the contemporary media with "extreme efficiency and extraordinary poetry" (Dorfman 256). Also, in these images, whether their content be private or political, complex iconographic alliances occur between past and present poses, past and present emotional regimes.

In Spain, most of the photographs of those executed decades ago used in these digitally recorded performances are either portraits from private family albums or sometimes framed and hung on the wall, taken before the war in photographers' studios or

Figure 14.3. Reburial in the municipal cemetery, organized by the Foro por la Memoria in 2011, of the remains of sixteen people recovered in a mass grave at Menasalbas (Toledo) the previous year. This type of staging, with contained emotion and the open display of Republican flags in a funerary landscape dominated by Catholic tombstones, encapsulates the Foro's activist approach to the past being unearthed. The ceremony ended with the singing of revolutionary songs. Courtesy of Foro por la Memoria.

by itinerant photographers, or else they have been extracted from official documents, such as military service records. The transnational connection with other similar poses and similar claims for recognition and justice enables the relatives who come to these graves or commemorative acts with photographs of their relatives to express their emotion and their political message under the globalized umbrella of "crimes against humanity" preestablished in international human rights legislation. Once uploaded in cyberspace, they become part of a global category of victims' portraits (see Fig. 14.4).

Third and finally, the most controversial poses are those we might call "*corps-à-corps* poses*," that is, those images circulating in cyberspace in which there is some form of direct contact with skeletal remains or with the spatial and biographical traces they have left behind. First of all, there is a series of poses which, owing to their proximity to open graves and the actual bones, express a kind of intimacy with the cadavers that may have precedents in Baroque painting and in broader funerary practices.[3] These images confer a sense of historicity on those posing ("I was there"), as well as digital identification with the historical experience of those executed. A second type of corps-à-corps pose takes place when relatives publicly come into direct physical contact with

Figure 14.4. Milagros (Burgos), 18 July 2009. Pedro Cancho poses for photographers with a portrait of his murdered grandfather, after whom he was named, next to the mass grave where the latter is believed to be buried. With his dignified stance, Pedro Cancho was unveiling for cyberspace an old and treasured family picture, while transferring its biographical content to the bare bones on the ground. Different takes of Pedro Cancho in this pose have circulated widely: one was used on the cover of the catalogue of the 2010 touring exhibition *Exhumando fosas, recuperando dignidades* (*Exhuming Mass Graves, Recovering Dignity*); another was reproduced on the cover of the February 2013 issue of the journal *American Ethnologist*. Photo by the author.

the verified bones or fragments of bones of their executed loved ones, after on-site or laboratory identification (Ferrándiz, *El pasado* 104–5). A third category that has become popular in some memorial circles is the pose of lying in the earth where the now exhumed bodies previously lay. This secular ritual was invented by Francisco Etxeberria, the main forensic scientist involved in the grave openings since 2000, and has proved a great if somewhat melodramatic success in rural communities. Archaeologists or forensic specialists instruct relatives, onlookers, and members of the technical team alike to lie in the former mass grave, adopting the approximate position of each of the exhumed corpses, based on anatomical reconstructions drawn by hand or reconstructed though specialized software (Ferrándiz, *El pasado* 242–44). This ritual was first performed in August 2005 at the exhumation of five bodies in Vadocondes, Burgos (Lourdes Herrasti and Francisco Etxeberria, personal communication). Unprecedented in Spanish forensic or political culture, the photograph of the reenactment was included in the forensic report, with the caption: "Interpretation of the way the bodies were left."[4] (For an example from 2009, see Figs. 14.5a and 14.5b.)

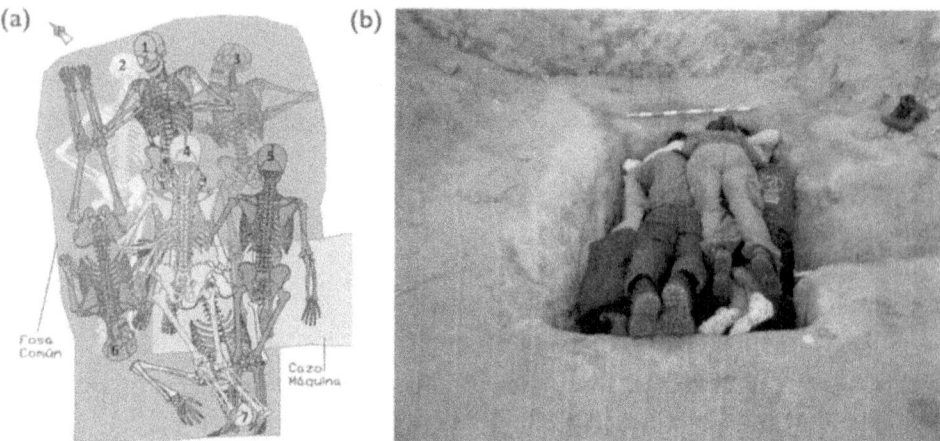

Figures 14.5a and b. Forensic ritual of emotional identification with the exhumed victims, with relatives (and sometimes activists or members of the technical team), under the direction of the archaeologists and forensic scientists, adopting the approximate positions of the bodies in the mass grave. This reconstruction took place at a mass grave in Casavieja (Ávila), where six people were exhumed in March 2009. The photograph was uploaded the same day to the blog of the association La Memoria Viva (*lamemoriaviva.wordpress.com/?s=Casavieja*). While primarily an empathic and scientifically informed ritual, it also performs the original moment when the mass grave was created, based on anatomical drawings. **(a)** Shows the drawing on which the reconstruction was based. **(b)** Note the archaeological precision provided by the ranging pole and the arrow pointing north at the bottom right of the grave. Images courtesy of archaeologist Trinidad Caballero.

This empathetic forensic ritual of occupying the very same place and position as the dead, of reversing the transition from flesh to bone, of returning to the very moment when the grave was created, with the bodies not yet decomposed and thus constructing a continuity with their historical experience as victims of the Francoist repression, is at times accompanied by the percussion of metal objects that reproduce the rhythm of the likely shots and the coup de grâce. During the celebration of this ritual, dominated by the solemnity of the participants, the silence is absolute. In the instances when I have seen this emotionally charged performance, it was considered neither undignified nor transgressive by those who participated or witnessed it, although some associations like the Foro consider it emotionally fraudulent. This is how Ana Fuentes, the great-grandniece of one of the six people exhumed in Casavieja (Ávila) in March 2009, described her feelings on participating in the reenactment illustrated in Fig. 14.5b:

> Al principio nos daba un poco de risa, íbamos bromeando, pero cuando pidieron silencio, un escalofrío me recorrió la espalda, y fue como dejar de estar donde estaba y estar en 1936 . . . fue súper emocionante . . . esa sensación de frío en la espalda . . . cuando hicieron esa foto, solamente se ve un trozo de mi camiseta, hay unos calcetines

rosas encima de mi cara . . . yo estaba abajo de espaldas contra el suelo . . . cierras los ojos y lo ves, yo no podía dejar de pensar en el miedo que debieron pasar aquella noche, sabiendo que les iban a dar el tiro de gracia . . . es una sensación como que le está pasando a otra persona . . . es difícil de explicar . . . impactó a todo el mundo.

(At first it felt like fun, we were even joking, but when there was a call for silence, I felt a shiver run down my spine, it was like being transported back to 1936 . . . it was incredibly emotional . . . that chill in the back . . . when the photo was taken, you can only see a bit of my T-shirt, there are someone else's pink socks on top of my face . . . I was lying face up underneath . . . you close your eyes and you can see it happening, I couldn´t stop thinking about how terrified they must have been that night, knowing they were going to be shot . . . it felt as though what was happening was happening to someone else . . . it's hard to put into words . . . everybody was hugely affected.)

It is crucial to take into account the potential misuse of emotions in the public sphere, as well as the far-reaching consequences of their increasing imbrication with digital technologies and flows—their transit from tear to pixel. But to regard emotions as by definition inferior forms of experience that simplify or obfuscate implies an incomplete understanding of the nature of social action. I believe it is important to make the effort to grasp the complexity of the diverse emotional regimes that are evolving and taking shape in the modern-day world; this case study has attempted to do so in relation to one specific instance: that of the memory movement in contemporary Spain. When analyzing emotions and the politics of emotion, we must consider their historical precedents, as well as their cultural and political referents, and their transformation in the context of globalization and the information society and society of the spectacle. If, as Innerarity suggests, their creative and productive management is integral to the configuration of a new contemporary public sphere; if we acknowledge that feelings, as an aspect of "mindful" bodies, can be forms of knowledge, experience, political action, and social knowledge; and if we accept that they partake of the synaptic connections that constitute the spasmodic nervous system of the contemporary age, then in the case of the exhumation process in Spain it is essential, indeed urgent, that we pay serious attention to the contemporary impact of the emotional life of dead bodies.

NOTES

This text is part of Research Project CSO2015-66104-R, funded by the Spanish Ministry of Economy and Competitivity (MINECO) and ISCH COST Action "In Search of Transcultural Memory in Europe" (ISTME, IS1203) and UNREST (H20202, REFLECTIVE-5-2015, ref. 693523).

1. I thank Francisco Etxeberria, Lourdes Herrasti, and Luis Ríos for providing me with these up-to-date figures.
2. See *www.foroporlamemoria.info/ideario/index.htm* (accessed 30 July 2014).

3. My thanks to Juan Pimentel and José Ramón Marcaida for this fertile suggestion, which requires further and more nuanced analysis.
4. See the last page of the 2006 Vadocondes forensic report at *www.sc.ehu.es/scrwwwsr/ Medicina-Legal/valladar/Exhumacion%20Valladar%20Burgos.htm* (accessed 4 October 2014).

WORKS CITED

Aguilar, Paloma. *Memory and Amnesia: The Role of the Spanish Civil War in the Transition to Democracy*. Oxford: Berghahn Books, 2002.

Asociación Archivo Guerra y Exilio et al. *Comunicado sobre las fosas comunes donde permanecen enterrados los restos de luchadores fusilados por la dictadura*. September 2002. *www.fosacomun.com/comunicado.htm* (accessed 29 October 2014).

Box, Zira. *España: Año cero*. Madrid: Alianza, 2010.

Dorfman, Ariel. "The Missing and Photography: The Uses and Misuses of Globalization." *Spontaneous Shrines and the Public Memorialization of Death*. Ed. Jack Santino. New York: Palgrave Macmillan, 2006. 255–60.

Ferrándiz, Francisco. "Exhuming the Defeated: Civil War Mass Graves in 21st-Century Spain." *American Ethnologist* 40.1 (2013): 38–54.

———. *El pasado bajo tierra: Exhumaciones contemporáneas de la Guerra Civil*. Barcelona: Anthropos; Siglo XXI, 2014.

Ferrándiz, Francisco, and Alejandro Baer. "Digital Memories: The Visual Recording of Mass Grave Exhumations in Contemporary Spain." *Forum Qualitative Sozialforschung/Forum: Qualitative Social Research* 9.3 (2008): article 35. *www.qualitative-research.net/index.php/ fqs/article/view/1152/2578* (accessed 29 October 2014).

Ferrándiz, Francisco, and Antonius C. G. M. Robben. "The Ethnography of Exhumations." In *Necropolitics: Mass Graves and Exhumations in the Age of Human Rights*. Ed. Francisco Ferrándiz and Antonius C. G. M. Robben. Philadelphia: U of Pennsylvania P, 2015. 1–38.

Harding, Jennifer, and E. Deidre Pribram. "Introduction: The Case for a Cultural Emotion Studies." *Emotions: A Cultural Studies Reader*. New York: Routledge, 2009. 1–23.

Hoskins, Andrew. "Digital Network Memory." *Mediation, Remediation and the Dynamics of Cultural Memory*. Ed. Astrid Erll and Ann Rigney. Berlin: De Gruyter, 2012. 91–106.

Innerarity, Daniel. "El gobierno emocional." *El País* 4 March 2009. *elpais.com/diario/ 2009/03/04/opinion/1236121204_850215.html* (accessed 29 October 2014).

———. *El nuevo espacio publico*. Madrid: Espasa, 2006.

"Ley 52/2007 de 26 de diciembre, por la que se reconocen y amplían derechos y se establecen medidas en favor de quienes padecieron persecución o violencia durante la guerra civil y la dictadura." *Boletín Oficial del Estado* 310.27 (December 2007): 53410–16. *www.boe.es/ diario_boe/txt.php?id=BOE-A-2007-22296* (accessed 24 May 2015).

Loureiro, Ángel. "Pathetic Arguments." *Journal of Spanish Cultural Studies* 9.2 (2008): 225–37.

Lutz, Catherine. *Unnatural Emotions: Everyday Sentiments on a Micronesian Atoll and Their Challenge to Western Theory*. Chicago: U of Chicago P, 1988.

Lutz, Catherine, and Geoffrey White. "The Anthropology of Emotions." *Annual Review of Anthropology* 15 (1986): 405–36.

Marcus, George E. "Ethnography in/of the World System: The Emergence of Multi-sited Ethnography." *Annual Review of Anthropology* 24 (1995): 95–117.
Mbembe, Achille. "Necropolitics." *Public Culture* 15.1 (2003): 11–40.
Preston, Paul. *El holocausto español: Odio y exterminio en la Guerra Civil y después*. Trans. Catalina Martínez Muñoz and Eugenia Vázquez Nacarino. Madrid: Debate, 2011.
Rabonovitz, Lauren, and Abraham Geil. "Introduction." *Memory Bytes: History, Technology, and Digital Culture*. Durham, NC: Duke UP, 2004. 1–19.
Rodrigo, Javier. *Hasta la raíz: Violencia durante la Guerra Civil y la dictadura franquista*. Madrid: Alianza, 2008.
Scheper-Hughes, Nancy, and Margaret M. Lock. "The Mindful Body: A Prolegomenon to Future Work in Medical Anthropology." *Medical Anthropology Quarterly* 1.1 (1987): 6–41.
Silva, Emilio, and Santiago Macías. *Las fosas de Franco*. Madrid: Temas de hoy, 2003.
Smaoui, Sélim. "Sortir du conflict ou asseoir la lutte? Exhumer et produire des 'victimes républicaines' en Espagne." *Revue Française de Science Politique* 64 (2014): 435–58.
Tarlow, Sarah. "Emotion in Archaeology." *Current Anthropology* 41.5 (2000): 713–46.
Taussig, Michael. *The Nervous System*. New York: Routledge, 1992.
Torchin, Leshu. *Creating the Witness: Documenting Genocide on Film, Video and the Internet*. Philadelphia: U of Pennsylvania P, 2012.
UN Human Rights Council. "Report of the Special Rapporteur on the Promotion of Truth, Justice, Reparations and Guarantees of Non-recurrence: Mission to Spain." 22 July 2014. A/HRC/27/56/Add. 1. *daccess-dds-ny.un.org/doc/UNDOC/GEN/G14/090/52/PDF/G1409052.pdf?OpenElement* (accessed 24 May 2015).
———. "Report of the Working Group on Enforced or Involuntary Disappearances. Addendum: Mission to Spain." 2 July 2014. A/HRC/27/49/Add. 1. *daccess-dds-ny.un.org/doc/UNDOC/GEN/G14/072/70/PDF/G1407270.pdf?OpenElement* (accessed 24 May 2015).
Verdery, Katherine. *The Political Lives of Dead Bodies*. New York: Columbia UP, 1999.
Williams, Raymond. *Marxism and Literature*. Oxford: Oxford UP, 1977.

CHAPTER 15

Public Tears and Secrets of the Heart

Political Emotions in a State of Crisis

LUISA ELENA DELGADO

The Heart Has Its Reasons

Fear, as is well known, is a fundamental political emotion, one with a long historical trajectory and distinguished commentators and critics: Machiavelli, Hobbes, Montesquieu, Tocqueville, Arendt, Shklar, to name a few. Fear has also become so characteristic of contemporary Western culture that it has been said to constitute "the ground of our public life" (Robin 3), a symptom of modern global anxieties. In her influential book *The Cultural Politics of Emotion*, Sara Ahmed has studied the politics of fear from a different angle, as an effect of the discourses of patriotic identification with the nation: a nation that distinguishes between those who threaten and those who feel threatened, and whose cohesion comes to adhere "as an effect of signs of love" (74). Along the same lines, Martha Nussbaum emphasizes the emotional component of patriotism, which should be understood as a form of love that considers the nation as one's own (208). Thus, the politics of fear and patriotic love are always intertwined, particularly in times of crisis. They are representative of the Janus-faced nature of patriotism, which looks outward in the name of the common good, and inward by separating deserving from undeserving citizens (Nussbaum 206). Bound together, love and fear contribute to an "ontology of insecurity within the constitution of the political" (Ahmed 76), which the defense of particular institutional and social forms, equated with the essence of the nation, attempts to neutralize. The 2014 Scottish referendum on independence provides a perfect example of how the expression of patriotic love is always interwoven with warnings about the costs of breaking an idealized national unity, as well as the importance of emotions and affects in mobilizing public opinion.

In September 2014, three days before the referendum on Scottish independence was due, and in light of polls that suggested the result would be a dead heat, Prime Minister David Cameron skipped a weekly parliamentary debate to head to Scotland, where he was to address the Scottish people. He had of course given speeches in Scotland before. In those earlier speeches, he had emphasized the economic and political dangers lurking on the horizon for an independent Scotland, in keeping with the relentless scare tactics used by the British government during the campaign. However, as polls began to suggest a close vote, the politics of fear (the insistence on all that Scotland had to lose) did not seem a good counterargument to those who stressed all that it had to gain (the politics of patriotic love defended by Alex Salmond as Scotland's first minister and leader of the Scottish National Party). At that point, Cameron's language became noticeably more emotional, a point he himself underlined by establishing a distinction between "arguments of the heart" versus "arguments of the head." Equating Scottish independence with a "painful divorce," Cameron stated that he would be "utterly heartbroken if this family of nations was torn apart" (Dearden). The message in favor of union was delivered not just by his choice of words and metaphors but also by his body language, including his voice, which was close to breaking at several points.

While the Scottish nationalist leader Alex Salmond considered both content and tone an indication of panic on the government's part, retrospectively there seems little doubt that the strategy was effective. Not as effective, though, as another speech by Scottish former Labour leader Gordon Brown, previously known for his outbursts of anger and awkwardness in public. Co-opted for the "No" campaign as a last resort, in September 2014 the irascible, reticent Scottish politician disappeared and instead a passionate, assertive leader emerged. Brown's "Better together" emotional address marked a "before and after" in the campaign. Successfully dismissing the notion that Scottish patriotism could thrive only in an independent Scotland, he insisted that love for Scotland was predicated on virtues and emotions like solidarity, civility, and compassion, all of which would be better served within a coalition of nations than in an independent Scotland. As in the case of David Cameron, the message was delivered both by words and by the speaker's passionate demeanor. Moreover, the speech was delivered in front of a background of images of hearts with the words "Love Scotland. Vote No." When the results of the vote were known, the *Telegraph* illustrated its headline "UK safe as Scotland rejects independence" with the image of a heart made of glass, whose broken pieces were precariously held together with band-aids.[1]

The Scottish independence referendum was followed very closely in Spain, where Catalonia's aspirations to a similar plebiscite had been blocked by the conservative Partido Popular (Popular Party) government in Madrid on the grounds of unconstitutionality. Supporters of the Catalan people's right to express their political will lamented how differently the situation had been handled in the two countries. While the United Kingdom had given the world a lesson in democracy by allowing the Scottish people to be heard, Spain effectively blocked every attempt to make the referendum official or to create a legal framework for it. The Spanish conservative press, on the other hand, was very critical of what they considered David Cameron's personal and political weakness. In their view, by allowing the referendum and making "concessions" to Scotland, he had opened a can of worms that could threaten the very stability of the United Kingdom. Far from acknowledging the strength of Cameron's democratic convictions, which took precedence over his own personal beliefs, Spanish conservative politicians—many of whom have limited democratic credentials at best—warned sternly of the dangers of political contagion by the virus of secessionism and the importance of isolating it throughout Europe. Moreover, most Spanish politicians outside of Catalonia, regardless of political affiliation, denied any similarity between the Scottish and Catalan cases.

Unquestionably, in both Scotland and Catalonia the independence referenda stirred a range of emotions, which were deployed for political ends. In this context, Cameron's and Brown's emotional performances are consistent with what Eva Illouz has labeled "the rise of Homo sentimentalis" (1). Indeed, the ubiquitous presence of visual and rhetorical hearts during the Scottish campaign is emblematic of the "emotional turn" that has characterized modernity and capitalism since the twentieth century. If that century witnessed the dissolution of the supposed separation between a rational public sphere and a private sphere saturated with emotion (Illouz 4), since then the emotional nature of capitalist culture has steadily intensified. The public sphere has been transformed into an arena for the display of what used to be private sentiments, and emotions are now understood not just as part of human subjectivity, but as a crucial tool needed to adequately manage professional and social interactions. Even France, a country that has built its national identity on the notion of the rational public sphere, witnessed one of its recent presidents disclose a new love relationship by having a very public date in (of all places) Disneyland Paris: an episode used by the critic Michaël Foessel to analyze the commercialization of emotions for public consumption in liberal democracies today. Both the display of what used to be intimate moments and the outbursts of emotion by public officials are consistent with a new understanding of citizenship linked to what critics in different disciplines have labeled the "emotional public sphere"—seen not as separate from the traditionally understood public sphere but as enmeshed with it (Richards; Pantti; Innerarity 32–39). The emotional public sphere is also linked to a therapeutic and confessional culture that has made emotions and their appropriate management into a new form of cultural capital (Illouz; Richards; Pantti).

In this context the nation, like any other form of interpersonal relationship, is "thought of, longed for, argued over, betrayed, fought for, and negotiated according to imaginary scripts which fill social closeness or distance with meaning" (Illouz 7). In the following pages I will analyze what types of scripts have circulated in the sentimental public sphere of today's Spain since the onset of economic crisis in 2008. My argument will be developed in relation to what Berlant calls "affective scenes"; that is to say, clusters of actions with great social resonance that invite political analysis (*Cruel Optimism* 3): the independence movement in Catalonia; sports successes and failures, specifically those related to the national soccer team; and, finally, the multiple social and political movements that are questioning the legitimacy of Spain's democratic regime and the politics of consensus born in 1978. Throughout my analysis, I will ask the same question that Sara Ahmed posed in relation to the sociality of emotions: what do emotions do? In order to answer that question, she calls attention to how emotions move us and move among us, but also how they *stick*, how they hold us in place, giving us a "dwelling place" but also anchoring us to specific positions (11). While many critics distinguish between emotion and affect, I follow Gould and Ahmed, among others, in considering how they are intertwined at the level of perception and effects. On the one hand, affective states are often followed by emotional reactions and are therefore perceived as a continuum. On the other hand, emotions translate vague sensations into structured systems of signification and cultural meanings. Along these lines, it is important to recognize the emotional dimension of collective political actions and the fact that "political attachments, sometimes, perhaps frequently, derive from visceral and inchoate fears, resentments, desires, aspirations, senses of belonging or non-belonging that an individual (or an ideal, or an organization) sometimes stirs up and addresses" (Gould 29). Accordingly, I will explore the emotional landscapes of a state of crisis in contemporary Spain, offering an "emotional" reading of the public sphere. I will allude to the impact of new social movements that appeal to a different understanding of the nation and acknowledge the importance of emotions in political mobilizations and transformative agency. While major political parties and the mainstream press insist on labeling these movements as "irrational" or a mere conduit for negative emotions (anger, indignation), my position is rather that they have been able to recognize and deploy the affective dimension of politics. Throughout my analysis, I will allude to the ubiquitous presence of heart-centered imagery in the "Spain of crisis" (as it has come to be known in Spanish) as an indication of the importance of the feeling subject in the emotional public sphere. Given the traditional association of heartfelt emotions with integrity and honesty, as well as the heart's status as the "informally acknowledged centre of cultural beliefs" (Bound 157), it is paradoxical that, in a historical moment marked by fraud and corruption scandals, political and commercial strategies should choose to appeal to visceral truths.

Masculine Tears and Excessive Subjects

If, as Lauren Berlant proposes, public spheres are always affect worlds "to which people are bound, when they are, by affective projections of a constantly negotiated common interestedness" (*Cruel Optimism* 226), there is no question that, in a Spain marked by severe political and social crisis, negotiations over what should be considered as being in the common interest are now routinely conducted in a highly charged, openly emotional context. Politicians trying to reconnect with disaffected or outraged citizens are resorting to a language of impassioned feeling and overt emotions that comes—purportedly—straight from their hearts. Such a strategy is not limited to the usual marginal or extremist suspects, left- or right-wing "populist" parties. Neither are the emotions at play limited to strong negative emotions, such as rage, contempt, or irritation, all traditionally accepted as legitimate in male political leaders. As we have seen in the context of the Scottish referendum, the current emotional turn is also affecting mature, respectable, and usually stoic white males: representatives of traditional mainstream (therefore conceived as "rational") politics who are now willing to display public vulnerability, appearing close to tears, begging citizens to listen to their message with their minds but also with their hearts. Indeed, the message they wish to convey is often transmitted by affective modalities expressed through the body and traditionally associated with femininity and loss of control: anxiety, anguish, grief. In Spain, a few recent moments are emblematic of that transition to a political "Homo sentimentalis," whether in the context of state politics or of the relation between the central government and the autonomous regions. One was the reaction of Catalan leader Oriol Junqueras, president of the proindependence left-wing party Esquerra Republicana de Catalunya (Republican Left of Catalonia), to the decision by his political ally Artur Mas, president of the conservative Convergència i Unió (Union and Convergence) and then president of the Catalan autonomous government),[2] not to hold an independence referendum on 9 November 2014, after Spain's Constitutional Court issued an injunction blocking it while the central government's legal challenge was considered. Junqueras, a history professor and customarily quite even-tempered, gave a radio interview on 17 October 2014 to a well-known Catalan journalist in which he was asked what should be done regarding the now officially banned plebiscite. His voice close to breaking, his eyes brimming with tears, and visibly moved (the interview was also filmed), Junqueras called on his fellow Catalan citizens, from the depths of his anguish but also "with hope," to do what had to be done: to call for elections and then proceed with a declaration of Catalan independence. Needless to say, this emotional display was understood very differently depending on the political tendencies of those judging it. Some attributed it to a legitimate expression of frustration with all the blocks placed by the state on the road to a new political reality for Catalonia, as well as to Junqueras's dismay at the possibility of losing the political momentum that had been built up in favor of independence. Others, while respecting the sincerity of the political leader's emotion, judged his broken voice to be a symbol of the fragility of the process itself (Gracia, "La voz"); yet others mocked what they considered "crocodile tears" used for political effect ("Millo").

Junqueras's were not the only tears of frustration and emotion shed in public in relation to the secessionist movement. Barely a year earlier, another Catalan official had had a similar reaction. On 12 December 2013, during the inauguration of what turned out to be a rather controversial symposium entitled "Spain against Catalonia: A Historical Approach (1714–2014)," Jaume Sobrequés, the president of Catalonia's Center for Contemporary History, broke down when alluding to the personal and political pressures he had had to endure while organizing the event, something he had done with "disciplinary rigor" but also compelled by a desire to serve the people of Catalonia. Again, reaction to this emotional display ranged from those who were moved by it to those who considered it part of an emotional manipulation of history characteristic of Catalan nationalism. Indeed, several political parties—Partido Popular; Ciutadans (Citizens); Unión, Progreso y Democracia (Union, Progress, and Democracy)—filed a legal complaint against the symposium on the grounds that it was hate speech ("incitación al odio") directed against Spain.

These two examples should be interpreted in the context of what has, without a doubt, been a highly charged political moment (2013–2014), both for relations between the Spanish state and Catalonia and for Catalan national self-definition. Obviously, any secessionist movement causes considerable tension (internal and external), with public discussion of political options inevitably bringing to the surface the fractures that are often hidden but exist in the social fabric of any society. Nevertheless, the reality is that daily life in Catalonia in past years has been remarkably peaceful, in stark contrast to the situation in the Basque Country when ETA was still active. Even at times of massive public demonstrations—such as those held on the Diadas (National Day of Catalonia) of 2012, 2013, and 2014, which saw as many as one million people on the streets of Barcelona—the most noticeable emotions were not negative (rage, indignation) but positive (hope, pride). These well-organized events, which were conducted without incident and in an atmosphere of civic festivity, also had their detractors. In 2014, some of the criticism was aimed precisely at the supposedly "excessive" degree of organization that went into forming a seven-mile-long "V" (for Vote and perhaps also for Victory) with people coming together from two of Barcelona's major avenues. For some, the combination of meticulous organization, joyous celebration, and patriotic fervor that characterized the day's events was reminiscent of North Korean aesthetics and emotional manipulation of citizenry, a disingenuous argument given the obvious differences between the two societies (Alonso Velarde; Pérez Andújar). Needless to say, had anything gone wrong and had there been any disruption of civic order, there would have been relentless criticisms of the event, of its organizers, and of course of unmanageable nationalist excesses.

The reality is that in Catalonia, as anywhere else, expressions of public emotion, including patriotic love, are subject to implicit "feeling rules" that are culturally and historically determined, as well as representative of power hierarchies in a given context (Pantti and van Zoonen). Given that one of the traditional stereotypical characteristics of the Catalan national character is "seny" (good sense, judiciousness, tempered wisdom), it could be argued that impassioned public reactions to the political situation—in particular by male public figures—carry a great deal of symbolic weight. Indeed, opposition to Catalan nationalism often asserts that one of the side effects of the Catalan proindependence movement has been the loss of seny and rationality in favor of their conceptual opposites, *rauxa* (rashness, fury) and irrational emotionality. But in reality rauxa has been present at many moments in Catalonia's past, as historian Jaume Vicens Vives insisted, as it is of course in all nations at moments of social or political upheaval. Indeed, if the rest of the Spanish state does not have a term that is the exact equivalent of rauxa, it has certainly experienced its share of political rage, in the past and in the present. Moreover, the significance of the affective dimension of the current proindependence process has been the subject of open critical debate in Catalonia. In this respect, there is recognition that a new Catalan nationalism should be "emotionally intelligent," that is to say, mindful of the capacity of emotions to motivate citizens to action, while being able to balance such emotions with more rational, pragmatic concerns and civic-democratic values (Espluga).

Masculine tears have also been visible in Spanish politics, albeit related to episodes of personal shame. In November 2014, the president of the autonomous region of Extremadura, José Antonio Monago, was obliged to defend his conduct in the face of allegations of misuse of public funds. Newspapers claimed that Monago had repeatedly flown to the Canary Islands to visit a lover, with the flights paid by the Spanish Senate. The politician first denied the accusations, stating that the trips had all been for business, then agreed to pay for those costs that were not related to business matters, and then presented press clippings depicting him at public political events on the islands. In the course of this maneuvering, Monago attended a political convention of his own party (Partido Popular) in Extremadura. Although the funding of those trips had not been properly explained, and despite the wave of public indignation created by the number of political corruption scandals in 2014, the reaction of Monago's colleagues was to give him a standing ovation. Visibly moved, Monago burst into tears and thanked his colleagues and the people of Extremadura for standing by him in difficult times. Prior to this episode, Monago was already notorious for his tendency to use sentimental rhetoric and trite metaphors of the kind found in self-help manuals. One of his most controversial moments was when he responded to Valencian government officials, who were complaining about their region's treatment by the central government, that perhaps what was needed was to create a "government department of love" (secretaría del amor), because what people really needed was hugs and kisses. Needless to say, the idea was not well received and he later had to apologize to the Valencian representatives. The effectiveness of Monago's tactics, including his emotional defense of his family's honor and his public tears, remains to be seen: he has remained in office and is his party's candidate for the next regional elections of May 2015, but public polls predict that he will not be reelected. The public scandal surrounding the case did force the Spanish Congress, reluctantly, to introduce controls on the free trips within Spain to which all public representatives had up to that point been entitled without any need for justification or auditing.[3]

What Becomes of the Brokenhearted?

As I have argued elsewhere, prior to official governmental acknowledgment of the economic crisis when the consensus was that Spain was doing very well ("España va bien")—that is, roughly speaking, from 1996 to 2008—the culture of democracy was correlated with normalcy and rationality (Delgado, "Settled"). Official discourses by mainstream politicians and intellectuals constantly invoked the impartiality of the rule of law and the unquestionable validity of consensus politics, which in turn implied the categorical acceptance of legal procedures already established, rather than the possibility of establishing new political agreements. At that time, the only cloud on the horizon seemed to be the dangers represented by nonstate nationalisms; not just in the Basque case—where nationalism as such was identified with the very real violence still employed by ETA—but in that of all nonstate nationalisms. State nationalism, firmly aligned with the rationality and normalcy symbolized by the 1978 Constitution, was categorized as "constitutional patriotism" but defended with a degree of emotionalism that contradicted the very premises of the original Habermasian concept, which, in its desire to avoid the emotionalist excess of fascism, ended up being criticized by some precisely for its abstractness and even "bloodless" quality (Müller). Those years saw a surge of political essays and national histories, many characterized by a highly emotional rhetoric that warned against political ruptures, the Balkanization of Spain, and even the loss of Spain's national essence (Delgado, "Settled," *La nación*).

Anxiety over the nation's threatened unity was nevertheless tempered by a generalized boastful public celebration of everything Spanish, which now, with hindsight, many regard as "nouveaux riche" excess. The decisive moment in this joyful celebration of Spanishness, which had hitherto eluded a country whose national self-definition has been so associated with an ethos of existential angst, was not a political moment per se although it certainly acquired political significance: it was 2010, the year that Spain won the World Soccer Cup in South Africa. With this victory, the national body—which had been diagnosed by José I. Wert, a well-known politician who would later become minister of education, culture, and sports, as suffering from "patriotic anorexia" (Delgado, *La nación* 131)—received such a big dose of collective pride that it became almost bloated. Even if the country was already in a midst of a recession (albeit officially denied), sports victories and in particular soccer victories functioned as a compensatory fantasy, a type of "national quixotism" sublimating material losses into spiritual gains (Labrador Méndez, "El Rey"). That continued to be the case until 2012. The first day of the European Soccer Cup, which Spain won for the second time running, coincided with the request by the conservative government for a European Union bailout of the Spanish financial sector, a bailout that Spanish taxpayers would ultimately have to pay back. The dilemma was then, for many citizens conscious of the country's dismal situation, what to do with the emotions that those victories triggered? The critic Germán Labrador Méndez pondered: "¿Cómo emocionarse ante las victorias de una selección que, si nos representa, lo hace al precio alto de tener que subordinarse a un esquema moral que pretende convencernos de que el coste de esa alegría es el sufrimiento o el dolor que nos habita en lo cotidiano, cuya razón, además, se nos escapa tanto como la suerte de un balón que flota sobre el área?" (What emotions should we feel at the victories of a national team that, if it represents us, does so at the high cost of subjecting us to a moral paradigm that attempts to convince us that the cost of that joy is our collective daily suffering, a suffering whose reasons are as hard to understand as those determining the trajectory of a ball in the penalty area?; "El Rey"). Yet, even he could not resign himself to not feeling that joy that was expressed so freely in the streets; even less could he rejoice at the thought that the team might not win. He summed up his dilemma with the question: "¿Es entonces, y allí, posible latir con un doble corazón?" (Is it possible then, in this case, for one's heart to beat with a double heartbeat?; "El Rey").

Hearts and "corazonadas" (heartbeats, gut feelings) had had an important symbolic role in the 2010 World Cup, and so they would in the debacle that was the 2014 event, when Spain lost its title in the first round. In 2010, after the final match and for the first time in the democratic period, the Spanish streets were inundated with flags not associated with any party: they were carried by young people chanting "I am Spanish, Spanish, Spanish." The emotional unity and patriotic pride associated with a diverse group of talented players was symbolized by the cover of the sports journal *Marca*: a huge heart in the colors of the national flag, with the words "46,745,807 corazonadas" (46,745,807 heartbeats), referring to the total population of Spain in June 2010.[4] In a similar vein, the newspaper *La Verdad* represented support for the team and patriotic pride as literally inscribed on the body of a (heavily made-up) male fan shown with his fists clenched in tension. On his abdomen, daubed in red and yellow, was the above-mentioned chant "Soy español, español, español" plus "Gracias por el sueño" (Thanks for the dream). Positioned roughly over his heart was the famous Osborne bull, one of the most stereotypical symbols of traditional Spanishness, with the phrase "A por ellos" ("Let's go get them").[5]

Had this visceral emotionality been used to support any expression of nonstate patriotism it would have been called excessive and irrational. Indeed, it *was* considered excessive and irrational by many Spaniards exasperated by the way soccer had taken over their lives and the news, relegating to invisibility the country's stark reality. Moreover, if it is accepted that expressions of patriotic love toward the nation-state and its symbols are, to a high degree, visceral and nonrational (gut feelings), then it should be clear that not everybody can be viscerally affected by the same emotions, or to the same degree. And yet, it is remarkable how often sports players, artists, or other citizens who express their affective attachment to their own autonomous communities are required to express a primary emotional allegiance to Spain, and are subject to attack if their loyalty is not unequivocal. It is relevant that in 2014, at a moment of generalized political anger, the conservative government appointed its vice president, Soraya Sáenz de Santamaría, as overseer of national symbols (including the flag and anthem), responsible for legal action resulting from their improper use (or nonuse). This appointment, unprecedented in the democratic period, took place just one day after the president of the Generalitat Artur Mas signed the legal announcement of the Catalan referendum, a decision that he then had to modify because of the legal block on the Spanish government's part.[6] The year 2014 was also when a significant percentage of the whole national population, fed up with corruption scandals and a stagnant economy, started to withdraw its support from the main political parties, prompting the spectacular rise of the new left-wing party Podemos (We Can) and the center-right Ciudadanos (Citizens), as well as a number of important civic initiatives—such as the Plataforma de Afectados por las Hipotecas (Mortgage Victims' Platform); the various "mareas" (waves) of citizens that have taken to the streets in protest; and the movement Democracia Real Ya (Real Democracy Now), among many others.

The government's decision to appoint the holder of the second highest political office in the country to defend the symbols of the nation-state is a clear example of its lack of understanding of how affective attachments have to be encouraged and promoted, not mandated. The Spanish government may win a legal battle over its right to impose on an official institution the use of one flag over another, but legal threats do nothing to promote the affective connectedness that is the basis for the construction of national cohesion. This rather obvious point has been acknowledged in public by politicians, intellectuals, and activists, many of whom are not necessarily in favor of Catalan independence and are not proponents of radical political movements. Indeed, the government's dismissal of plural patriotic feelings, as well as its obstinate insistence on adhering to the letter of current laws instead of finding the political resources to modify them, has backfired by considerably increasing the number of supporters of Catalan independence, even among citizens who a few years ago would not have chosen that option. Along those lines, Jordi Gracia, a well-known essayist and proponent of political reform rather than rupture, lamented that outside of Catalonia it was assumed that Catalans' heads and hearts had been "colonized in a unanimous manner" ("Reforma política").

A Hopeful Indignation

Catalan nationalism is not the only political affect that has been pathologized by the Spanish government and significant sectors of the media. The same condemnation, indeed near criminalization, has been directed at the social movements and collective protests that have expressed their indignation and lack of trust in their public representatives and the state of Spanish democracy. In fact, if the emotional habitus of the period 2008–2014 could be summed up in one word it would be precisely "Indignados" ("Outraged"), the label used by the social movement 15-M in Spain and shared with similar movements in other countries.[7] As is well known, Stéphane Hessel's 2010 book *Indignez-vous!* (translated to English as *Time for Outrage!*) provided the intellectual framework for the 15-M movement. While criticized for its "emotional ramblings" and for presenting as patriotic a negative emotion such as indignation, the book became a worldwide bestseller, attributed precisely to the emotional connection that it established with indignant citizens everywhere at a time of crisis and political outrage. Yet the Spanish establishment's interpretation of that indignation has been to label it an antidemocratic negative affect, a merely reactive condition with no true political content. Indeed, it is interesting to note that, in the initial moments of the crisis, the establishment spoke more of voters' "desafección" (disaffection), interpreted as passive and apolitical in its condemnation of all major political forces. And yet, the year 2012 saw almost daily protests converge in Madrid: multiple waves of indignant citizens that included professors, doctors, nurses, judges, janitorial staff, miners, students, and metro workers, among many others. In fact, it is hard to say who was *not* protesting. The sociologist Amparo Lasén has noted the contradiction between citizens' supposed political "disaffection" and the high level of public mobilization and participation. Lasén regrets that interest in politics is measured only through formal affiliation to established political groups, when what we are witnessing is a redefinition of the nature of the political and an important civil interpellation of those in power. In other words, there is not so much a disaffection as a lack of adhesion to traditional politics, and an attempt to find ways of publicly channeling a range of affects and emotions that can be negative (such as indignation, anger, or spite) but also positive (such as happiness, sympathy, or hope).

The condemnation by current mainstream politicians of anger, pessimism, and mistrust as failures of good citizenship is disingenuous at best. Such emotions should not be equated with apathy, much less with inaction. They have mobilized people to action in the past and will do so again, not to sustain the structure of inherited legal procedures and boundaries but precisely to question them. As Javier Krauel reminds us, indignation differs from anger in that it implies moral judgment, the belief that a particular situation is unjust at a suprapersonal level. Indignation also attributes responsibility and, perhaps because of this, is a more politically effective emotion than anger (Innerarity 43). The continual insistence on the part of public officials in Spain on the importance of not "giving in" to negative affects like pessimism should be framed within what Berlant has called the affective structure of an optimistic attachment that returns time and time again to the scene of fantasy—"España es un gran país" (Spain is a great country)—hoping that, eventually, the expectations that sustain the structure of the fantasy will be fulfilled. Berlant gives the term "cruel optimism" to this loyalty to a problematic object, to a condition of possibility whose realization is impossible, toxic, or a fantasy. And it is surely cruel optimism that is asserted when politicians from different parties keep extolling the "quality of life" that can be had in Spain, insisting that it is superior to that of other countries. In this respect one needs to ask what indicators are being used to measure the quality of life in a country where for many people the quotidian has become a "landfill for overwhelming and impending crisis of life-building," a scenario of economic and intimate contingency (Berlant, *Cruel* 3).

While different Spanish governments have refused to acknowledge the political importance of emotions and affects, they have nevertheless been very active in promoting what Berlant has called national sentimentality: "a rhetoric of promise that a nation can be built across fields of social difference through channels of affective identification and empathy" ("Subject" 53). While the emotional dimension of legitimate political actions is ignored or considered excessive, bland sentimentality is promoted to create a cultural national normativity, whose goal is to mend a fractured society through personal empathy. Social antagonisms and concrete political problems are therefore displaced onto a utopian space "ideally void of struggle and ambivalence" (Berlant, "The Subject" 59), whose internal cohesion is based on the connection established among subjects who share the same feelings (Berlant, "Poor Eliza," *Cruel Optimism*). A good example of the substitution of sentimental plots and individual initiatives for what should be dealt with politically (following the principles clearly set out in the so-often-invoked but so-little-respected Constitution) was the Spanish state television program *Entre todos* (*If We All Pull Together*, 2013–2014). The program presented cases of families in desperate situations who appeared on-screen to ask for help to pay for their most basic necessities and to start small businesses that would help them escape poverty. A panel of experts (lawyers, consultants, psychologists, coaches) gave their opinion while the guests, often with evident reticence, had to talk about the most private details of their lives in front of millions of viewers. In every case, the focus of the narrative was on the unemployed as victims of a personal trauma. In the exposition of their suffering, there was no room for any explicit reflection on the structural conditions of their situation, on the root causes of the circumstances that force millions of people to beg for basic necessities in what is still considered "a great country" by its political leaders. The program also allowed no consideration of responsibilities or blame, and certainly no expression of anger, just personal grief. Indeed such was the need to Photoshop reality that when one particular woman alluded to the fact that her troubles started as the result of domestic abuse, the program's host (also a woman) abruptly cut her short, declaring stiffly "I'm not getting into that" (she had to apologize later). In this model of sentimental culture, the only legitimate reaction is acceptance and hope that individual (rather than institutional) solidarity will alleviate the effects of a social disaster. As many articles dedicated to the program pointed out, the problem is not the cultivation of solidarity, a laudable objective, but that charity and private initiatives should replace what until recently were responsibilities and essential services of the state, such as school lunches or home care for people in need, including the elderly and minors with disabilities.

In its tone and focus, *Entre todos* recalled Francoism's famous slogan "Ponga un pobre en su mesa" (Seat a Poor Person at Your Table) satirized so wonderfully by Luis García Berlanga in his 1961 film *Plácido*, or the program *Ustedes son formidables* (*You're the Greatest*) broadcast by the radio network SER from 1960 to 1977. However, as befits today's historical moment, charity is no longer presented as a moral Christian virtue but as a message from experts in personal and business management who assure us that the future and happiness are ours if we know how to take charge of our lives and manage our emotions adequately (Illouz), without succumbing to despair. The same uncritical sentimentalism, reminiscent of the Francoist imaginary, was also portrayed in a series of commercials from the cured meats company Campofrío that were broadcast in 2011, 2012, and 2013, respectively. These commercials all ended with the on-screen message "Que nada ni nadie nos quite nuestra manera de disfrutar la vida" (Don't let anything or anyone rob us of our way of enjoying life). If sports victories have taught us anything, it is that collective, context-specific enjoyment does indeed play a fundamental role in national cohesion. In this commercial's case, the enemy threatening to rob the Spanish people of enjoyment was, as during Francoism, foreign institutions that have the power to evaluate *our* economy and *our* legal system, but who do not understand *our* values or *our* way of doing things.

The emphasis on a given community's customary way of doing things and enjoying life has also been used as a marketing tool in several autonomous communities, in a series of very successful advertisements aimed at creating a sense of emotional cohesion in viewers. In Galicia the supermarket chain Gadis made marketing history by pegging a series of ads (2008–present) onto the idea of a Galician specificity identified with material and emotional endurance: "Vivamos como galegos" (Let's live as Galicians). In Catalonia, the Estrella Dam beer company started a series of television commercials in 2006 with the title "Mediterràniament" (In the Mediterranean way), appealing to an emotional, seemingly apolitical and nonideological Mediterranean reduced to its European elements. Set in beautiful natural locations, these advertisements show attractive people responsible for their own happiness (that is to say, people who adequately manage their emotions) enjoying the landscape while sharing a few beers. The cultural plurality and historical complexity of the Mediterranean, not to mention the fact that it is now the scenario of a tragic migrant crisis, are lost in the re-creation of a Eurocentric, cosmopolitan, and unconflicted scenario that appeals to an ideal of apolitical universal enjoyment and timeless leisure (Bardera and Espluga).

Affective Networks

In 1976, a song by the Andalusian group Jarcha used to promote the newly created *Diario 16* became one of the unofficial anthems of the Transition: "Libertad sin ira" (Freedom without Wrath). The lyrics spoke of a people who wanted to enjoy the pleasures of life peacefully, trying to achieve a freedom without anger, which, then as now, was perceived as a dangerous social emotion. It was the perfect musical counterpart to the hegemonic narrative and spirit of the period. Another of the group's songs, "Habla pueblo habla" (Speak, People, Speak), was used in the referendum for the 1976 Law of Political Reform and is widely believed to have contributed to Adolfo Suárez's first (decisive) political victory. Almost forty years later, neither of these emblematic songs could be used as political propaganda by the present government, which has just blocked the second attempt by the Catalan government to let the Catalan people speak and has introduced severe legal limitations on the right of all Spaniards to dissent and protest in public (Congress in Madrid is now protected by metal barriers). And yet the latest CIS (Center for Sociological Research) government opinion poll shows that the new political parties Podemos (despite relentless media accusations of dangerous radicalism) and Ciudadanos have become, as of early May 2015, key players in an electoral map previously characterized by an unassailable two-party system. The majority opinion expressed in the national press has been that the upsurge in "populist" politics is driven by anger and indignation, which of course is part of the story but not the whole story. What Podemos, Guanyem Barcelona, Ganemos Madrid, and other movements are also offering is hope. "Primero estaba indignada, ahora estoy ilusionada" (First I was outraged, now I am hopeful) could be read on banners during the 15-M public protests. Other banners asked for a smile to restart a broken system; in almost all public expressions of support for the movement, solidarity and empathy were identified as the qualities needed to start a peaceful revolution based on acts of civil disobedience (Delgado, *La nación* 241–50).

As Labrador Méndez notes, the 15-M movement's rapid social growth was supported by expansive waves of affectivity ("Si te pasa"). Between 2011 and 2012, a group of researchers at the Internet Interdisciplinary Institute of the Universitat Oberta de Catalunya, directed by Javier Toret, undertook an investigation into the range and deployment of new technologies and media involved in the movement's expansion. The authors of this highly technical study, which deserves more attention than can be given here, describe the process as the collective affective commotion of a connected body that generated a technologically structured contagion, causing an escalation of the #15m network system (Toret et al. 2). They insist that the 15-M movement should be understood not as an event or brand, but as a mobilization of collective emotions that went "viral" thanks to new technologies. In this respect, one of the questions the researchers asked of media users was "What emotions has 15-M created?" Their analysis of tweets sent between April 2011 and July 2012 showed that, from an initial sense of anger, paralysis, fear, and isolation, the movement had generated a sense of community, hope, and, above all, empowerment. Indeed, "empowerment" was the word that appeared most frequently in tweets, more than indignation (second), fear (third), and happiness (fourth). Moreover, the tweets sent during the 15-M movement had considerably higher emotional peaks than regular tweets. The authors of the study conclude that highly emotionally charged messages went viral faster and had more impact than other messages, even those sent at key moments during the movement. The goal of their analysis of the "emotional peaks of engagement" of the 15-M tweets is to understand how collective emotions are activated through technology so that this affective energy can be deployed for positive political change.

As Labrador Méndez had previously argued, the Spanish Revolution that started in the streets on 15 May 2011 had already begun in the hearts of all of those who took to the streets that day, and the columns of outraged citizens that marched on Madrid functioned as a type of "homeopathy" of a collective heart that had not been functioning properly ("Si te pasa"). Indeed, one of the characteristic features of 15-M was its vindication of a "sensitive democracy" (Monedero; Foessel) that acknowledges the importance of emotions and affects in the forging of democratic bonds, and depathologizes the political significance of "negative" emotions, which should be understood in terms of their proper context and function.

All We Need Is Love

In her latest study of political emotions, Martha Nussbaum maintains that what liberalism needs is love. She argues that emotions are an important part of political life and that, if liberals cede the strong emotion of patriotism, which she identifies with a form of love, to "power hungry nationalists," they are making a big mistake. She then wonders what is truly required of a good citizen: someone acting correctly but whose actions are not sustained by real feeling, or rather someone who truly *has* love? She further ponders: "So nations need those things [economic thought, military thought, good use of computer science and technology] but do they not need the heart? They need the expertise, but do we not need the daily emotion, the sympathy, tears and laughter that we require of ourselves as parents, lovers and friends, or the wonder with which we contemplate beauty?" (397). Her answer is, of course, that liberalism needs love even if that is not all it needs.[8] And yet, she acknowledges how countries with a fascist past, like Germany for instance, have avoided legislating on the basis of emotional attachments, given how successfully fascism had mobilized intense emotions for spurious political purposes. Spain would be a similar case, given how skillfully the Falange (Spanish Fascist Party) and Francoism co-opted passionate patriotic love and the rhetoric of national affective ties as the basis for incontestable unity and cohesion. At the same time, Nussbaum also admits that productive citizenship might not require heartfelt feelings all the time, and that, since there are many kinds of love, we should imagine "a family of sentiments" and not a single emotion.

The importance of the heart for good citizenship is now being asserted in different intellectual and political quarters in the context of the corruption scandals that shook an already weak Spanish democracy in the fall of 2014. On 1 November, immediately after yet another high-ranking politician (Francisco Granados) was arrested, charged with a multimillion euro fraud, the conservative newspaper *ABC* quoted philosopher Javier Gomá Lanzón to propose a "sentimental education of the heart" as a partial solution to the problem, since, without such an education, the heart might react in a negative, destructive way (González 5). What is needed in times of socioeconomic crisis, Gomá Lanzón had stated in a previous article in *La Vanguardia*, is a "visión culta y corazón educado" (cultivated vision and educated heart), an approach reminiscent of the Enlightenment ideal of sensibility tempered by reason in order to avoid the dangers of excessive emotions.

A few days after the 2014 Diada, journalist and author Juan Cruz wrote an article entitled "'Heart,' 'cor,' corazón" ("Heart" in English, Catalan, and Spanish) which alluded to David Cameron's strategy of appealing to the heart in order to convince the Scottish people to stay in the United Kingdom. It also mentioned a speech by Mariano Rajoy, given on 11 September, on the occasion of the twenty-fifth anniversary of the National Transplant Organization but also the National Day of Catalonia. The fact that Spain is a world leader in organ donations and transplants has been used throughout the crisis to support the idea of the emotional strength of the networks of love and solidarity binding Spanish citizens together. Rajoy took the argument a step further, claiming that the country was morally and emotionally interconnected ("vertebrada") and offering a concrete example: an Andalusian could live with a heart donated by a Catalan, or a Galician with the heart of someone from Madrid ("Rajoy"). Needless to say, the example was particularly ill timed and led to all kinds of comments and jokes: all that was needed for national solidarity was for Catalans or Madrileños to rip out their hearts and become spare parts for other citizens. There is a long-standing debate on whether a transplanted heart gives the recipient "something other than a mere pump: a sense of identity, perhaps a change of soul" (Bound 1). If so, mass transplants would allow all our hearts to beat with a single heartbeat, there would be no conflicting loyalties, no uncertainties as to what we feel. Cruz used these examples to state that the possibility of Catalonia not being part of his country broke his heart.[9] Ironically, the logo for the fastest-growing political party in Spain, Ciudadanos, which started out in Catalonia under the name Ciutadans (Citizens), is precisely a heart divided equally between the Catalan and Spanish flags, with both of them joined together by the European Union logo.

Rajoy's metaphor was not the only one of its kind. Prior to the celebration of the 2014 World Soccer Cup, before the Spanish team (the reigning world champions) was defeated in the first round, shattering all expectations that sport could work its magic as a social glue again, there was a beer publicity campaign—entitled "Préstanos tu corazón" ("Lend us your heart") and analyzed brilliantly by Labrador Méndez ("El Rey")—that seemed to sense that drastic measures would be needed to repeat the historic feat. The ads showed different players worried that, owing to the economic crisis, fans would not be able to travel to Brazil to support them. The solution was to ask fans to donate their hearts: that is, to cut out the logo on the official T-shirt (identifying the team as world champion) and send it to a specific address, where the pieces would be stitched together to form a huge heart that would unite forty-six million people in a single heartbeat (the hashtag used to promote the event was #AsilateEspaña). The commercials acknowledged that fans might be reluctant to tear out their figurative hearts, associated with so many important emotions, not to mention the fact that the expensive T-shirt would be ruined; to convince them, the players promised they would see their generosity rewarded with yet another star (the symbol of the world championship). As we know, what the Spanish fans got was a humiliating defeat in the tournament's first round, a broken heart, and another broken promise. Upon the team's inglorious return home, many commentators pointed to the lack of commitment of some players to the very idea of a national Spanish team, with the Catalan Piqué and the naturalized-Spanish, Brazilian-born Diego Costa being particularly targeted: their lackluster performances were linked to their "true" national (Catalan and Brazilian, respectively) feelings. Needless to say, Piqué had played with the same feelings before to great effect and to the benefit of the Spanish national team. Costa had chosen to play for Spain instead of for his native Brazil (he was taunted for that choice by Brazilian fans throughout the tournament).

The fact of the matter is that "corazonadas" (gut feelings) are not what leads to success in any endeavor, much less to long-term national cohesion. It must be noted in this respect that the disastrous campaign for Madrid's failed bid to organize the 2016 Olympic Games was also structured around the slogan "Tengo una corazonada" ("I have a gut feeling"): the writer Rafael Sánchez Ferlosio criticized the hyperbolic emotional tone of what turned out to be another failed economic and affective investment. Constructive democratic citizenship should not require an unconflicted heart, or the unveiling of its secrets, contradictions, and conflicts before a tribunal of public opinion. Indeed, as Daniel Innerarity states, a well-articulated public sphere requires that certain questions be discussed in public, while allowing for others to be protected from public scrutiny. There should be areas where it is irrelevant whether the reasons for someone's actions conform to "common sense" (37–38). The fact that national belonging is now associated with a sentimentality based on the public exposure of the (usually subaltern) citizen's pain or frustration, or with the normative framing of emotional reactions by public figures, should be contextualized as part of the distraction tactics involved in the "neoliberal orchestration of political emotion's intimate viscera" (Berlant, *Cruel* 262). Moreover, the norms that might be relevant in the context of close personal relationships are not necessarily useful in the public arena (Innerarity 37). Public tears and admissions of personal regret should not bypass political obligations to the civic body, or the legal consequences of the failure to comply with them. Instead of focusing on the display of individual emotions, their sincerity or lack thereof, it would be more productive to pay attention to how and why certain emotions are mobilized in the public sphere, whether to positive or negative effect. If anything positive has come out of the current state of crisis in Spain, it is recognition of the urgent need "to take the measure of the impact of the present" (Berlant, *Cruel* 263) and to tackle the constraints imposed by fantasy scenes of national completeness and singularity. In that context, it might be time to acknowledge that it is possible to live "with and beside each other, and yet not as one" (Ahmed 39). Substantive dissent in the political realm should be negotiated politically, and not diverted into a maze of legal procedures or pathologized as inherently destructive of democratic coexistence, for the affective connectedness of a society is not enhanced by the public exposure of the secrets of its citizens' hearts. Rather, it is based on the conscious acceptance of an ongoing civic obligation to a community understood not as a point of convergence, but as a point of departure toward ways of being-in-relation that are both singular and plural.[10]

NOTES

1. The image can be seen at *www.telegraph.co.uk/news/uknews/scottish-independence/11108852/Scottish-independence-referendum-10-things-you-may-have-missed.html* (accessed 1 November 2014).
2. Mas and Junqueras had a "governability agreement" that allowed the former to become president of the Catalan government by providing the votes necessary to win a majority. This agreement included Mas's commitment to hold a referendum on the question of Catalonia's independence.
3. There are many other instances of male politicians on the verge of tears when having to explain publicly their involvement in cases of corruption, misuse of public funds, tax evasion, etc. Perhaps the most disturbing is that of the archbishop of Granada, Francisco Javier Martínez, who had ignored a case of sexual abuse in his archdiocese, resulting in the Vatican ordering an inquiry. Insisting that the presumption of innocence of the accused must be respected, Martínez agreed to cooperate with the inquiry, stating that "he could not contain his tears" because the situation had wounded him so deeply ("El arzobispo").
4. "Corazonada" here also means "gut feeling" or "premonition" since the cover was created at the tournament's start (15 June 2010), before the final victory. The image can be seen at *www.especialmundial.com/wp-content/uploads/portada-marca-Mundial-de-f%C3%BAtbol-16-de-Junio.jpg* (accessed 28 September 2014).
5. *La Verdad* (10 July 2010). The cover won the award for best cover of the year in Spain and Portugal. It can be seen at *maquetadores.blogspot.com.es/2010/10/la-voz-de-cadiz-el-correo-gallego-i-y.html* (accessed 15 November 2014).
6. As is well known, ultimately a nonbinding "procés de participació ciutadana" (citizen's participation process) was held on 9 November 2014, when an estimated two million people voted, roughly one-third of the population of Catalonia. On 18 November 2014, the central state general prosecutor issued charges against Mas and other members of the Catalan government for allowing the process to take place.
7. The 15-M movement refers to a series of protests starting on 15 May 2011 and continuing through 2012, which questioned the functioning of Spanish democracy and demanded a series of radical changes to it. The grassroots activism and solidarity networks promoted by the movement have had a very significant impact on the development of alternatives to the political system established in 1978. For a good analysis of the movement, as well as the role of indignation and hope in it, see the double issue of the *Journal of Spanish Cultural Studies* edited by Bryan Cameron.
8. The importance of love in democratic politics had been recognized in the 1930s by María Zambrano, who also builds her argument around the metaphor of the heart (see Introduction to this volume).
9. The fantasy of an emotionally cohesive community, made possible by technology, was also enacted in Barcelona's 2015 New Year celebrations. The well-known theater group La Fura dels Baus constructed *L'Ésser del Mil·lenni* (*The Millennium Being*), a huge iron human figure that was then "fleshed out" with *castellers* (traditional Catalan human towers). Once the *castellers* had humanized the structure, the thousands of spectators gathered for the performance were instructed to turn on their cell phones at the same moment to

"activate" the iron man's heart, thus becoming a collective working in unison to produce a single heartbeat.
10. The notion of community as a point of departure is developed by Roberto Esposito (see also Delgado, *La nación* 293–97).

WORKS CITED

Ahmed, Sara. *The Cultural Politics of Emotion*. Edinburgh: Edinburgh UP, 2004.
Alonso Velarde, Juan. "Estética coreana en la Diada." *Blogia* 16 September 2014. *juanvelarde.blogia.com/2014/091601-estetica-coreana-en-la-diada.php* (accessed 28 September 2014).
"El arzobispo de Granada admite que los abusos sexuales denunciados son 'verosímiles.'" *RTVE.es* 20 November 2014. *www.rtve.es/noticias/20141120/arzobispo-granada-admite-abusos-sexuales-denunciados-son-verosimiles/1051502.shtml* (accessed 20 November 2014).
Bardera, Damià, and Eudald Espluga. *Mediterràneament: La catalanitat emocional*. Barcelona: Biblioteca del Núvol, 2013.
Berlant, Lauren. *Cruel Optimism*. Durham, NC: Duke UP, 2011.
———. "Poor Eliza." *No More Separate Spheres*. Spec. issue of *American Literature* 70.3 (1998): 635–68.
———. "The Subject of True Feeling." *Cultural Pluralism, Identity Politics and the Law*. Ed. Austin Sarat and Thomas Kearns. Ann Arbor: U of Michigan P, 1999. 49–84.
Bound, Fay. *Matters of the Heart: History, Medicine and Emotion*. Oxford: Oxford UP, 2010.
Cameron, Bryan, ed. *Spain in Crisis: 15-M and the Culture of Indignation*. Spec. issue of *Journal of Spanish Cultural Studies* 15.1–2 (2014).
Cruz, Juan. "'Heart,' 'Cor,' corazón." *El País* 14 September 2014. *elpais.com/elpais/2014/09/12/opinion/1410521655_841160.html* (accessed 6 December 2014).
Cvetkovich, Ann. "On Affect and Protest." *Political Emotions: New Agendas in Communication*. Ed. Janet Staiger, Ann Cvetkovich, and Ann Reynolds. New York: Routledge, 2010. 4–12.
Dearden, Lizzie. "Scottish Independence: Full text of David Cameron's 'No Going Back' Speech." *Independent* 16 September 2014. *www.independent.co.uk/news/uk/scottish-independence/scottish-independence-full-text-of-david-camerons-no-going-back-speech-9735902.html* (accessed 14 November 2014).
Delgado, Luisa Elena. *La nación singular: Fantasías de la normalidad democrática española (1996–2011)*. Madrid: Siglo XXI, 2014.
———. "Settled in Normal: Narratives of a Prozaic (Spanish) Nation." *Nationalisms*. Spec. issue of *Arizona Journal of Spanish Cultural Studies* 4.1 (2003): 3–11.
Espluga, Eudald. *Las pasiones ponderadas: O cómo el nacionalismo catalán se volvió emocionalmente inteligente*. Madrid: Capitán Swing Libros, 2015. Kindle edition.
Esposito, Roberto. *Communitas: The Origin and Destiny of Community*. Trans. Timothy Campbell. Stanford, CA: Stanford UP, 2010.
Foessel, Michaël. *La privación de lo íntimo: Las representaciones políticas de los sentimientos*. Trans. Jordi Terré. Barcelona: Ediciones Península, 2010.
Gomá Lanzón, Javier. "Visión culta y corazón educado: Lecciones de la crisis." *Cultura/s* (supplement of *La Vanguardia*) 22 October 2014: 3–5.
González, Jaime. "El asesinato del Sistema." *ABC* 1 November 2014: 5.

Gould, Deborah. "On Affect and Protest." *Political Emotions: New Agendas in Communication.* Ed. Janet Staiger, Ann Cvetkovich, and Ann Reynolds. New York: Routledge, 2010. 18–44.

Gracia, Jordi. "Reforma política o ruptura." *El País* 2 November 2014. *politica.elpais.com/politica/2014/10/31/actualidad/1414780597_840153.html* (accessed 6 December 2014).

———. "La voz rota de Oriol Junqueras." *El País* 23 October 2014. *www.caffereggio.net/2014/10/23/la-voz-rota-de-oriol-junqueras-de-jordi-gracia-en-el-pais/* (accessed 6 December 2014).

Hessell, Stéphane. *Indignez-vous!* Montpellier: Indigène, 2010.

Illouz, Eva. *Cold Intimacies: The Making of Emotional Capitalism.* Cambridge: Polity, 2007.

Innerarity, Daniel. *El nuevo espacio público.* Madrid: Espasa, 2006.

Krauel, Javier. "The Anatomy of Imperial Indignation: Ramiro de Maeztu's *Hacia otra España.*" *Imperial Emotions: Cultural Responses to Myths of Empire in Fin-de Siècle Spain.* Liverpool: Liverpool UP, 2013. 124–39.

Labrador Méndez, Germán. "Si te pasa a ti, me pasa a mí y le pasa al operario: Gramática de afectos y poéticas de lo común; Del hip hop al movimiento 15-M." Paper presented at the session "Emotions and Affects in Twentieth- and Twenty-First-Century Spanish Culture," MLA Convention. Boston. January 2013.

———. "El Rey y el deporte rey: Simulacros políticos y crisis monárquicas en la España del Mundial de 2014." *FronteraD: Revista Digital* 21 August 2014. *www.fronterad.com/?q=rey-y-deporte-rey-simulacros-politicos-y-crisis-monarquicas-en-espana-mundial-2014* (accessed 6 December 2014).

Lasén, Amparo. "Las nuevas formas de acción colectiva desafían la lógica de la representación." *Fuera de lugar: Conversaciones entre crisis y transformación.* Ed. Amador Fernández Savater. Madrid: Antonio Machado Libros, 2013. 257–71.

"Millo critica les "llàgrimes de cocodril" de Junqueras." *E-notícies* 18 October 2014. *politica.e-noticies.cat/millo-critica-les-llagrimes-de-cocodril-de-junqueras-89200.html* (accessed 6 December).

Monedero, Juan Carlos. *Dormíamos y despertamos: El 15 M, la reinvención de la democracia.* Madrid: Nueva Utopía, 2012.

Müller, Jan-Werner. "On the Origins of Constitutional Patriotism." *Contemporary Political Theory* 5 (2006): 278–96.

Nussbaum, Martha C. *Political Emotions: Why Love Matters for Justice.* Cambridge, MA: Belknap–Harvard UP, 2013.

Pantti, Mervi. "Disaster News and Public Emotions." *The Routledge Handbook of Emotions and Mass Media.* Ed. Katrin Döveling, Christian von Scheve, and Elly A. Konijn. Abingdon, UK: Routledge, 2011. 221–36.

Pantti, Mervi, and Liesbet van Zoonen. "Do Crying Citizens Make Good Citizens?" *Social Semiotics* 16.2 (2006): 205–24.

Pérez Andújar, Javier. "Parque temático del independentismo." *El País* 12 September 2014. *ccaa.elpais.com/ccaa/2014/09/11/catalunya/1410464415_800460.html* (accessed 14 September 2014).

"Rajoy: 'Un andaluz puede vivir con el corazón de un catalán con un transplante.'" *El País* 11 September 2014. *politica.elpais.com/politica/2014/09/11/actualidad/1410436004_674269.html* (accessed 6 December 2014).

Richards, Barry. "News and the Emotional Public Sphere." *The Routledge Companion to News and Journalism*. Ed. Stuart Allan. Abingdon, UK: Routledge, 2010. 301–10.

Robin, Corey. *Fear: The History of a Political Idea*. Oxford: Oxford UP, 2006.

Sánchez Ferlosio, Rafael. "Corazón arriba, corazón abajo." *El País* 14 October 2009. *elpais.com/diario/2009/10/14/opinion/1255471211_850215.html* (accessed 20 January 2015).

Toret, Javier, et al. "Lanzamiento: 'Tecnopolítica y 15-M. La potencia de las multitudes conectadas. Un nuevo paradigma de la política distribuida." *DatAnalysis15M* 20 June 2013. *datanalysis15m.wordpress.com/2013/06/20/lanzamiento-tecnopolitica-y-15m-la-potencia-de-las-multitudes-conectadas-el-sistema-red-15m-un-nuevo-paradigma-de-la-politica-distribuida/* (accessed 18 September 2014).

Vicens Vives, Jaume. "Catalans and the Minotaur." *Catalonia, a Self-Portrait*. Ed. and trans. Josep Miquel Sobrer. Bloomington: Indiana UP, 1992. 95–105.

Žižek, Slavoj. *The Universal Exception*. London: Continuum, 2006.

AFTERWORD

Shameless Emotions

ANTONIO MUÑOZ MOLINA

Memory is quite good at storing minor grudges. Some twenty-five years ago, soon after my first novel came out, and at the first literary dinner I attended in Madrid, a famous critic of the time turned to me across the table and said rather patronizingly: "Yours is a good first novel. Too bad you didn't leave the love story out." The remark puzzled me, since, according to my understanding, if the love story were taken out of the novel, very little would be left. By and large the love story was the story, the cornerstone the whole narrative stood on; not one but two love stories to be precise, mirroring each other over the time span unfolding in the novel. When you are young and a newcomer, people tend to bestow their unsolicited advice on you. I believe it was at that same dinner that someone else told me that my novel was quite good, if only I had done without that boring subject, the Spanish Civil War. Emotional displays and the Spanish Civil War were not fashionable topics for novels at that time, the cheerfully forgetful mid-1980s. Many years later the war would become an enduringly hot topic in Spanish letters and cinema, but what has remained not so common are human emotions such as love, tenderness, jealousy, yearning, unless they quickly lead to sex. A very clever reader of literature and good friend of mine told me when he finished my last novel: "I have enjoyed most of it, but I had difficulties getting through all that stuff about childrearing and feverish little babies crying all night." It is true that my friend has had no children, but still I found it intriguing that, out of the almost one thousand pages of a novel that may well be too long, he would deem superfluous only those dealing with the very common although perhaps not too literary predicaments of young parenthood.

To the extent of my knowledge, no Spanish film produced in the last thirty years fails to include at least one explicit sex scene, usually involving athletic couplings of sweaty bodies noisily banging against a wall or a door. But surprisingly few of them care to address in any detail the emotional complexities of desire, the nuances of adult love. And I don't say adult in the sense so pervasively attached to the word by the porn industry. In many novels, some of them written by the most prestigious authors, embarrassingly graphic sexual descriptions are as conspicuous as the lack of any meaningful insights into the feelings of the characters, especially the female partners of the usually male heroes. And I don't mean authors belonging to the paleolithic generation of Camilo José Cela and such, whose erotic expertise went no further than the drab intimacy of brothels. There is much to be said for Manuel Vázquez Montalbán's Carvalho novels, which so vividly convey the tone of urban life and shifting social and political mores at the outset of democracy in contemporary Spain. But in each and every one of these novels a moment comes when the bitterly disillusioned detective engages in long episodes of sexual intercourse with obliging young ladies. Much as I find boring the other fixed ingredient in the Carvalho stories, the part about morosely cooking and eating and digressing on food, there is far more emotional intensity in those scenes than in the usually gynecological sex encounters. Sometimes I suspect that men of Montalbán's generation never managed to get over the guilty masturbatory fantasies of Catholic postwar Spain.

Modern art was partially born out of a healthy rejection of fin de siècle sentimentality, of uncontrolled outbursts of postromantic languor. The sharp, unforgiving eye of Toulouse-Lautrec, the sexual and social ironies of Manet, the thick, spare forms of Cézanne dealt a merciless blow to the bland sentimental conventions of academic art. By the late nineteenth century, French music was drowning in the sugary repertoire of grand opera, with its regular doses of oriental or medieval kitsch. It took Debussy, Satie, and Ravel, among others, to shake up almost a century of numbing musical conformism. To be modern meant to be furiously iconoclastic, antibourgeois, antisentimental. When it premiered in 1913, Stravinsky's *Rite of Spring* was as far removed from any middle-class melodic emotionalism as Picasso's *Demoiselles d'Avignon*. Almost overnight, lush orchestrations became as outdated as the virtuoso mellowness of academic or even early Impressionist painting.

But even then the canonical narrative of modernism misses a part of the picture worth paying attention to. What about Mary Cassat's portraits of mothers and children? Not to mention the many openly emotional Picasso drawings and paintings of his son Paolo. For shouldn't the modern artist, rather than be a responsible husband or parent (being a mother or wife is almost out of the question), be a madman and a visionary, a drunkard, an outcast, "un artist maudit" in the by then hallowed tradition of Lautréamont or Rimbaud? A few years ago, at the Prado Museum in Madrid, I gave some thought to these issues while viewing in amazement one of the best and most overlooked paintings of the late 1890s: Joaquín Sorolla's stunning portrait of his wife in bed after giving birth to one of their daughters. The young mother, her wet black hair spread out on the pillow, turns her gaze to her baby, a smudge of reddish oils that renders with surprising accuracy the round, blotchy face of a newborn. The faces of mother and child barely emerge from the heavy white bedcover. The bed is large and white; the wall, pale blue behind the headboard. But then you pay a little more attention and there is no such thing as pure white or pure blue on the canvas, only nervous smudges of different shades of almost gray and almost white and almost blue: what seemed at first sight a cozy family scene turns out to be as daring and original in its composition and colors as any sketch of gas-lit nocturnal debauchery by Toulouse-Lautrec.

The problem is this: Sorolla, a family man, a middle-class, cheerful, hardworking painter, doesn't shy away from his open emotional commitment. Had he chosen to paint, instead of his beloved wife and daughter, some aloof society lady, some emaciated absinthe drinker, some despondent fellow artist, that same unmatched technique would have landed him in New York's Museum of Modern Art.

In order to qualify as cool, you must refrain from any show of warmth. You play safe while pretending to be daring, to break boundaries, to do away with sentimental conventions. But in fact, rather than subverting anything, you are embracing a different orthodoxy, abiding by another set of rules, according to which darkness is more modern and profound than light, meanness more so than generosity, despair more so than happiness, tortured narcissism more so than gregarious joy, disruption more so than harmony, resentment more so than gratitude. Is that really so? How many of us have accepted, without any further personal inquiry, that Buster Keaton is a much better artist than Charles Chaplin, that the Rolling Stones are better than the Beatles, that Sarah Vaughan is better than Ella Fitzgerald, that Godard is better than Truffaut? Not to mention, in the narrow confines of Spanish literature, that Juan Benet is better than Luis Martín Santos (let alone Carmen Laforet), that Baroja is better than Galdós, that almost anyone is better than poor old sentimental Antonio Machado? And what great poet has been more consistently underrated or despised than Jorge Guillén, almost solely on the grounds of his unapologetic celebration of the small comforts and joys of living, his fondness for common sense and passionate monogamy?

François Truffaut is a case in point. No other contemporary filmmaker has more used the screen as a blank page to pour out the most intimate confessions. Starting out with the squalor and lovelessness of his childhood, he went on to document the episodes of his own sentimental education, his love of women, his love of falling in love and being in love and suffering for love and being carried away by the many blessings and curses of love, both requited and unrequited. His former friend Jean-Luc Godard cruelly scorned him for not being ideological enough, at a time when ideologies were so very much in fashion, when it was so chic to declare oneself a Maoist in Paris while millions of people were being imprisoned or humiliated or starved to death in Mao's paradise in China. Godard was making erratic propaganda films, which was the right thing to do at the time. Truffaut, a man out of step with the times, kept telling stories of people passionately in love, overflowing with petit bourgeois sentimentality. It is not unlikely that, at the time of his death, Truffaut may have felt a neglected has-been, someone left behind by his contemporaries. In one of his very last films, *La femme d'à coté* (*The Woman Next Door*), his muse and lover Fanny Ardant says something that I love to recall: "I like the songs they play on the radio. They alone tell the truth."

This is a statement that resonates with me since, long before I learned to read and write, I was raised on a steady diet of popular songs broadcast on the radio, daily installments of popular *radionovelas* (radio serials), and double feature-film sessions at the nearby open-air movie theaters that my mother, grandmother, and aunt loved to attend every night in the summer. No emotional detachment, no Brechtian programmatic estrangement for us back in those years. I still have to come to terms with the startling fact that I am no longer an up-and-coming young man, but, truth be told, I have memories of a time in Spain prior to the arrival of TV, prior to the universal overtaking of the radio waves by mass-produced English-language global pop music. Popular, sentimental, flamenco-inspired, homegrown songs were the regular fare on radio stations when I was a child. Working-class people, men and women alike, recognized themselves in them. Lola Flores, Antonio Molina, Juanito Valderrama, the most popular singers, were working-class heroes in their own right. First thing in the morning my mother or grandmother or aunt would turn on the radio and sing along to the familiar *coplas* as they went about their daily chores, making beds, dusting the floor, lighting the fire, cooking lunch, stuffing preserves in glass jars. Almost the whole afternoon was taken up by radionovelas: they would listen intensely to every word, they would weep or cheer, they would endlessly discuss the nuances of the plot or its likely outcome. And, at their side, the child I was would end up hooked forever on those two not-so-different forms of emotional fiction: novels and songs. Coplas and radionovelas alike dared to tell the truth at a time when the truth was not otherwise allowed to be told: the longing of the huge number of migrants forced to leave their villages for the city or overseas in order to find jobs and feed their families, the ravages and the raptures of love, the shameless love for a mother or father or child, the cruelty of injustice, the humble happiness on the occasion of a beloved's *día del santo* (saint's day)—no birthdays among the working class back then—or a child's first communion.

No high culture was available for us at the time: no classical music, no literature, no art. We went to the movies and listened to the radio and that was that. Women and girls would sing old traditional songs, medieval romances that had survived by word of mouth for centuries and would very soon disappear leaving no trace, as so often happens with popular culture. Men would lower their voices to tell stories of the war. And they, especially the women, were never afraid of sounding sentimental, of repeating in their own beautiful illiterate words the songs and stories they had heard on the radio or seen in the movies, stories of love and loss, pain and joy, the very vulgar stuff that human lives and cheap novels and great works of art are made of. When dealing with basic emotions in your writing, you walk on a tightrope and risk a catastrophic fall if you take a single wrong step. But I don't think there is a way to reach for the best in any art without accepting the possibility of failure. As the old American song goes, all or nothing at all, you shouldn't settle for less. Deep down, these are the kind of stories I try to tell when I write my own novels.

Contributors

Enrique Álvarez is associate professor of Spanish at Florida State University, where he teaches Spanish literature, film, cultural studies, and critical theory. He is a specialist in twentieth-century Spanish poetry with particular emphasis on the representation of space, gender, and sexuality. He is the author of *Dentro/Fuera: El espacio homosexual masculino en la poesía española del siglo XX* (Madrid: Biblioteca Nueva, 2010). His new book project *Homotional Men: Affective Masculinites in Twentieth-Century Spain* explores the role played by emotions in relationships between men, history, and cultural practice.

Mónica Bolufer is associate professor of modern history at the University of Valencia. She has worked on discourses of gender in Enlightenment culture; women's intellectual practices; concepts of intimacy, privacy, and the public sphere; travel literature; the regulation of conduct (civility, hygiene); and the construction of the self. Her six monographs and edited books include *Educar los sentimientos y las costumbres: Una mirada desde la historia* (coedited with Juan Gomis and Carolina Blutrach, 2014), *La vida y la escritura en el siglo XVIII* (2008), and *Mujeres e Ilustración* (1998).

Lou Charnon-Deutsch is professor emerita of the Department of Hispanic languages and literature at Stony Brook University. She specializes in visual culture, feminist theory, and nineteenth-century Spanish narrative. Her books include *Hold That Pose: Visual Culture in the Nineteenth-Century Spanish Press* (2008), *The Spanish Gypsy: History of a European Obsession* (2004), *Fictions of the Feminine in the Nineteenth-Century Spanish Press* (2000), *Culture and Gender in Nineteenth-Century Spain* (coedited with Jo Labanyi, 1995), *Narratives of Desire: Nineteenth-Century Spanish Fiction by Women* (1994), and *Gender and Representation: Women in Spanish Realist Fiction* (1990).

Luisa Elena Delgado is professor of Spanish literatures and cultures, criticism and interpretive theory, and gender and women's studies at the University of Illinois, Urbana-Champaign. She is the author of *La nación singular: Fantasías de la normalidad democrática española (1996–2011)* (2014) and *La imagen elusiva: Lenguaje y representación en la narrativa de Galdós* (2000). Her main research interests are the cultural construction of Spanish national identity; Spanish literature and culture of the nineteenth, twentieth, and twenty-first centuries; and emotions and affects in/as culture. She is a member of the Editorial Collective of the *Journal of Spanish Cultural Studies* and editor of a book series on contemporary Hispanic studies for Liverpool University Press.

Pura Fernández is research professor in the Center for the Humanities and Social Sciences at Spain's National Research Council (CSIC), Madrid. She has directed various collaborative projects on the history of the modern literary and cultural field, focusing on the history of publishing and reading; the professionalization of the writer and of women writers in particular; transatlantic cultural and publishing networks; and the intersections of literature, scientific discourse, and public policy. Her books include *"No hay nación para este sexo." La Re(d)pública trasatlántica de las Letras: Escritoras españolas y latinoamericanas (1824–1936)* (an edited volume, 2015), *La mujer de letras o la letraherida: Discursos y representaciones sobre la mujer escritora en el siglo XIX* (coedited with Marie-Linda Ortega, 2008), *Mujer pública y vida privada: Del arte eunuco a la novela lupanaria* (2008), and *Eduardo López Bago y el naturalismo radical: Literatura y mercado editorial en el siglo XIX* (1995). She also coordinated the publication of Ramón Gómez de la Serna's *Obras completas* (twenty volumes, 1996–2014), in which she edited the volume *Total de Greguerías* (2014).

Francisco Ferrándiz is a tenured researcher at Spain's National Research Council (CSIC), Madrid. He has a PhD in social and cultural anthropology from the University of California, Berkeley, funded by a Fulbright Scholarship. Since 2002, he has conducted research on the politics of memory in contemporary Spain through analysis of exhumations of mass graves from the Spanish Civil War. On this topic, he has recently published the monograph *El pasado bajo tierra: Exhumaciones contemporáneas de la Guerra Civil* (2014) and coedited with Antonius C. G. M. Robben the comparative volume *Necropolitics: Mass Graves and Exhumations in the Age of Human Rights* (2015).

Rebecca Haidt is professor of Spanish at the Ohio State University. Her work covers eighteenth- and nineteenth-century topics such as gender, labor history, fashion, and visual cultures. She has published three books: *Women, Work and Clothing in Eighteenth-Century Spain* (2011); *Seduction and Sacrilege: Rhetorical Power in "Fray Gerundio de Campazas"* (2002); and *Embodying Enlightenment: Knowing the Body in Eighteenth-Century Spanish Literature and Culture* (1998), awarded the Modern Language Associations's Katherine Singer Kovacs prize.

Juli Highfill is professor of Spanish literature and culture at the University of Michigan. In her teaching and research, she focuses on Spanish literature, culture, and film in the 1920s and 1930s. Her most recent book, *Modernism and Its Merchandise: The Spanish Avant-Garde and Material Culture, 1920–1930*, was published in 2014. Her current book project, *Images in Flight: Popular and Political Affect in Spanish Film, 1920–1940*, examines the evolution of popular film and spectatorship from the early years of mass spectacle through the Spanish Civil War.

Rafael Huertas is research professor at Spain's National Research Council (CSIC), Madrid. His research has focused principally on the history of psychiatry and public health. He has been director of the Department of History of Science in the Institute of History, CSIC; president of the Spanish Society of History of Medicine; and a member of the Executive Committee of the European Association for the History of Psychiatry. He is currently the editor of *Asclepio: Revista de Historia de la Medicina y de la Ciencia*. His most recent book publications include *Historia cultural de la psiquiatría: (Re)pensar la locura* (2012), *Los laboratorios de la norma: Medicina y regulación social en el estado liberal* (2008), and *El siglo de la clínica: Para una teoría de la práctica psiquiátrica* (2005).

Javier Krauel is associate professor of Spanish and comparative literature at the University of Colorado Boulder. His current research focuses on the theory of emotions and on twentieth-century Spanish and Catalan literatures. In 2013, he published *Imperial Emotions: Cultural Responses to Myths of Empire in "Fin-de-Siècle" Spain*. He is currently working on a book project on public emotions in the works of Francisco Ayala.

Jo Labanyi is professor of Spanish at New York University, where she teaches modern Spanish cultural history. Her most recent publications are *Europe and Love in Cinema* (coedited with Karen Diehl and Luisa Passerini, 2012), *A Companion to Spanish Cinema* (coedited with Tatjana Pavlović, 2012), and *Spanish Literature* (in Oxford University Press's Very Short Introduction series, 2010). She is currently coauthoring a *Cultural History of Modern Spanish Literature* and *Cinema and Everyday Life in 1940s and 1950s Spain: An Oral History*. In 2002–2004, she was a researcher for the international project *Europe: Emotions, Identities, Politics*, directed by Luisa Passerini. She is the coordinating editor of the *Journal of Spanish Cultural Studies* and directs the book series *Remapping Cultural History* for Berghahn Books. In 2005 she was elected a fellow of the British Academy.

Helena Miguélez-Carballeira is senior lecturer in Hispanic studies at Bangor University, UK. She has authored the monograph *Galicia, a Sentimental Nation: Gender, Culture and Politics* (2013), which has been translated into Portuguese. She has also edited *A Companion to Galician Culture* (2014) and has published on contemporary Spain, women's writing, and translation studies. She directs the Centre for Galician Studies in Wales.

Javier Moscoso is research professor of the history and philosophy of science at Spain's National Research Council (CSIC), Madrid. His latest book, *Pain: A Cultural History*, has been published in Spanish (2011), English (2012), and French (2015). At the CSIC he leads the research group HIST-EX, which brings together scholars and artists interested in the history and philosophy of emotions. He is currently preparing a book on passions of rivalry in the early nineteenth century.

Antonio Muñoz Molina is one of Spain's major contemporary novelists. He has been awarded the Premio Nacional de Narrativa (1987, 1992), Premio Planeta (1991), and Premio Príncipe de Asturias de las Letras (2013). His most recent novels are *Como sombra que se va* (2014), *La noche de los tiempos* (2010), and *Sefarad* (2001). He is a regular contributor to *El País* and in 2004–2005 was director of the Instituto Cervantes in New York. In 2010–2015 he was Banco Santander Global Professor of Creative Writing in Spanish at New York University. He has been awarded honorary doctorates by Villanova and Brandeis Universities and was elected a fellow of the Real Academia Española in 1995.

Wadda C. Ríos-Font is professor of Spanish and Latin American cultures at Barnard College, Columbia University. Her area of specialty is the literature and culture of modern Spain, including the transatlantic relationship with its American possessions through 1898. She is the author of two books: *The Canon and the Archive: Configuring Literature in Modern Spain* (2004) and *Rewriting Melodrama: The Hidden Paradigm in Modern Spanish Theater* (1997). Currently, she is completing a book project provisionally entitled *Quasimodo's Bell: Puerto Rican National Culture and the Spanish Empire, 1808–1898*.

Maite Zubiaurre is a professor of Spanish and German and associate dean for Equity, Diversity and Inclusion, Humanities Division at the University of California, Los Angeles. Her areas of interest are gender studies, urban studies, visual studies, and cultural history. She is the author of two books, *Cultures of the Erotic in Spain, 1898–1939* (2012; Spanish translation 2014) and *El espacio en la novela realista: Paisajes, miniaturas, perspectivas* (2000). She is also the coeditor with Roberta Johnson of *Antología del pensamiento feminista español: 1726–2008* (2012). She is a literary translator of nineteenth- and twentieth-century novels in German into Spanish and is currently writing a book on contemporary cultural representations of trash and rubble.

Index

Numbers in **bold** refer to figures.

Acción Republicana, 147
Ackermann, Rudolph, 79
Acquaviva, Claudio, 97
Adorno, Theodor, 176
affect, 5–7, 23, 176, 177–78, 188n2, 189n3, 192
    as bodily intensity, 63, 66, 121–22, 126, 154, 202–3, 204
    as strong emotional impact, 85, 136, 148, 154, 248, 264, 265–66, 268, 271–72, 275–76
    See also sensory experience
Ahern, Stephen, 212
Ahmed, Sara, 2–3, 5, 6, 95–96, 195, 196–97, 262, 264–65
Alarcón, Pedro de, 104, 105
Alas, Leopoldo, 64, 105
Alberti, Rafael, 211
Alcaina Guirao, Antonio, 41
Alcalá Galiano, Antonio, 26
Alcalá Zamora, Niceto, 145, 149, 151
Alianza Popular, 217
Alighieri, Salvador, 195
Álvarez de Sotomayor, Fernando, 218
Amar en tiempos revueltos (TV series), 8, 14
anarchism, 10, 11, 12, 143, 150, 152–53, 154, 228
Andalusia, 193, 199, 200, 207n5, 213–16, 219, 274, 277
Anderson, Benedict, 4, 44
Anento, Julián, 58, 59, 67
Aner d'Esteve, Felip, 40, 41
anger, 176, 194
    at church, 97
    as negative emotion, 265, 267, 272, 274, 275
    as protest, 13, 16, 270, 273
    See also indignation
Annales school, 23

anticlericalism, 97–98, 101, 106, 107–8, 152
anti-Semitism, 96–97, 98, 101–3, 106, 107
Arconada, César, 154
Ardant, Fanny, 285
Arenal, Concepción, 10, 79, 80, 86–87, 89
Arendt, Hannah, 262
Argentina, 229, 255
Argüelles y Álvarez, Agustín, 40, 42–43, 45–46, 48, 51
Aristotle, 142, 149, 156n8
Artières, Philippe, 111
Augé, Marc, 113
Austin, J. L., 65
autobiography. *See* self-writing
avant-garde, 3, 120, 126, 154
Ayala, Francisco, 120, 121, 127–31, 135, 137n6, 144, 146–54, 155n5
Ayguals de Izco, Wenceslao, 64
Azaña, Manuel, 145, 147, 155n5
Azar, Xosé, 218
Azorín (José Martínez Ruiz), 212

Balázs, Béla, 124, 126
Balbín de Unquera, Antonio, 86
Balibrea, Mari Paz, 194, 211
Barber, Antonio, 132
Bardem, Pilar, 230
Baroja, Pío, 285
Barruel, Agustín, 103
Barthes, Roland, 112
Basque Country, 16, **30**, 45, 213–16, 250, 267. *See also under* nationalism
Baudelaire, Charles, 124
Beatles, the, 285
Benda, Julien, 143
Benedetti, Mario, 112
Benet, Juan, 285
Benjamin, Walter, 124, 126–27, 141
Bennett, Alan, 57
Bentham, 83, 88

291

Berlant, Lauren, 16, 17, 264, 265, 272–73, 278
binary oppositions, 2, 8, 15, 35, 77, 136, 194, 202, 204, 206
Blanchard, Phyllis, 169
Blanco-White, José, 26
Blasco Ibáñez, Vicente, 105–6
Bloch, Marc, 179
body
    embarrassment at, 195–97
    historicity of, 6
    inseparability from mind, 5–6, 9, 10, 13, 161, 266
    politics of dead, 242, 244, 245, 249, **253**, 257–59, **258**
    reading with, 57, 65–70
    writing on, 108
    writing with, 201–6
    See also affect; contagion; hapticity; homosexuality; race; sensory experience; sexuality
Boone, Joseph Allen, 194, 205, 206
Bourdieu, Pierre, 5
Brazil, 277–78
Brennan, Teresa, 6, 7
Bresciani, Antonio, 103
Brierre de Boismont, Alexandre Jacques François, 111
Brown, Gordon, 263, 264
Bruno, Giuliana, 127, 128–29
Buck-Morss, Susan, 127
Burke, Peter, 11, 23, 177
Butler, Judith, 219, 222

Cabanis, Pierre, 77, 78, 83, 86, 89
Cabrera, Miguel, 53n7
Cádiz, Cortes de, 2, 11, 15, 39, 46, 48, 50
    Constitution of Cádiz, 60
Cameron, David, 262–64, 277
Campbell, Peter R., 41
Campoamor, Clara, 154
Camporesi, Piero, 179
Capmany y Montpalau, Antonio, 40
Carlists, 98
    Wars, 11, 72–73, 81, 97, 99
Carlos III, 30
Carlos IV, 53n3
Carvajal, Beatriz, 214–15
Casas Viejas, 143, 152–53

Cassat, Mary, 284
Castelar, Emilio, 149
Castellanos, Basilio Sebastián, 58, 59, 67
Castillo, Antonio, 115, 117n8
Castillo, Santiago, 32
Castro, Rosalía de, 215, 217
Catalonia, 45, 146, 162, 164, 213–16, 274
    Acció Catalana, 147
    Convergència i Unió, 266
    Ciutadans, 267, 277 (*See also* Ciudadanos)
    Esquerra Republicana de Catalunya, 266
    government of (Generalitat), 12, 152, 159
    Lliga Regionalista, 147
    political autonomy, 143, 151, 152
    proindependence movement, 210, 263–64, 266–68, 270–71, 274, 276–77, 279n2
    See also under nationalism
Catholicism, 10, 25, 58, 167, 168, 201, 227–29, 243, 284
    Catholic Church, 34, 86, 97, 104, 143, 144, 151–52, 226
    See also anticlericalism
Caveda y Solares, Rita, 29
Cela, Camilo José, 283
censorship, 24–25, 34, 44, 59–60, 274
Cernuda, Luis, 2, 11, 193–94, 195, 200, 202
Cézanne, Paul, 284
Chadwick, Edwin, 83
Chambers, Ross, 124–25
Chaplin, Charles, 285
charity, 41, 80, 84–87, 89, 273
Charles IV, 53n3
Chaves Nogales, Manuel, 144, 146–47, 148–50, 152–54, 155n5
Chile, 229, 255
cholera, 77, 79–83, 87–89
Chow, Rey, 107–8
cinema, 2, 3, 4, 14, 227, 248, 283, 285, 286
Ciudadanos, 17, 271, 275, 277
Cixous, Hélène, 66
class, 13, 16, 25, 34, 153, 154
    others, 9, 200, 286
    working, 5, 80, 83–85, 233, 234, 235, 284
Coloma, Luis, 104, 105
colonialism. *See* empire

Communist Party (Partido Comunista de España, PCE), 154, 230, 251–52
Condillac, Étienne Bonnot de, 21
Confederación Española de Derechas Autónomas (CEDA), 146
consensus, culture of, 212, 222, 264, 269
contagion, 7, 9, 10, 11, 34, 81, 82–83, 264, 275
Corbin, Alain, 179
Costa, Diego, 278
Cruz, Juan, 276–77
Cuba, 45
Cuéntame cómo pasó (TV series), 226
Cuisin, J. R. P., 59, 62, 71–72
Culture of the Transition (CT). *See* consensus, culture of; regime of 1978

Dalí, Salvador, 120
David, Monsieur, 58
Debussy, Claude, 284
de Cosca Vayo, Estanislao de, 98–100, 105, 108n1
de la Cruz, Vicente, 103, 105, 106
Delgado, Luisa Elena, 207n4, 210
Derrida, Jacques, 116n4
Descartes, René, 142
Destutt de Tracy, Antoine, 77
de Torre, Guillermo, 121
digital culture, 136, 242, 243, 246, 249
    Internet, 4, 245
    new media, 2, 3, 14, 97, 252–58
    social media, 219, 275
    See also globalization
Dilthey, Wilhelm, 187, 189n4
Dixon, Thomas, 7, 177
Dorfman, Ariel, 255
Dueñas y Castro, Domingo, 40
Dumas, Alexandre, 98
Durkheim, Émile, 179

Eco, Umberto, 99
Eisenberg, Daniel, 199
Elías Riquelme, Francisco, 121, 132–36
Elizabeth II, 57
Ellis, Havelock, 66
Elsaesser, Thomas, 230, 239
emotional community, 4, 7, 29, 35n1, 63–64, 188n1, 255, 275, 279n9
    creating, 5, 41, 73

emotional competence, 8, 14, 226, 227, 232–33, 239, 273–74
empathy, 232, 245, 248
    as basis of citizenship, 17, 26, 41, 50, 272, 275
    as transhistorical identification, 250, 258
    See also emotional community; sympathy
empire, 43, 51, 52n1, 73, 155
Enlightenment, 57, 21–33, 100
    balance of sensibility and reason, 68, 276
    humanitarianism, 177
    sensibility, 2, 17, 78–79
    sociability, 8
    sympathy, 77–94
envy, 9, 107
Eribon, Didier, 198
Espina, Antonio, 122
Etxeberria, Francisco, 257
exhumations, 14, 229, 243–44, 247, 249–50, **253**, **257**, **258**

Faber, Sebastiaan, 198, 201–2
Fabra Soldevila, Francisco, 70
fascism, 142, 144, 155, 229, 251, 269, 276
    Falange Española, 144, 155, 226, 227–28, 229, 230, 231–32, 276
fear, 3, 60, 176, 265, 275
    of social others, 154
    of threats to nation, 10, 97, 262
    in war, 184
Febvre, Lucien, 178, 179, 188n1
Feijóo y Montenegro, Benito, 41
Felipe VI, 56
Fernández, Pura, 104, 106
Fernández de Moratín, Leandro, 32
Fernando VII, 42–43, 57, 58, 59, 60, 78, 79, 100, 108n1
Fish, Stanley, 11, 64, 195
Fitzgerald, Ella, 285
Flatley, Jonathan, 145
Flores, Lola, 286
Foessel, Michaël, 264
Foucault, Michel, 176, 179
Fraga, Manuel, 212, 216
Franco, Francisco, 229, **235**, 243, 244
    dictatorship, 187, 195, 207, 225, 227, 239, 243, 244

Franco, Francisco (*continued*)
   Francoist ideology, 193, 198, 199, 207n1, 210, 250, 273–74, 276
   Francoist repression, 2, 14, 226–31, 237, 240n8, 243, 250, **253**, 258
   See also exhumations
Freemasons, 2, 3, 5, 96, 97, 103–4, 107–8
French Revolution, 8, 34, 77, 79, 95, 103
Freud, Sigmund, 14, 66, 112, 117n5, 168, 169, 231, 233, 235
Frevert, Ute, 6
friendship, 7, 25–26, 29–30
frigidity, 169, 170, 172
Fris Ducos, Luis, 103
Frosh, Stephen, 149
Fura dels Baus, La, 279n9

Gala, Antonio, 212–16
Galdós. *See* Pérez Galdós, Benito
Galería fúnebre. See Pérez Zaragoza y Godínez, Agustín
Galicia, 16, 45, 184, 211–12, 215, 222, 274, 277
   Bloque Nacionalista Galego, 218–19
   Galician language, 212, 217, 220–21, 222n6
   government (Xunta de Galicia), 216–19, 220
   Partido Socialista de Galicia 218–19
   political autonomy, 216
   See also under nationalism
Garbo, Greta, 127, 132–33
García Aristegui, David, 217
García Berlanga, Luis, 273
García Lorca, Federico, 199
García Malo, Ignacio, 25, 27–29, **33**
García Martí, Victoriano, 212
Garlinger, Patrick, 199
Garrido, Fernando, 97
Garzón, Baltasar, 244
Gatrey, 24
Geertz, Clifford, 187
gender
   feminization, 212, 218, 221, 232, 234, 266
   gender distinctions, 8, 26–27, 30–34, 153
   gender implications, 13, 16–17, 207
   gender studies, 8, 23

   See also homosexuality; lesbianism; queer desire; readership; women
Generation of 27, 199
Generation of 98, 192
Genlis, Stéphanie de, 24
genocide, 231, 232, 246
Germany, 12, 141, 144, 155n2, 276
Gilbert, Pamela K., 80
Gil de Biedma, Jaime, 195
Ginger, Andrew, 134, 137n7
globalization
   of human rights discourse, 229, 242, 243, 248
   of information, 14, 107, 121, 238, 252–59
Goddard, Jean–Luc, 285
Goethe, Johann Wolfgang von, 31, 65
Gomá Lanzón, Javier, 276
Gómez de la Serna, Ramón, 57
gothic, 59, 60, 65, 71. *See also* horror
Gould, Deborah, 13, 15, 17, 265
Goya y Lucientes, Francisco José de, 21, **22**, 25, 26, 32–33, **34**, 68
Gracia, Jordi, 271
Granados, Francisco, 276
grief. *See* mourning; suffering
Guillén, Jorge, 211, 285

Haidt, Rebecca, 65
Hamon, Philippe, 69–70
Hansen, Miriam, 121, 137n9
happiness, 176, 272
   collective, 275
   as goal of citizenship, 29, 42, 46, 49, 51, 84, 148
   personal, 195, 273, 274, 285, 286
hapticity, 4, 68, 73, 123, 126–27, 129, 133, 135
Hardt, Michael, 5
hatred, 9, 176
   and paranoia, 114
   political, 145, 151, 152, 153
   social, 2, 3, 5, 10, 17, 95–96, 107–8
   See also anticlericalism; anti-Semitism
heart
   morality of, 10, 17, 21–22, 26, 27, 85, 236–37, 265, 276
   as physical organ, 63, 65, 69–70, 148, 185, 277

as seat of the emotions, 23, 28–29, 33, 46–48, 51, 95, 99, 210, 266
as symbol, 222n1, 263, 270, 275, 277, 279nn8–9
Heidegger, Martin, 145
Heine, Heinrich, 81
Hessell, Stéphane, 271
Hispanidad, 192–93, 194, 196–207
historical memory, 225, 226, 229–30, 245, 246
historical memory activism, 242, 249
   Archivo Guerra y Exilio, 247, 248
   Asociación de Familiares y Amigos de la Fosa Común de Oviedo, 247, 248
   Asociación para la Recuperación de la Memoria Histórica (ARMH), 229, 249–52, 254
   Foro por la Memoria, 249, 251, 254, 255, **256**
   Sociedad de Ciencias Aranzadi, 254
   See also exhumations
History of the Emotions
   research centers, 1, 7
   research groups, 1
Hobbes, Thomas, 142
homosexuality, 198–99, 204, 237, 238
   homophobia, 193–94
   as problem, 159, 167, 168, 170
   See also lesbianism; queer desire
hope, 176, 180, 183, 185, 186, 214
   political 15, 52, 142, 143, 144, 145, 148, 149, 153, 266, 267, 272, 275, 279n7
Horkheimer, Max, 176
horror
   at atrocities, 49, 81, 83, 141, 226, 248
   as literary genre, 2, 4, 8, 11, 56–76
Huizinga, Johan, 179
humanity, 8, 79, 80, 84, 87, 88, 89, 143, 167
   crimes against, 244, 256
Hume, David, 21
Hutcheson, Francis, 21
hygiene, 2, 8–9, 10, 73, 77, 78, 79, 81, 84, 89
hysteria, 9, 113, 154, 156n6, 160, 172

Iarocci, Michael, 71
Ideologues, the, 77–78, 80, 83
Iglesias, Pablo, 210
Illouz, Eva, 14–15, 148, 226, 227, 232–33, 235, 238–39, 264, 273
indignation, 15, 16, 17, 180, 265, 267, 268, 271–72, 275, 279n7. *See also* anger
Inguanzo y Rivero, Pedro, 40
Innerarity, Daniel, 246, 248, 259, 264, 272, 278
intellectuals, 25, 79, 159, 164, 168, 196–97, 198, 269
   and emotional engagement, 13, 142–43, 155, 271
   and emotional restraint, 12–13, 144, 146–47, 150
Internet. *See* digital culture
Irigaray, Luce, 66
Isabel II, 58, 81, 101, 108n1
Italy, 144, 155n2
Izquierdo Martín, Jesús, 239

Jaggar, Alison, 144, 150, 156n6
Jameson, Fredric, 107
Jarcha, 274
jealousy, 9, 114, 283
Jesuits, 2, 3, 5, 10, 96, 97–99, 100, 103–6, 108n2, 151
Jews, 2, 3, 5, 10, 96–97, 101–2, **102**, 106, 108
Jovellanos, Gaspar Melchor de, 10, 21–22, 25–26, 28, 29, 89n4
Juliá, Santos, 229
Junqueras, Oriol, 266, 279n2

Kant, Immanuel, 57
Keaton, Buster, 285
Knott, Sarah, 24, 26
Koselleck, Reinhart, 178–79
Kracauer, Siegfried, 126
Krauel, Javier, 272

Labanyi, Jo, 60, 178
Labrador Méndez, Germán, 269–70, 275, 277
Laforet, Carmen, 285
Lamazares, Antón, 217
Larra, Mariano José de, 7, 56–57, 196
Lasén, Amparo, 272
Lautréamont, Comte de, 284
Lazarte, Juan, 170

Ledesma Ramos, Ramiro, 155
Leganés (Santa Isabel Madhouse), 9–10, 111–17
Legouvé, Ernest, 62–63
Lejeune, Philippe, 116
Leprince de Beaumont, Jeanne-Marie, 24
lesbianism, 159, 160, 167, 168, 198, 238
Levene, Mark, 231
Lewis, Tom, 107
Leys, Ruth, 6
liberalism, 10, 17, 42, 58, 81, 100, 142, 264, 276
    as belief-system, 7, 78, 80, 97, 104, 141, 152, 201, 232
    intellectuals, 12, 79, 98–99, 143, 144, 164
    neoliberalism, 226, 239, 251, 278
literature, 2, 7, 9, 14, 56–57, 227, 283–84, 285
    poetry, 53, 121, 122–27, 193, 195, 196, 198, 201, 203–4
    popular fiction, 3, 5, 10, 57, 64, 65, 68, 96–97, 100, 108
    realist novels, 4, 5, 98, 107
    sentimental fiction, 7, 21, 24–25, 27–29, 31, 60, 65
    theater, 24, 25, 31, 32, 212–16
    See also avant-garde; self-writing
Littau, Karen, 57
Lock, Margaret M., 246
Lomana, Carmen, 217
Lorca. *See* García Lorca, Frederico
Los de Río, 219
Loureiro, Ángel, 248–49, 252
love, 30, 87, 96, 105, 112, 161, 176, 180, 194, 227, 268
    as basis of community, 17, 28–39, 143, 210, 251, 276–78, 279n8
    charitable, 86–87, 228
    of family, 233, 284–85, 286
    of land, 2, 50–51, 52, 53, 197, 202, 204–6
    patriotic, 2, 11, 15–16, 67, 221, 262–63, 267, 270, 276, 277
    romantic, 31–32, 56, 107, 127, 130, 177, 195–96, 197, 198, 234–38, 239, 283, 285, 286
    sexual, 60, 160, 161–62, 166–67, 168–72, 203
    See also friendship; passions

Machado, Antonio, 285
Machiavelli, Niccolò, 262
Macías, Santiago, 250
Macías-Fernández, Paz, 60
madness, 9, 111–17, 184
Maffesoli, Michel, 64
Manet, Édouard, 284
Marañón, Gregorio, 164–65, 167, 170
Marcé, Louis-Victor, 111
Marchena, José, 35
María Cristina, 58, 60, 68, 73
marriage, 28–29, 30, 32, 169, 171, 234
Martí Ibáñez, Félix, 10, 11, 12, 13
Martínez, Francisco Javier, 279n3
Martínez, Guillem, 211
Martín López, Pedro, 98
Martín Santos, Luis, 285
Marx, Karl, 95
    Marxism 142, 155
    See also Communist Party
Mas, Artur, 266, 270, 279
Massumi, Brian, 5–6, 61, 121, 178
Maura, Miguel, 151
McClintock, Anne, 206, 207
medicine, 2, 12, 25, 70, 78, 111, 115–16, 160, 168, 177, 178. *See also* hygiene
Medina Domènech, Rosa María, 1
melancholia, 9, 113, 115, 185, 194, 218, 248
Meléndez Bruna, Salvador, 49
Meléndez Valdés, Juan, 23, 25, 29, 32–33
melodrama, 14, 134, 226, 227, 230, 233, 239, 248, 249, 257
Méndez Álvaro, Francisco, 10, 79–80, 83, 84–86, 87, 89
Mesonero Romanos, Ramón, 81, 87–88
Mexico, 2, 11
Misterio de la Puerta del Sol, El (film), 121, 132–36
Mistral, Gabriela, 185, 189n8
Molina, Antonio, 286
Molinari, Augusta, 115
Monago, José Antonio, 268
Monedero, Juan Carlos, 210
Monita secreta, 96–97, 98, 106
Monlau, Pedro Felipe, 10, 78–80, 83–85, 86, 89
Montengón, Pedro de, 24
Moore, Alison, 172

Morant, Isabel, 24, 28
Mor de Fuentes, José, 25, 31–32, 35
Moreno, Salvador, 202
Moscoso, Javier, 1, 61
mourning, 176, 243–46, 248, 251–52
Muñoz, José Esteban, 207
Murguía, Manuel, 212
music, 4, 16, 28, 64, 219–22, 250, 274, 284, 285

national identity, 11, 16–17, 45
nationalism, 2, 17, 39–40
    Basque, 250, 269
    Catalan, 15–16, 147, 222n1, 250, 267–68
    ETA (Basque Homeland and Freedom), 215, 267
    Galician, 212
    Mexican, 193
    nonstate, 269, 270
    Scottish, 262–64, 266
    Spanish, 194, 199, 201, 211, 269, 276
    See also Catalonia; love: patriotic
nation formation, 4, 10
Navarro Navarro, Javier, 165
Navarro Villoslada, Antonio, 99, 101–2, 103, 106
new media. *See* digital culture
new social movements, 265
    Democracia Real Ya, 271
    15-M, 219, 271, 275–76, 279n7
    Ganemos Madrid, 17, 275
    Guanyem Barcelona, 17, 275
    Plataforma de los Afectados por las Hipotecas, 17
    See also Podemos
Ngai, Sianne, 9
Nieland, Justus, 132
Nietzsche, Friedrich, 176, 187
normalcy, 13, 17, 148, 268–69
Normante y Carcavillas, Lorenzo, 78
nostalgia, 52, 53n7, 185, 194, 204, 226, 251
Núñez, Toribio, 78
Núñez Feijóo, Alberto, 221
Nussbaum, Martha, 15, 17, 262, 276

Olavide, Pablo de, 24
Olender, Maurice, 96
Oliveira Pires, A. de, 97
Ónega, Fernando, 222n5
Ónega, José Ramón, 217, 222n5
orality, 4, 42, 62–63, 64
Orduña, Juan de, 132
Orientalism, 35, 194, 202, 205–6
Ortega y Gasset, José, 142–43, 144, 147, 155, 155–56n6, 161
Ortiz, Letizia, 56
Os da Ría, 219–22

Pagés-Rangel, Roxana, 9
paranoia, 113, 114, 115
paratopia, 112, 114, 117n6
Pardo Bazán, Emilia, 106
passions, 12, 17, 18, 27–28, 31, 33, 58, 65, 68, 73, 78, 84, 160
    negative, 9, 176, 177
    premodern, 7, 21, 23, 81–82
Payne, Stanley, 144
Pedreño, José María, 251
Penagos, Rafael de, 185–86
Pennac, Daniel, 57
Pérez Escrich, Enrique, 64
Pérez Galdós, Benito, 62, 104, 106–7, 196, 285
Pérez Touriño, Emilio, 218
Pérez Zaragoza y Godínez, Agustín, 4, 8, 11
performance, 13, 251
    of emotions, 3, 4, 14, 178, 196–99, 243, 247, 252–59, 264
    language as, 24, 52, 65, 195
    oral reading, 62, 64
photography, 2, 5, 14, 218, 243, 252–58
Picasso, Pablo, 284
Picón, Javinto Octavio, 105
Piqué, Gerard, 278
Plamper, Jan, 5, 6, 24
Plato, 142
Podemos, 16, 17, 210, 222n1, 271, 275
politics, 2, 225, 226, 239
    emotions in, 12–13, 15–18, 25, 210–12, 215, 216–19
Popular Front, 14, 225
Popular Party (Partido Popular), 217, 219, 226, 244, 263, 267, 268
Porter, Roy, 111
Power y Giralt, Ramón, 2, 11, 15, 44–53
Pratt, Mary Louise, 44

Preston, Paul, 240n8, 243
pride, 11, 26, 150, 153, 194, 197–98, 214, 267, 269, 270
Primo de Rivera, José Antonio, 144, 155
Primo de Rivera, Miguel, 145
private sphere, 2, 7, 8, 10, 33, 62, 106, 151, 242, 249, 264
prostitution, 83, 160, 163, 168
Protocols of the Elders of Zion, The, 96–97, 98, 103
public sphere, 13, 62, 106, 121, 227, 242, 244–46, 248, 249, 250, 259, 265, 278
    sentimental, 16, 264, 268, 272–73, 276, 284
Puerta Martín, Adolfo, 240
Puerto Rico, 2, 11, 15, 39–53

Quaggio, Giulia, 211
queer desire, 11, 199, 202, 204, 207

race, 9, 11, 52–53n1, 193–94, 199–200, 204
Radcliffe, Ann, 60, 66
Radical Party, 154
radio, 4, 132, 220, 235, 273
    serials, 235, 285–86
rage. *See* anger; indignation
Rajoy, Mariano, 277
Ravel, Maurice, 284
readership, 4, 5, 25, 59, 67, 96, 195
    female, 5, 8, 35–36n2, 57, 59–60, 62, 63, 65–66, 68–70, 73
reason, 2, 15, 17, 142, 147, 151, 154, 155, 248
    balanced with sensibility, 8, 40–41, 276
    rationality, 13, 149, 164, 176, 266, 267–68, 269
Reddy, William, 24, 28, 35n1, 64, 70
Redondo, Onésimo, 155
regime of 1978, 15–16, 264, 269, 279n7. *See also* consensus, culture of; Transition
Reig, Ramiro, 106
religion, 10, 25, 40, 41, 85, 88, 107, 251
    discourse, 14, 27, 79, 80, 86–87, 89, 228, 232, 273
    question, 104, 151
    See also Catholicism
Republic, Second, 12–13, 143–45, 148, 200, 225, 234, 239, 243

resentment, 9, 72, 114, 150, 265, 285
Retortillo Imbrecht, Ángel, 88
Revuelta González, Manuel, 108
Richardson, Samuel, 24, 25, 27, 65
Riera y Comas, José Mariano, 99, 103, 104
Rimbaud, Arthur, 284
Robert, L. J. M., 80–81
Rodríguez, Joaquín, 97
Rodríguez Zapatero, José Luis, 226, 244
Rolland, Romain, 156n6
Rolling Stones, 285
Romero, María Rosario, 23
Romero Quiñones, Ubaldo, 103, 106
Rorty, Richard, 179, 189n5
Rosenwein, Barbara, 4, 23, 24, 177, 188n1
Rothschild, Jakob, **102**
Rousseau, Jean-Jacques, 26, 31, 65, 142
Rueda, Ana, 21, 24, 34

Sáenz de Santamaría, Soraya, 270
Sagarra, Josep Maria de, 144, 146–47, 148, 150–54
Sagrera, Juana, 114, 117n7
Salinas, Pedro, 121, 122–27, 131, 137n3
Salmond, Alex, 263
Sánchez Ferlosio, Rafael, 278
Sánchez León, Pablo, 239
Sánchez-Saornil, Lucía, 120–21
Sarabia, Luis, 179–80, **181**, **182**, 183, 185–87, **185**, **186**
Satie, Erik, 284
Scarry, Elaine, 179
Scheer, Monique, 5
Scheper-Hughes, Nancy, 246
Schmitt, Carl, 142, 155
Scott, Joan W., 13
Sedgwick, Eve Kosofsky, 197–98
self-writing, 7, 9, 24, 26, 28, 35, 112, 116, 117n6, 179
    personal letters, 2, 9–10, 25–26, 31, 112, 114, 115–16
Seneca, 142
Sennet, Richard, 9
sensibility, 6, 68, 70, 177, 193, 276
    Enlightenment concept of, 2, 7–8, 17, 21, 27, 32, 41, 77–79, 82, 87, 89
sensory experience, 3–4, 57, 62–63, 64–65, 73, 122, 131, 177, 180, 187

sensory perception, 23, 67–70, 78
  See also affect; body; hapticity
sentimentality, 14, 27, 32, 162, 184–85, 235, 247–48, 251, 268, 272–73, 278, 284, 285, 286
  associated with women, 7, 16, 33, 163, 168, 171, 212, 218, 221
  See also literature; public sphere
Seoane, Mateo, 78–79, 83, 88
Serafina, La. See Mor de Fuentes, José
Serrano Suñer, Ramón, **245**
sexuality, 10, 130, 159, 160–61, 163, 167, 170–71, 173, 283. *See also* homosexuality; lesbianism; queer desire
Shaftesbury, 3rd Earl of, 21
shame, 12, 176, 194, 232, 233, 236, 268, 283, 286
  national, 11, 196–98, 206
  sexual, 199, 203, 207n3
Shaviro, Steven, 126, 135, 137n10
Shklar, Judith N., 262
Sicot, Bernard, 193, 199, 200, 203, 204, 205
Sierra, Verónica, 115, 117n8
Silva, Emilio, 243–44, 250
Simmel, Georg, 187
Sinués, Pilar, 60
Sjöström, Victor, 123
Smith, Adam, 9, 21, 82, 83, 87, 89, 89n4, 142
Smith, Paul Julian, 226, 238
Snediker, Michael D., 197
Sobrequés, Jaume, 266–67
sociability, 8, 26, 29–30, 35, 64, 68, 73, 77–78
Socialist Party (Partido Socialista Obrero Español, PSOE), 225–26, 230, 244
social media. *See* digital culture.
Society of Friends of the Nation
  Basque, 29–30
  Madrid, 30
Sorel, Georges, 142
Sorrolla, Joaquín, 284–85
Spanish Civil War, 5, 12, 159, 162–64, 165–68, 193, 227–28, 239, 240n8, 243, 250, 286
  representations of, 6, 13, 14, 179, 180–81, 189, 225
  See also historical memory

spectatorship, 4, 14, 63, 68, 226–27, 234, 238, 240n7
  cinematic, 121, 126, 129, 131, 135–36
Stekel, Wilhelm, 169
Stravinsky, Igor, 284
structure of feeling, 2, 5, 64, 145, 194, 200, 202
Suárez, Adolfo, 274
subjectivity, 3, 7, 18, 25–26, 29, 62, 111, 179, 188, 197, 253, 264
Sue, Eugène, 98–99, **99**, 100, 105, 106
suffering, 60, 87, 250, 255, 269–70, 274
  and Francoist repression, 13–14, 230–31, 237, 239, 244, 247–48, 273
  See also mourning
sympathy, 65, 70, 194, 197, 198, 199–200, 201, 204, 216, 272, 276
  Enlightenment concept of, 8, 23, 78, 80, 276

Taussig, Michael, 247
tears, 48, 166, 182, 183, 202, 265–68, 276, 279n3
television, 2, 4, 56, 210, 211, 214–15, 217, 220, 245, 248, 273–74
  series, 8, 14
terminology (for emotions), 6–8, 22–23, 177–78
Terrero Monesterio, Vicente, 40, 41
terror. *See* horror
Teruel, José, 196
Thrift, Nigel, 192
Tissot, Claude-Joseph, 82
Tocqueville, Alexis de, 262
Toreno, Count of, 98
Toret, Javier, 275
Torné, Gonzalo, 211, 219
Torres del Hoyo, Luis, 161
Toulouse-Lautrec, Henri de, 284
Toussenel, Alphonse, 101–2
Transition, 13, 16, 210–11, 226, 243–44, 250, 274. *See also* consensus, culture of; regime of 1978
translations 23, 28, 58, 60, 78, 82, 88, 89, 98
  translators, 25, 27, 31, 59, 79
transnational connections, 2, 3, 78, 107, 200, 243, 256. *See also* globalization
trauma, 61, 170, 210, 229, 231–32, 243, 247, 273

Tresserra, Ceferino, 98–99, 100–101, 105, 107
Trigo, Felipe, 170
Trigueros, Cándido María, 31
Truffaut, François, 285
Tully, Carol, 79
Turiel, Mariano, 217
Turner, Victor, 181, 187, 188

Unamuno, Miguel de, 144, 155
Unión, Progreso y Democracia, 267

Valderrama, Juanito, 286
Valender, James, 192–93, 195, 196, 200
Valentino, Rudolph, 133
Valis, Noël, 85, 87, 194
Valladares de Sotomayor, Antonio, 24
Vaughan, Sarah, 285
Vázquez Montalbán, Manuel, 284
Vega Armentero, Remigio 114
Vela, Fernando, 126, 129, 130
Venezuela, 46, 47–48, 53n5
Verdery, Katherine, 245, 249
Vertov, Dziga, 126
Vicens Vives, Jaume, 267
Vidal, Ignacio, 159
Vietnam War, 231
Villacañas Berlanga, José Luis, 143, 146, 156
Villanueva y Astengo, Joaquín, 40, 41
Vincent, Mary, 144, 145–46, 154
violence, 12, 16, 72, 141, 180, 211, 229, 242, 243, 247, 248, 249, 269
   anticlerical, 100, 108n3, 146, 147
   See also war

Virilio, Paul, 135
Viroli, Maurizio, 40, 41
vision, 4, 67–68, 70, 122. *See also* hapticity; spectatorship
visual culture, 2, 6, 13, 176–77, 179, 181, 185, 256, 284–85

war, 67–68, **69**, 70–72, 72–73, 84. *See also* Carlists; *specific conflicts*
War of Independence, 8, 11, 12, 13, 21, 34–35, 40, 57, 60, 67
Weber, Max, 4, 63, 142, 144, 147–48, 154, 155n1, 156n7
Wert, José Ignacio, 269
Wetherell, Margaret, 122
Williams, Raymond, 2, 8, 64, 145, 194. *See also* structure of feeling
women, 7, 8, 21, 24, 61, 70, 80, 154, 185, 226, 238
   in combat, 12, 34–35, 72, 162–64
   See also readership
Woolf, Virginia, 57
World War I, 141, 142, 143, 164, 176–77
World War II, 238

Zambrano, María, 17–18, 143, 211, 279n8
Zapater, Martín, 26
Zavala y Zamora, Gaspar, 24, 29, 31
Žižek, Slavoj, 98
Zugazagoitia y Frías, Antonio, 152
Zúñiga, Josefa de (Marquesa de Sarria), 24
Zweig, Stefan, 141, 156n6

www.ingramcontent.com/pod-product-compliance
Lightning Source LLC
Chambersburg PA
CBHW081800300426
44116CB00014B/2190